PENGUIN

SELECTED PLAYS

William Butler Yeats, the Irish poet, dramatist, autobiographer, critic and occult philosopher, was born in Dublin in 1865. He came from an artistic middle-class family and spent his childhood in Sligo, Dublin and London. He enrolled at the Metropolitan School of Art in Dublin in 1884. The next year he became a founder member of the Dublin Hermetic Society; in time this led him to the Esoteric Section of the Theosophical Society and the Hermetic Order of the Golden Dawn (1890). He developed a life-long interest in magic, the occult and the supernatural, which influenced much of his thinking and writing, and which achieved its most complete expression in the expository speculations of *A Vision* (1925; revised version 1937).

Yeats's home was most often in London, though he visited Ireland frequently. For a while he was close to the politics of Irish nationalism, not least because of his long infatuation with the revolutionary Maud Gonne, to whom he unsuccessfully proposed on many occasions throughout his life. From an early stage, he devoted his energies much less to direct political action than to the cause of an imaginative nationalism which involved him in the collection of folklore (notably in *The Celtic Twilight*, 1893), in the creation and management of a national theatre for which he wrote a body of plays (five of which presented the epic hero Cuchulain), and in the critical reinterpretation and advancement of the Irish literary tradition.

In 1915 Yeats refused a knighthood from the British government; in 1922 he became a Senator of the newly founded Irish Free State, and finally settled in Dublin with Georgie Hyde-Lees, whom he had married in 1917 and whose automatic writing became the basis of *A Vision*. In 1917 he also purchased a Norman stone tower in Ballylee, Co. Galway, and this provided the symbolic focus for *The Tower* (1928) which is, perhaps, his richest collection of poetry. Yeats left a vivid record of his life and of his friends and acquaintances in the volumes which were collected as *Autobiographies* and in the franker *Memoirs* (not published until 1972). He died at Roquebrune, France, in January 1939.

Richard Aller   oyal
Holloway, U   and

educated at St Catharine's College, Cambridge. His many publications include works on Renaissance and Modern theatre and on the relation between dance and drama. Anglo-Irish theatre has been his special interest for many years, both as critic and as director (he has staged most of Yeats's plays). He has also edited Oscar Wilde's *The Importance of Being Earnest and Other Plays* and is currently editing a volume of Yeats's writings on theatre, also for Penguin.

W. B. YEATS

Selected Plays

Edited by
RICHARD ALLEN CAVE

PENGUIN BOOKS

PENGUIN BOOKS

Published by the Penguin Group
Penguin Books Ltd, 80 Strand, London, WC2R 0RL, England
Penguin Putnam Inc., 375 Hudson Street, New York, New York 10014, USA
Penguin Books Australia Ltd, Ringwood, Victoria, Australia
Penguin Books Canada Ltd, 10 Alcorn Avenue, Toronto, Ontario, Canada M4V 3B2
Penguin Books India (P) Ltd, 11, Community Centre, Panchsheel Park, New Delhi – 110 017, India
Penguin Books (NZ) Ltd, Private Bag 102902, NSMC, Auckland, New Zealand
Penguin Books (South Africa) (Pty) Ltd, 5 Watkins Street, Denver Ext 4, Johannesburg 2094, South Africa

Penguin Books Ltd, Registered Offices: 80 Strand, London, WC2R 0RL, England

This edition first published in Penguin Books 1997

10

Amateur and professional repertory rights in these plays are handled by
Samuel French Ltd of 52 Fitzroy Street, London W1P 6JR

Texts copyright © Michael B. Yeats, 1997
Editorial material copyright © Richard Allen Cave, 1997
All rights reserved

The moral right of the editor has been asserted

Set in 9.75/11.75pt Monotype Sabon
Typeset by Rowland Phototypesetting Ltd, Bury St Edmunds, Suffolk
Printed and bound in Great Britain by Antony Rowe Ltd, Chippenham, Wiltshire

ISBN 978-0-14-018374-0

CONTENTS

FOR KATHARINE WORTH AND COLIN SMYTHE
two valued friends and admired scholars

ACKNOWLEDGEMENTS

I wish to thank David Ward of the library at Royal Holloway, who produced relevant books for me almost quicker than I realized I needed them to solve particular problems; and Professor Warwick Gould who kindly invited me to review for *Yeats Annual* the various volumes relating to the plays that have so far appeared in the Cornell Yeats (in tracing the evolution of the texts through the manuscript materials and early editions, these proved an invaluable aid in writing the commentaries and notes). Unusually perhaps in respect of editorial work, I would like to express a massive debt of gratitude to the numerous casts – amateur, student and professional – whose creative exploration of Yeats's plays under my direction has over the years taught me so much about the dynamic of these works in performance. Finally and most importantly I thank the two friends to whom this edition is dedicated: their scholarship, wit, advice and lively debate about matters Yeatsian have been a lasting inspiration. It was an interest in Irish theatre and literature that brought us together in 1970 on the day that the International Association for the Study of Irish Literature was founded; time sealed an instant rapport by steadily transforming it to an abiding friendship.

R.A.C.

LIST OF ILLUSTRATIONS

INTRODUCTION

Friendship meant a great deal to Yeats. Frequently throughout his life, when moved to take stock of his achievements, it was of the value of friendship that he was inspired to write, even seeing it in one of the last of his poems, 'The Municipal Gallery Revisited', as the true 'glory' of his existence and his work. This was not mere rhetoric. Friends inspired, sustained, challenged, assisted, sponsored, in fact *gave* (and gave willingly) in all the myriad ways in which that simple but psychologically intricate verb can be motivated into action. In one of Yeats's last plays, *The King of the Great Clock Tower*, a Stroller extols the beauty of a Queen and foretells that out of gratitude she will dance for him and that he, grateful in his turn, will sing. Yeats, grateful for the beauty of friendship, sang; and sang with a scruple that kept praise meticulously free of flattery.

It is noticeable, however, that few of these poems record friendships which advanced his career in the theatre as playwright and practitioner. That particular range of inspirational debts is recorded, perhaps more appropriately, in the dedications to his many plays. Yet one cannot but be struck, in taking stock of Yeats's achievements as a dramatist, by the determining power which certain friendships had to shape his development in the particular ways in which it evolved. In one of his late poems, 'An Acre of Grass', Yeats writes of an imperative and continuing need he experiences in respect of his inspiration: 'Myself must I remake,' he asserts, and wills himself to find the energies, despite old age, to make such a renewal possible. His whole career in the theatre was a quite remarkable process of making and remaking the self; and new friends invariably appeared as required to aid his efforts at renewal and transformation. It is astonishing how frequently the process that Jung termed synchronicity operated in Yeats's life: he had an amazing propensity for being in the right place at the right time, enabling him to gravitate towards the artist or theatre practitioner most capable of helping him over the next hurdle he confronted. When no one suitable was at hand, Yeats never intemperately forced an issue to a resolution but could wait, in some instances for over a decade, till a chance encounter occurred that would revitalize suddenly and profitably a long-standing preoccupation, exciting his creativity to move in a new direction.

The first, truly momentous meeting came early in the summer of 1897 when, out of a talk between Yeats, Lady Gregory and Edward Martyn, came the joint decision to found the Irish Literary Theatre, to seek sponsorship for an annual season of plays over a three-year period, and to work to establish in the fullness of time an indigenous national theatre. The ambition was realized on all three counts (though at the cost of the friendship with Martyn), the culminating achievement being the opening at Christmas-time in 1904 of the Abbey Theatre as the permanent Dublin home of a company of Irish actors with Irish producers under an Irish management (a new friend, the dramatist John Millington Synge, now joined Lady Gregory and Yeats in that capacity). Though an important sequence of events, it is – as the elderly Yeats himself asserted – an oft-told tale and one that can be studied elsewhere. Lady Gregory remained a life-long friend and mentor, whose own career as dramatist took shape alongside Yeats's as they pooled ideas, offered each other responsive criticism, debated problems of dramatic structure, assisted with dialogue and several times negotiated the stresses involved in wholesale collaboration.

But if that encounter in 1897 was so quickly productive, it was because Yeats had begun to conceive of the idea of a national drama and of a company pledged to stage it long before. Reviewing John Todhunter's pastoral drama *A Sicilian Idyll* as early as 1891, Yeats had praised the poetic staging of a poetic play but concluded, 'I should very much like to see what Dr Todhunter could do with an Irish theme written for and acted before an Irish audience.' That ambition was one he was himself at the time endeavouring to fulfil: *The Countess Cathleen* was all but complete (it was to be published and granted the Lord Chamberlain's licence in 1892); and the folklore that Yeats was then collecting for inclusion in *The Celtic Twilight* (1893) was to inspire him with the subject for a second play, *The Land of Heart's Desire* (staged in 1894). From our standpoint in the 1990s when we have benefited from decades of first-rate Irish playwriting, it is perhaps difficult to gauge just how daring, culturally and ideologically, Yeats's ambition was a century ago.

Throughout the eighteenth century, theatre in Ireland had meant theatre in Dublin: establishments like the Fishamble Street or Smock Alley theatres were decidedly select in their audiences and the province of the Protestant Ascendancy; dramatists and performers of any calibre gravitated quickly to London houses. After the Act of Union of 1800 theatres began to multiply but the drama on offer totally reflected London taste: increasingly the stages were occupied with English touring companies; where there were resident troupes, they played in revivals of English successes. Theatrical culture was as much a vehicle for colonial domination and exhibitionism as were more overtly political and social dimensions of life in Ireland. There was no such thing as an *Irish* theatre. (One consequence of this was that the Irish Literary Theatre had to resort to English actors in casting plays for all three of their seasons, simply because there were not adequately trained Irish professionals capable of tackling the roles on offer.) It is not surprising, therefore, that the theatre should have been the focus for much Catholic, nationalist criticism throughout the century.

It would be wrong to suggest that Yeats alone initiated a change in this situation. From the mid-1880s the old Queen's Theatre in Dublin had set out to attract Irish audiences with a repertoire designed to appeal to nationalist sympathies. The theatre gathered a group of dramatists – Hubert O'Grady, J. W. Whitbread, P. J. Bourke – who established a recognizable house style that drew heavily, almost at times to the point of plagiarism, on the plays of Dion Boucicault, which were repeatedly revived alongside their own work. Here lay the weakness that undermined their efforts to break new ground culturally. All three dramatists imitated a form of melodrama, the conventions of which had been established in England, but they lacked Boucicault's brilliant wit, which had enabled him to interrogate and subvert that form to make it define Irish experience as distinct from British. The opening scene of Boucicault's *The Shaughraun*, for example, presents the audience with a picture-book image of Ireland (an elegant ruin on a rocky coastline beside a picturesque, thatched cottage) which an English army officer proceeds to interpret in a nonchalantly superior, colonial fashion, till forcefully reprimanded and corrected by two spirited Irish women, who teach him how to read the landscape as emblematic of harsh political realities. O'Grady, Whitbread and Bourke never achieved such sophisticated control of audience-response as this, largely because, where Boucicault was attempting to persuade English audiences to take Ireland and Irish characters seriously, they were addressing Irish audiences of a republican disposition. What was wanted was a completely new form and style of drama that admitted no English influence whatever.

If Yeats wholeheartedly disparaged the plays of the Queen's

dramatists, it was because he found their brand of nationalism as suspect as their artistry. The stock Queen's melodramas generally took for subject matter the lives of failed patriots who suffered defeat at the hands of the British (the likes of Wolfe Tone, Edward Fitzgerald, Henry McCracken or Michael Dwyer). The form soon became merely a formula through its continual repetition, which had the effect of promoting a sense that rebellion, however noble-spirited, was doomed to failure. Increasingly the plays popularized a particular kind of rhetoric apostrophizing 'This land of Emerald green . . . beloved country watered by the tears of thy daughters and nurtured by the blood of thy sons!' The defeatism and self-pity implicit in such rhetoric, far from inspiring active revolutionary ardour in audiences, were likely to be disabling in their effect, which is presumably why the Queen's plays were never censored by Dublin Castle or the Lord Chamberlain in London.

The Irish Literary Theatre would have no truck with this kind of enervating sentimentality: they worked, in Lady Gregory's phrase, 'to add *dignity* to Ireland'. If Yeats saw the need for an Irish drama written on Irish themes for Irish audiences, he appreciated that the change had to be wholesale, that the innovations had to be intellectual, political, ideological, as well as aesthetic. His quest was for a form of drama that owed no debts to English models. A crucial influence throughout the 1890s (before Yeats's meetings with Lady Gregory, Martyn and Synge) was the poet and critic Arthur Symons, who introduced him to the work of the French Symbolists (especially Mallarmé and Villiers de l'Isle Adam), to the aesthetic writings of Wagner and the plays of Maurice Maeterlinck; and it was Symons who accompanied Yeats to the performance in Paris of Alfred Jarry's *Ubu Roi* in 1896 which challenged his romantic sensibility profoundly. Symons, himself an eclectic enthusiast, steered Yeats towards the most innovatory continental art of the day; significantly much of it was theatrical; and Yeats learnt some valuable lessons.

Though *The Countess Catheen*, Yeats's first published play (1892), has an Irish setting, its form is that of the old morality drama with Pre-Raphaelite inspiration behind its chosen style of setting and with some pretensions to spectacle in its closing scene. The real breakthrough came with *The Land of Heart's Desire*, which Yeats wisely designed for performance in a small venue (it was mounted by Florence Farr as a curtain-raiser first to Todhunter's *A Comedy of Sighs* and subsequently to Shaw's *Arms and the Man* at the Avenue Theatre in 1894). The setting is of the simplest: the interior of a peasant cottage with table and hearth and little decoration except a crucifix on the wall and a bough of quicken-wood on the open door, which are in consequence immediately invested with significance. While most of the characters are grouped around the table eating and discussing the daily round of tasks, the young wife, Mary Bruin, is drawn repeatedly to the doorway, where a strange light can be seen glimmering through a wood. She gazes steadfastly out into this beyond with a rapt attentiveness that excites the criticism of the others, who express superstitious fears about the dangers of living in the imagination and not applying one's consciousness wholly to work and prayer. In time an unknown and unnamed child enters whose seeming innocence seduces the family into indulging her every whim; unwittingly they have invited a 'faery', one of the Sidhe, or ever-living ones, into their midst. Steadily the child gains control of the entire stage-space and the disposition of all the characters within it, whereupon she dances in a circle about young Mary, carrying her spirit off to fairyland while her body drops lifeless.

The subject is very much of its period; but before too readily dismissing the play as dated, it is worth noting how skilfully Yeats evokes the tone of dangerous innocence that characterizes the speech of the child and weaves dance and song into the texture of the play to define the supernatural world while not apparently breaking with the realistic mode in which the play overall is conceived (singing and dancing are plausible activities of a wayward, vivacious child). The most striking feature of Yeats's artistry, however, is the assured handling of stage-space and in particular the sustained focus of attention on the doorway as the threshold between different dimensions of reality: the known which is mundane and a beyond which, being unknown, is charged with imaginative potential. That focus on the door as threshold allows the setting to be at once the realistic representation of Mary's home and a symbolic evocation of her consciousness, her soul, and the pressures and impulses in conflict there. Stage-space has become metaphorical; this is drama of the interior (in both senses of the word).

It might be argued that, despite the Irish setting, a fairy enchantment is not an especially Irish subject. What makes it peculiarly so for an Irish audience is the focus on the threshold, for the concept of the threshold means much to the Gaelic sensibility. According to Celtic belief, states of in-between-ness, physical and temporal, were respected as times for acquiring or losing great personal powers. In dramatic terms they afforded Yeats a context for achieving what under his father's guidance he had long considered the primary objective of theatre: the staging of moments of intense life, 'passionate action or somnambulistic reverie'. They were states not of being but of becoming and as such were decisive, irrevocable. The actual doorway on stage here becomes the correlative of the central character's access to self-awareness, since it gives entrance to a representative of some challenging, alien nature or world, the Other in Jungian terms, against which Mary Bruin's self has to seek definition. Whether consciously or not, Yeats had hit on a powerful, archetypal symbol in the threshold which in terms of drama had its roots less in English than in classical Greek theatre. It was too a stage-image which at this exact point in time Maeterlinck was reviving and exploring with a vibrant and eerie immediacy in his plays *The Intruder*, *Interior* and *The Death of Tintagiles*. Ancient and modern usage endowed this focus on the ominous doorway with considerable authority.

It was characteristic of Yeats that he should make a creative virtue out of a practical necessity: he had shrewdly judged that a new Irish drama designed to challenge the mainstream of British theatre could initially expect to see performance only in random venues, infrequently and in what professionally were known as fit-up conditions. Simplicity of staging was essential; subtlety, complexity and richness were to be the work of the players' imaginations and the audiences'. A few flats with a windowpiece and doorway were easily obtainable, and they are sufficient to create the settings for most of Yeats's early plays and for Lady Gregory's and Synge's. When in 1904 their company acquired the old Mechanics' Institute in Dublin and converted it into a permanent base as the Abbey Theatre, they were all working on a stage measuring only twenty-one feet by sixteen.

What is impressive is the range of significance that Yeats invited audiences to read into his various thresholds. In *Cathleen ni Houlihan* (first staged in 1902) a peasant comedy about dowries and wedding clothes is invaded by an elderly woman whose strange talk mesmerizes the son of the house, Michael Gillane, and draws him away from the hearth and his bride-to-be. In contrast with the realism of the room and the relaxed postures of the Gillane household, she seems an alien presence, tense, rhetorical, insistent, with her tales from legend and history about men who have died for her cause, her songs and her prophetic exhortations about an army that is massing outside. Yet by the end of the play when her true identity stands revealed as Cathleen ni Houlihan, she has transformed Michael's way of seeing his home: it becomes *unreal* to him in contrast with the image of a patriotic destiny that Cathleen awakens in his imagination and promises might soon be his. She has given him an Irish virility and sense of purpose. As he grows keener to join the rising in preparation without (it is 1798) so she grows in stature and presence till she leaves the stage transfigured, having effected a similar transformation in Michael's soul.

Yeats's play attempts to initiate a change in perception for his audiences too by posing them a challenge in respect of how they interpret the image of Cathleen's departing figure with arm upraised: is she a maundering crone or a heroic but dispossessed queen, icon of a national ideal? The play is unquestionably Irish in form, technique and feeling, since to be interpreted at all adequately it requires an understanding of Irish political and cultural history. In consequence it has sustained an enduring popularity, even after Ireland's independence, since with the division of the kingdom into North and South Cathleen is still not in possession of all her 'beautiful green fields'. The strength of *Cathleen ni Houlihan* lies in its confronting a tragic situation without recourse to the defeatist rhetoric characteristic of the old Queen's melodramas.

In *The Hour-Glass* (first staged 1903, revised 1912) the doorway marks the intersection of the timeless with the time-bound, of the divine with the mortal, of the numinous with the rational: it admits a supernatural visitor (the Angel) who razes a dogmatic, though intricately developed, human consciousness (the Wise Man's) to its foundations, the better to build it again to a less egocentric design. By contrast the threshold in *Deirdre* (staged 1906, revised text 1907) is the focus of all the heroine's fear and self-pity; and when it ultimately admits the object of her dread, her enemy, the jealous king Conchubar, she is compelled to transcend herself and accomplish the suicide that has long been prophesied as her end. Here the doorway is Yeats's means of concentrating the audience's attention on the psychological implications of the plot: *Deirdre* explores the intricate strategies by which the heroine's mind seeks at first to evade but subsequently comes to accept, even choose, the death which she senses to be threateningly imminent. The image of billowing sea-mist framed by the 'big door' of the 'great hall at Dundealgan', the setting for *On Baile's Strand* (staged 1904), is Yeats's means of discriminating in that play between his two central characters, Cuchulain and King Conchubar. To the latter that 'beyond' is a place to be feared against which he must prepare defences now he chooses to establish a settled kingdom; to the hero it emblematizes the challenge of the unknown and a source of exhilaration, since to survive there Cuchulain must needs keep his awareness at a pitch of attention. The whole tragedy will grow out of that distinction of temperament.

Yeats, through this run of early plays, found and developed a dramatic strategy which allowed him with the utmost economy to create a playing space that, as the audience perceived it, was at once realistic and symbolic. In each of the plays discussed a precise social world is evoked with considerable immediacy which, when viewed from a particular perspective, also defines the state of one character's subjective awareness. Though the central characters in these plays move towards an intense perception of selfhood, they do this in contexts which prevent them being described as solipsistic. It is worth stressing this point, as it helps to draw a necessary contrast between Yeats's plays and those of the French Symbolists, especially Villiers de l'Isle Adam and Maeterlinck, who were described above as influencing his early practice as dramatist. They too explored stage-space to create a drama of the interior, alternating outdoor and indoor settings, thresholds, labyrinthine passageways, vaults and turrets to define the intricate movements of their characters' subconscious: the fears, apprehensions, sudden mood-swings, moments of inexplicable illumination that shape awareness and modify perception in ways that determine what is the essence of the self. But, though their plays have a remarkable intensity and concentration of effect, the characters are largely revealed as the victims of circumstance, driven by inexplicable forces of doom. By contrast, in Yeats's plays the characters are the creators of their own destinies by virtue of passionately made choices in their social lives, the consequences of which bring them to varying degrees of insight into the nature of being, chance and fate; states of what Yeats later termed 'excited reverie' repeatedly mark the climax of his dramas.

Yeats believed fervently that metaphysical, symbolic or imagistic art of any kind, running always the risk of being diffuse or vague, needed a sharp edge to its definitions of experience; only through an absolute clarity in the presentation of subject and theme would a play capture an audience's imagination and reverberate in their memories after a performance. A play, he argued, should trouble the mind of a spectator not only through its strangeness but also, and paradoxically, its immediacy. In a late poem, 'The Circus Animals' Desertion' (1939), Yeats meditates on the achievement of his earliest plays in just these terms: their themes were 'heart-mysteries', yet the presentation of those themes required particularity:

Character isolated by a deed
To engross the present and dominate memory.

And Yeats revised those early plays rigorously till he had achieved that artistic ideal to his satisfaction. While he admired Maeterlinck's strategies for making the experience of drama in performance a kind of lived poetry, Yeats considered that few if any of Maeterlinck's plays achieved the status of total symbol which could encompass both an elasticity and precision of reference. What gave Yeats's own plays that necessary hard edge would seem to be his unshaken determination to make the stage not only a place for poetry but also an expression of a nationalist identity and intent.

The force of this contrast becomes apparent if one considers Yeats's *The Shadowy Waters* (first staged 1904, revised staging 1906; but in composition throughout the 1890s), his one full-scale attempt at the symbolist style. The play went through numerous redraftings in an effort to achieve a simple plot-line that would best convey Yeats's complex theme about the psychological and emotional pressures that compel individuals to devote their lives to questing after seemingly impossible ideals; Forgael's zeal, while it alienates his fellow-pirates, infects the captive queen, Dectora, till she identifies wholly with his ambitions. Though the play is set in a remote, mythical world and is fundamentally a mood-piece that rises to a rapturous close as Dectora and Forgael embrace in celebration of their commitment to pursue a shared ideal, *The Shadowy Waters* never loses its focus on the workings of the human psyche: Forgael's quest exacts of him a relentless process of depersonalization which Yeats defines with a scrupulous exactitude; and when Dectora comes under his spell, she is required to submit to that process too. The mythical reference is wholly Irish, and this offsets the immediacy of the action during a performance to a covert propagandist end: the play is situated in Ireland's saga past but is realized (through the devices of the theatre) in the present time that the spectator's imagination inhabits, where the dramatist's ideas about the nature of commitment might hopefully take root and inspire a future action. An influence from contemporary French drama has undergone a sea-change into something richer than the prototype and strangely Irish.

Continual revision of the manuscripts of *The Shadowy Waters* to produce a genuinely stageable version taught Yeats a great deal about dramatic verse. He became convinced that 'all the finest poetry comes logically out of the fundamental action' and that it was erroneous 'to believe that some things are inherently poetical and to try and pull them on to the scene at every moment', since 'it is just these seeming inherently poetical things that wear out'. The weakness of the first drafts was that 'there was no internal life pressing for expression through the characters'. Such a new form of drama and mode of characterization clearly demanded performers prepared to evolve a technique that was very different from the style of externalized emotionalism then current in the playing of melodrama. Histrionic mannerism needed to be discarded in favour of an intense inwardness, and a power of suggestion in favour of forceful presentation. Actors had to be aware of how everything on stage existed in both a realistic and a symbolic dimension and how they were the mediators taking their audiences on a journey into consciousness that would expand each spectator's awareness too till it comfortably inhabited both dimensions.

With the founding of first the Irish Literary Theatre and then the Irish National Theatre Society over the period 1899 to 1904 Yeats got the chance to observe his work in performance, and he became increasingly preoccupied with discovering ways of controlling the look and sound of a production to avoid unnecessary distractions and too intrusive and modish a theatricality. As his opinions ripened into theories, he decided to start a regular theatre-publication in which he and his fellow dramatists might argue their position and justify their practice: *Beltaine* ran through three issues between May 1899 and April 1900; and the more substantial *Samhain*, which included texts of plays as well as articles, achieved seven numbers between October 1901 and November 1908. The impressive array of subjects Yeats covered in these publications steadily amounted to a manifesto about how he wished to revolutionize Irish theatre and make it partake of the best of contemporary European innovation. The articles (like many of his letters and essays of this time) expound ideas about the proper functions of director, actor and designer within a production; about vocal control and modulation; the stylizing of gesture and movement; about the value of stillness. Yeats saw good grounds for changing the whole practice of theatre.

Yeats's prime need in the early 1900s was for performers, preferably Irish and of nationalist sympathies, who were untutored in the ways of the professional (Anglicized) theatre and willing to commit themselves enthusiastically to innovation. Experimental 'laboratory' theatres are so regular a part of our experience of drama in performance today that it is perhaps difficult to imagine how daring, startling even, Yeats's ambition to found such a theatre was in the Dublin of 1901. Fortuitously, one like-minded man came to Yeats's aid: Frank Fay. For some months in the columns of the *United Irishman* Fay had been writing criticism of the routine nature of most Dublin theatrical fare; he contrasted it with the situation in Paris, where Antoine and Lugné-Poë had set about training a company of actors expressly to create a new production style; and he asked why the Irish Literary Theatre could not do the same rather than rely (as they had felt obliged to do throughout their first three seasons) on English performers such as May Whitty or Frank Benson's company. Actually Fay already had such a group in training under his direction, Inghínidhe na hÉireann (The Daughters of Erin); they were in time to form the nucleus of the Abbey company.

Fay as a director set great store by the primacy of the spoken text and musical delivery by technically accomplished voices that did not self-consciously spurn their Irish accents or rhythms. To focus attention on the vocal riches of a performance, he had evolved a mode of acting that eschewed exaggerated, overtly theatrical gesture. Movement was to be sparing, simple and rarely timed to coincide with speech unless on the part of the actual speaker. Delivery under these circumstances had to be worth the listening, hence Fay's concern with musicality and rhythm. It was a self-consistent theory of performance and it perfectly matched Yeats's ambitions.

Such a style of acting and direction required a complementary style of stage design: unassertive, aesthetically satisfying, sensitive to the dramatist's symbolic deployments of spatial relations. Fortuitously again, Yeats's circle of friends and colleagues was expanding to include a group of artist–designers with the right skills and pioneering spirit: Lady Gregory's son, Robert, the poet and engraver Thomas Sturge Moore, Charles Ricketts and Edward Gordon Craig. All believed theatre design to be an art not a craft and considered that stage-settings should not merely inform as to place and time or provide an illustrative background to the action but should lead the audience to engage through carefully selected visual stimuli with the poetic dimensions of the play being performed. The objective was to find spatially dynamic and aesthetically suggestive means of encouraging an audience to inhabit the play as at once an immediate and a symbolic entity. Financial considerations made simple settings imperative; aesthetic consider-ations demanded a simplicity that did not look amateurish or obviously cheap; a principle of consciously refined simplicity in design would introduce an order of imaginative richness into a production which had little to do with the conventionally spectacular, but which offered instead a wealth of implication. At every level of performance this was an art theatre appealing directly to the imagination, wholly unified in its means the better to effect the creation of a drama exploring the nature of consciousness.

Throughout the first decade of this century, despite a series of political controversies that led to the secession of some prominent members of the original Abbey company (including, in time, Frank Fay), Yeats was consolidating his achievement by virtue of his new friendships and gaining increasing confidence in all branches of the art of theatre, thereby strengthening his command of dramatic form and expression as a playwright. The stage began to speak for him in a uniquely distinctive way, and particularly so when he turned to dramatizing material relating to the old Irish sagas; Yeats showed himself utterly confident in mustering to his aid a variety of dramatic styles, verbal and theatrical. *On Baile's Strand* (first staged 1904, revised 1906) is a tragedy in the Shakespearean mould, exploring the conflict between two destructively antipathetic modes of being: the carefree, impulsive life of the warrior (Cuchulain) who thinks with his entire body is set against the calculating, politic mind that delights only in cerebral scheming and values only material security (Conchubar). *Deirdre* (staged 1906, revised staging 1908) is a tense, psychological game of power that is also a profound study of the way the human mind prepares itself for death; the chosen form of the play is a neoclassical tragedy akin to Racine. *The Green Helmet* (staged 1910) is a heroic farce negotiating brilliant transitions of mood between the uproarious, the knockabout, the amorous, the chivalric, the downright eerie and the transcendently supernatural. In none of these works are we experiencing what has come to be known pejoratively as 'costume drama', comfortably remote because undemanding emotionally or intellectually.

To study these early plays in chronological sequence shows Yeats exuberantly exploring possible ways of effecting surprising, often audacious transitions of tone to bring an audience into a deeper awareness of a character's psyche. The exciting theatricality always sharpens one's powers of discrimination; and the effects are often dazzling for the economy with which they are achieved in terms of stage-time. Particularly thrilling and purposeful are the shifts of mood that accompany the developing action of *On Baile's Strand*, as the focus moves back and forth between the heroic characters and that strange pairing of

Blind Man and Fool (the one teasing and coldly malicious; the other full of a visionary understanding yet incapable of adequately articulating his perceptions). We seem at times to be watching a grotesque caricaturing of the main action that repeatedly challenges our sense of Cuchulain and Conchubar as heroic. In the final sequences of the play the two worlds fuse, so that Cuchulain confronts the horror of learning that the young man he has slain is his unknown son while seated in the company of Blind Man and Fool, who will not or cannot identify with his suffering out of fellow-feeling. Far from denigrating his tragic stature, their darkly comic insinuations endorse it by stressing the utter isolation of his sensibility as it embraces an all-consuming grief. The artistry here goes way beyond what conventionally passes for dramatic irony.

Equally exciting in performance is Yeats's decision to present Deirdre as a consummate actress who is compelled by cruel circumstance to define her heart's truth (the absolute constancy of her love for Naoise) through role-play. When Deirdre realizes her lover has been slain by Conchubar's men, she is at first frantic and turns away from the king to hide her passionate grief; turning back to him, she has gained a sudden, chilling calm which as rapidly changes to feline sensuality. The transitions keep an audience in rapt attention to every nuance of the ensuing dialogue, anxious to learn the truth about this seeming shape-changer; and Yeats handles the blank verse with a wonderful elasticity to create a new mode of speech to complement each of the personalities that Deirdre chooses to assume. The outstanding technical accomplishment of *The Green Helmet* is often undervalued by critics: Yeats places a heroic character, Cuchulain, at the centre of a farce which presents a once decorous community in the grip of a particular form of madness. Every other character's dignity has been undermined and till the last moment the audience is left uncertain whether circumstances will compel the hero to succumb to the prevailing lunacy or whether he will have the tenacity to remain self-possessed and transcend the pressures to conform. The technical brilliance in all three of these plays is wholly at the service of a profound psychological inquiry.

By the time he completed *Deirdre* and *The Green Helmet*, Yeats had evolved an approach to dramatic form and related theories about style in performance that were firmly opposed to what conventionally passed for realism and naturalism on the contemporary stage. His preoccupation was with returning qualities of wonder and strangeness (a word that for Yeats always carried decidedly metaphysical overtones or intimations of the numinous) to the art of theatre. To this end his plays increasingly pursued modes of stylization: songs as detached commentary on the action, dance and mime, varieties of intoned or sung speech, moments of ritual and of sustained stillness, the deliberate exploitation of role-play and a deployment of certain characters within the action for their symbolic potential. One final aid to stylization (one with a long provenance in the theatre) had yet to be added to the list of Yeats's technical experiments: masks. His friendship with Edward Gordon Craig had matured over the decade, and in consequence the Abbey had been privileged to receive the gift of a set of Craig's newly invented system of screens, which would enable Yeats to create an endless series of abstract architectural settings in which to stage the range of his plays. Craig, in exploring and advising how the screens might be deployed for *The Hour-Glass*, *Deirdre* and *On Baile's Strand* (some of his suggested designs were included by Yeats in *Plays for an Irish Theatre* in 1911), read Yeats's plays with great sensitivity and suggested it would be appropriate for certain characters such as the Angel or the Blind Man and the Fool to wear masks to enhance an audience's perception of them as serving a symbolic function. He designed three magnificent masks for them to prove his point. Though all the constituent elements of Yeats's later plays had now been identified and their dramatic possibilities severally assessed, they had not yet come together to cohere within one autonomous, unified structure. Yeats seemed to be looking for some stimulus to inspire that next creative leap.

A recurring desire on Yeats's part from the moment the company was established at the Abbey had been to mount a Greek tragedy to create the taste in Dublin audiences by which his own art might be enjoyed and understood, just as he had encouraged productions of Molière's and Goldoni's comedies to foster appreciation of Lady Gregory's work and Synge's. It was a way of establishing the (non-English) traditions which the Abbey dramatists saw themselves as continuing. Greek tragedies like Sophocles' *Oedipus the King* (Yeats's preferred choice) use song, dance, mime, masks, patterned speech and a setting reduced to little more than one vast threshold to create a drama that is at once social and deeply psychological. Yeats pushed on with his *Oedipus* project assiduously after 1908, as if its completion would answer some personal need. The problem was to find a speakable, terse, non-academic translation. When in 1911/12 Nugent Monck finally put the play into rehearsal at the Abbey, Yeats decided to create a stage-version himself; large sections of the play other than the choruses were completed enthusiastically; but the project was suddenly shelved, chiefly one supposes for want of an actor in the Abbey company sufficiently accomplished to tackle the demanding title role.

How Yeats's career as playwright would have developed had *Oedipus* been staged in 1912 is a matter of guesswork, but involvement in actually staging a Greek tragedy would have taught him much about the mechanics of such a form of drama; Yeats learned rapidly through listening to, and participating in, rehearsals. None of the extant information about Monck's plans suggests, however, that he intended to use masks, which are so central a feature of the performance-dynamic of Greek drama, effectively depersonalizing the actors while giving the characters' predicaments a rare immediacy. The mask had long fascinated Yeats but more as an idea, as a cerebral metaphor through which to define psychological evasions and duplicities, than as a tangible entity with extraordinary powers of expression in the theatre. Given that Monck's intentions with *Oedipus* appear to have been rather prosaic and literal, it is perhaps as well that they were not realized (to judge the situation from Yeats's standpoint): a production of the tragedy might have halted without properly satisfying Yeats's search for a tradition of drama where stylization and ritual were the guiding and unifying creative principles. Two new friendships suddenly enabled Yeats to make a momentous discovery that would transform his expectations of what theatre might achieve not as a stage for verse but as a stage for embodied symbol. Those friends, Ezra Pound and Michio Ito, brought him to an awareness of Japanese Noh, a drama which in the staging became a kind of living poetry, where all the arts that together constitute performance were stylized to such an extreme degree that they became charged with profound metaphorical resonances. Crucially, Noh was a theatre where the abiding focus was on the dynamic potential of masks.

During 1913 Mary Fenollosa invited Ezra Pound to edit her late husband's papers, the product of many years' study of aspects of Japanese culture; the bulk of them related to his major interest, the Noh drama. Ernest Fenollosa had not only attended performances regularly during two long visits to the country (1878–86 and 1897–1900) but had received personal instruction in the art of acting in the Noh style. He had studied the operatic but guttural delivery; the special stance that dictates the elegant, gliding movement of the body; the evocative use of the fan; the carriage of the head when masked. Above all he had learnt the discipline underlying the fundamental principle of Noh that less achieves more, which in the accomplished performer is manifest in a stillness that is alive with tensions implying so many possibilities for action that any gesture or motion is both surprising and inevitable. The papers included descriptions of the theatres, the typical programme of a performance, the costumes and masks, and numerous translations of plays (each accompanied by annotations, many in the form of sketches, defining the particular techniques and skills required of the actors). Pound moved that November to a Sussex cottage to begin the undertaking which he was to publish in 1916 as *Noh – or, Accomplishment*. Some of the material appeared a few months prior to the Macmillan volume as a Cuala Press publication, entitled *Certain Noble Plays of Japan*, where the translations were prefaced by an essay from Yeats. Pound had invited Yeats to share Stone Cottage with him at Coleman's Hatch, Sussex; the ensuing two months were a rite of passage for Yeats into maturity as a playwright, as he found an ancient theatre that practised what he had believed was only an imagined ideal. Five 'plays for dancers', composed and revised between 1916 and 1921, were his direct response, but the dramatic form he created at this time continued to influence his playwriting till the end of his career.

Yeats had known of the Japanese art of the print since the 1890s and had observed its influence at work in the setting and costume designs of Charles Ricketts for some years. Longing to get away from the literal-mindedness of painted backdrops for outdoor scenes that were the convention of the time, he had encouraged Robert Gregory to study Japanese water-colours and prints to discover ways of stylizing observations of nature into aesthetic patterns before he began designing the first woodland setting the Abbey required in 1905. Of Japanese theatre forms Yeats appears to have known little before his encounter with the Noh. Here was a theatre in which drama coalesced with ritual, where centuries-old traditions in performing demanded the total depersonalization of the actor as inheritor of particular roles and where the wearing of masks ensured the loss of the performer's subjective self except in the expressiveness of his body-language in gesture, mime and dance. Noh offers a mode of performance in which voice and movement make their appeal to the spectator's imagination through the mask as mediator and shaper of meaning rather than through the interpretational skills and stage-personality of the individual actor as in most modern forms of Western theatre. Though poetic and literary in inspiration, Noh freely admits that there are invariably moments in drama when words fall short of the power of song, dance and stillness to communicate intricacy of meaning.

Equally exciting for Yeats must have been the discovery of a drama where ghosts and gods, daimons and demons, mingle confidently with human characters without the stage having recourse to trick lighting, spectacular traps, flying devices or specially cued musical effects. Noh is a theatre that eschews all conventions of realism, the better to engage with the nature of the mind in its subtlest operations; all the action is psychological in its intent and focuses on the central character of the drama, the role assumed by the principal actor, or *shite*. This character is invariably caught in a crisis of identity and is searching for the innermost truths about the self in an effort to find release from the spiritual torment that is his or her present condition of being; ghosts and gods become aspects of that questing self, projections of fears, hopes, unconscious and conflicting impulses that keep the mind in thrall to self-pity or despair. The climactic dance towards which the performance moves inexorably can be expressive of continuing anguish or, less frequently, of the peace of enlightenment as the self finds the means of transcending its obsession with identity.

Then too there was the unusual form of the Noh play with its series of framing devices to detach the audience from realistic preoccupations: the trance-inducing rhythms of drums and flute; a chorus which lyrically evokes the atmosphere of the scene, establishes the basic situation and at times speaks for the central character as if from the very depths of that character's being; and the subordinate *waki*-figure, often a priest or weary, benighted traveller, who is the occasion for the *shite*-character's appearance and on-stage audience for that character's self-communing. Even that process of inner exploration may involve a further degree of detachment, since it is often cast in the form of a dreaming-back over past experience, with the character's present self watching the drama of his or her former life as it is played out in the private theatre of memory and imagination. Noh is a theatre where reverie is tense and excited; and a theatre that is addressed by a deliberate series of strategies to 'the eye of the mind' of the spectator. Masks are appropriately the main visual means of communication, since the plays are chiefly about the personae created by a particular mind to meet its changing needs. Noh pursues an overt theatricality in terms of its structure and mode of performance in order to bring the audience into an engagement with the poetic, psychological and symbolic content of the plays. It exactly realized what Yeats considered theatre should endeavour to be.

Yeats is often criticized for not directly copying the form of Noh, but it was not his way to be derivative in respect of influences. *At the Hawk's Well*, his first attempt at a dance-drama, is the closest he came to creating a traditional Noh; but even then there are notable differences, particularly the development of the *waki*-like Old Man as a character who is not just a spectator of Cuchulain's drama but has a distinctive contribution to make to the thematic organization of the play. Yeats's way with the Noh is not so much a case of cultural appropriation as creative improvising on a traditional ground-base to further his ambition for a uniquely Irish drama. The subject matter of his dance-dramas is never oriental, nor were the productions mounted in his lifetime orientalized in terms of their performance techniques, style of design, choreography or musical accompaniment. (One possible exception was the dance of the Hawk-Woman in the 1916 staging of *At the Hawk's Well*, which was created by Michio Ito, a young Japanese dancer who chanced to be visiting London after studying the Dalcroze method on the continent; he assisted Pound with the Fenollosa papers and in time demonstrated to Yeats what he could recall of the movements in Noh drama.) What Yeats took from Noh was its fundamental principles of stylization to achieve a union of myth, dream and psychological symbolism; the myths and their psychological interpretation were, however, to be wholly Irish.

Of the initial group of four plays for dancers, *At the Hawk's Well* and *The Only Jealousy of Emer* examine incidents from the saga accounts of the life of Cuchulain; *The Dreaming of the Bones* investigates the relationship between Irish history and the contemporary revolutionary consciousness; and *Calvary*, while taking the Passion of Christ as its ostensible subject, explores the nature of martyrdom in a manner that makes its thinking applicable to the fate of a number of Irish patriots, especially Parnell. All four centre on a moment of choice that irrevocably determines the future identity of the protagonist. Cuchulain, hoping for immortality by drinking from the waters of the mystic well, commits himself to a heroic warrior's existence that offers him instead undying fame in legend. Emer confronts her growing jealousy and learns how her possessiveness distorts her perception of Cuchulain; she gives him his freedom by transcending her innermost longings in an act that defines the nature of selfless love. The Soldier, a gunman on the run from the failed Easter Rising of 1916, meets the ghosts of Diarmuid and Dervorgilla who, when living, were responsible for inviting an English invasion of Ireland to support their authority which had been compromised by their adulterous relationship; they appeal to his pity, since his forgiveness would bring their souls release from the horror of knowing the consequences of their intimacy; and he wrestles with antagonistic impulses, unsure whether to be compassionate or to reaffirm his patriotic stance. Christ repeatedly dreams through the events that marked his progress to Calvary and crucifixion in an effort to understand the refusal of the people he meets to accept his sacrifice on the terms in which he makes it. Obsessively self-centred intellectually, emotionally and physically, Lazarus, Judas, the women and the Roman soldiers cannot appreciate the effort of will that enables him so to depersonalize himself that he can face death with equanimity; his selflessness arouses only apathy, derision, hero-worship, envy or indifference, because nothing Christ can do can affect the biased perceptions of the spectators of his Passion; and that awareness crucifies him again and again spiritually, making him doubt the value of his life's purpose and dedication to others.

What is immediately apparent from this short summary of the plays is how far they depart with increasing confidence from the traditional format of the Noh: they deploy far larger casts (at least nine actors are required for *Calvary*) and are shaped in at least two instances to a sequence of episodes within the one main action without any loss of concentration or intensity. Less apparent from the summaries is Yeats's ambitious experimentation with the possibilities of the mask. In *At the Hawk's Well*, the masks simply define youth, age and the bird-woman. In *Calvary* the mask of a dreaming Christ is thrown into sharp contrast with the aggressively life-hungry features defining the masks of the other characters and with the anguished voice and racked body of the actor playing the central role; the difficulty of sustaining the spiritual repose which is the play's subject has a precise visual correlative achieved within the very circumstances of the performance.

The Dreaming of the Bones is distinctive for having one unmasked character, the rebel soldier, accompanied by two, the ghosts, who are masked. At first this seems to define their supernatural condition; but as their story is told and their purgatorial anguish becomes known, so the masks augment our sense of the horror of their fixed state of being, caught seemingly throughout eternity between longing and loathing for each other. Our response to the young man's unmasked face similarly undergoes change as the action develops; at first it intimates his palpably sentient humanity, which encourages the ghosts to make their desperate appeal to his apparently innocent, kindly nature; later the actor's moving, troubled features define the character's capacity for choice, while the contrast between his face and the ghosts' masks amplifies our sense of the danger of choice when its consequences can prove so far-reaching and emotionally stultifying. Ultimately his choice endorses the political status quo, and one is left wondering whether his want of a mask exposes his lack of a truly heroic potential that would have enabled him to rise imaginatively above the situation and find a solution to break the cycles of destiny. The theatrical strategies of the play exactly complement the thematic and psychological objectives.

The Only Jealousy of Emer involves even more sophisticated strategies with masks. One actor is required first to represent the near drowned Cuchulain; then after Emer draws the curtains around the bed on which he reclines, he changes a suitably heroic mask for one with the distorted features of the god, Bricriu; once Emer makes her tragic renunciation, the actor collapses within the bed to reappear moments later sporting the original mask as Cuchulain newly restored to consciousness. This actor's heroic mask has an exact double on stage worn by the Ghost of Cuchulain in the play-within-the-play that Bricriu conjures up to show Emer how Fand in the spirit world is trying desperately to gain total possession of the warrior's being. The exchange of masks by the one actor, whose stance must shift to match from the upright to the contorted, renders in precise dramatic terms the way that perception is affected by fluctuating emotions and in so doing shows the audience how to see the play overall as dramatizing the levels of Emer's consciousness. All the characters are as it were projections of her mind, defining her conflicting attitudes to Cuchulain and her marriage; as she rises above her fanatical desire to constrain and shape Cuchulain to her personal liking, so the stage clears of the phantoms that haunt her and we are left to contemplate her mask undistracted as the chorus sing of the nature of tragic beauty. By a great effort of courage and imagination, Emer has experienced the process of catharsis in the depths of her being. Yeats has exploited the use of the mask to dramatize the subtlest movements of the psyche to a nicety.

The dance too was an aspect of Noh that Yeats began to use differently from the prototype. In the Noh it is always performed by the *shite*-actor and is the final expression of his character's innermost self. In Yeats's dance-plays this is rarely the case; usually Yeats deploys the dance to express a new kind of awareness that afflicts or confronts his protagonist and challenges all previous sense that that character possessed of his or her identity. The youthfully arrogant Cuchulain is mesmerized by the hawk, whose attacks then rouse his own fierce spirit, compelling him to assert an identity very different from that which till then has been determined by his quest after magic waters which will give him an eternity of indolent pleasure. In *At the Hawk's Well* Cuchulain is required at least to participate in the dance; in the three remaining *Plays for Dancers* the protagonist is a spectator in whose personal interpretation of a danced episode lies a means to achieve greater self-definition. Emer watches the sinuous Fand trying to seduce the Ghost of Cuchulain into her power; this woman of the Sidhe is beautiful but awesome, being perfect of form yet like an idol of bronze or silver. She at once attracts and repels, since she tempts with pleasures that will be all-consuming: in return for Cuchulain's complete submission Fand promises oblivion and the extinction of self. Fand is an emblem of possessiveness – overwhelming, enveloping in her intent – who teaches Emer to recognize such qualities in herself. Christ on his cross observes the Roman soldiers mime a complicated scenario involving a game of dice for possession of his cloak before they reel jubilantly about him in a dance expressive of mindless vitality; they celebrate the life of the body in a fashion that sets them in direct opposition to his intellectual preoccupations with piety and dedication to an ideal.

Movement permeates a performance of *The Dreaming of the Bones* more extensively than in the other plays in this group with a correspondingly greater complexity of significance. The play enacts a journey: the Soldier is anxious to reach the west coast of Ireland by morning to take ship for America and gain safety from the British authorities. The ghosts guide him in the darkness over a mountain from the summit of which they perceive below them a landscape of ruins and wasted fields that are one consequence of the English conquest. This journey is represented in a stylized form: the three characters circle the stage three times before pausing for breath in their rapid 'ascent' and this action is itself repeated three times, making it a kind of ritual. The numbers have, of course, magical connotations and the ghosts can be seen to be working a charm on the young man, preparing his mind to be sympathetic to their plight; but their hypnotic hold over him is somewhat broken when he sees the vista below and lyrically keens the ravaged land. They tell him their tale and make their appeal but withhold at first their actual names. To his persistent inquiries they reveal their identities and are rejected and denounced for their treachery to Ireland. The lovers' response is a stunned silence before they break into a different pattern of movement: they turn restlessly about each other, at first with gestures suggestive of passionate longing, but these are soon dispelled by others intimating a horror at what that passion impelled them to do. The sequence is repeated endlessly, getting faster and faster; the ghosts' circling about the stage gets ever wider, till finally they disappear from view. The continual image of encircling comes to represent a horrifying kind of completeness: entrapment within a deterministic cycle of events and of behaviour. All three characters are trapped within the process of history: the Soldier is granted a visionary awareness of that fact and for such knowledge he can find no forgiveness; he vaunts his patriotism as he views the spectacle of the ghosts dancing out their despair and his seemingly inhuman ardour is seen as one tragic consequence of the past that is being re-created before us. How are we, the greater audience of the dance, to judge the event? The simplest of dance patterns, the circle, is here charged with a complexity of meaning carrying social, historical, emotional and intellectual resonances. Yeats's use of movement in this play was a brilliant and daring invention: extreme simplicity wedded to a conceptual and aesthetic sophistication of the highest order.

It is traditional in Japan for Noh plays to be performed in groups of three or five. Their sheer intensity demands some element of relief, so the principal dramas are interspersed in the programme with short *kyogen* plays, earthy farce-like creations involving much knockabout. It was customary Abbey policy from the first to have regular programmes of one-act works which were carefully selected to cover a wide tonal and emotional range. Yeats, wishing to see his plays for dancers make up a complete evening's programme and realizing the need for tonal variety, next expanded the form he had devised into the genre of comedy. *The Cat and the Moon* takes the stand-up comic routine that is a hallmark of Irish theatre (O'Casey was soon to exploit the device in some notable pairings: Shields and Davoren, Joxer and the Paycock) and by a characteristic Yeatsian irony uses it as the basis for a play about miracle and the power of faith to transfigure the earthy into the sublime. The transformation is effected before our eyes by the power of the mask and the dance as the Lame Man, till now quick only in his wits, discovers with the Saint's aid the joys of movement. It is a wonderful exploration of the capacity of the actor's art to convince us imaginatively first of the reality of the character's lameness, then of the reality of the miracle; and all is achieved through his physical prowess, shaping meaning by the meticulous and richly inventive deployment of a flexible body-language.

In 1926 chance again played a part in furthering Yeats's development as a dramatist: Mrs Yeats found the abandoned manuscript of her husband's version of Sophocles' *King Oedipus* and encouraged him to complete it. In F. J. McCormick the Abbey now had an actor capable of sustaining the demanding central role and in Lennox Robinson a director sensitive to the play's formalities and to Yeats's concern for a direct delivery of the speech uncontaminated by archly 'poetic' voices. A successful production set Yeats translating *Oedipus at Colonus* immediately. What impresses from a study of the manuscripts of *King Oedipus* is Yeats's concern to highlight the horror the other characters feel on realizing how Oedipus is being singled out by Apollo to be a means of demonstrating the god's power. Motivated by a well-meaning compassion, they tried long ago, or are trying now, to stave off the king's own discovery of his fate, but in so doing only make that moment of recognition the more terrible; they are made agents of the god's decree by virtue of what defines their humanity. Yeats's version makes the play as much a social as an individual tragedy; the metaphysical issue of fate compromises every character's integrity. That issue continued to resonate in Yeats's thinking and in varying degrees informs all his subsequent plays.

After the completion of his five dance-plays, the early years of the 1920s proved a fallow period for Yeats the dramatist but working on the Oedipus plays restored to him a wonderful creative exuberance. This energy was further enhanced by the discovery in May 1927 of a new friend, just as the work on Sophocles was coming to an end. Ninette de Valois was to be the last shaping influence on his career as playwright, a muse of a surprising but fitting kind, whose extraordinary gifts as a dancer and choreographer exactly matched Yeats's creative needs of the moment. Her cousin Terence Gray had mounted a production of *On Baile's Strand* at his theatre in Cambridge that January, for which she created the movement work involved in the oath-taking ritual and, more importantly, for the two masked figures of the Blind Man and the Fool. Gordon Bottomley, the English poet who had been inspired to devise dance-plays in imitation of Yeats's recent work, saw the production and wrote excitedly to Yeats about it, enclosing photographs of the performance in his letter. Gray and de Valois had a trained cast that enabled them to stage the play with a physical flamboyance that the Abbey could never have attempted; even from the photographs Yeats must have seen that the performance came nearer to his ideals in terms of staging than any other production had managed to do. Learning that the company were to perform *The Player Queen* in May, he travelled to the Festival Theatre in Cambridge to view their next efforts with his work at first hand. De Valois' contribution to this particular production was slight, but the programme was completed with dances in the modern style of abstract expressionism performed by herself and members of her dancing school. Yeats asked to meet her, invited her to come regularly to Dublin to help establish a school of dance at the Abbey and join him in staging his plays for dancers. This she did, to Yeats's immense satisfaction, and in gratitude he devised for her *Fighting the Waves* (a version of *The Only Jealousy of Emer*, staged 1929) and *The King of the Great Clock Tower* (1934). Inspired by the art and artistry of the Greek tragedian and the modern dancer, Yeats yet again undertook the process of remaking the self as playwright. The resulting series of late plays was as boldly innovative, strange and challenging as this combination of influences would suggest; they placed Yeats firmly in the vanguard of modern experimental theatre.

The remarkable feature about the final plays is the extent to which they use techniques evolved in the composition of the earlier Noh-inspired plays for dancers but with a freedom and audacity that carry them beyond any direct influence from the Japanese prototype. Masks, ghosts, dances, songs, rituals, mimes appear now in startling juxtapositions or disrupt scenes progressing in a style suggestive of conventional stage realism. Yeats appears to have abandoned all his previous concerns for stylistic unity in the drama; traditional concepts of artistic decorum are shattered deliberately in the interest of depicting in dramatic terms the greater ordering of the process that is destiny. Chance and choice are shown in operation in individual lives and work for the most part, as in *Oedipus*, in cruelly deterministic ways; the hope and the quest of the characters would seem always for some release from this tyranny that would allow individuals scope to assert a personal will. The tone of the plays shifts uneasily between the comic and the tragic, the absurd and the enraptured, but always the effect is of a deepening pathos at the dilemma of the human mind that finds itself compromised either by the precarious evolutions and revolutions of history or by its own state of restless ecstasy where metaphysical, intellectual and sensual imperatives are in endless conflict. 'Excited reverie', Yeats's preferred mode of being, here presages disaster more frequently than it heralds inner release from selfhood bringing transcendence. Destiny usually frustrates the characters' efforts at depersonalizing the self.

The Resurrection seems at first a kind of Shavian comedy of ideas as the Greek and the Hebrew discuss the nature of godhead and their characters are sharply distinguished by their very different views of the recently crucified Christ's life and practice. The Greek laughs at Calvary 'because they thought they were nailing the hands of a living man upon the Cross, and all the time there was nothing there but a phantom'; he exemplifies what Yeats in the final chorus calls 'Platonic tolerance', even to the point of being somewhat patronizing towards the Hebrew who believes that in worshipping the Messiah one is honouring a principle of supreme abnegation and suffering as the highest achievement of which humankind is capable. Their talk while guarding Christ's disciples in the inner room is continually disrupted by the sounds the Musicians make, which evoke a Dionysiac rite that we are invited to imagine as taking place in the street outside. It is a wild fertility ritual enacting a death and a rebirth in which nothing is what it seems: the celebrants are men dressed as women; a boy actor dons a mask and seems to be possessed by the god; a woman gives herself sexually to a stranger but clearly in a state of religious ecstasy; an intensely physical experience has a profound symbolic significance. A sacrificial dance-play is conjured up in our imaginations even as our intellects are engaging in the metaphysical debate being enacted before us, and so we experience an unsettling division in our response as audience. The Syrian arrives elated with the news of Christ's seeming resurrection; the strangeness previously associated with the cult taking place outside seems to be invading the apparent discipline of the playing space.

Before Greek and Hebrew can dismiss the Syrian's claims, a masked figure begins slowly to traverse the stage; it is an actor depersonalized by the mask which depicts the face of Christ, whose identity has temporarily displaced his. The paradoxical image that confronts us as well as the characters is both man and godhead, a perception that sends the Greek reeling with terror. He and the Hebrew are totally compromised intellectually and emotionally by this new perception of divinity. A powerful archetypal symbol quite at odds with the rational tenor and realistic presentation of the action takes complete possession of the space, subverting what seemed the established dramatic decorum of the play. *The Resurrection* enacts a momentous occasion of historical and cultural change which the Syrian accepts in awe; but the moment reduces the Hebrew to silence and the Greek to hysteria; they are totally broken by the event. Destiny has destroyed their faith. The dramatic method of the play, with its breaking of one kind of stage illusion the better to endorse another based on extreme stylization, is a superbly judged correlative for the subject being presented.

This bold experiment with form was carried even further in *The Words upon the Window-Pane*, which begins in a style reminiscent of many an Abbey comedy: we are in a Dublin tenement room in which are collected a motley assortment of eccentrics attending a seance. The tone is carefully pitched to syphon off potential scepticism in the audience which might express itself through mocking laughter. Two of the characters talk with some authority about spiritualism and ideas of purgatory, but the prevailing mood is one of tense excitement as more mundane individuals vent their frustration over the fact that previous sessions have been disturbed by a 'hostile influence'. The seance begins and the singing of a hymn heightens and ritualizes the tone. When the contact speaks through the medium, the middle-aged Mrs Henderson, it is incongruously with the high-pitched voice of a child, Lulu. Again this is a brilliantly calculated effect to allow the audience to vent any last impulse to laugh out of nervousness or derision before Lulu's voice is displaced suddenly by a baritone bark of sheer fury. The stage-image is disconcerting in the extreme: a sleeping woman whose mouth is possessed by voices alien to herself and a circle of auditors who claim to believe in spiritualism but who are horrified by the black vision of purgatory that is revealed by the male voice issuing from the medium's lips, because it wholly challenges their rather cosy view of the spirit world. The characters next find that their comfortable space is shared by a couple of angry ghosts who reveal their identities as Swift and Vanessa. Stage realism is supplanted by a new surreal play that takes place for us wholly in 'the eye of the mind': we hear two voices and, hearing, imagine an encounter. The sheer intensity of the passions that impel the two new characters into speech through the medium endows these historical figures with a rare immediacy: they seem of a higher order of reality than the characters we can actually see.

The couple are quarrelling about destiny and the individual will; Swift, fearing inherited madness, refuses to wed Vanessa for all her seductive, cajoling talk about trusting to the chance that she has inherited healthy blood; he has tried, we discover, to educate her in classical precepts of stoicism and self-discipline in the hope of avoiding a scene such as the one she has now forced on him, which steadily reduces him to impotent rage and desperation. Her humanity undermines his intellectual stance and unmans him. Swift seeks succour in the calming presence of his other companion, Stella, but the relaxed tenor of their scene together is set at risk by his repeatedly wanting assurance that she will tend his dying and will close his eyes. Stella has taken his classical philosophy as hers and found a personal freedom and inner beauty in it that have eluded her tutor, who patently dreads the processes of ageing and death. It is a painful play that we are asked to act out in our imaginations; it is about the rage of a man who could not live up to his own impossible ideals, whose choice of the intellect as the supreme expression of himself compelled him into a life of endless compromise. His choice made a purgatory of life and subsequently was to make purgatory his destiny.

The image of Swift is *masterful* (to deploy the term used in 'The Circus Animals' Desertion') in every sense. In the past Swift was possessed with an idea, and with chauvinist imperiousness he shaped Stella's, then Vanessa's mind to its pattern; within the time-span of the play he first takes possession of Mrs Henderson's voice, next the stage-space, then our imaginations and finally the medium's very body and personality. Once seen, this play is not easily forgotten: it fulfils Yeats's desire that a play should 'engross the present and dominate memory' in the most potent and challenging way. *The Words upon the Window-Pane* is highly theatrical; yet the theatricality is an exact metaphor for the implacable working of fate in individual lives, since it is indeed a form of psychological invasion.

Swift endeavoured to shape destiny to his liking and failed; the Stroller in *The King of the Great Clock Tower* succeeds because he chooses to shape his life to fulfil a vow for which he has got divine sanction. His oath transforms physical desire (his love of the Queen's beauty) into a spiritual quest so that his life is pledged to the attainment of an ideal, which he pursues confidently to the point of death. The vow exacts of him a complete depersonalization of the self; he can laugh even at the potential absurdity of his position, but he never loses faith in the vow itself; and his faith is rewarded, though not in the manner he might have expected. Men who die for their faith are deemed martyrs, especially if in dying they instil faith in others: the Stroller's destiny touches the heart of the still, silent Queen and stirs her from the apathy into which she has been thrown by the King's relentless, intrusive questioning. Where the King wishes to *know* the Queen utterly and seeks to determine her identity, the Stroller respects her mystery and extols her with a devotion that yet leaves her free to choose whether or not to respond. In responding, she completes his destiny in a way that is at once profoundly intimate yet selfless: she returns his rapture as he wishes in a dance, knowing he has the sensibility to understand her unique mode of address.

Dance is expressed by the body, yet its motivation comes from some inner impulse and its effect is other-worldly, transcendent; the Queen gives herself completely to the Stroller in the dance without transgressing her private mystery; and that renews her strength to resist the King's aggression. The King is defeated ultimately by his want of imagination, trust and generosity, which are the source of the Stroller's success in communing with the Queen. *The King of the Great Clock Tower* is a highly ambitious work in exploring the nature of sexuality and in its frankly admitting how incapable words are of communicating true intimacy. For over half the playing-time communication is not by speech but by mime, dance, song, snatches of choric utterance and tableaux; words create a context which opens up an audience's receptivity to other modes of theatrical expression; like the Queen, we too are stirred by the action to extend our means of perception, thereby enriching our powers of understanding. We are encouraged to apprehend and embrace the symbolic without reaching after precise and potentially limiting definitions. We live imaginatively within a mystery, which is the nature of faith.

If a vow creates for the Stroller a destiny that is to his liking, a curse imposes on Congal in *The Herne's Egg* a fate that he is powerless to change or to resist, though he chooses to do battle with a god, the Great Herne, to see who is master of his future. *The Herne's Egg* is the strangest, most exotic of Yeats's plays: it is a black farce with touches of pantomime; dance, song and mimed battles permeate the action to achieve a degree of spectacle unparalleled in his other work; it demands an intense physicality in performance, yet sacrilege, blasphemy, religious frenzy and metaphysical ecstasy are its subject. A potent influence on Yeats's theme is clearly Sophocles' *Oedipus*, but equally strong an influence on his dramatic method and vision is Jarry's *Ubu Roi*, the first performance of which Yeats chanced to see in Paris in 1896. *Ubu Roi* is a grotesque, knockabout drama about the abuse of power (it was conceived as a Punch-and-Judy-style puppet-play, though performed when Yeats saw it with actors). Recalling the experience in *Autobiographies* causes Yeats to meditate on the state of culture at the time, on the passing of a conception of art as subtle and celebratory with the upsurge of a new, passionately satirical art designed to challenge, subvert and denigrate; he concludes with a cry of outrage: 'After us the Savage God.'

There could be no more savage god than the Herne, for whom humankind are mere playthings, especially if, like Congal, they question his authority and provoke his 'red rage'. Congal is cursed by the Herne's priestess, Attracta, to die at the hands of a fool, and much of the play is taken up with his attempts to elude this fate. A born warrior, he cannot conceive of life except in terms of 'bouts'; his every effort to wage war on divinity is cunningly turned by the Herne into an expression of the god's own power. Congal and his men claim they have raped Attracta, but she, brought to them mysteriously in a trance, asserts that she has fulfilled her sacred destiny and coupled with the god himself. She has (in Yeats's words) completed her task, her circle; Congal in a last bid to avoid completing his promised circle commits suicide, only to realize too late that he may himself be the fool prophesied to bring about his demise. Attracta tries to prevent the god's cruelty and derision from pursuing Congal beyond death but is frustrated.

The play abounds in ironies, appropriately since the world we are introduced to is presided over by a cruel joker in the Herne. But there is one irony that builds cumulatively through the action, which finally subverts the god's power: the more Attracta and Congal become pawns in the Herne's bizarre games with fate, the more dignity they acquire in their suffering. Both undergo a total transformation of personality: she, a prim postulate with an over-zealous sense of vocation, grows into a warm, compassionate woman; and he, all brawn and little brain, banal, unscrupulous, aggressively chauvinist, begins steadily to grapple with metaphysical issues and ends accepting the justice of his death and honouring Attracta's integrity. Both appear somewhat caricatured figures at first, but their entanglement in the Herne's schemes to vindicate his godhead invests each of them with a developing humanity that by the end arouses our pity. *The Herne's Egg* is a superbly crafted play: incisive, succinct, full of theatrical surprises that dazzle the eye and the mind while advancing Yeats's argument about humanity's intricate relationship with its spiritual yearnings and apprehensions. Farce would seem an odd form to choose for so serious a meditation; but farce is conventionally a determining, mechanistic structure and so an apt correlative for the workings of fate. The form allows the god's authority to manifest itself as all-powerful while exposing it to our judgement as at once awesome and awful.

The Old Man in *Purgatory* acts always in the belief that he lives under a curse by virtue of the facts of his birth. He rages against the past because he cannot shape it differently yet cannot accept what it offers him as his inheritance. In his view his mother married beneath her out of blind lust for a stable groom ('Looked at him and married him'), who, after her death in childbirth, proceeded to squander her wealth and property 'on horses, drink and women'. At sixteen the Old Man had put paid to the past by murdering his father and firing the ancestral home, totally obliterating his given identity before becoming a vagrant. All of this new self that he has to give to the future is a lad, now sixteen, that he 'got/Upon a tinker's daughter in a ditch'.

Much of the play is taken up with the Old Man's story of the past, which does not lie buried in his consciousness but lives on inexorably in his memory. His narrative is spoken with the voice of omniscient authority, appropriately since the story shows how he took on himself the role of god-like arbiter of his father's fate. Yet the dramatic method of the play begins increasingly to subvert that authority. A silent play of ghosts is glimpsed in the ruins of the family home: first the dead mother is seen framed in a window, then the father; they are like icons which, far from promoting veneration, aggravate the Old Man's anger. What disturbs an audience is the disparity between the visual effect of the images and the Old Man's spoken commentary on them. He sees the mother as physically racked both with desire and purgatorial remorse at reliving her past 'transgressions'; the father as a 'beast', drunken, witless. The figures, however, have a composure that makes his words seem perversely ungenerous. So, similarly, do the Boy's responses to the tale: he has no awareness of loss or guilt, no sensed personal involvement with the past to overlay his speech with judgemental tones; and when he finally turns and sees his grandfather's ghost, he expresses pure terror at the surreal strangeness of the experience ('A dead, living, murdered man!'); the words are spontaneous but noticeably free of blame. The Boy's innocence of the burden of original sin sets him poles apart from his father, who now callously butchers him.

For a second time the Old Man has assumed the role of destiny with the intent of ending 'all that consequence' of his mother's marriage; and the second time has so many parallels with the first that it seems to be a calculated re-enactment. Ritualizing the event is the Old Man's way of attempting to depersonalize himself; the Boy's murder is to be a placatory sacrifice to release the grandmother's soul into bliss, or so the Old Man's logic would have us and himself believe; time, place and action have been chosen with scrupulous exactitude; the death has to have the decorum of high art. Yet the elation the Old Man finds in its accomplishment is quickly displaced by horror ('Twice a murderer and all for nothing'), for what stands revealed as the real motive of it all is an obsessive yearning for revenge on the past bred of an intensifying self-loathing. Cursing the hour of his birth is to curse his progenitors and himself. Depersonalizing the self cannot suppress to extinction the story that resonates in his consciousness; all his mind's efforts at doing so only draw the Old Man deeper into a labyrinth of despair. He is the architect of his own destiny, an insight for which he can find no grounds for forgiveness.

The play is remarkable for its compression and lucidity, and for the way it makes an engrossing narrative intensely dramatic by using it as a means to effect a journey deep into the psyche of the Old Man as teller till we know why he is compelled to tell his story and must seek to shape it to a personally satisfying conclusion. His words throughout are juxtaposed with stage-images that qualify and undercut his assertions, alerting us to the possibility that his perceptions are distorted: the impassive ghosts; the genial, down-to-earth nature and healthy movements of the Boy; the glint of scattered coins and then the unsheathed jack-knife in the moonlight; the climactic tableau of the father cradling his murdered son while tunelessly mouthing a nursery-ditty, a pose caricaturing the conventional Pietà, which defines precisely the Old Man's madness and sacrilege; and the ensuing darkness out of which a shaft of light isolates the stunted tree blasted by lightning, which at first seemed merely naturalistic scene-setting but now emblematizes the Old Man's innermost self. What to us is an image of complete desolation is to him an image of grace, till a sudden mood-swing teaches him the bitter truth. The extent of this mind's betrayal of itself makes *Purgatory* Yeats's most profound tragedy.

The Death of Cuchulain was written while Yeats was himself dying, but there is no slackening of inspiration, rigour or innovative audacity. At a first encounter it seems perhaps an oddly disconnected sequence of scenes. A wild old man 'looking like something out of mythology' speaks a prologue clearly intended through mockery of 'this vile age' to alienate the audience. Next come confrontations between Cuchulain and three figures who seem to challenge his self-possession; the last, the hideous Blind Man from *On Baile's Strand*, deals him a death blow and severs his head. Then a genuine figure out of mythology, the Morrigu, goddess of war and fate, appears amidst an arrangement of black parallelograms, each 'the size of a man's head', which she informs us are to represent the decapitated skulls of Cuchulain and his six opponents in battle. Claiming that she 'arranged the dance', the pattern of Cuchulain's death, she summons Emer, the hero's wife, to perform his funeral rite, which is represented by a long, danced scenario in which rage against Cuchulain's murderers gives place to veneration of her husband and then to a rapt stillness in which her posture exactly mirrors his at the moment of his death. The final scene plunges us into a twentieth-century fair where a street-singer celebrates a tradition of Irish heroism stemming from the legendary age of Cuchulain to the martyrs of the Easter Rising of 1916 (a tradition that inspired those martyrs, a fact honoured in the choice of a statue of Cuchulain to mark the site of their rebellion, the Dublin Post Office). The play has subtly defined that heroism as a physical and spiritual fearlessness which invests an individual with a power of self-transcendence.

In each of his scenes with Eithne, Aoife and the Blind Man, Cuchulain rises above the perplexities their presence provokes, which might have reduced him respectively to a jealous rage, self-pity and despair. In the face of Eithne's apparent treachery he shows only the magnanimity of a contented lover; to Aoife's vengefulness he brings compassion and understanding, acknowledging her intent as just; and the Blind Man's obsessive malice he counters with a wit that relishes the absurd incongruity of their situation ('Twelve pennies! What better reason for killing a man?'). The Morrigu may have arranged the dance that is his destiny, but she has no power to determine the mind-set in which he will approach his end. What we watch is a process in which Cuchulain gains increasing self-possession by paradoxically depersonalizing all his responses to the point with the Blind Man where, far from railing against fate, he can jest under the pressure of death. His reward is the gift of vision:

> There floats out there
> The shape that I shall take when I am dead,
> My soul's first shape, a soft feathery shape . . .
> I say it is about to sing.

And Emer undergoes a similar journey beyond the self-centredness of heartache, which expresses itself as rage against her enemies; through selfless veneration of her husband, Emer so identifies with Cuchulain that she is suddenly transfixed by the same vision that attended his dying ('There is silence, and in the silence a few faint bird notes'). That the vision continues to inspire is the theme of the final song which unites the legendary with the modern, the artistic with the political in celebrating what elsewhere Yeats called the 'indomitable Irishry'. The play was a superb culmination of all Yeats's ambitions for a uniquely Irish drama.

SELECT BIBLIOGRAPHY

In preparing this edition I have chiefly used *The Collected Plays of W. B. Yeats* (Macmillan, 1952, reprinted 1969) and *The Variorum Edition of the Plays of W. B. Yeats*, edited by Peter Allt and Russell K. Alspach (Macmillan, 1966). These have been supplemented where possible by the texts, including manuscript materials, which have been published in the Cornell Yeats (Cornell University Press). To date this series includes *The Death of Cuchulain* (edited by Phillip L. Marcus); *Purgatory* (edited by Sandra F. Siegel); *The Herne's Egg* (edited by Alison Armstrong); and *The Hour-Glass* (edited by Catherine Phillips). I have also consulted *W. B. Yeats: The Writing of 'Sophocles' King Oedipus'* by David R. Clark and James B. McGuire (The American Philosophical Society, 1989); *Druid Craft: The Writing of 'The Shadowy Waters'* by Michael J. Sidnell, George P. Mayhew and David R. Clark (Dolmen Press, 1972); and the edition of *The Herne's Egg* by Andrew Parkin for the series Irish Dramatic Texts (Catholic University of America Press and Colin Smythe Ltd, 1991).

Of Yeats's other writings consulted, these include: *Autobiographies* (Macmillan, 1955); *Beltaine* (Frank Cass, 1970); *Essays and Introductions* (Macmillan, 1961); *Four Plays for Dancers* (Macmillan, 1921); *Letters*, edited by Allan Wade (Rupert Hart-Davis, 1954); *Mythologies* (Macmillan, 1959); *Memoirs*, edited by Denis Donoghue (Macmillan, 1972); *Plays for an Irish Theatre* (A. H. Bullen, 1911); *Samhain* (Frank Cass, 1970); *The Variorum Edition of the Poems of W. B. Yeats*, edited by Peter Allt and Russell K. Alspach (Macmillan, 1957); *Wheels and Butterflies* (Macmillan, 1934); and the editions of the later plays published by the Cuala Press.

Amongst the critical studies and commentaries on the plays I have consulted, the following proved the most valuable (some are cited by author in the annotations):

Curtis Bradford, *W. B. Yeats at Work* (Carbondale, 1965)

Ursula Bridge, *W. B. Yeats and T. Sturge Moore: Their Correspondence 1901–1937* (Routledge & Kegan Paul, 1953)

S. B. Bushrui, *Yeats's Verse Plays: The Revisions 1900–1910* (Clarendon, 1965)

D. J. Gordon, *Images of a Poet* (Manchester University Press, 1961)

Augusta, Lady Gregory, *Cuchulain of Muirthemne* (Colin Smythe Ltd, 1970) and *Gods and Fighting Men* (Colin Smythe Ltd, 1970)

Robert Hogan and Michael J. O'Neill (eds.), *Joseph Holloway's Abbey Theatre* (Carbondale, 1967)

Robert Hogan et al., *The Modern Irish Drama: A Documentary History*, 5 vols. (Dolmen Press, 1976–84)

A. Norman Jeffares and A. S. Knowland, *A Commentary on the Collected Plays of W. B. Yeats* (Macmillan, 1975)

Liam Miller, *The Noble Drama of W. B. Yeats* (Dolmen Press, 1977)

Robert O'Driscoll and Lorna Reynolds (eds.), *Yeats and the Theatre* (Macmillan, 1975)

Ann Saddlemyer, *Theatre Business* (Colin Smythe Ltd, 1982)

Peter Ure, *Yeats the Playwright* (Routledge & Kegan Paul, 1963)

Katharine J. Worth, *The Irish Drama of Europe from Yeats to Beckett* (Athlone Press, 1978)

Yeats Annuals (edited since Number 3 by Warwick Gould and published by Macmillan) are an on-going source of specialist information and recent scholarship on all aspects of Yeatsian studies.

The titles listed here all specifically relate to Yeats's plays in performance and his work in the theatre; I have not included critical studies of the plays, however excellent, where the bias is more towards literary analysis.

A NOTE ABOUT THIS EDITION

For many readers Yeats is predominantly, even for some exclusively, viewed as a poet; and yet when he received the Nobel Prize for Literature he chose to define himself on that occasion as theatre practitioner, founder of the Abbey and playwright. This edition is designed to allow the reader to approach the plays either as dramatic literature or as texts for performance. The selected texts are offered in the form in which they appeared in *The Collected Plays of W. B. Yeats* as published by Macmillan initially in 1952 with no editorial intrusions beyond a small number of textual emendations. In the second part of the volume a short commentary on each play outlines the circumstances of its composition, the nature of revisions to the text where these are relevant and the history of its performance in the theatre. The body of notes that follows each commentary is devoted in part to elucidating textual cruces but is chiefly preoccupied with intimating the theatrical power of the play when it is staged. From early in his career as dramatist Yeats was conscious of the need to control inventively the visual as distinct from the verbal dynamics of communication between actor and audience. It is on this aspect of the stageability of the dramas that the annotations focus to enable readers to begin imaginatively to see the plays in performance with what Yeats himself would term 'the eye of the mind'. Sketches and line-drawings have been included where these help to clarify how Yeats appeared to envisage the performance of a particular play.

It may be questioned why as many as eighteen plays are included in this selection when the entire canon numbers twenty-six (twenty-seven, if you include *Grania*, the collaborative venture with George Moore). The intention has been to show the sheer range and diversity of Yeats's achievement as a playwright. Selection is always problematic and vexing; and, doubtless, there will be questions as to why some plays have not been included in the volume while others have. Viability in performance has been the guiding principle behind this particular selection. Only three of Yeats's early plays have been included (*Cathleen ni Houlihan*, *The Shadowy Waters* and *The Hour-Glass*) from among his prentice work through which he was discovering the precise contributions to a performance made by the various constituent arts of the theatre; they show Yeats already confidently manipulating the conventions of turn-of-the-century drama to define experiences vastly different from what those conventions were originally designed to convey. It is Yeats as theatrical innovator that this selection seeks to celebrate.

Plays such as *The Player Queen* and *A Full Moon in March* have been omitted because, though they have excited much critical comment and interpretation respecting their intricate verbal symbolism, it is open to question whether the ideas that Yeats is exploring in these works find a proper dramatic correlative. On stage, for example, the sheer physicality of the act of performance tends to confine the communicated meaning of *A Full Moon in March* to its narrative line rather than to its symbolic resonances, so it is less what critics have seen as an allegory of the depersonalizing relationship between poet and inspirational muse that impresses itself on an audience's awareness than the representation of a sexual encounter which seems in dubious taste because overly phallocentric in its bias. This is not a criticism one could level at *The King of the Great Clock Tower*, Yeats's first exploration of the same body of material, where theme and dramatic method are meticulously matched.

Sophocles' King Oedipus has been included since it was the culmination of a project which had preoccupied Yeats for many years, and after its staging (a triumph for all concerned) the tragedy had a considerable impact in terms of theme and structure on Yeats's last and finest works for the theatre. The companion-piece, *Sophocles' Oedipus at Colonus* (though as brilliant an adaptation for the modern stage), is not represented here, however, since its major impact subsequently was on Yeats's philosophical works, such as *On the Boiler*, rather than on his drama.

Yeats was an inveterate reviser; and this poses problems about choice of available texts for particular plays. Should one include the earliest complete version of a play since that roots it precisely in the time of its composition? Revisions even to his first plays were rarely so large scale as to change the nature, style and structure of the work substantially, rather Yeats refined his initial inspiration (usually after scrutinizing the impact of the piece in performance) to clarify and strengthen the dramaturgy. The texts published ultimately in *Collected Plays* are therefore the versions which he was known to have considered most *stageworthy*; these have been reproduced here, even when such final acting versions were realized a decade or more after the original date of composition.

This creates another problem respecting the order in which the plays are grouped. Macmillan's *Collected Plays* follows no logical pattern. An early play, *The Shadowy Waters*, is given the date of its preferred acting version (1911) and placed at the end of a group arranged otherwise chronologically in order of composition, when it ought by such a principle of organization to come earlier in the sequence. (*The Hour-Glass*, by a similarly misguided logic, is positioned roughly appropriate to the date assigned it on the title-page of 1914, though versions of the play – initially wholly in prose – were being staged from as early as 1903. Moreover, the version with its passages in Latin printed in *Collected Plays* actually dates from 1922.) This vaguely chronological principle of ordering is eventually broken so that the saga-plays relating to Deirdre and Cuchulain can appear in an arrangement that respects their on-going narrative line, even though this means that plays of different periods of invention and style are grouped haphazardly with no respect for date of composition. However, even this attempt at a sequence is not properly sustained, since *The Death of Cuchulain* is situated at the end of the entire volume, being Yeats's last completed play, rather than after *The Only Jealousy of Emer*, where it belongs in terms of narrative development. Such an arrangement most unfortunately breaks up the group of *Plays for Dancers*, which were originally published as a distinct unit because they share a set of creative and structural principles.

The present edition groups the plays chronologically according to the completion dates of their *initial* composition, even when a revised acting version of a later date is the text selected for printing. This arrangement allows one to study Yeats's remarkable development as a playwright most clearly. The one set-back with this method of ordering is that the Cuchulain plays are spaced out over the volume and do not appear in narrative sequence; but then Yeats never thought of all five plays being played together as a cycle and they were not conceived and written as such in one creative burst. This seems a small price to pay for the deepening insight a properly chronological arrangement brings into how Yeats built upon his discoveries through the practice of theatre and integrated new influences and sources of inspiration into a confidently sustained dramaturgy that placed him in the vanguard of early twentieth-century dramatists and practitioners seeking an alternative mode of drama to the prevailing ethos of naturalism.

The Plays

THE SHADOWY WATERS

Persons in the Play

FORGAEL
AIBRIC
SAILORS
DECTORA

A mast and a great sail, a large tiller, a poop rising several feet above the stage, and from the overhanging stern a lanthorn hangs. The sea or sky is represented by a semicircular cloth of which nothing can be seen except a dark abyss. The persons move but little. Some sailors are discovered crouching by the sail. Forgael is asleep and Aibric standing by the tiller on the raised poop.

FIRST SAILOR: It is long enough, and too long, Forgael has been bringing us through the waste places of the great sea.[1]

SECOND SAILOR: We did not meet with a ship to make a prey of these eight weeks, or any shore or island to plunder or to harry. It is a hard thing, age to be coming on me, and I not to get the chance of doing a robbery that would enable me to live quiet and honest to the end of my lifetime.

FIRST SAILOR: We are out[2] since the new moon. What is worse again, it is the way we are in a ship, the barrels empty and my throat shrivelled with drought, and nothing to quench it but water only.

FORGAEL [*in his sleep*]: Yes; there, there; that hair that is the colour of burning.[3]

FIRST SAILOR: Listen to him now, calling out in his sleep.

FORGAEL [*in his sleep*]: That pale forehead, that hair the colour of burning.

FIRST SAILOR: Some crazy dream he is in, and believe me it is no crazier than the thought he has waking. He is not the first that has had the wits drawn out from him through shadows and fantasies.

SECOND SAILOR: That is what ails him. I have been thinking it this good while.

3

FIRST SAILOR: Do you remember that galley we sank at the time of the full moon?

SECOND SAILOR: I do. We were becalmed the same night, and he sat up there playing that old harp of his until the moon had set.

FIRST SAILOR: I was sleeping up there by the bulwark, and when I woke in the sound of the harp a change came over my eyes, and I could see very strange things. The dead were floating upon the sea yet, and it seemed as if the life that went out of every one of them had turned to the shape of a man-headed bird[4] – grey they were, and they rose up of a sudden and called out with voices like our own, and flew away singing to the west. Words like this they were singing: 'Happiness beyond measure, happiness where the sun dies'.

SECOND SAILOR: I understand well what they are doing. My mother used to be talking of birds of the sort. They are sent by the lasting watchers to lead men away from this world and its women to some place of shining women that cast no shadow,[5] having lived before the making of the earth. But I have no mind to go following him to that place.

FIRST SAILOR: Let us creep up to him and kill him in his sleep.

SECOND SAILOR: I would have made an end of him long ago, but that I was in dread of his harp. It is said that when he plays upon it he has power over all the listeners, with or without the body, seen or unseen, and any man that listens grows to be as mad as himself.[6]

FIRST SAILOR: What way can he play it, being in his sleep?

SECOND SAILOR: But who would be our captain then to make out a course from the Bear and the Polestar, and to bring us back home?

FIRST SAILOR: I have that thought out. We must have Aibric with us. He knows the constellations as well as Forgael. He is a good hand with the sword. Join with us; be our captain, Aibric. We are agreed to put an end to Forgael, before he wakes. There is no man but will be glad of it when it is done. Join with us, and you will have the captain's share and profit.

AIBRIC: Silence! for you have taken Forgael's pay.

FIRST SAILOR: Little pay we have had this twelvemonth. We would never have turned against him if he had brought us, as he promised, into seas that would be thick with ships. That was the bargain. What is the use of knocking about and fighting as we do unless we get the chance to drink more wine and kiss more women than lasting

peaceable men through their long lifetime? You will be as good a
leader as ever he was himself, if you will but join us.

AIBRIC: And do you think that I will join myself
To men like you, and murder him who has been
My master from my earliest childhood up?
No! nor to a world of men like you
When Forgael's in the other scale. Come! come!
I'll answer to more purpose when you have drawn
That sword out of its scabbard.

FIRST SAILOR: You have awaked him.
We had best go, for we have missed this chance.
  [*Sailors go out.*]

FORGAEL: Have the birds passed us? I could hear your voice
But there were others.

AIBRIC: I have seen nothing pass.

FORGAEL: You are certain of it? I never wake from sleep
But that I am afraid they may have passed;
For they're my only pilots. I have not seen them
For many days, and yet there must be many
Dying at every moment in the world.

AIBRIC: They have all but driven you crazy, and already
The sailors have been plotting for your death;
Whatever has been cried into your ears
Has lured you on to death.

FORGAEL: No; but they promised—

AIBRIC: I know their promises. You have told me all.
They are to bring you to unheard-of passion,
To some strange love the world knows nothing of,
Some Ever-living woman as you think,
One that can cast no shadow, being unearthly.
But that's all folly. Turn the ship about,
Sail home again, be some fair woman's friend;
Be satisfied to live like other men,
And drive impossible dreams away. The world
Has beautiful women to please every man.

FORGAEL: But he that gets their love after the fashion
Loves in brief longing and deceiving hope
And bodily tenderness, and finds that even

The bed of love, that in the imagination
Had seemed to be the giver of all peace,
Is no more than a wine-cup in the tasting,
And as soon finished.

AIBRIC: All that ever loved
Have loved that way – there is no other way.

FORGAEL: Yet never have two lovers kissed but they
Believed there was some other near at hand,
And almost wept because they could not find it.

AIBRIC: When they have twenty years; in middle life
They take a kiss for what a kiss is worth,
And let the dream go by.

FORGAEL: It's not a dream,
But the reality that makes our passion
As a lamp shadow – no – no lamp, the sun.
What the world's million lips are thirsting for
Must be substantial somewhere.

AIBRIC: I have heard the Druids
Mutter such things as they awake from trance.
It may be that the dead have lit upon it,
Or those that never lived; no mortal can.

FORGAEL: I only of all living men shall find it.

AIBRIC: Then seek it in the habitable world,
Or leap into that sea and end a journey
That has no other end.

FORGAEL: I cannot answer.
I can see nothing plain; all's mystery.
Yet sometimes there's a torch inside my head
That makes all clear, but when the light is gone
I have but images, analogies,
The mystic bread, the sacramental wine,
The red rose where the two shafts of the cross,
Body and soul, waking and sleep, death, life,
Whatever meaning ancient allegorists
Have settled on, are mixed into one joy.
For what's the rose but that? miraculous cries,
Old stories about mystic marriages,
Impossible truths?[7] But when the torch is lit

All that is impossible is certain,
I plunge in the abyss.
    [*Sailors come in.*]

FIRST SAILOR: Look there![8] there in the mist! A ship of spices!

SECOND SAILOR: We would not have noticed her but for the sweet
    smell through the air. Ambergris and sandalwood, and all the herbs
    the witches bring from the sunrise.

FIRST SAILOR: No; but opoponax and cinnamon.

FORGAEL [*taking the tiller from Aibric*]: The Ever-living have kept my
    bargain; they have paid you on the nail.

AIBRIC: Take up that rope to make her fast while we are plundering
    her.

FIRST SAILOR: There is a king on her deck and a queen. Where there
    is one woman it is certain there will be others.

AIBRIC: Speak lower or they'll hear.

FIRST SAILOR: They cannot hear; they are too much taken up with
    one another. Look! he has stooped down and kissed her on the lips.

SECOND SAILOR: When she finds out we have as good men aboard
    she may not be too sorry in the end.

FIRST SAILOR: She will be as dangerous as a wild cat. These queens
    think more of the riches and the great name they get by marriage
    than of a ready hand and a strong body.

SECOND SAILOR: There is nobody is natural but a robber. That is the
    reason the whole world goes tottering about upon its bandy legs.

AIBRIC: Run upon them now, and overpower the crew while yet asleep.
    [*Sailors and Aibric go out. The clashing of swords and confused
    voices are heard from the other ship, which cannot be seen because
    of the sail.*][9]

FORGAEL [*who has remained at the tiller*]: There! there! They come!
    Gull, gannet, or diver,
But with a man's head, or a fair woman's.
They hover over the masthead awhile
To wait their friends, but when their friends have come
They'll fly upon that secret way of theirs,
One – and one – a couple – five together.
And now they all wheel suddenly and fly
To the other side, and higher in the air,

They've gone up thither, friend's run up by friend;
They've gone to their beloved ones in the air,
In the waste of the high air, that they may wander
Among the windy meadows of the dawn.
But why are they still waiting? Why are they
Circling and circling over the masthead?
Ah! now they all look down – they'll speak of me
What the Ever-living put into their minds,
And of that shadowless unearthly woman
At the world's end. I hear the message now,
But it's all mystery. There's one that cries,
'From love and hate'. Before the sentence ends
Another breaks upon it with a cry,
'From love and death and out of sleep and waking'.
And with the cry another cry is mixed,
'What can we do, being shadows?' All mystery,
And I am drunken with a dizzy light.
But why do they still hover overhead?
Why are you circling there? Why do you linger?
Why do you not run to your desire,
Now that you have happy winged bodies?
Being too busy in the air, and the high air,
They cannot hear my voice. But why that circling?
   [*The Sailors have returned. Dectora is with them.*]
   [*Turning and seeing her.*] Why are you standing with your eyes upon
      me?
You are not the world's core. O no, no, no!
That cannot be the meaning of the birds.
You are not its core. My teeth are in the world,
But have not bitten yet.

DECTORA: I am a queen,
   And ask for satisfaction upon these
   Who have slain my husband and laid hands upon me.

FORGAEL: I'd set my hopes on one that had no shadow: –
   Where do you come from? who brought you to this place?
   Why do you cast a shadow? Answer me that.

DECTORA: Would that the storm that overthrew my ships,
   And drowned the treasures of nine conquered nations,
   And blew me hither to my lasting sorrow,

Had drowned me also. But, being yet alive,
I ask a fitting punishment for all
That raised their hands against him.

FORGAEL: There are some
That weigh and measure all in these waste seas –
They that have all the wisdom that's in life,
And all that prophesying images
Made of dim gold rave out in secret tombs;
They have it that the plans of kings and queens
Are dust on the moth's wing; that nothing matters
But laughter and tears – laughter, laughter and tears –
That every man should carry his own soul
Upon his shoulders.

DECTORA: You've nothing but wild words,
And I would know if you would give me vengeance.

FORGAEL: When she finds out that I'll not let her go –
When she knows that.

DECTORA: What is that you are muttering?
That you'll not let me go? I am a queen.

FORGAEL: Although you are more beautiful than any,
I almost long that it were possible;
But if I were to put you on that ship,
With sailors that were sworn to do your will,
And you had spread a sail for home, a wind
Would rise of a sudden, or a wave so huge
It had washed among the stars and put them out,
And beat the bulwark of your ship on mine,
Until you stood before me on the deck –
As now.

DECTORA: Has wandering in these desolate seas
And listening to the cry of wind and wave
Driven you mad?

FORGAEL: But, queen, I am not mad.

DECTORA: And yet you say the water and the wind
Would rise against me.

FORGAEL: No, I am not mad –
If it be not that hearing messages
From lasting watchers that outlive the moon

At the most quiet midnight is to be stricken.

DECTORA: And did those watchers bid you take me captive?

FORGAEL: Both you and I are taken in the net.
It was their hands that plucked the winds awake
And blew you hither; and their mouths have promised
I shall have love in their immortal fashion.
They gave me that old harp of the nine spells
That is more mighty than the sun and moon,
Or than the shivering casting-net of the stars,
That none might take you from me.

DECTORA [first trembling back from the mast where the harp is, and
then laughing]: [10]   For a moment
Your raving of a message and a harp
More mighty than the stars half troubled me.
But all that's raving. Who is there can compel
The daughter and granddaughter of a king
To be his bedfellow?

FORGAEL: Until your lips
Have called me their beloved, I'll not kiss them.

DECTORA: My husband and my king died at my feet,
And yet you talk of love.[11]

FORGAEL: The movement of time
Is shaken in these seas, and what one does
One moment has no might upon the moment
That follows after.

DECTORA: I understand you now.
You have a Druid craft of wicked music,
Wrung from the cold women of the sea –[12]
A magic that can call a demon up,
Until my body give you kiss for kiss.

FORGAEL: Your soul shall give the kiss.

DECTORA: I am not afraid
While there's a rope to run into a noose
Or wave to drown. But I have done with words,
And I would have you look into my face
And know that it is fearless.

FORGAEL: Do what you will,
For neither I nor you can break a mesh

Of the great golden net that is about us.

DECTORA: There's nothing in the world that's worth a fear.

> [*She passes Forgael and stands for a moment looking into his face.*]

I have good reason for that thought.

> [*She runs suddenly on to the raised part of the poop.*]

And now
I can put fear away as a queen should.

> [*She mounts on the bulwark, and turns towards Forgael.*]

Fool, fool! Although you have looked into my face
You did not see my purpose. I shall have gone
Before a hand can touch me.

FORGAEL [*folding his arms*]: My hands are still;
The Ever-living hold us. Do what you will,
You cannot leap out of the golden net.

FIRST SAILOR: There is no need for you to drown. Give us our pardon and we will bring you home on your own ship, and make an end of this man that is leading us to death.

DECTORA: I promise it.

AIBRIC: I stand upon his side.
I'd strike a blow for him to give him time
To cast his dreams away.

FIRST SAILOR: He has put a sudden darkness over the moon.

DECTORA: Nine swords with handles of rhinoceros horn
To him that strikes him first!

FIRST SAILOR: I will strike him first. No! for that music of his might put a beast's head upon my shoulders, or it may be two heads and they devouring one another.

DECTORA: I'll give a golden galley full of fruit
That has the heady flavour of new wine
To him that wounds him to the death.

FIRST SAILOR: I'll strike at him.[13] His spells, when he dies, will die with him and vanish away.

SECOND SAILOR: I'll strike at him.

THE OTHERS: And I! And I! And I!

> [*Forgael plays upon the harp.*]

FIRST SAILOR [*falling into a dream*]: It is what they are saying, there is some person dead in the other ship; we have to go and wake him. They did not say what way he came to his end, but it was sudden.

SECOND SAILOR: You are right, you are right. We have to go to that wake.

DECTORA: He has flung a Druid spell upon the air,
And set you dreaming.

SECOND SAILOR: What way can we raise a keen, not knowing what name to call him by?

FIRST SAILOR: Come on to his ship. His name will come to mind in a moment. All I know is he died a thousand years ago, and was never yet waked.

SECOND SAILOR: How can we wake him having no ale?

FIRST SAILOR: I saw a skin of ale aboard her – a pigskin of brown ale.

THIRD SAILOR: Come to the ale, a pigskin of brown ale, a goatskin of yellow!

FIRST SAILOR [singing]: Brown ale and yellow; yellow and brown ale; a goatskin of yellow!

ALL [singing]: Brown ale and yellow; yellow and brown ale!
[Sailors go out.]

DECTORA: Protect me now, gods that my people swear by!
[Aibric has risen from the ground where he had fallen. He has begun looking for his sword as if in a dream.]

AIBRIC: Where is my sword that fell out of my hand
When I first heard the news? Ah, there it is!
[He goes dreamily towards the sword, but Dectora runs at it and takes it up before he can reach it.]
[Sleepily.] Queen, give it me.

DECTORA: No, I have need of it.

AIBRIC: Why do you need a sword? But you may keep it.
Now that he's dead I have no need of it,
For everything is gone.

A SAILOR [calling from the other ship]: Come hither, Aibric,
And tell me who it is that we are waking.

AIBRIC [half to Dectora, half to himself]: What name had that dead king? Arthur of Britain?
No, no – not Arthur. I remember now.

It was golden-armed Iollan, and he died
Broken-hearted, having lost his queen
Through wicked spells. That is not all the tale,
For he was killed. O! O! O! O! O! O!
For golden-armed Iollan has been killed.[14]

[*He goes out. While he has been speaking, and through part of what follows, one hears the singing of the Sailors from the other ship. Dectora stands with the sword lifted in front of Forgael. He changes the tune.*]

DECTORA: I will end all your magic on the instant.[15]

[*Her voice becomes dreamy, and she lowers the sword slowly, and finally lets it fall. She spreads out her hair. She takes off her crown and lays it upon the deck.*]

The sword is to lie beside him in the grave.
It was in all his battles. I will spread my hair,
And wring my hands, and wail him bitterly,
For I have heard that he was proud and laughing,
Blue-eyed, and a quick runner on bare feet,
And that he died a thousand years ago.
O! O! O! O!

[*Forgael changes the tune.*]

        But no, that is not it.
I knew him well, and while I heard him laughing
They killed him at my feet. O! O! O! O!
For golden-armed Iollan that I loved.
But what is it that made me say I loved him?
It was that harper put it in my thoughts,
But it is true. Why did they run upon him,
And beat the golden helmet with their swords?

FORGAEL: Do you not know me, lady? I am he
That you are weeping for.

DECTORA: No, for he is dead.
O! O! O! O! for golden-armed Iollan.

FORGAEL: It was so given out, but I will prove
That the grave-diggers in a dreamy frenzy
Have buried nothing but my golden arms.
Listen to that low-laughing string of the moon
And you will recollect my face and voice,
For you have listened to me playing it

These thousand years.

[*He starts up, listening to the birds. The harp slips from his hands, and remains leaning against the bulwarks behind him.*]

                What are the birds at there?
Why are they all a-flutter of a sudden?
What are you calling out above the mast?
If railing and reproach and mockery
Because I have awakened her to love
By magic strings, I'll make this answer to it:
Being driven on by voices and by dreams
That were clear messages from the Ever-living,
I have done right. What could I but obey?
And yet you make a clamour of reproach.

DECTORA [*laughing*]: Why, it's a wonder out of reckoning
That I should keen him from the full of the moon
To the horn, and he be hale and hearty.

FORGAEL: How have I wronged her now that she is merry?
But no, no, no! your cry is not against me.
You know the councils of the Ever-living,
And all the tossing of your wings is joy,
And all that murmuring's but a marriage song;
But if it be reproach, I answer this:
There is not one among you that made love
By any other means. You call it passion,
Consideration, generosity;
But it was all deceit, and flattery
To win a woman in her own despite,[16]
For love is war, and there is hatred in it;
And if you say that she came willingly –

DECTORA: Why do you turn away and hide your face
That I would look upon for ever?

FORGAEL: My grief!

DECTORA: Have I not loved you for a thousand years?

FORGAEL: I never have been golden-armed Iollan.

DECTORA: I do not understand. I know your face
Better than my own hands.

FORGAEL: I have deceived you
Out of all reckoning.

DECTORA: Is it not true
　　That you were born a thousand years ago,
　　In islands where the children of Aengus[17] wind
　　In happy dances under a windy moon,
　　And that you'll bring me there?

FORGAEL: I have deceived you;
　　I have deceived you utterly.

DECTORA: How can that be?
　　Is it that though your eyes are full of love
　　Some other woman has a claim on you,
　　And I've but half?

FORGAEL: O no!

DECTORA: And if there is,
　　If there be half a hundred more, what matter?
　　I'll never give another thought to it;
　　No, no, nor half a thought; but do not speak.
　　Women are hard and proud and stubborn-hearted,
　　Their heads being turned with praise and flattery;
　　And that is why their lovers are afraid
　　To tell them a plain story.

FORGAEL: That's not the story;
　　But I have done so great a wrong against you,
　　There is no measure that it would not burst.
　　I will confess it all.

DECTORA: What do I care,
　　Now that my body has begun to dream,
　　And you have grown to be a burning coal[18]
　　In the imagination and intellect?
　　If something that's most fabulous were true –
　　If you had taken me by magic spells,
　　And killed a lover or husband at my feet –
　　I would not let you speak, for I would know
　　That it was yesterday and not to-day
　　I loved him; I would cover up my ears,
　　As I am doing now. [A pause.] Why do you weep?

FORGAEL: I weep because I've nothing for your eyes
　　But desolate waters and a battered ship.

DECTORA: O, why do you not lift your eyes to mine?

FORGAEL: I weep – I weep because bare night's above,
  And not a roof of ivory and gold.

DECTORA: I would grow jealous of the ivory roof,
  And strike the golden pillars with my hands.
  I would that there was nothing in the world
  But my beloved – that night and day had perished,
  And all that is and all that is to be,
  And all that is not the meeting of our lips.

FORGAEL: Why do you turn your eyes upon bare night?
  Am I to fear the waves, or is the moon
  My enemy?

DECTORA: I looked upon the moon,
  Longing to knead and pull it into shape
  That I might lay it on your head as a crown.
  But now it is your thoughts that wander away,
  For you are looking at the sea. Do you not know
  How great a wrong it is to let one's thought
  Wander a moment when one is in love?
    [*He has moved away. She follows him. He is looking out over the
    sea, shading his eyes.*]
  Why are you looking at the sea?

FORGAEL: Look there!
  There where the cloud creeps up upon the moon.

DECTORA: What is there but a troop of ash-grey birds
  That fly into the west?
    [*The scene darkens, but there is a ray of light upon the figures.*]

FORGAEL: But listen, listen!

DECTORA: What is there but the crying of the birds?

FORGAEL: If you'll but listen closely to that crying
  You'll hear them calling out to one another
  With human voices.

DECTORA: Clouds have hid the moon.
  The birds cry out, what can I do but tremble?

FORGAEL: They have been circling over our heads in the air,
  But now that they have taken to the road
  We have to follow, for they are our pilots;
  They're crying out. Can you not hear their cry? –
  'There is a country at the end of the world

Where no child's born but to outlive the moon.'
   [*The Sailors come in with Aibric. They carry torches.*]

AIBRIC: We have lit upon a treasure that's so great
  Imagination cannot reckon it.
  The hold is full – boxes of precious spice,
  Ivory images with amethyst eyes,
  Dragons with eyes of ruby. The whole ship
  Flashes as if it were a net of herrings.
  Let us return to our own country, Forgael,
  And spend it there. Have you not found this queen?
  What more have you to look for on the seas?

FORGAEL: I cannot – I am going on to the end.
  As for this woman, I think she is coming with me.

AIBRIC: Speak to him, lady, and bid him turn the ship.
  He knows that he is taking you to death;
  He cannot contradict me.[19]

DECTORA: Is that true?

FORGAEL: I do not know for certain.

DECTORA: Carry me
  To some sure country, some familiar place.
  Have we not everything that life can give
  In having one another?

FORGAEL: How could I rest
  If I refused the messengers and pilots
  With all those sights and all that crying out?

DECTORA: I am a woman, I die at every breath.

AIBRIC [*to the Sailors*]: To the other ship, for there's no help in
    words.
  And I will follow you and cut the rope
  When I have said farewell to this man here,
  For neither I nor any living man
  Will look upon his face again.
    [*Sailors go out, leaving one torch perhaps in a torch-holder on the
    bulwark.*]

FORGAEL [*to Dectora*]:   Go with him,
  For he will shelter you and bring you home.

AIBRIC [*taking Forgael's hand*]: I'll do it for his sake.

DECTORA: No. Take this sword
And cut the rope, for I go on with Forgael.

AIBRIC: Farewell! Farewell!
   [*He goes out. The light grows stronger.*]

DECTORA: The sword is in the rope –
The rope's in two – it falls into the sea,
It whirls into the foam. O ancient worm,
Dragon that loved the world and held us to it,
You are broken, you are broken. The world drifts away,
And I am left alone with my beloved,
Who cannot put me from his sight for ever.
We are alone for ever, and I laugh,
Forgael, because you cannot put me from you.
The mist has covered the heavens, and you and I
Shall be alone for ever. We two – this crown –
I half remember. It has been in my dreams.
Bend lower, O king, that I may crown you with it.
O flower of the branch, O bird among the leaves,
O silver fish that my two hands have taken
Out of the running stream, O morning star,
Trembling in the blue heavens like a white fawn ·
Upon the misty border of the wood,
Bend lower, that I may cover you with my hair,
For we will gaze upon this world no longer.[20]
   [*The harp begins to burn as with fire.*]

FORGAEL [*gathering Dectora's hair about him*]:[21] Beloved, having
   dragged the net about us,
And knitted mesh to mesh, we grow immortal;
And that old harp awakens of itself
To cry aloud to the grey birds, and dreams,
That have had dreams for father, live in us.

THE END

CATHLEEN NI HOULIHAN

Persons in the Play

PETER GILLANE
MICHAEL GILLANE, *his son, going to be married*
PATRICK GILLANE, *a lad of twelve, Michael's brother*
BRIDGET GILLANE, *Peter's wife*
DELIA CAHEL, *engaged to Michael*
THE POOR OLD WOMAN
NEIGHBOURS

Interior of a cottage close to Killala, in 1798. Bridget is standing at a table undoing a parcel. Peter is sitting at one side of the fire, Patrick at the other.

PETER: What is that sound I hear?

PATRICK: I don't hear anything. [*He listens.*] I hear it now. It's like cheering. [*He goes to the window and looks out.*] I wonder what they are cheering about. I don't see anybody.

PETER: It might be a hurling.[1]

PATRICK: There's no hurling to-day. It must be down in the town the cheering is.

BRIDGET: I suppose the boys must be having some sport of their own. Come over here, Peter, and look at Michael's wedding clothes.

PETER [*shifts his chair to table*]: Those are grand clothes, indeed.

BRIDGET: You hadn't clothes like that when you married me, and no coat to put on of a Sunday more than any other day.

PETER: That is true, indeed. We never thought a son of our own would be wearing a suit of that sort for his wedding, or have so good a place to bring a wife to.

PATRICK [*who is still at the window*]: There's an old woman coming down the road. I don't know is it here she is coming.

BRIDGET: It will be a neighbour coming to hear about Michael's wedding. Can you see who it is?

PATRICK: I think it is a stranger, but she's not coming to the house. She's turned into the gap that goes down where Maurteen and his sons are shearing sheep.[2] [*He turns towards Bridget.*] Do you remember what Winny of the Cross-Roads was saying the other night about the strange woman that goes through the country whatever time there's war or trouble coming?

BRIDGET: Don't be bothering us about Winny's talk, but go and open the door for your brother. I hear him coming up the path.

PETER: I hope he has brought Delia's fortune with him safe, for fear the people might go back on the bargain and I after making it. Trouble enough I had making it.

[*Patrick opens the door and Michael comes in.*]

BRIDGET: What kept you, Michael? We were looking out for you this long time.

MICHAEL: I went round by the priest's house to bid him be ready to marry us to-morrow.

BRIDGET: Did he say anything?

MICHAEL: He said it was a very nice match, and that he was never better pleased to marry any two in his parish than myself and Delia Cahel.

PETER: Have you got the fortune, Michael?

MICHAEL: Here it is.

[*Michael puts bag on table and goes over and leans against chimney-jamb. Bridget, who has been all this time examining the clothes, pulling the seams and trying the lining of the pockets, etc., puts the clothes on the dresser.*]

PETER [*getting up and taking the bag in his hand and turning out the money*]: Yes, I made the bargain well for you, Michael. Old John Cahel would sooner have kept a share of this a while longer. 'Let me keep the half of it until the first boy is born,' says he. 'You will not,' says I. 'Whether there is or is not a boy, the whole hundred pounds must be in Michael's hands before he brings your daughter to the house.' The wife spoke to him then, and he gave in at the end.

BRIDGET: You seem well pleased to be handling the money, Peter.

PETER: Indeed, I wish I had had the luck to get a hundred pounds, or twenty pounds itself, with the wife I married.

BRIDGET: Well, if I didn't bring much I didn't get much. What had you the day I married you but a flock of hens and you feeding them, and a few lambs and you driving them to the market at Ballina? [*She is vexed and bangs a jug on the dresser.*] If I brought no fortune I worked it out in my bones, laying down the baby, Michael that is standing there now, on a stook of straw, while I dug the potatoes, and never asking big dresses or anything but to be working.

PETER: That is true, indeed.

[*He pats her arm.*]

BRIDGET: Leave me alone now till I ready the house for the woman that is to come into it.

PETER: You are the best woman in Ireland, but money is good, too. [*He begins handling the money again and sits down.*] I never thought to see so much money within my four walls. We can do great things now we have it. We can take the ten acres of land we have the chance of since Jamsie Dempsey died, and stock it. We will go to the fair at Ballina to buy the stock. Did Delia ask any of the money for her own use, Michael?

MICHAEL: She did not, indeed. She did not seem to take much notice of it, or to look at it at all.

BRIDGET: That's no wonder. Why would she look at it when she had yourself to look at, a fine, strong young man? It is proud she must be to get you; a good steady boy that will make use of the money, and not be running through it or spending it on drink like another.

PETER: It's likely Michael himself was not thinking much of the fortune either, but of what sort the girl was to look at.

MICHAEL [*coming over towards the table*]: Well, you would like a nice comely girl to be beside you, and to go walking with you. The fortune only lasts for a while, but the woman will be there always.

PATRICK [*turning round from the window*]: They are cheering again down in the town. Maybe they are landing horses from Enniscrone.[3] They do be cheering when the horses take the water well.

MICHAEL: There are no horses in it. Where would they be going and no fair at hand? Go down to the town, Patrick, and see what is going on.

PATRICK [*opens the door to go out, but stops for a moment on the threshold*]: Will Delia remember, do you think, to bring the greyhound pup she promised me when she would be coming to the house?

MICHAEL: She will surely.

[*Patrick goes out, leaving the door open.*]

PETER: It will be Patrick's turn next to be looking for a fortune, but he won't find it so easy to get it and he with no place of his own.

BRIDGET: I do be thinking sometimes, now things are going so well with us, and the Cahels such a good back to us in the district, and Delia's own uncle a priest, we might be put in the way of making Patrick a priest some day, and he so good at his books.

PETER: Time enough, time enough. You have always your head full of plans, Bridget.

BRIDGET: We will be well able to give him learning, and not to send him tramping the country like a poor scholar that lives on charity.

MICHAEL: They're not done cheering yet.

[*He goes over to the door and stands there for a moment, putting up his hand to shade his eyes.*]

BRIDGET: Do you see anything?

MICHAEL: I see an old woman coming up the path.

BRIDGET: Who is it, I wonder? It must be the strange woman Patrick saw a while ago.

MICHAEL: I don't think it's one of the neighbours anyway, but she has her cloak over her face.

BRIDGET: It might be some poor woman heard we were making ready for the wedding and came to look for her share.

PETER: I may as well put the money out of sight. There is no use leaving it out for every stranger to look at.

[*He goes over to a large box in the corner, opens it and puts the bag in and fumbles at the lock.*]

MICHAEL: There she is, father! [*An Old Woman passes the window slowly. She looks at Michael as she passes.*] I'd sooner a stranger not to come to the house the night before my wedding.

BRIDGET: Open the door, Michael; don't keep the poor woman waiting. [*The Old Woman comes in. Michael stands aside to make way for her.*]

OLD WOMAN: God save all here!

PETER: God save you kindly!

OLD WOMAN: You have good shelter here.

PETER: You are welcome to whatever shelter we have.

BRIDGET: Sit down there by the fire and welcome.

OLD WOMAN [*warming her hands*]: There is a hard wind outside.
[*Michael watches her curiously from the door. Peter comes over to the table.*]

PETER: Have you travelled far to-day?

OLD WOMAN: I have travelled far, very far; there are few have travelled so far as myself, and there's many a one that doesn't make me welcome. There was one that had strong sons I thought were friends of mine, but they were shearing their sheep, and they wouldn't listen to me.

PETER: It's a pity indeed for any person to have no place of their own.

OLD WOMAN: That's true for you indeed, and it's long I'm on the roads since I first went wandering.

BRIDGET: It is a wonder you are not worn out with so much wandering.

OLD WOMAN: Sometimes my feet are tired and my hands are quiet, but there is no quiet in my heart. When the people see me quiet, they think old age has come on me and that all the stir has gone out of me. But when the trouble is on me I must be talking to my friends.

BRIDGET: What was it put you wandering?

OLD WOMAN: Too many strangers in the house.

BRIDGET: Indeed you look as if you'd had your share of trouble.

OLD WOMAN: I have had trouble indeed.

BRIDGET: What was it put the trouble on you?

OLD WOMAN: My land that was taken from me.[4]

PETER: Was it much land they took from you?

OLD WOMAN: My four beautiful green fields.[5]

PETER [*aside to Bridget*]: Do you think could she be the widow Casey that was put out of her holding at Kilglass a while ago?

BRIDGET: She is not. I saw the widow Casey one time at the market in Ballina, a stout fresh woman.

PETER [*to Old Woman*]: Did you hear a noise of cheering, and you coming up the hill?

OLD WOMAN: I thought I heard the noise I used to hear when my friends came to visit me.
[*She begins singing half to herself.*]

> I will go cry with the woman,

> For yellow-haired Donough is dead,
> With a hempen rope for a neckcloth,
> And a white cloth on his head,—

MICHAEL [*coming from the door*]: What is it that you are singing, ma'am?

OLD WOMAN: Singing I am about a man I knew one time, yellow-haired Donough that was hanged in Galway.

   [*She goes on singing, much louder.*]

> I am come to cry with you, woman,
> My hair is unwound and unbound;
> I remember him ploughing his field,
> Turning up the red side of the ground,
> And building his barn on the hill
> With the good mortared stone;
> O! we'd have pulled down the gallows
> Had it happened in Enniscrone![6]

MICHAEL: What was it brought him to his death?

OLD WOMAN: He died for love of me: many a man has died for love of me.

PETER [*aside to Bridget*]: Her trouble has put her wits astray.

MICHAEL: Is it long since that song was made? Is it long since he got his death?

OLD WOMAN: Not long, not long. But there were others that died for love of me a long time ago.

MICHAEL: Were they neighbours of your own, ma'am?

OLD WOMAN: Come here beside me and I'll tell you about them. [*Michael sits down beside her on the hearth.*] There was a red man of the O'Donnells from the north,[7] and a man of the O'Sullivans from the south,[8] and there was one Brian that lost his life at Clontarf[9] by the sea, and there were a great many in the west, some that died hundreds of years ago, and there are some that will die to-morrow.

MICHAEL: Is it in the west that men will die to-morrow?

OLD WOMAN: Come nearer, nearer to me.

BRIDGET: Is she right, do you think? Or is she a woman from beyond the world?

PETER: She doesn't know well what she's talking about, with the want and the trouble she has gone through.

BRIDGET: The poor thing, we should treat her well.

PETER: Give her a drink of milk and a bit of the oaten cake.

BRIDGET: Maybe we should give her something along with that, to bring her on her way. A few pence or a shilling itself, and we with so much money in the house.

PETER: Indeed I'd not begrudge it to her if we had it to spare, but if we go running through what we have, we'll soon have to break the hundred pounds, and that would be a pity.

BRIDGET: Shame on you, Peter. Give her the shilling and your blessing with it, or our own luck will go from us.

[*Peter goes to the box and takes out a shilling.*]

BRIDGET [*to the Old Woman*]: Will you have a drink of milk, ma'am?

OLD WOMAN: It is not food or drink that I want.

PETER [*offering the shilling*]: Here is something for you.

OLD WOMAN: This is not what I want. It is not silver I want.

PETER: What is it you would be asking for?

OLD WOMAN: If any one would give me help he must give me himself, he must give me all.

[*Peter goes over to the table staring at the shilling in his hand in a bewildered way, and stands whispering to Bridget.*]

MICHAEL: Have you no one to care you in your age, ma'am?

OLD WOMAN: I have not. With all the lovers that brought me their love I never set out the bed for any.

MICHAEL: Are you lonely going the roads, ma'am?

OLD WOMAN: I have my thoughts and I have my hopes.

MICHAEL: What hopes have you to hold to?

OLD WOMAN: The hope of getting my beautiful fields back again; the hope of putting the strangers out of my house.

MICHAEL: What way will you do that, ma'am?

OLD WOMAN: I have good friends that will help me. They are gathering to help me now. I am not afraid. If they are put down to-day they will get the upper hand to-morrow.[10] [*She gets up.*] I must be going to meet my friends. They are coming to help me and I must be there to welcome them. I must call the neighbours together to welcome them.

MICHAEL: I will go with you.

BRIDGET: It is not her friends you have to go and welcome, Michael; it is the girl coming into the house you have to welcome. You have plenty to do; it is food and drink you have to bring to the house. The woman that is coming home is not coming with empty hands; you would not have an empty house before her. [*To the Old Woman.*] Maybe you don't know, ma'am, that my son is going to be married to-morrow.

OLD WOMAN: It is not a man going to his marriage that I look to for help.

PETER [*to Bridget*]: Who is she, do you think, at all?

BRIDGET: You did not tell us your name yet, ma'am.

OLD WOMAN: Some call me the Poor Old Woman,[11] and there are some that call me Cathleen, the daughter of Houlihan.[12]

PETER: I think I knew some one of that name, once. Who was it, I wonder? It must have been some one I knew when I was a boy. No, no; I remember, I heard it in a song.

OLD WOMAN [*who is standing in the doorway*]: They are wondering that there were songs made for me; there have been many songs made for me. I heard one on the wind this morning.
 [*sings*]

> Do not make a great keening
> When the graves have been dug to-morrow.
> Do not call the white-scarfed riders
> To the burying that shall be to-morrow.
>
> Do not spread food to call strangers
> To the wakes that shall be to-morrow;
> Do not give money for prayers
> For the dead that shall die to-morrow. . . .

They will have no need of prayers, they will have no need of prayers.

MICHAEL: I do not know what that song means, but tell me something I can do for you.

PETER: Come over to me, Michael.

MICHAEL: Hush, father, listen to her.

OLD WOMAN: It is a hard service they take that help me. Many that are red-cheeked now will be pale-cheeked; many that have been free to walk the hills and the bogs and the rushes will be sent to walk hard streets in far countries;[13] many a good plan will be broken;

many that have gathered money will not stay to spend it; many a
child will be born and there will be no father at its christening to
give it a name. They that have red cheeks will have pale cheeks for
my sake, and for all that, they will think they are well paid.[14]

[*She goes out; her voice is heard outside singing.*]

> They shall be remembered for ever,
> They shall be alive for ever,
> They shall be speaking for ever,
> The people shall hear them for ever.

BRIDGET [*to Peter*]: Look at him, Peter; he has the look of a man that
has got the touch.[15] [*Raising her voice.*] Look here, Michael, at the
wedding clothes. Such grand clothes as these are! You have a right
to fit them on now; it would be a pity to-morrow if they did not fit.
The boys would be laughing at you. Take them, Michael, and go
into the room and fit them on.

[*She puts them on his arm.*]

MICHAEL: What wedding are you talking of? What clothes will I be
wearing to-morrow?

BRIDGET: These are the clothes you are going to wear when you marry
Delia Cahel to-morrow.

MICHAEL: I had forgotten that.

[*He looks at the clothes and turns towards the inner room, but
stops at the sound of cheering outside.*]

PETER: There is the shouting come to our own door. What is it has
happened?

[*Neighbours come crowding in, Patrick and Delia with them.*]

PATRICK: There are ships in the Bay; the French are landing at Killala!

[*Peter takes his pipe from his mouth and his hat off, and stands
up. The clothes slip from Michael's arm.*]

DELIA: Michael! [*He takes no notice.*] Michael! [*He turns towards
her.*] Why do you look at me like a stranger?

[*She drops his arm. Bridget goes over towards her.*]

PATRICK: The boys are all hurrying down the hillside to join the
French.

DELIA: Michael won't be going to join the French.

BRIDGET [*to Peter*]: Tell him not to go, Peter.

PETER: It's no use. He doesn't hear a word we're saying.

BRIDGET: Try and coax him over to the fire.

DELIA: Michael, Michael! You won't leave me! You won't join the French, and we going to be married!

[*She puts her arms about him, he turns towards her as if about to yield.*]

[*Old Woman's voice outside.*]

> They shall be speaking for ever,
>
> The people shall hear them for ever.

[*Michael breaks away from Delia, stands for a second at the door, then rushes out, following the Old Woman's voice. Bridget takes Delia, who is crying silently, into her arms.*]

PETER [*to Patrick, laying a hand on his arm*]: Did you see an old woman going down the path?

PATRICK: I did not, but I saw a young girl, and she had the walk of a queen.[16]

THE END

THE HOUR-GLASS

Persons in the Play

A WISE MAN
BRIDGET, *his wife*
TEIGUE, *a Fool*
ANGEL
CHILDREN AND PUPILS

The stage is brought out into the orchestra so as to leave a wide space in front of the stage curtain. Pupils come in and stand before the stage curtain, which is still closed. One Pupil carries a book.

FIRST PUPIL: He said we might choose the subject for the lesson.

SECOND PUPIL: There is none of us wise enough to do that.

THIRD PUPIL: It would need a great deal of wisdom to know what it is we want to know.

FOURTH PUPIL: I will question him.

FIFTH PUPIL: You?

FOURTH PUPIL: Last night I dreamt that some one came and told me to question him. I was to say to him, 'You were wrong to say there is no God and no soul – maybe, if there is not much of either, there is yet some tatters, some tag on the wind – so to speak – some rag upon a bush, some bob-tail of a god.' I will argue with him – nonsense though it be – according to my dream, and you will see how well I can argue, and what thoughts I have.

FIRST PUPIL: I'd as soon listen to dried peas in a bladder as listen to your thoughts.

[*Teigue the Fool[1] comes in.*]

FOOL: Give me a penny.

SECOND PUPIL: Let us choose a subject by chance. Here is his big book. Let us turn over the pages slowly. Let one of us put down his finger without looking. The passage his finger lights on will be the subject for the lesson.

29

FOOL: Give me a penny.

THIRD PUPIL [*taking up book*]: How heavy it is!

FOURTH PUPIL: Spread it on Teigue's back, and then we can all stand round and see the choice.

SECOND PUPIL: Make him spread out his arms.

FOURTH PUPIL: Down on your knees. Hunch up your back. Spread your arms out now, and look like a golden eagle in a church.[2] Keep still, keep still.

FOOL: Give me a penny.

THIRD PUPIL: Is that the right cry for an eagle-cock?

SECOND PUPIL: I'll turn the pages – you close your eyes and put your finger down.

THIRD PUPIL: That's it, and then he cannot blame us for the choice.

FIRST PUPIL: There, I have chosen. Fool, keep still – and if what's wise is strange and sounds like nonsense, we've made a good choice.

FIFTH PUPIL: The Master has come.

FOOL: Will anybody give a penny to a fool?

[*One of the Pupils draws back the stage curtains showing the Master sitting at his desk. There is an hour-glass upon his desk or in a bracket on the wall. One Pupil puts the books before him.*]

FIRST PUPIL: We have chosen the passage for the lesson, Master. 'There are two living countries, one visible and one invisible, and when it is summer there, it is winter here, and when it is November with us, it is lambing-time there.'

WISE MAN: That passage, that passage! What mischief has there been since yesterday?

FIRST PUPIL: None, Master.

WISE MAN: Oh yes, there has; some craziness has fallen from the wind, or risen from the graves of old men, and made you choose that subject. – Diem noctemque contendo, sed quos elegi, quos amavi, in tirocinium vel hi labuntur.[3]

FOURTH PUPIL: I knew that it was folly, but they would have it.

THIRD PUPIL: Had we not better say we picked it by chance?

SECOND PUPIL: No; he would say we were children still.

FIRST PUPIL: I have found a sentence under that one that says – as though to show it had a hidden meaning – a beggar wrote it upon the walls of Babylon.[4]

WISE MAN: Then find some beggar and ask him what it means, for I will have nothing to do with it.

FOURTH PUPIL: Come, Teigue, what is the old book's meaning when it says that there are sheep that drop their lambs in November?

FOOL: To be sure – everybody knows, everybody in the world knows, when it is spring with us, the trees are withering there, when it is summer with us, the snow is falling there, and have I not myself heard the lambs that are there all bleating on a cold November day – to be sure, does not everybody with an intellect know that? And maybe when it's night with us, it is day with them, for many a time I have seen the roads lighted before me.

WISE MAN: The beggar who wrote that on Babylon wall meant that there is a spiritual kingdom that cannot be seen or known till the faculties, whereby we master the kingdom of this world, wither away like green things in winter. A monkish thought, the most mischievous thought that ever passed out of a man's mouth. – Virgas ut partus educant colligunt aves, mens hominis nugas.[5]

FIRST PUPIL: If he meant all that, I will take an oath that he was spindle-shanked, and cross-eyed, and had a lousy itching shoulder, and that his heart was crosser than his eyes, and that he wrote it out of malice.

SECOND PUPIL: Let's come away and find a better subject.

FOURTH PUPIL: And maybe now you'll let me choose.

FIRST PUPIL: Come.

WISE MAN: Were it but true, 'twould alter everything
Until the stream of the world had changed its course,
And that and all our thoughts had run
Into some cloudy thunderous spring
They dream to be its source –
Aye, to some frenzy of the mind;
And all that we have done would be undone,
Our speculation but as the wind.[6]
    [A pause.]
I have dreamed it twice.

FIRST PUPIL: Something has troubled him.
    [Pupils go out.]

WISE MAN: Twice have I dreamed it in a morning dream,
Now nothing serves my pupils but to come

With a like thought. Reason is growing dim;
A moment more and Frenzy will beat his drum
And laugh aloud and scream;
And I must dance in the dream.[7]
No, no, but it is like a hawk, a hawk of the air,
It has swooped down – and this swoop makes the third –
And what can I, but tremble like a bird?

FOOL: Give me a penny.

WISE MAN: That I should dream it twice, and after that, that they should pick it out!

FOOL: Won't you give me a penny?

WISE MAN: What do you want? What can it matter to you whether the words I am reading are wisdom or sheer folly?

FOOL: Such a great, wise teacher will not refuse a penny to a fool.

WISE MAN: Seeing that everybody is a fool when he is asleep and dreaming, why do you call me wise?

FOOL: O, I know, – I know, I know what I have seen.

WISE MAN: Well, to see rightly is the whole of wisdom, whatever dream be with us.

FOOL: When I went by Kilcluan, where the bells used to be ringing at the break of every day, I could hear nothing but the people snoring in their houses. When I went by Tubber-vanach, where the young men used to be climbing the hill to the blessed well, they were sitting at the cross-roads playing cards. When I went by Carrick-orus, where the friars used to be fasting and serving the poor, I saw them drinking wine and obeying their wives. And when I asked what misfortune had brought all these changes, they said it was no misfortune, but that it was the wisdom they had learned from your teaching.

WISE MAN: And you too have called me wise – you would be paid for that good opinion doubtless. – Run to the kitchen; my wife will give you food and drink.

FOOL: That's foolish advice for a wise man to give.

WISE MAN: Why, Fool?

FOOL: What is eaten is gone – I want pennies for my bag. I must buy bacon in the shops, and nuts in the market, and strong drink for the time the sun is weak, and snares to catch the rabbits and the hares, and a big pot to cook them in.

WISE MAN: I have more to think about than giving pennies to your like, so run away.

FOOL: Give me a penny and I will bring you luck. The fishermen let me sleep among their nets in the loft because I bring them luck; and in the summer-time, the wild creatures let me sleep near their nests and their holes. It is lucky even to look at me, but it is much more lucky to give me a penny. If I was not lucky I would starve.

WISE MAN: What are the shears for?

FOOL: I won't tell you. If I told you, you would drive them away.

WISE MAN: Drive them away? Whom would I drive away?

FOOL: I won't tell you.

WISE MAN: Not if I give you a penny?

FOOL: No.

WISE MAN: Not if I give you two pennies?

FOOL: You will be very lucky if you give me two pennies, but I won't tell you.

WISE MAN: Three pennies?

FOOL: Four, and I will tell you.

WISE MAN: Very well – four, but from this out I will not call you Teigue the Fool.

FOOL: Let me come close to you, where nobody will hear me; but first you must promise not to drive them away. [*Wise Man nods.*] Every day men go out dressed in black and spread great black nets over the hills, great black nets.

WISE MAN: A strange place that to fish in.

FOOL: They spread them out on the hills that they may catch the feet of the angels; but every morning, just before the dawn, I go out and cut the nets with the shears and the angels fly away.

WISE MAN [*speaking with excitement*]: Ah, now I know that you are Teigue the Fool. You say that I am wise, and yet I say there are no angels.

FOOL: I have seen plenty of angels.

WISE MAN: No, no, you have not.

FOOL: They are plenty if you but look about you. They are like the blades of grass.

WISE MAN: They are plenty as the blades of grass – I heard that phrase when I was but a child and was told folly.

FOOL: When one gets quiet. When one is so quiet that there is not a thought in one's head maybe, there is something that wakes up inside one, something happy and quiet, and then all in a minute one can smell summer flowers, and tall people go by, happy and laughing, but they will not let us look at their faces. O no, it is not right that we should look at their faces.

WISE MAN: You have fallen asleep upon a hill; yet even those that used to dream of angels dream now of other things.

FOOL: I saw one but a moment ago – that is because I am lucky. It was coming behind me, but it was not laughing.

WISE MAN: There's nothing but what men can see when they are awake. Nothing, nothing.

FOOL: I knew you would drive them away.

WISE MAN: Pardon me, Fool,
I had forgotten whom I spoke to.
Well, there are your four pennies – Fool you are called,
And all day long they cry, 'Come hither, Fool'.
    [*The Fool goes close to him.*]
Or else it's, 'Fool, be gone'.
    [*The Fool goes further off.*]
Or, 'Fool, stand there'.
    [*The Fool straightens himself up.*]
Or, 'Fool, go sit in the corner'.
    [*The Fool sits in the corner.*]
                              And all the while
What were they all but fools before I came?
What are they now but mirrors that seem men
Because of my image? Fool, hold up your head.
    [*The Fool does so.*]
What foolish stories they have told of the ghosts
That fumbled with the clothes upon the bed,
Or creaked and shuffled in the corridor,
Or else, if they were pious bred,
Of angels from the skies,
That coming through the door,
Or, it may be, standing there,
Would solidly out-stare
The steadiest eyes with their unnatural eyes,
Aye, on a man's own floor.[8]

[*An Angel has come in. It may be played by a man if a man can be found with the right voice, and in that case 'she' should be changed to 'he' throughout and may wear a little golden domino and a halo made of metal. Or the whole face may be a beautiful mask, in which case the sentence in lines 5 and 6 on page 34 should not be spoken.*]

Yet it is strange, the strangest thing I have known,
That I should still be haunted by the notion
That there's a crisis of the spirit wherein
We get new sight, and that they know some trick
To turn our thoughts for their own needs to frenzy.
Why do you put your finger to your lip,
And creep away?

[*The Fool goes out.*]

[*Wise Man sees Angel.*] What are you? Who are you?
I think I saw some like you in my dreams,
When but a child. That thing about your head, –
That brightness in your hair – that flowery branch;[9]
But I have done with dreams, I have done with dreams.

ANGEL: I am the crafty[10] one that you have called.

WISE MAN: How that I called?

ANGEL: I am the messenger.

WISE MAN: What message could you bring to one like me?

ANGEL [*turning the hour-glass*]: That you will die when the last grain of sand
Has fallen through this glass.[11]

WISE MAN: I have a wife,
Children and pupils that I cannot leave:
Why must I die, my time is far away?

ANGEL: You have to die because no soul has passed
The heavenly threshold since you have opened school,
But grass grows there, and rust upon the hinge;
And they are lonely that must keep the watch.

WISE MAN: And whither shall I go when I am dead?

ANGEL: You have denied there is a Purgatory,
Therefore that gate is closed; you have denied
There is a Heaven, and so that gate is closed.

WISE MAN: Where then? For I have said there is no Hell.

ANGEL: Hell is the place of those who have denied;
  They find there what they planted and what dug,
  A Lake of Spaces, and a Wood of Nothing,
  And wander there and drift, and never cease
  Wailing for substance.

WISE MAN: Pardon me, blessed Angel,
  I have denied and taught the like to others.
  But how could I believe before my sight
  Had come to me?

ANGEL: It is too late for pardon.

WISE MAN: Had I but met your gaze as now I meet it –
  But how can you that live but where we go
  In the uncertainty of dizzy dreams
  Know why we doubt? Parting, sickness, and death,
  The rotting of the grass, tempest, and drouth,
  These are the messengers that came to me.
  Why are you silent? You carry in your hands
  God's pardon,[12] and you will not give it me.
  Why are you silent? Were I not afraid,
  I'd kiss your hands – no, no, the hem of your dress.

ANGEL: Only when all the world has testified,
  May soul confound it, crying out in joy,
  And laughing on its lonely precipice.
  What's dearth and death and sickness to the soul
  That knows no virtue but itself? Nor could it,
  So trembling with delight and mother-naked,
  Live unabashed if the arguing world stood by.

WISE MAN: It is as hard for you to understand
  Why we have doubted as it is for us
  To banish doubt. – What folly have I said?
  There can be nothing that you do not know.
  Give me a year – a month – a week – a day,
  I would undo what I have done – an hour –
  Give me until the sand has run in the glass.

ANGEL: Though you may not undo what you have done,
  I have this power – if you but find one soul,
  Before the sands have fallen, that still believes,
  One fish to lie and spawn among the stones

Till the great Fisher's net is full again,
You may, the purgatorial fire being passed,
Spring to your peace.

    [*Pupils sing in the distance.*]

                      Who stole your wits away
                      And where are they gone?

WISE MAN: My pupils come.
Before you have begun to climb the sky
I shall have found that soul. They say they doubt,
But what their mothers dinned into their ears
Cannot have been so lightly rooted up;
Besides, I can disprove what I once proved –
And yet give me some thought, some argument,
More mighty than my own.

ANGEL: Farewell – farewell,
  For I am weary of the weight of time.

    [*Angel goes out. Wise Man makes a step to follow and pauses.
    Some of his Pupils come in at the other side of the stage.*]

FIRST PUPIL: Master, Master, you must choose the subject.

    [*Enter other Pupils with Fool,*[13] *about whom they dance; all the
    Pupils may have little cushions on which presently they seat them-
    selves.*]

SECOND PUPIL: Here is a subject – Where have the Fool's wits gone?
    [*singing*]

                      Who dragged your wits away
                      Where no one knows?
                      Or have they run off
                      On their own pair of shoes?

FOOL: Give me a penny.

FIRST PUPIL: The Master will find your wits.

SECOND PUPIL: And when they are found, you must not beg for
  pennies.

THIRD PUPIL: They are hidden somewhere in the badger's hole,
  But you must carry an old candle-end
  If you would find them.

FOURTH PUPIL: They are up above the clouds.

FOOL: Give me a penny, give me a penny.

FIRST PUPIL [*singing*]:

> I'll find your wits again.
> Come, for I saw them roll
> To where old badger mumbles
> In the black hole.

SECOND PUPIL [*singing*]:

> No, but an angel stole them
> The night that you were born,
> And now they are but a rag
> On the moon's horn.

WISE MAN: Be silent.

FIRST PUPIL: Can you not see that he is troubled?
[*All the Pupils are seated.*]

WISE MAN: Nullum esse deum dixi, nullam dei matrem: mentitus vero:
nam recte intelligenti sunt et deus et dei mater.[14]

FIRST PUPIL: Argumentis igitur proba; nam argumenta poscit qui
rationis est particeps.[15]

WISE MAN: Pro certo habeo e vobis unum quidem in fide perstitisse,
unum altius quam me vidisse.[16]

SECOND PUPIL: You answer for us.

THIRD PUPIL [*in a whisper to First Pupil*]: Be careful what you say;
If he persuades you to an argument,
He will but turn us all to mockery.

FIRST PUPIL: We had no minds until you made them for us.

WISE MAN: Quae destruxi necesse est omnia reaedificem.[17]

FIRST PUPIL: Haec rationibus nondum natis opinabamur: nunc vero
adolevimus: exuimus incunabula.[18]

WISE MAN: You are afraid to tell me what you think
Because I am hot and angry when I am crossed.
I do not blame you for it; but have no fear,
For if there's one that sat on smiling there
As though my arguments were sweet as milk,
Yet found them bitter, I will thank him for it,
If he but speak his mind.

FIRST PUPIL: There is no one, Master.
There is not one but found them sweet as milk.

WISE MAN: The things that have been told us in our childhood

Are not so fragile.

SECOND PUPIL: We are not children now.

FIRST PUPIL: Non iam pueri sumus; corpus tantummodo ex matre fictum est.[19]

SECOND PUPIL: Docuisti; et nobis persuadetur.[20]

WISE MAN: Mendaciis vos imbui, mentisque simulacris.[21]

SECOND PUPIL: Nulli non persuasisti.

OTHER PUPILS [*speaking together*]: Nulli, nulli, nulli.[22]

WISE MAN: I have deceived you – where shall I go for words? –
I have no thoughts – my mind has been swept bare.
The messengers that stand in the fiery cloud
Fling themselves out, if we but dare to question,
And after that the Babylonian moon
Blots all away.

FIRST PUPIL [*to other Pupils*]: I take his words to mean
That visionaries and martyrs, when they are raised
Above translunary things, and there enlightened,
As the contention is, may lose the light,
And flounder in their speech when the eyes open.

SECOND PUPIL: How well he imitates their trick of speech.

THIRD PUPIL: Their air of mystery.

FOURTH PUPIL: Their empty gaze
As though they'd looked upon some wingéd thing,
And would not condescend to mankind after.

FIRST PUPIL: Master, we all have learnt that truth is learnt
When the intellect's deliberate and cold,
As it were a polished mirror that reflects
An unchanged world; not when the steel dissolves
Bubbling and hissing, till there's naught but fume.

WISE MAN: When it is melted, when it all fumes up,
They walk as when beside those three in the furnace
The form of the fourth.[23]

FIRST PUPIL: Master, there's none among us
That has not heard your mockery of these,
Or thoughts like these, and we have not forgot.

WISE MAN: Something incredible has happened – some one has come
Suddenly like a grey hawk out of the air,

And all that I declared untrue is true.

FIRST PUPIL [*to other Pupils*]: You'd think, the way he says it, that
    he felt it.
There's not a mummer[24] to compare with him.
He's something like a man.

SECOND PUPIL: Argumentum, domine, profer.[25]

WISE MAN: What proof have I to give, but that an angel
  An instant ago was standing on that spot?
    [*The Pupils rise.*]

THIRD PUPIL: You dreamed it.

WISE MAN: I was awake as I am now.

FIRST PUPIL [*to the others*]: I may be dreaming now for all I know.
He wants to show we have no certain proof
Of anything in the world.

SECOND PUPIL: There is this proof
That shows we are awake – we have all one world
While every dreamer has a world of his own,
And sees what no one else can.

THIRD PUPIL: Teigue sees angels.
So when the Master says he has seen an angel,
He may have seen one.

FIRST PUPIL: Both may still be dreamers,
Unless it's proved the angels were alike.

SECOND PUPIL: What sort are the angels, Teigue?

THIRD PUPIL: That will prove nothing,
Unless we are sure prolonged obedience
Has made one angel like another angel
As they were eggs.

FIRST PUPIL: The Master's silent now:
For he has found that to dispute with us –
Seeing that he has taught us what we know –
Is but to reason with himself. Let us away,
And find if there is one believer left.

WISE MAN: Yes, Yes. Find me but one that still can say:
Credo in patrem et filium et spiritum sanctum.[26]

THIRD PUPIL: He'll mock and maul him.

FOURTH PUPIL: From the first I knew
  He wanted somebody to argue with.
    [*They go.*]

WISE MAN: I have no reason left. All dark, all dark!
    [*Pupils return laughing. They push forward Fourth Pupil.*]

FIRST PUPIL: Here, Master, is the very man you want.
  He said, when we were studying the book,
  That maybe after all the monks were right,
  And you mistaken, and if we but gave him time,
  He'd prove that it was so.

FOURTH PUPIL: I never said it.

WISE MAN: Dear friend, dear friend, do you believe in God?

FOURTH PUPIL: Master, they have invented this to mock me.

WISE MAN: You are afraid of me.

FOURTH PUPIL: They know well, Master,
  That all I said was but to make them argue.
  They've pushed me in to make a mock of me,
  Because they knew I could take either side
  And beat them at it.

WISE MAN: If you can say the creed
  With but a grain, a mustard-grain of faith,[27]
  You are my soul's one friend.
    [*Pupils laugh.*]
                          Mistress or wife
  Can give us but our good or evil luck
  Amid the howling world, but you shall give
  Eternity, and those sweet-throated things
  That drift above the moon.
    [*Pupils look at one another and are silent.*]

SECOND PUPIL: How strange he is!

WISE MAN: The angel that stood there upon that spot
  Said that my soul was lost unless I found
  One that had faith.

FOURTH PUPIL: Cease mocking at me, Master,
  For I am certain that there is no God
  Nor immortality, and they that said it
  Made a fantastic tale from a starved dream
  To plague our hearts. Will that content you, Master?

WISE MAN: The giddy glass is emptier every moment,
  And you stand there, debating, laughing and wrangling.
  Out of my sight! Out of my sight, I say.
    [*He drives them out.*[28]]
  I'll call my wife, for what can women do,
  That carry us in the darkness of their bodies,
  But mock the reason that lets nothing grow
  Unless it grow in light? Bridget, Bridget!
  A woman never gives up all her faith,
  Say what we will. Bridget, come quickly, Bridget.
    [*Bridget comes in wearing her apron. Her sleeves are turned up
    from her arms, which are covered with flour.*]
  Wife, what do you believe in? Tell me the truth,
  And not – as is the habit with you all –
  Something you think will please me. Do you pray?
  Sometimes when you're alone in the house, do you pray?

BRIDGET: Prayers – no, you taught me to leave them off long ago. At
  first I was sorry, but I am glad now, for I am sleepy in the evenings.

WISE MAN: Do you believe in God?

BRIDGET: O, a good wife only believes in what her husband tells her.

WISE MAN: But sometimes, when the children are asleep
  And I am in the school, do you not think
  About the martyrs and the saints and the angels,
  And all the things that you believed in once?

BRIDGET: I think about nothing. Sometimes I wonder if the linen is
  bleaching white, or I go out to see if the crows are picking up the
  chickens' food.

WISE MAN: My God, – my God! I will go out myself.
  My pupils said that they would find a man
  Whose faith I never shook – they may have found him.
  Therefore I will go out – but if I go,
  The glass will let the sands run out unseen.
  I cannot go – I cannot leave the glass.
  Go call my pupils – I can explain all now.
  Only when all our hold on life is troubled,
  Only in spiritual terror can the Truth
  Come through the broken mind – as the pease burst
  Out of a broken pease-cod.

[*He clutches Bridget as she is going.*]
Say to them

That Nature would lack all in her most need,
Could not the soul find truth as in a flash,
Upon the battle-field, or in the midst
Of overwhelming waves, and say to them –
But no, they would but answer as I bid.

BRIDGET: You want somebody to get up an argument with.

WISE MAN: Look out and see if there is any one
There in the street – I cannot leave the glass,
For somebody might shake it, and the sand
If it were shaken might run down on the instant.

BRIDGET: I don't understand a word you are saying. There's a crowd of people talking to your pupils.

WISE MAN: Go out and find if they have found a man
Who did not understand me when I taught,
Or did not listen.

BRIDGET: It is a hard thing to be married to a man of learning that must always be having arguments.
[*She goes out.*]

WISE MAN: Strange that I should be blind to the great secret,
And that so simple a man might write it out
Upon a blade of grass with the juice of a berry,
And laugh and cry, because it was so simple.
[*Enter Bridget followed by the Fool.*]

FOOL: Give me something; give me a penny to buy bacon in the shops and nuts in the market, and strong drink for the time when the sun is weak.

BRIDGET: I have no pennies. [*To Wise Man.*] Your pupils cannot find anybody to argue with you. There's nobody in the whole country with religion enough for a lover's oath. Can't you be quiet now, and not always wanting to have arguments? It must be terrible to have a mind like that.

WISE MAN: Then I am lost indeed.

BRIDGET: Leave me alone now, I have to make the bread for you and the children.
[*She goes into kitchen. The Fool follows her.*]

WISE MAN: Children, children!

BRIDGET: Your father wants you, run to him.
  [*Children run in.*]

WISE MAN: Come to me, children. Do not be afraid.
  I want to know if you believe in Heaven,
  God or the soul – no, do not tell me yet;
  You need not be afraid I shall be angry;
  Say what you please – so that it is your thought –
  I wanted you to know before you spoke
  That I shall not be angry.

FIRST CHILD: We have not forgotten, father.

SECOND CHILD: O no, father,

BOTH CHILDREN [*as if repeating a lesson*]: There is nothing we cannot
  see, nothing we cannot touch.

FIRST CHILD: Foolish people used to say that there was, but you have
  taught us better.

WISE MAN: Go to your mother, go – yet do not go.
  What can she say? If I am dumb you are lost;
  And yet, because the sands are running out,
  I have but a moment to show it all in. Children,
  The sap would die out of the blades of grass
  Had they a doubt. They understand it all,
  Being the fingers of God's certainty,
  Yet can but make their sign into the air;
  But could they find their tongues they'd show it all;
  But what am I to say that am but one,
  When they are millions and they will not speak? –
    [*Children have run out.*]
  But they are gone; what made them run away?
    [*The Fool comes in with a dandelion.*]
  Look at me, tell me if my face is changed,
  Is there a notch of the Fiend's nail upon it
  Already? Is it terrible to sight
  Because the moment's near?
    [*Going to glass.*]   I dare not look,
  I dare not know the moment when they come.
  No, no, I dare not. [*Covers glass.*] Will there be a footfall,
  Or will there be a sort of rending sound,
  Or else a cracking, as though an iron claw

Had gripped the threshold-stone?
[*The Fool has begun to blow the dandelion.*]
                                    What are you doing?

FOOL: Wait a minute – four – five – six –

WISE MAN: What are you doing that for?

FOOL: I am blowing the dandelion to find out what hour it is.

WISE MAN: You have heard everything and that is why
You'd find what hour it is – you'd find that out
That you may look upon a fleet of devils ·
Dragging my soul away. You shall not stop,
I will have no one here when they come in,
I will have no one sitting there – no one!
And yet – and yet – there is something strange about you.
I half remember something. What is it?
Do you believe in God and in the soul?

FOOL: So you ask me now. I thought when you were asking your
pupils, 'Will he ask Teigue the Fool? Yes, he will, he will; no, he will
not – yes, he will'. But Teigue will say nothing. Teigue will say
nothing.

WISE MAN: Tell me quickly.

FOOL: I said, 'Teigue knows everything, not even the green-eyed cats
and the hares that milk the cows have Teigue's wisdom'; but Teigue
will not speak, he says nothing.

WISE MAN: Speak, speak, for underneath the cover there
The sand is running from the upper glass,
And when the last grain's through, I shall be lost.

FOOL: I will not speak. I will not tell you what is in my mind. I will
not tell you what is in my bag. You might steal away my thoughts.
I met a bodach[29] on the road yesterday, and he said, 'Teigue, tell me
how many pennies are in your bag; I will wager three pennies that
there are not twenty pennies in your bag; let me put in my hand and
count them'. But I gripped the bag the tighter, and when I go to sleep
at night I hide the bag where nobody knows.

WISE MAN: There's but one pinch of sand, and I am lost
If you are not he I seek.

FOOL: O, what a lot the Fool knows, but he says nothing.

WISE MAN: Yes, I remember now. You spoke of angels.

You said but now that you had seen an angel.
You are the one I seek, and I am saved.

FOOL: O no. How could poor Teigue see angels? O, Teigue tells one
tale here, another there, and everybody gives him pennies. If Teigue
had not his tales he would starve.[30]

[*He breaks away and goes out.*]

WISE MAN: The last hope is gone,
And now that it's too late I see it all:
We perish into God and sink away
Into reality – the rest's a dream.

[*The Fool comes back.*]

FOOL: There was one there – there by the threshold, waiting there;
and he said, 'Go in, Teigue, and tell him everything that he asks you.
He will give you a penny if you tell him.'

WISE MAN: I know enough, that know God's will prevails.

FOOL: Waiting till the moment had come – That is what the one out
there was saying, but I might tell you what you asked. That is what
he was saying.

WISE MAN: Be silent.[31] May God's will prevail on the instant,
Although His will be my eternal pain.
I have no question:
It is enough, I know what fixed the station
Of star and cloud.
And knowing all, I cry
That whatso God has willed
On the instant be fulfilled,
Though that be my damnation.
The stream of the world has changed its course,
And with the stream my thoughts have run
Into some cloudy thunderous spring
That is its mountain source –
Aye, to some frenzy of the mind,
For all that we have done's undone,
Our speculation but as the wind.[32]

[*He dies.*]

FOOL: Wise Man – Wise Man, wake up and I will tell you everything
for a penny. It is I, poor Teigue the Fool. Why don't you wake up,
and say, 'There is a penny for you, Teigue'? No, no, you will say

nothing. You and I, we are the two fools, we know everything, but we will not speak.

[*Angel enters holding a casket.*]

O, look what has come from his mouth! O, look what has come from his mouth – the white butterfly![33] He is dead, and I have taken his soul in my hands; but I know why you open the lid of that golden box. I must give it to you. There then [*he puts butterfly in casket*], he has gone through his pains, and you will open the lid in the Garden of Paradise. [*He closes curtain and remains outside it.*] He is gone, he is gone, he is gone, but come in, everybody in the world, and look at me.

> I hear the wind a-blow,
> I hear the grass a-grow,
> And all that I know, I know.

But I will not speak, I will run away.

[*He goes out.*]

THE END

ON BAILE'S STRAND

TO

WILLIAM FAY

because of the beautiful fantasy of his
playing in the character of the Fool

Persons in the Play

A FOOL
A BLIND MAN
CUCHULAIN, *King of Muirthemne*
CONCHUBAR, *High King of Uladh*
A YOUNG MAN, *son of Cuchulain*
KINGS AND SINGING WOMEN

*A great hall at Dundealgan, not 'Cuchulain's great ancient house' but
an assembly-house nearer to the sea. A big door at the back, and
through the door misty light as of sea-mist. There are many chairs and
one long bench. One of these chairs, which is towards the front of the
stage, is bigger than the others. Somewhere at the back there is a table
with flagons of ale upon it and drinking-horns. There is a small door
at one side of the hall. A Fool and Blind Man, both ragged, and their
features made grotesque and extravagant by masks, come in through
the door at the back. The Blind Man leans upon a staff.*

FOOL: What a clever man you are though you are blind! There's nobody
  with two eyes in his head that is as clever as you are. Who but you
  could have thought that the henwife sleeps every day a little at noon?
  I would never be able to steal anything if you didn't tell me where
  to look for it. And what a good cook you are! You take the fowl out
  of my hands after I have stolen it and plucked it, and you put it into
  the big pot at the fire there, and I can go out and run races with the
  witches at the edge of the waves and get an appetite, and when I've

got it, there's the hen waiting inside for me, done to the turn.

BLIND MAN [*who is feeling about with his stick*]: Done to the turn.

FOOL [*putting his arm round Blind Man's neck*]: Come now, I'll have a leg and you'll have a leg, and we'll draw lots for the wish-bone. I'll be praising you, I'll be praising you while we're eating it, for your good plans and for your good cooking. There's nobody in the world like you, Blind Man. Come, come. Wait a minute. I shouldn't have closed the door. There are some that look for me, and I wouldn't like them not to find me. Don't tell it to anybody, Blind Man. There are some that follow me. Boann¹ herself out of the river and Fand² out of the deep sea. Witches they are, and they come by in the wind, and they cry, 'Give a kiss, Fool, give a kiss', that's what they cry. That's wide enough. All the witches can come in now. I wouldn't have them beat at the door and say, 'Where is the Fool? Why has he put a lock on the door?' Maybe they'll hear the bubbling of the pot and come in and sit on the ground. But we won't give them any of the fowl. Let them go back to the sea, let them go back to the sea.

BLIND MAN [*feeling legs of big chair with his hands*]: Ah! [*Then, in a louder voice as he feels the back of it.*] Ah – ah –

FOOL: Why do you say 'Ah-ah'?

BLIND MAN: I know the big chair. It is to-day the High King Conchubar is coming. They have brought out his chair. He is going to be Cuchulain's master in earnest from this day out. It is that he's coming for.

FOOL: He must be a great man to be Cuchulain's master.

BLIND MAN: So he is. He is a great man. He is over all the rest of the kings of Ireland.

FOOL: Cuchulain's master! I thought Cuchulain could do anything he liked.

BLIND MAN: So he did, so he did. But he ran too wild, and Conchubar is coming to-day to put an oath upon him that will stop his rambling and make him as biddable as a house-dog and keep him always at his hand. He will sit in this chair and put the oath upon him.

FOOL: How will he do that?

BLIND MAN: You have no wits to understand such things. [*The Blind Man has got into the chair.*] He will sit up in this chair and he'll say: 'Take the oath, Cuchulain. I bid you take the oath. Do as I tell you. What are your wits compared with mine, and what are your riches compared with mine? And what sons have you to pay your debts and to put a stone over you when you die? Take the oath, I tell you. Take a strong oath.'

FOOL [crumpling himself up and whining]: I will not. I'll take no oath. I want my dinner.

BLIND MAN: Hush, hush! It is not done yet.

FOOL: You said it was done to a turn.

BLIND MAN: Did I, now? Well, it might be done, and not done. The wings might be white, but the legs might be red. The flesh might stick hard to the bones and not come away in the teeth. But, believe me, Fool, it will be well done before you put your teeth in it.

FOOL: My teeth are growing long with the hunger.

BLIND MAN: I'll tell you a story – the kings have storytellers while they are waiting for their dinner – I will tell you a story with a fight in it, a story with a champion in it, and a ship and a queen's son that has his mind set on killing somebody that you and I know.

FOOL: Who is that? Who is he coming to kill?

BLIND MAN: Wait, now, till you hear. When you were stealing the fowl, I was lying in a hole in the sand, and I heard three men coming with a shuffling sort of noise. They were wounded and groaning.

FOOL: Go on. Tell me about the fight.

BLIND MAN: There had been a fight, a great fight, a tremendous great fight. A young man had landed on the shore, the guardians of the shore had asked his name, and he had refused to tell it, and he had killed one, and others had run away.

FOOL: That's enough. Come on now to the fowl. I wish it was bigger. I wish it was as big as a goose.

BLIND MAN: Hush! I haven't told you all. I know who that young man is. I heard the men who were running away say he had red hair, that he had come from Aoife's[3] country, that he was coming to kill Cuchulain.

FOOL: Nobody can do that.

　　　　[to a tune[4]]

> Cuchulain has killed kings,
> Kings and sons of kings,
> Dragons out of the water,
> And witches out of the air,

Banachas and Bonachas[5] and people of the woods.

BLIND MAN: Hush! hush!

FOOL [*still singing*]:

> Witches that steal the milk,
> Fomor[6] that steal the children,
> Hags that have heads like hares,
> Hares that have claws like witches,
> All riding a-cock-horse

[*spoken*]

Out of the very bottom of the bitter black North.

BLIND MAN: Hush, I say!

FOOL: Does Cuchulain know that he is coming to kill him?

BLIND MAN: How would he know that with his head in the clouds? He doesn't care for common fighting. Why would he put himself out, and nobody in it but that young man? Now if it were a white fawn that might turn into a queen before morning –

FOOL: Come to the fowl. I wish it was as big as a pig; a fowl with goose grease and pig's crackling.

BLIND MAN: No hurry, no hurry. I know whose son it is. I wouldn't tell anybody else, but I will tell you, – a secret is better to you than your dinner. You like being told secrets.

FOOL: Tell me the secret.

BLIND MAN: That young man is Aoife's son. I am sure it is Aoife's son, it flows in upon me that it is Aoife's son. You have often heard me talking of Aoife, the great woman-fighter Cuchulain got the mastery over in the North?

FOOL: I know, I know. She is one of those cross queens that live in hungry Scotland.

BLIND MAN: I am sure it is her son. I was in Aoife's country for a long time.

FOOL: That was before you were blinded for putting a curse upon the wind.

BLIND MAN: There was a boy in her house that had her own red colour on him, and everybody said he was to be brought up to kill Cuchulain, that she hated Cuchulain. She used to put a helmet on a pillar-stone and call it Cuchulain and set him casting at it. There is a step outside – Cuchulain's step.

[*Cuchulain passes by in the mist outside the big door.*]

FOOL: Where is Cuchulain going?

BLIND MAN: He is going to meet Conchubar that has bidden him to take the oath.

FOOL: Ah, an oath, Blind Man. How can I remember so many things at once? Who is going to take an oath?

BLIND MAN: Cuchulain is going to take an oath to Conchubar who is High King.

FOOL: What a mix-up you make of everything, Blind Man! You were telling me one story, and now you are telling me another story. . . . How can I get the hang of it at the end if you mix everything at the beginning? Wait till I settle it out. There now, there's Cuchulain [*he points to one foot*], and there is the young man [*he points to the other foot*] that is coming to kill him, and Cuchulain doesn't know. But where's Conchubar? [*Takes bag from side.*] That's Conchubar with all his riches – Cuchulain, young man, Conchubar. – And where's Aoife? [*Throws up cap.*] There is Aoife, high up on the mountains in high hungry Scotland. Maybe it is not true after all. Maybe it was your own making up. It's many a time you cheated me before with your lies. Come to the cooking-pot, my stomach is pinched and rusty. Would you have it to be creaking like a gate?[7]

BLIND MAN: I tell you it's true. And more than that is true. If you listen to what I say, you'll forget your stomach.

FOOL: I won't.

BLIND MAN: Listen. I know who the young man's father is, but I won't say. I would be afraid to say. Ah, Fool, you would forget everything if you could know who the young man's father is.

FOOL: Who is it? Tell me now quick, or I'll shake you. Come, out with it, or I'll shake you.

[*A murmur of voices in the distance.*]

BLIND MAN: Wait, wait. There's somebody coming. . . . It is Cuchulain is coming. He's coming back with the High King. Go and ask Cuchulain. He'll tell you. It's little you'll care about the cooking-pot when you have asked Cuchulain that . . .

[*Blind Man goes out by side door.*]

FOOL: I'll ask him. Cuchulain will know. He was in Aoife's country. [*Goes up stage.*] I'll ask him. [*Turns and goes down stage.*] But, no, I won't ask him, I would be afraid. [*Going up again.*] Yes, I will ask him. What harm in asking? The Blind Man said I was to ask him. [*Going down.*] No, no. I'll not ask him. He might kill me. I have but killed hens and geese and pigs. He has killed kings. [*Goes up again almost to big door.*] Who says I'm afraid? I'm not afraid. I'm no coward. I'll ask him. No, no, Cuchulain, I'm not going to ask you.

> He has killed kings,
> Kings and the sons of kings,
> Dragons out of the water,
> And witches out of the air,
> Banachas and Bonachas and people of the woods.

[*Fool goes out by side door, the last words being heard outside. Cuchulain and Conchubar enter through the big door at the back. While they are still outside, Cuchulain's voice is heard raised in anger. He is a dark man, something over forty years of age. Conchubar is much older and carries a long staff, elaborately carved or with an elaborate gold handle.*]

CUCHULAIN: Because I have killed men without your bidding
And have rewarded others at my own pleasure,
Because of half a score of trifling things,
You'd lay this oath upon me, and now – and now
You add another pebble to the heap,
And I must be your man, well-nigh your bondsman,
Because a youngster out of Aoife's country
Has found the shore ill-guarded.

CONCHUBAR: He came to land
While you were somewhere out of sight and hearing,
Hunting or dancing with your wild companions.

CUCHULAIN: He can be driven out. I'll not be bound.
I'll dance or hunt, or quarrel or make love,
Wherever and whenever I've a mind to.
If time had not put water in your blood,
You never would have thought it.

CONCHUBAR: I would leave
A strong and settled country to my children.

CUCHULAIN: And I must be obedient in all things;
Give up my will to yours; go where you please;
Come when you call; sit at the council-board
Among the unshapely bodies of old men;

I whose mere name has kept this country safe,
I that in early days have driven out
Maeve[8] of Cruachan and the northern pirates,[9]
The hundred kings of Sorcha, and the kings
Out of the Garden in the East of the World.[10]
Must I, that held you on the throne when all
Had pulled you from it, swear obedience
As if I were some cattle-raising king?
Are my shins speckled with the heat of the fire,
Or have my hands no skill but to make figures
Upon the ashes with a stick? Am I
So slack and idle that I need a whip
Before I serve you?

CONCHUBAR: No, no whip, Cuchulain,
But every day my children come and say:
'This man is growing harder to endure.
How can we be at safety with this man
That nobody can buy or bid or bind?
We shall be at his mercy when you are gone;
He burns the earth[11] as if he were a fire,
And time can never touch him.'

CUCHULAIN: And so the tale
Grows finer yet; and I am to obey
Whatever child you set upon the throne,
As if it were yourself!

CONCHUBAR: Most certainly.
I am High King, my son shall be High King;
And you for all the wildness of your blood,
And though your father came out of the sun,[12]
Are but a little king and weigh but light
In anything that touches government,
If put into the balance with my children.

CUCHULAIN: It's well that we should speak our minds out plainly,
For when we die we shall be spoken of
In many countries. We in our young days
Have seen the heavens like a burning cloud
Brooding upon the world, and being more
Than men can be now that cloud's lifted up,
We should be the more truthful. Conchubar,

I do not like your children – they have no pith,
No marrow in their bones, and will lie soft
Where you and I lie hard.

CONCHUBAR: You rail at them
Because you have no children of your own.

CUCHULAIN: I think myself most lucky that I leave
No pallid ghost or mockery of a man
To drift and mutter in the corridors
Where I have laughed and sung.

CONCHUBAR: That is not true,
For all your boasting of the truth between us;
For there is no man having house and lands,
That have been in the one family, called
By that one family's name for centuries,
But is made miserable if he know
They are to pass into a stranger's keeping,
As yours will pass.

CUCHULAIN: The most of men feel that,
But you and I leave names upon the harp.[13]

CONCHUBAR: You play with arguments as lawyers do,
And put no heart in them. I know your thoughts,
For we have slept under the one cloak and drunk
From the one wine-cup. I know you to the bone,
I have heard you cry, aye, in your very sleep,
'I have no son', and with such bitterness
That I have gone upon my knees and prayed
That it might be amended.

CUCHULAIN: For you thought
That I should be as biddable as others
Had I their reason for it; but that's not true;
For I would need a weightier argument
Than one that marred me in the copying,
As I have that clean hawk out of the air[14]
That, as men say, begot this body of mine
Upon a mortal woman.

CONCHUBAR: Now as ever
You mock at every reasonable hope,
And would have nothing, or impossible things.

What eye has ever looked upon the child
Would satisfy a mind like that?

CUCHULAIN: I would leave
My house and name to none that would not face
Even myself in battle.

CONCHUBAR: Being swift of foot,
And making light of every common chance,
You should have overtaken on the hills
Some daughter of the air, or on the shore
A daughter of the Country-under-Wave.[15]

CUCHULAIN: I am not blasphemous.

CONCHUBAR: Yet you despise
Our queens, and would not call a child your own,
If one of them had borne him.

CUCHULAIN: I have not said it.

CONCHUBAR: Ah! I remember I have heard you boast,
When the ale was in your blood, that there was one
In Scotland, where you had learnt the trade of war,
That had a stone-pale cheek and red-brown hair;
And that although you had loved other women,
You'd sooner that fierce woman of the camp
Bore you a son than any queen among them.

CUCHULAIN: You call her a 'fierce woman of the camp',
For, having lived among the spinning-wheels,
You'd have no woman near that would not say,
'Ah! how wise!' 'What will you have for supper?'
'What shall I wear that I may please you, sir?'
And keep that humming through the day and night
For ever. A fierce woman of the camp!
But I am getting angry about nothing.
You have never seen her. Ah! Conchubar, had you seen her
With that high, laughing, turbulent head[16] of hers
Thrown backward, and the bowstring at her ear,
Or sitting at the fire with those grave eyes
Full of good counsel as it were with wine,
Or when love ran through all the lineaments
Of her wild body – although she had no child,
None other had all beauty, queen or lover,

Or was so fitted to give birth to kings.

CONCHUBAR: There's nothing I can say but drifts you farther
From the one weighty matter. That very woman –
For I know well that you are praising Aoife –
Now hates you and will leave no subtlety
Unknotted that might run into a noose
About your throat, no army in idleness
That might bring ruin on this land you serve.

CUCHULAIN: No wonder in that, no wonder at all in that.
I never have known love but as a kiss
In the mid-battle, and a difficult truce
Of oil and water, candles and dark night,
Hillside and hollow, the hot-footed sun –
And the cold, sliding, slippery-footed moon –
A brief forgiveness between opposites
That have been hatreds for three times the age
Of this long-'stablished ground.[17]

CONCHUBAR: Listen to me.
Aoife makes war on us, and every day
Our enemies grow greater and beat the walls
More bitterly, and you within the walls
Are every day more turbulent; and yet,
When I would speak about these things, your fancy
Runs as it were a swallow on the wind.

> [Outside the door in the blue light of the sea-mist are many old
> and young Kings; amongst them are three Women, two of whom
> carry a bowl of fire. The third, in what follows, puts from time
> to time fragrant herbs into the fire so that it flickers up into brighter
> flame.]

Look at the door and what men gather there –
Old counsellors that steer the land with me,
And younger kings, the dancers and harp-players
That follow in your tumults, and all these
Are held there by the one anxiety.
Will you be bound into obedience
And so make this land safe for them and theirs?
You are but half a king and I but half;
I need your might of hand and burning heart,
And you my wisdom.

CUCHULAIN [*going near to door*]: Nestlings of a high nest,
    Hawks that have followed me into the air
    And looked upon the sun, we'll out of this
    And sail upon the wind once more. This king
    Would have me take an oath to do his will,
    And having listened to his tune from morning,
    I will no more of it. Run to the stable
    And set the horses to the chariot-pole,
    And send a messenger to the harp-players.
    We'll find a level place among the woods,
    And dance awhile.

A YOUNG KING: Cuchulain, take the oath.
    There is none here that would not have you take it.

CUCHULAIN: You'd have me take it? Are you of one mind?

THE KINGS: All, all, all, all!

A YOUNG KING: Do what the High King bids you.

CONCHUBAR: There is not one but dreads this turbulence
    Now that they're settled men.

CUCHULAIN: Are you so changed,
    Or have I grown more dangerous of late?
    But that's not it. I understand it all.
    It's you that have changed. You've wives and children now,
    And for that reason cannot follow one
    That lives like a bird's flight from tree to tree. –
    It's time the years put water in my blood
    And drowned the wildness of it, for all's changed,
    But that unchanged. – I'll take what oath you will:
    The moon, the sun, the water, light, or air,
    I do not care how binding.[18]

CONCHUBAR: On this fire
    That has been lighted from your hearth and mine;
    The older men shall be my witnesses,
    The younger, yours. The holders of the fire
    Shall purify the thresholds of the house
    With waving fire, and shut the outer door,
    According to the custom; and sing rhyme
    That has come down from the old law-makers
    To blow the witches out. Considering

That the wild will of man could be oath-bound,[19]
But that a woman's could not, they bid us sing
Against the will of woman at its wildest
In the Shape-Changers[20] that run upon the wind.
   [*Conchubar has gone on to his throne.*]

THE WOMEN [*They sing in a very low voice after the first few words
   so that the others all but drown their words.*]:

                    May this fire have driven out
                    The Shape-Changers that can put
                    Ruin on a great king's house
                    Until all be ruinous.
                    Names whereby a man has known
                    The threshold and the hearthstone,
                    Gather on the wind and drive
                    The women none can kiss and thrive,
                    For they are but whirling wind,
                    Out of memory and mind.
                    They would make a prince decay
                    With light images of clay
                    Planted in the running wave;
                    Or, for many shapes they have,
                    They would change them into hounds
                    Until he had died of his wounds,
                    Though the change were but a whim;
                    Or they'd hurl a spell at him,
                    That he follow with desire
                    Bodies that can never tire
                    Or grow kind, for they anoint
                    All their bodies, joint by joint,
                    With a miracle-working juice
                    That is made out of the grease
                    Of the ungoverned unicorn.
                    But the man is thrice forlorn,
                    Emptied, ruined, wracked, and lost,
                    That they follow, for at most
                    They will give him kiss for kiss
                    While they murmur, 'After this
                    Hatred may be sweet to the taste'.
                    Those wild hands that have embraced

All his body can but shove
At the burning wheel of love
Till the side of hate comes up.
Therefore in this ancient cup
May the sword-blades drink their fill
Of the home-brew there, until
They will have for masters none
But the threshold and hearthstone.[21]

CUCHULAIN [*speaking, while they are singing*]: I'll take and keep
      this oath, and from this day
I shall be what you please, my chicks, my nestlings.
Yet I had thought you were of those that praised
Whatever life could make the pulse run quickly,
Even though it were brief, and that you held
That a free gift was better than a forced. –
But that's all over. – I will keep it, too;
I never gave a gift and took it again.
If the wild horse should break the chariot-pole,
It would be punished. Should that be in the oath?
      [*Two of the Women, still singing, crouch in front of him holding
      the bowl over their heads. He spreads his hands over the flame.*]
I swear to be obedient in all things
To Conchubar, and to uphold his children.

CONCHUBAR: We are one being, as these flames are one:
I give my wisdom, and I take your strength.
Now thrust the swords into the flame, and pray
That they may serve the threshold and the hearthstone
With faithful service.
      [*The Kings kneel in a semicircle before the two Women and
      Cuchulain, who thrusts his sword into the flame. They all put the
      points of their swords into the flame. The third Woman is at the
      back near the big door.*]

CUCHULAIN: O pure, glittering ones
That should be more than wife or friend or mistress,
Give us the enduring will, the unquenchable hope,
The friendliness of the sword! –
      [*The song grows louder, and the last words ring out clearly. There
      is a loud knocking[22] at the door, and a cry of 'Open! open!'*]

CONCHUBAR: Some king that has been loitering on the way.
Open the door, for I would have all know
That the oath's finished and Cuchulain bound,
And that the swords are drinking up the flame.
   [*The door is opened by the third Woman, and a Young Man with
   a drawn sword enters.*[23]]

YOUNG MAN: I am of Aoife's country.
   [*The Kings rush towards him. Cuchulain throws himself between.*]

CUCHULAIN: Put up your swords.
He is but one. Aoife is far away.

YOUNG MAN: I have come alone into the midst of you
To weigh this sword against Cuchulain's sword.

CONCHUBAR: And are you noble? for if of common seed,
You cannot weigh your sword against his sword
But in mixed battle.

YOUNG MAN: I am under bonds
To tell my name to no man; but it's noble.

CONCHUBAR: But I would know your name and not your bonds.
You cannot speak in the Assembly House,
If you are not noble.

FIRST OLD KING: Answer the High King!

YOUNG MAN: I will give no other proof than the hawk gives
That it's no sparrow!
   [*He is silent for a moment, then speaks to all.*]
                    Yet look upon me, kings.
I, too, am of that ancient seed, and carry
The signs about this body and in these bones.

CUCHULAIN: To have shown the hawk's grey feather is enough,
And you speak highly, too. Give me that helmet.
I'd thought they had grown weary sending champions.
That sword and belt will do. This fighting's welcome.
The High King there has promised me his wisdom;
But the hawk's sleepy till its well-beloved
Cries out amid the acorns, or it has seen
Its enemy like a speck upon the sun.
What's wisdom to the hawk, when that clear eye
Is burning nearer up in the high air?
   [*Looks hard at Young Man; then grasps Young Man by shoulder.*[24]]

Hither into the light.
[*To Conchubar.*]   The very tint
Of her that I was speaking of but now.
Not a pin's difference.
[*To Young Man.*]   You are from the North,
Where there are many that have that tint of hair –
Red-brown, the light red-brown. Come nearer, boy,
For I would have another look at you.
There's more likeness – a pale, a stone-pale cheek.
What brought you, boy? Have you no fear of death?

YOUNG MAN: Whether I live or die is in the gods' hands.

CUCHULAIN: That is all words, all words; a young man's talk.
I am their plough, their harrow, their very strength;
For he that's in the sun begot this body
Upon a mortal woman, and I have heard tell
It seemed as if he had outrun the moon
That he must follow always through waste heaven,
He loved so happily. He'll be but slow
To break a tree that was so sweetly planted.
Let's see that arm. I'll see it if I choose.
That arm had a good father and a good mother,
But it is not like this.

YOUNG MAN: You are mocking me;
You think I am not worthy to be fought.
But I'll not wrangle but with this talkative knife.

CUCHULAIN: Put up your sword; I am not mocking you.
I'd have you for my friend, but if it's not
Because you have a hot heart and a cold eye,
I cannot tell the reason.
[*To Conchubar.*]   He has got her fierceness,
And nobody is as fierce as those pale women.
But I will keep him with me, Conchubar,
That he may set my memory upon her
When the day's fading. – You will stop with us,
And we will hunt the deer and the wild bulls;
And, when we have grown weary, light our fires
Between the wood and water, or on some mountain
Where the Shape-Changers of the morning come.
The High King there would make a mock of me

Because I did not take a wife among them.
Why do you hang your head? It's a good life:
The head grows prouder in the light of the dawn,
And friendship thickens in the murmuring dark
Where the spare hazels meet the wool-white foam.
But I can see there's no more need for words
And that you'll be my friend from this day out.[25]

CONCHUBAR: He has come hither not in his own name
But in Queen Aoife's, and has challenged us
In challenging the foremost man of us all.

CUCHULAIN: Well, well, what matter?

CONCHUBAR: You think it does not matter,
And that a fancy lighter than the air,
A whim of the moment, has more matter in it.
For, having none that shall reign after you,
You cannot think as I do, who would leave
A throne too high for insult.

CUCHULAIN: Let your children
Re-mortar their inheritance, as we have,
And put more muscle on. – I'll give you gifts,
But I'd have something too – that arm-ring, boy.
We'll have this quarrel out when you are older.

YOUNG MAN: There is no man I'd sooner have my friend
Than you, whose name has gone about the world
As if it had been the wind; but Aoife'd say
I had turned coward.

CUCHULAIN: I will give you gifts
That Aoife'll know, and all her people know,
To have come from me.
   [Showing cloak.]
                         My father gave me this.
He came to try me, rising up at dawn
Out of the cold dark of the rich sea.
He challenged me to battle, but before
My sword had touched his sword, told me his name,
Gave me this cloak, and vanished. It was woven
By women of the Country-under-Wave
Out of the fleeces of the sea. O! tell her

I was afraid, or tell her what you will.
No; tell her that I heard a raven croak
On the north side of the house, and was afraid.

CONCHUBAR: Some witch of the air has troubled Cuchulain's mind.

CUCHULAIN: No witchcraft. His head is like a woman's head
I had a fancy for.

CONCHUBAR: A witch of the air
Can make a leaf confound us with memories.
They run upon the wind and hurl the spells
That make us nothing, out of the invisible wind.
They have gone to school to learn the trick of it.

CUCHULAIN: No, no – there's nothing out of common here;
The winds are innocent. – That arm-ring, boy.

A KING: If I've your leave I'll take this challenge up.

ANOTHER KING: No, give it me, High King, for this wild Aoife
Has carried off my slaves.

ANOTHER KING: No, give it me,
For she has harried me in house and herd.

ANOTHER KING: I claim this fight.

OTHER KINGS [together]:   And I! And I! And I!

CUCHULAIN: Back! back! Put up your swords! Put up your swords!
There's none alive that shall accept a challenge
I have refused. Laegaire,[26] put up your sword!

YOUNG MAN: No, let them come. If they've a mind for it,
I'll try it out with any two together.

CUCHULAIN: That's spoken as I'd have spoken it at your age.
But you are in my house. Whatever man
Would fight with you shall fight it out with me.
They're dumb, they're dumb. How many of you would meet
          [Draws sword.]
This mutterer, this old whistler, this sand-piper,
This edge that's greyer than the tide, this mouse
That's gnawing at the timbers of the world,
This, this – Boy, I would meet them all in arms
If I'd a son like you. He would avenge me
When I have withstood for the last time the men
Whose fathers, brothers, sons, and friends I have killed

Upholding Conchubar, when the four provinces[27]
Have gathered with the ravens over them.
But I'd need no avenger. You and I
Would scatter them like water from a dish.

YOUNG MAN: We'll stand by one another from this out.
Here is the ring.

CUCHULAIN: No, turn and turn about.
But my turn's first because I am the older.
    [*Spreading out cloak.*[28]]
Nine queens out of the Country-under-Wave
Have woven it with the fleeces of the sea
And they were long embroidering at it. – Boy,
If I had fought my father, he'd have killed me,
As certainly as if I had a son
And fought with him, I should be deadly to him;
For the old fiery fountains are far off
And every day there is less heat o' the blood.

CONCHUBAR [*in a loud voice*]: No more of this. I will not have this
    friendship.
Cuchulain is my man, and I forbid it.
He shall not go unfought, for I myself –

CUCHULAIN: I will not have it.

CONCHUBAR: You lay commands on me?

CUCHULAIN [*seizing Conchubar*]: You shall not stir, High King. I'll
    hold you there.

CONCHUBAR: Witchcraft has maddened you.

THE KINGS [*shouting*]:   Yes, witchcraft! witchcraft!

FIRST OLD KING: Some witch has worked upon your mind,
    Cuchulain.
The head of that young man seemed like a woman's
You'd had a fancy for. Then of a sudden
You laid your hands on the High King himself!

CUCHULAIN: And laid my hands on the High King himself?

CONCHUBAR: Some witch is floating in the air above us.

CUCHULAIN: Yes, witchcraft! witchcraft! Witches of the air!
    [*To Young Man.*] Why did you? Who was it set you to this work?
    Out, out! I say, for now it's sword on sword!

YOUNG MAN: But . . . but I did not.

CUCHULAIN: Out, I say, out, out!

[*Young Man goes out followed by Cuchulain. The Kings follow them out with confused cries, and words one can hardly hear because of the noise. Some cry, 'Quicker, quicker!' 'Why are you so long at the door?' 'We'll be too late!' 'Have they begun to fight?' 'Can you see if they are fighting?' and so on. Their voices drown each other. The three Women are left alone.*]

FIRST WOMAN: I have seen, I have seen!

SECOND WOMAN: What do you cry aloud?

FIRST WOMAN: The Ever-living have shown me what's to come.

THIRD WOMAN: How? Where?

FIRST WOMAN: In the ashes of the bowl.

SECOND WOMAN: While you were holding it between your hands?

THIRD WOMAN: Speak quickly!

FIRST WOMAN: I have seen Cuchulain's roof-tree
Leap into fire, and the walls split and blacken.

SECOND WOMAN: Cuchulain has gone out to die.

THIRD WOMAN: O! O!

SECOND WOMAN: Who could have thought that one so great as he
Should meet his end at this unnoted sword!

FIRST WOMAN: Life drifts between a fool and a blind man
To the end, and nobody can know his end.

SECOND WOMAN: Come, look upon the quenching of this greatness.
[*The other two go to the door, but they stop for a moment upon the threshold and wail.*]

FIRST WOMAN: No crying out, for there'll be need of cries
And rending of the hair when it's all finished.[29]
[*The Women go out. There is the sound of clashing swords from time to time during what follows.*
Enter the Fool, dragging the Blind Man.]

FOOL: You have eaten it, you have eaten it! You have left me nothing but the bones.
[*He throws Blind Man down by big chair.*]

BLIND MAN: O, that I should have to endure such a plague! O, I ache all over! O, I am pulled to pieces! This is the way you pay me all the good I have done you.

FOOL: You have eaten it! You have told me lies. I might have known
you had eaten it when I saw your slow, sleepy walk. Lie there till
the kings come. O, I will tell Conchubar and Cuchulain and all the
kings about you!

BLIND MAN: What would have happened to you but for me, and you
without your wits? If I did not take care of you, what would you do
for food and warmth?

FOOL: You take care of me? You stay safe, and send me into every
kind of danger. You sent me down the cliff for gulls' eggs while you
warmed your blind eyes in the sun; and then you ate all that were
good for food. You left me the eggs that were neither egg nor bird.

[Blind Man tries to rise; Fool makes him lie down again.]

Keep quiet now, till I shut the door. There is some noise outside –
a high vexing noise, so that I can't be listening to myself. [Shuts the
big door.] Why can't they be quiet? Why can't they be quiet? [Blind
Man tries to get away.] Ah! you would get away, would you? [Follows
Blind Man and brings him back.] Lie there! lie there! No, you won't
get away! Lie there till the kings come. I'll tell them all about you. I
will tell it all. How you sit warming yourself, when you have made
me light a fire of sticks, while I sit blowing it with my mouth. Do
you not always make me take the windy side of the bush when it
blows, and the rainy side when it rains?

BLIND MAN: O, good Fool! listen to me. Think of the care I have taken
of you. I have brought you to many a warm hearth, where there was
a good welcome for you, but you would not stay there; you were
always wandering about.

FOOL: The last time you brought me in, it was not I who wandered
away, but you that got put out because you took the crubeen[30] out
of the pot when nobody was looking. Keep quiet, now!

CUCHULAIN [rushing in]: Witchcraft! There is no witchcraft on the
earth, or among the witches of the air, that these hands cannot break.

FOOL: Listen to me, Cuchulain. I left him turning the fowl at the fire.
He ate it all, though I had stolen it. He left me nothing but the
feathers.

CUCHULAIN: Fill me a horn of ale!

BLIND MAN: I gave him what he likes best. You do not know how
vain this Fool is. He likes nothing so well as a feather.

FOOL: He left me nothing but the bones and feathers. Nothing but the
feathers, though I had stolen it.

CUCHULAIN: Give me that horn. Quarrels here, too! [*Drinks.*] What is there between you two that is worth a quarrel? Out with it!

BLIND MAN: Where would he be but for me? I must be always thinking – thinking to get food for the two of us, and when we've got it, if the moon is at the full or the tide on the turn, he'll leave the rabbit in the snare till it is full of maggots, or let the trout slip back through his hands into the stream.

[*The Fool has begun singing while the Blind Man is speaking.*]

FOOL [*singing*]:

> When you were an acorn on the tree-top,
>   Then was I an eagle-cock;
> Now that you are a withered old block,
>   Still am I an eagle-cock.

BLIND MAN: Listen to him, now. That's the sort of talk I have to put up with day out, day in.

[*The Fool is putting the feathers into his hair. Cuchulain takes a handful of feathers out of a heap the Fool has on the bench beside him, and out of the Fool's hair, and begins to wipe the blood from his sword with them.*]

FOOL: He has taken my feathers to wipe his sword. It is blood that he is wiping from his sword.

CUCHULAIN [*goes up to door at back and throws away feathers*]: They are standing about his body. They will not awaken him, for all his witchcraft.

BLIND MAN: It is that young champion that he has killed. He that came out of Aoife's country.[31]

CUCHULAIN: He thought to have saved himself with witchcraft.

FOOL: That Blind Man there said he would kill you. He came from Aoife's country to kill you. That Blind Man said they had taught him every kind of weapon that he might do it. But I always knew that you would kill him.

CUCHULAIN [*to the Blind Man*]: You knew him, then?

BLIND MAN: I saw him, when I had my eyes, in Aoife's country.

CUCHULAIN: You were in Aoife's country?

BLIND MAN: I knew him and his mother there.

CUCHULAIN: He was about to speak of her when he died.[32]

BLIND MAN: He was a queen's son.

CUCHULAIN: What queen? what queen? [*Seizes Blind Man, who is now sitting upon the bench.*] Was it Scathach?[33] There were many queens. All the rulers there were queens.

BLIND MAN: No, not Scathach.

CUCHULAIN: It was Uathach,[34] then? Speak! speak!

BLIND MAN: I cannot speak; you are clutching me too tightly. [*Cuchulain lets him go.*] I cannot remember who it was. I am not certain. It was some queen.

FOOL: He said a while ago that the young man was Aoife's son.

CUCHULAIN: She? No, no! She had no son when I was there.

FOOL: That Blind Man there said that she owned him for her son.

CUCHULAIN: I had rather he had been some other woman's son. What father had he? A soldier out of Alba?[35] She was an amorous woman – a proud, pale, amorous woman.

BLIND MAN: None knew whose son he was.

CUCHULAIN: None knew! Did you know, old listener at doors?

BLIND MAN: No, no; I knew nothing.

FOOL: He said a while ago that he heard Aoife boast that she'd never but the one lover, and he the only man that had overcome her in battle.

　　[*Pause.*]

BLIND MAN: Somebody is trembling, Fool! The bench is shaking. Why are you trembling? Is Cuchulain going to hurt us? It was not I who told you, Cuchulain.

FOOL: It is Cuchulain who is trembling. It is Cuchulain who is shaking the bench.

BLIND MAN: It is his own son he has slain.[36]

CUCHULAIN: 'Twas they that did it, the pale windy people.
Where? where? where? My sword against the thunder!
But no, for they have always been my friends;
And though they love to blow a smoking coal
Till it's all flame, the wars they blow aflame
Are full of glory, and heart-uplifting pride,
And not like this. The wars they love awaken
Old fingers and the sleepy strings of harps.
Who did it then? Are you afraid? Speak out!

For I have put you under my protection,
And will reward you well. Dubthach[37] the Chafer?
He'd an old grudge. No, for he is with Maeve.
Laegaire did it! Why do you not speak?
What is this house? [*Pause.*] Now I remember all.
  [*Comes before Conchubar's chair, and strikes out with his sword,
  as if Conchubar was sitting upon it.*]
'Twas you who did it – you who sat up there
With your old rod of kingship, like a magpie
Nursing a stolen spoon. No, not a magpie,
A maggot that is eating up the earth!
Yes, but a magpie, for he's flown away.
Where did he fly to?

BLIND MAN: He is outside the door.

CUCHULAIN: Outside the door?

BLIND MAN: Between the door and the sea.

CUCHULAIN: Conchubar, Conchubar! the sword into your heart!
  [*He rushes out. Pause. Fool creeps up to the big door and looks
  after him.*]

FOOL: He is going up to King Conchubar. They are all about the young
  man. No, no, he is standing still. There is a great wave going to
  break, and he is looking at it. Ah! now he is running down to the
  sea, but he is holding up his sword as if he were going into a fight.
  [*Pause.*] Well struck! well struck!

BLIND MAN: What is he doing now?

FOOL: O! he is fighting the waves!

BLIND MAN: He sees King Conchubar's crown on every one of them.

FOOL: There, he has struck at a big one! He has struck the crown off
  it; he has made the foam fly. There again, another big one!

BLIND MAN: Where are the kings? What are the kings doing?

FOOL: They are shouting and running down to the shore, and the
  people are running out of the houses. They are all running.

BLIND MAN: You say they are running out of the houses? There will
  be nobody left in the houses. Listen, Fool!

FOOL: There, he is down! He is up again. He is going out in the deep
  water. There is a big wave. It has gone over him. I cannot see him
  now. He has killed kings and giants, but the waves have mastered
  him, the waves have mastered him!

BLIND MAN: Come here, Fool!

FOOL: The waves have mastered him.

BLIND MAN: Come here!

FOOL: The waves have mastered him.[38]

BLIND MAN: Come here, I say.

FOOL [*coming towards him, but looking backwards towards the door*]:
   What is it?

BLIND MAN: There will be nobody in the houses. Come this way; come
   quickly! The ovens will be full. We will put our hands into the ovens.
      [*They go out.*]

THE END

THE GREEN HELMET

AN HEROIC FARCE

Persons in the Play

LAEGAIRE (*pronounced* Leary)
CONALL
CUCHULAIN (*pronounced* Cuhoolin)
RED MAN, *a Spirit*
EMER
LAEGAIRE'S WIFE
CONALL'S WIFE
LAEG, *Cuchulain's chariot-driver*
STABLE BOYS AND SCULLIONS
BLACK MEN, etc.

A house made of logs. There are two windows at the back and a door which cuts off one of the corners of the room. Through the door one can see low rocks which make the ground outside higher than it is within, and beyond the rocks a misty moon-lit sea. Through the windows one can see nothing but the sea. There is a great chair at the opposite side to the door, and in front of it a table with cups and a flagon of ale. Here and there are stools.

At the Abbey Theatre the house is orange-red and the chairs and tables and flagons black, with a slight purple tinge which is not clearly distinguishable from the black. The rocks are black with a few green touches. The sea is green and luminous, and all the characters except the Red Man and the Black Men are dressed in various shades of green, one or two with touches of purple which look nearly black. The Black Men all wear dark purple and have eared caps, and at the end their eyes should look green from the reflected light of the sea. The Red Man is altogether in red. He is very tall, and his height increased by horns on the Green Helmet. The effect is intentionally violent and startling.

LAEGAIRE: What is that? I had thought that I saw, though but in the
wink of an eye,

A cat-headed man out of Connacht go pacing and spitting by;
But that could not be.

CONALL: You have dreamed it – there's nothing out there.
I killed them all before daybreak – I hoked them out of their lair;
I cut off a hundred heads with a single stroke of my sword,
And then I danced on their graves and carried away their hoard.

LAEGAIRE: Does anything stir on the sea?

CONALL: Not even a fish or a gull:
I can see for a mile or two, now that the moon's at the full.[1]
    [A distant shout.]

LAEGAIRE: Ah – there – there is some one who calls us.

CONALL: But from the landward side,
And we have nothing to fear that has not come up from the tide;
The rocks and the bushes cover whoever made that noise,
But the land will do us no harm.

LAEGAIRE: It was like Cuchulain's voice.

CONALL: But that's an impossible thing.

LAEGAIRE: An impossible thing indeed.

CONALL: For he will never come home, he has all that he could need
In that high windy Scotland[2] – good luck in all that he does.
Here neighbour wars on neighbour, and why there is no man knows,
And if a man is lucky all wish his luck away,
And take his good name from him between a day and a day.

LAEGAIRE: I would he'd come for all that, and make his young wife
    know
That though she may be his wife, she has no right to go
Before your wife and my wife, as she would have done last night
Had they not caught at her dress, and pulled her as was right;
And she makes light of us though our wives do all that they can.
She spreads her tail like a peacock and praises none but her man.

CONALL: A man in a long green cloak[3] that covers him up to the chin
Comes down through the rocks and hazels.

LAEGAIRE: Cry out that he cannot come in.

CONALL: He must look for his dinner elsewhere, for no one alive
    shall stop
Where a shame must alight on us two before the dawn is up.

LAEGAIRE: No man on the ridge of the world must ever know that
    but us two.

CONALL [*outside door*]: Go away, go away, go away.

YOUNG MAN [*outside door*]: I will go when the night is through
  And I have eaten and slept and drunk to my heart's delight.

CONALL: A law has been made that none shall sleep in this house
  to-night.

YOUNG MAN: Who made that law?

CONALL: We made it, and who has so good a right?
  Who else has to keep the house from the Shape-Changers till day?

YOUNG MAN: Then I will unmake the law, so get you out of the way.
  [*He pushes past Conall and goes into house.*]

CONALL: I thought no living man could have pushed me from the
  door,
  Nor could any living man do it but for the dip in the floor;
  And had I been rightly ready there's no man living could do it,
  Dip or no dip.

LAEGAIRE: Go out – if you have your wits, go out,
  A stone's throw further on you will find a big house where
  Our wives will give you supper, and you'll sleep sounder there,
  For it's a luckier house.

YOUNG MAN: I'll eat and sleep where I will.

LAEGAIRE: Go out or I will make you.

YOUNG MAN [*forcing up Laegaire's arm, passing him and putting
    his shield on the wall over the chair*]: Not till I have drunk my
    fill,
  But may some dog defend me, for a cat of wonder's up.
  Laegaire and Conall are here, the flagon full to the top,
  And the cups——

LAEGAIRE: It is Cuchulain.

CUCHULAIN: The cups are dry as a bone.
  [*He sits on chair and drinks.*]

CONALL: Go into Scotland again, or where you will, but begone
  From this unlucky country that was made when the Devil spat.

CUCHULAIN: If I lived here a hundred years, could a worse thing
    come than that
  Laegaire and Conall should know me and bid me begone to my
  face?

CONALL: We bid you begone from a house that has fallen on shame
  and disgrace.

CUCHULAIN: I am losing patience, Conall – I find you stuffed with
    pride,
  The flagon full to the brim, the front door standing wide;
  You'd put me off with words, but the whole thing's plain enough,
  You are waiting for some message to bring you to war or love
  In that old secret country beyond the wool-white waves,
  Or it may be down beneath them in foam-bewildered caves
  Where nine forsaken sea-queens fling shuttles to and fro;
  But beyond them, or beneath them, whether you will or no,
  I am going too.

LAEGAIRE: Better tell it all out to the end;
  He was born to luck in the cradle, his good luck may amend
  The bad luck we were born to.

CONALL: I'll lay the whole thing bare.
  You saw the luck that he had when he pushed in past me there.
  Does anything stir on the sea?[4]

LAEGAIRE: Not even a fish or a gull.

CONALL: You were gone but a little while. We were there and the
    ale-cup full.
  We were half drunk and merry, and midnight on the stroke,
  When a wide, high man came in with a red foxy cloak,
  With half-shut foxy eyes and a great laughing mouth,
  And he said, when we bid him drink, that he had so great a drouth
  He could drink the sea.

CUCHULAIN: I thought he had come for one of you
  Out of some Connacht rath,[5] and would lap up milk and mew;
  But if he so loved water I have the tale awry.

CONALL: You would not be so merry if he were standing by,
  For when we had sung or danced as he were our next of kin
  He promised to show us a game, the best that ever had been;
  And when we had asked what game, he answered, 'Why, whip off
    my head!
  Then one of you two stoop down, and I'll whip off his', he said.
  'A head for a head', he said, 'that is the game that I play'.

CUCHULAIN: How could he whip off a head when his own had been
    whipped away?

CONALL: We told him it over and over, and that ale had fuddled his
    wit,

But he stood and laughed at us there, as though his sides would
    split,
Till I could stand it no longer, and whipped off his head at a blow,
Being mad that he did not answer, and more at his laughing so,
And there on the ground where it fell it went on laughing at me.

LAEGAIRE: Till he took it up in his hands –

CONALL: And splashed himself into the sea.

CUCHULAIN: I have imagined as good when I've been as deep in the
    cup.

LAEGAIRE: You never did.

CUCHULAIN: And believed it.

CONALL: Cuchulain, when will you stop
Boasting of your great deeds and weighing yourself with us two,
And crying out to the world, whatever we say or do,
That you've said or done a better? – Nor is it a drunkard's tale,
Though we said to ourselves at first that it all came out of the ale,
And thinking that if we told it we should be a laughing-stock
Swore we should keep it secret.

LAEGAIRE: But twelve months upon the clock –

CONALL: A twelvemonth from the first time –

LAEGAIRE: And the jug full up to the brim:
For we had been put from our drinking by the very thought of
    him –

CONALL: We stood as we're standing now –

LAEGAIRE: The horns were as empty –

CONALL: When
He ran up out of the sea with his head on his shoulders again.

CUCHULAIN: Why, this is a tale worth telling.

CONALL: And he called for his debt and his right,
And said that the land was disgraced because of us two from that
    night
If we did not pay him his debt.

LAEGAIRE: What is there to be said
When a man with a right to get it has come to ask for your head?

CONALL: If you had been sitting there you had been silent like us.

LAEGAIRE: He said that in twelve months more he would come again
    to this house

And ask his debt again. Twelve months are up to-day.

CONALL: He would have followed after if we had run away.

LAEGAIRE: Will he tell every mother's son that we have broken our
word?

CUCHULAIN: Whether he does or does not, we'll drive him out with
the sword,
And take his life in the bargain if he but dare to scoff.

CONALL: How can you fight with a head that laughs when you've
whipped it off?

LAEGAIRE: Or a man that can pick it up and carry it out in his hand?

CONALL: He is coming now, there's a splash and a rumble along the
strand
As when he came last.

CUCHULAIN: Come, and put all your backs to the door.
[*A tall red-headed, red-cloaked man stands upon the threshold
against the misty green of the sea; the ground, higher without than
within the house, makes him seem taller even than he is. He leans
upon a great two-handed sword.*]

LAEGAIRE: It is too late to shut it, for there he stands once more
And laughs like the sea.

CUCHULAIN: Old herring[6] – You whip off heads! Why, then,
Whip off your own, for it seems you can clap it on again.
Or else go down in the sea, go down in the sea, I say,
Find that old juggler Manannan[7] and whip his head away;
Or the Red Man of the Boyne, for they are of your own sort,
Or if the waves have vexed you and you would find a sport
Of a more Irish[8] fashion, go fight without a rest
A caterwauling phantom among the winds of the West.
But what are you waiting for? Into the water, I say!
If there's no sword can harm you, I've an older trick to play,
An old five-fingered trick to tumble you out of the place;
I am Sualtim's son,[9] Cuchulain – What, do you laugh in my face?

RED MAN: So you too think me in earnest in wagering poll for poll!
A drinking joke and a gibe and a juggler's feat, that is all,
To make the time go quickly – for I am the drinker's friend,
The kindest of all Shape-Changers from here to the world's end,
The best of all tipsy companions. And now I bring you a gift:
I will lay it there on the ground for the best of you all to lift

[*He lays his Helmet on the ground.*]
And wear upon his own head, and choose for yourselves the best.
O, Laegaire and Conall are brave, but they were afraid of my jest.
Well, maybe I jest too grimly when the ale is in the cup.
There, I'm forgiven now –
    [*Then in a more solemn voice as he goes out.*]
                          Let the bravest[10] take it up.
    [*Conall takes up Helmet and gazes at it with delight.*]

LAEGAIRE [*singing, with a swaggering stride*]:

> Laegaire is best;
> Between water and hill,
> He fought in the West
> With cat-heads, until
> At the break of day
> All fell by his sword,
> And he carried away
> Their hidden hoard.

    [*He seizes the Helmet.*]

CONALL: Laegaire, that Helmet is mine, for what did you find in the
    bag
  But the straw and the broken delf and the bits of dirty rag
  You'd taken for good money?

CUCHULAIN: No, no, but give it me.
    [*He takes Helmet.*]

CONALL: The Helmet's mine or Laegaire's – you're the youngest of
    us three.

CUCHULAIN [*filling Helmet with ale*]: I did not take it to keep it –
    the Red Man gave it for one,
  But I shall give it to all – to all of us three or to none;
  That is as you look upon it – we will pass it to and fro,
  And time and time about, drink out of it and so
  Stroke into peace this cat that has come to take our lives.
  Now it is purring again, and now I drink to your wives,
  And I drink to Emer, my wife.
    [*A great noise without and shouting.*]
                      Why, what in God's name is that noise?

CONALL: What else but the charioteers and the kitchen and stable
    boys

Shouting against each other, and the worst of all is your own,
That chariot-driver, Laeg, and they'll keep it up till the dawn,
And there's not a man in the house that will close his eyes to-night,
Or be able to keep them from it, or know what set them to fight.

[*A noise of horns without.*]

There, do you hear them now? Such hatred has each for each
They have taken the hunting-horns to drown one another's speech
For fear the truth may prevail. – Here's your good health and long life
And, though she be quarrelsome, good health to Emer, your wife.

[*The Charioteers, Stable Boys and Scullions come running in. They carry great horns and other instruments, ladles and the like.*[11]]

LAEG: I am Laeg, Cuchulain's driver, and my master's cock of the yard.

ANOTHER CHARIOTEER: Conall would scatter his feathers.

[*Confused murmurs.*]

LAEGAIRE [*to Cuchulain*]:   No use, they won't hear a word.

CONALL: They'll keep it up till the dawn.

ANOTHER CHARIOTEER: It is Laegaire that is the best,
For he fought with cats in Connacht while Conall took his rest
And drained his ale-pot.

ANOTHER: Laegaire – what does a man of his sort
Care for the like of us? He did it for his own sport.

ANOTHER: It was all mere luck at the best.

ANOTHER: But Conall, I say –

ANOTHER: Let me speak.

LAEG: You'd be dumb if the cock of the yard would but open his beak.

ANOTHER: Before your cock was born, my master was in the fight.

LAEG: Go home and praise your grand-dad. They took to the horns for spite,
For I said that no cock of your sort had been born since the fight began.

ANOTHER: Conall has got it, the best man has got it, and I am his man.

CUCHULAIN: Who was it started this quarrel?

A STABLE BOY: It was Laeg.

ANOTHER: It was Laeg done it all.

LAEG: A high, wide, foxy man came where we sat in the hall,
  Getting our supper ready, with a great voice like the wind,
  And cried that there was a helmet, or something of the kind,
  That was for the foremost man upon the ridge of the earth.
  So I cried your name through the hall,
    [*The others cry out and blow horns, partly drowning the rest of his speech.*]
                                but they denied its worth,
Preferring Laegaire or Conall, and they cried to drown my voice;
But I have so strong a throat that I drowned all their noise
Till they took to the hunting-horns and blew them into my face,
And as neither side would give in – we would settle it in this place.
Let the Helmet be taken from Conall.

A STABLE BOY: No, Conall is the best man here.

ANOTHER: Give it to Laegaire that made the murderous cats pay
      dear.

CUCHULAIN: It has been given to none: that our rivalry might cease,
  We have turned that murderous cat into a cup of peace.
  I drank the first; and then Conall; give it to Laegaire now
    [*Conall gives Helmet to Laegaire.*]
  That it may purr in his hand and all of our servants know
  That, since the ale went in, its claws went out of sight.

A SERVANT: That's well – I will stop my shouting.

ANOTHER: Cuchulain is in the right;
  I am tired of this big horn that has made me hoarse as a rook.

LAEGAIRE: Cuchulain, you drank the first.

ANOTHER: By drinking the first he took
  The whole of the honours himself.

LAEGAIRE: Cuchulain, you drank the first.

ANOTHER: If Laegaire drink from it now, he claims to be last and
      worst.

ANOTHER: Cuchulain and Conall have drunk.

ANOTHER: He is lost if he taste a drop.

LAEGAIRE [*laying Helmet on table*]: Did you claim to be better than
      us by drinking first from the cup?

CUCHULAIN [*his words are partly drowned by the murmurs of the
      crowd though he speaks very loud*]: That juggler from the sea,
      that old red herring it is

Who has set us all by the ears – he brought the Helmet for this,
And because we would not quarrel he ran elsewhere to shout
That Conall and Laegaire wronged me, till all had fallen out.
 [*The murmur grows less so that his words are heard.*]
Who knows where he is now or whom he is spurring to fight?
So get you gone, and whatever may cry aloud in the night,
Or show itself in the air, be silent until morn.

A SERVANT: Cuchulain is in the right – I am tired of this big horn.

CUCHULAIN: Go!
 [*The Servants turn towards the door but stop on hearing the voices of women outside.*]

LAEGAIRE'S WIFE [*without*]: Mine is the better to look at.

CONALL'S WIFE [*without*]:   But mine is better born.

EMER [*without*]: My man is the pithier man.

CUCHULAIN: Old hurricane, well done!
You've set our wives to the game that they may egg us on;
We are to kill each other that you may sport with us.
Ah, now they've begun to wrestle as to who'll be first in the house.
 [*The women come to the door struggling.*[12]]

EMER: No, I have the right of place, for I married the better man.

CONALL'S WIFE [*pulling Emer back*]: My nails in your neck and
  shoulder.

LAEGAIRE'S WIFE: And go before me if you can.
My husband fought in the West.

CONALL'S WIFE [*kneeling in the door so as to keep the others out
  who pull at her*]:   But what did he fight with there
But sidelong and spitting and helpless shadows of the dim air?
And what did he carry away but straw and broken delf?

LAEGAIRE'S WIFE: Your own man made up that tale trembling alone
  by himself,
Drowning his terror.

EMER [*forcing herself in front*]: I am Emer, it is I go first through the
  door.
No one shall walk before me, or praise any man before
My man has been praised.

CUCHULAIN [*putting his spear across the door so as to close it*]:
        Come, put an end to their quarrelling:

One is as fair as the other, each one the wife of a king.
Break down the painted walls, break them down, down to the floor!
Our wives shall come in together, each one at her own door.

[*Laegaire and Conall begin to break down the walls. Their wives go each to the hole her husband is making. Emer stands at the door and sings. Some of those who carry musical instruments may play an accompaniment.*]

EMER:

> Nothing that he has done;
> His mind that is fire,
> His body that is sun,
> Have set my head higher
> Than all the world's wives.
> Himself on the wind
> Is the gift that he gives,
> Therefore women-kind,
> When their eyes have met mine,
> Grow cold and grow hot,
> Troubled as with wine
> By a secret thought,
> Preyed upon, fed upon
> By jealousy and desire,
> For I am moon to that sun,
> I am steel to that fire.[13]

[*Holes have been broken in the walls. Cuchulain takes his spear from the door, and the three women come in at the same moment.*]

EMER: Cuchulain, put off this sloth and awake:
I will sing till I've stiffened your lip against every knave that would take
A share of your honour.

LAEGAIRE'S WIFE: You lie, for your man would take from my man.

CONALL'S WIFE [*to Laegaire's Wife*]: You say that, you double-face, and your own husband began.

CUCHULAIN [*taking up Helmet from table*]: Townland may rail at townland till all have gone to wrack,
The very straws may wrangle till they've thrown down the stack;
The very door-posts bicker till they've pulled in the door,

The very ale-jars jostle till the ale is on the floor,
But this shall help no further.
[*He throws Helmet into the sea.*]

LAEGAIRE'S WIFE: It was not for your head,
And so you would let none wear it, but fling it away instead.

CONALL'S WIFE: But you shall answer for it, for you've robbed my
man by this.

CONALL: You have robbed us both, Cuchulain.

LAEGAIRE: The greatest wrong there is
On the wide ridge of the world has been done to us two this day.

EMER [*drawing her dagger*]: Who is for Cuchulain?

CUCHULAIN: Silence!

EMER: Who is for Cuchulain, I say?
[*She sings the same words as before, flourishing her dagger about.
While she is singing, Conall's Wife and Laegaire's Wife draw their
daggers and run at her, but Cuchulain forces them back. Laegaire
and Conall draw their swords to strike Cuchulain.*]

LAEGAIRE'S WIFE [*crying out so as to be heard through Emer's
singing*]: Deafen her singing with horns!

CONALL'S WIFE]: Cry aloud! blow horns! make a noise!

LAEGAIRE'S WIFE: Blow horns, clap hands, or shout, so that you
smother her voice!
[*The Stable Boys and Scullions blow their horns or fight among
themselves. There is a deafening noise and a confused fight. Suddenly three black hands come through the windows and put out
the torches.[14] It is now pitch-dark, but for a faint light outside the
house which merely shows that there are moving forms, but not
who or what they are, and in the darkness one can hear low
terrified voices.*]

A VOICE: Coal-black, and headed like cats, they came up over the
strand.

ANOTHER VOICE: And I saw one stretch to a torch and cover it with
his hand.

ANOTHER VOICE: Another sooty fellow has plucked the moon from
the air.
[*A light gradually comes into the house from the sea, on which
the moon begins to show once more. There is no light within the*

house, and the great beams of the walls are dark and full of shadows, and the persons of the play dark too against the light. The Red Man is seen standing in the midst of the house. The black cat-headed men crouch and stand about the door. One carries the Helmet, one the great sword.[15]]

RED MAN: I demand the debt that's owing. Let some man kneel down there

That I may cut his head off, or all shall go to wrack.

CUCHULAIN: He played and paid with his head, and it's right that we pay him back,

And give him more than he gave, for he comes in here as a guest:

So I will give him my head.

[*Emer begins to keen.*]

Little wife, little wife, be at rest.

Alive I have been far off in all lands under the sun,

And been no faithful man; but when my story is done

My fame shall spring up and laugh, and set you high above all.

EMER [*putting her arms about him*]: It is you, not your fame that I love.

CUCHULAIN [*tries to put her from him*]: You are young, you are wise, you can call

Some kinder and comelier man that will sit at home in the house.

EMER: Live and be faithless still.

CUCHULAIN [*throwing her from him*]: Would you stay the great barnacle-goose

When its eyes are turned to the sea and its beak to the salt of the air?

EMER [*lifting her dagger to stab herself*]: I, too, on the grey wing's path!

CUCHULAIN [*seizing dagger*]: Do you dare, do you dare, do you dare?[16]

Bear children and sweep the house.

[*Forcing his way through the servants who gather round.*]

Wail, but keep from the road.

[*He kneels before Red Man. There is a pause.*]

Quick to your work, old Radish, you will fade when the cocks have crowed.

[*A black cat-headed man holds out the Helmet. The Red Man takes it.*]

RED MAN: I have not come for your hurt, I'm the Rector of this land,
And with my spitting cat-heads, my frenzied moon-bred band,
Age after age I sift it, and choose for its championship
The man who hits my fancy.

[*He places the Helmet on Cuchulain's head.*]

                                        And I choose the laughing lip
That shall not turn from laughing, whatever rise or fall;
The heart that grows no bitterer although betrayed by all;
The hand that loves to scatter; the life like a gambler's throw;
And these things I make prosper, till a day come that I know,
When heart and mind shall darken that the weak may end the strong,
And the long-remembering harpers have matter for their song.

THE END

DEIRDRE

TO

MRS. PATRICK CAMPBELL

who in the generosity of her genius has played my Deirdre in Dublin and London
with the Abbey Company, as well as with her own people, and

IN MEMORY OF

ROBERT GREGORY

who designed the beautiful scene she played it in.

Persons in the Play

MUSICIANS
FERGUS, *an old man*
NAOISE (*pronounced* Neesh-e), *a young king*
DEIRDRE, *his queen*
A DARK-FACED MESSENGER
CONCHUBAR (*pronounced* Conohar), *the old King of Uladh, who is still
strong and vigorous*
A DARK-FACED EXECUTIONER

*A Guest-house in a wood. It is a rough house of timber; through the
doors and some of the windows one can see the great spaces of the
wood, the sky dimming, night closing in. But a window to the left
shows the thick leaves of a coppice; the landscape suggests silence and
loneliness. There is a door to right and left, and through the side
windows one can see anybody who approaches either door, a moment
before he enters. In the centre, a part of the house is curtained off; the
curtains are drawn. There are unlighted torches in brackets on the
walls. There is, at one side, a small table with a chess-board and
chessmen upon it. At the other side of the room there is a brazier with
a fire; two women, with musical instruments beside them, crouch about
the brazier: they are comely women of about forty. Another woman,*

87

*who carries a stringed instrument, enters hurriedly; she speaks, at first
standing in the doorway.*

FIRST MUSICIAN:[1] I have a story right, my wanderers,
That has so mixed with fable in our songs
That all seemed fabulous. We are come, by chance,
Into King Conchubar's country, and this house
Is an old guest-house for travellers
From the seashore to Conchubar's royal house,[2]
And there are certain hills among these woods
And there Queen Deirdre grew.

SECOND MUSICIAN: That famous queen
   Who has been wandering with her lover Naoise
   Somewhere beyond the edges of the world?

FIRST MUSICIAN [*going nearer to the brazier*]: Some dozen years
         ago, King Conchubar found
   A house upon a hillside in this wood,
   And there a child with an old witch[3] to nurse her,
   And nobody to say if she were human,
   Or of the gods, or anything at all
   Of who she was or why she was hidden there,
   But that she'd too much beauty for good luck.
   He went up thither daily, till at last
   She put on womanhood, and he lost peace,
   And Deirdre's tale began. The King was old.
   A month or so before the marriage-day,
   A young man, in the laughing scorn of his youth,
   Naoise, the son of Usna, climbed up there,
   And having wooed, or, as some say, been wooed,
   Carried her off.

SECOND MUSICIAN: The tale were well enough
   Had it a finish.

FIRST MUSICIAN: Hush! I have more to tell;
   But gather close about that I may whisper
   The secrets of a king.

SECOND MUSICIAN: There's none to hear!

FIRST MUSICIAN: I have been to Conchubar's house and followed
         up

A crowd of servants going out and in
With loads upon their heads: embroideries
To hang upon the walls, or new-mown rushes
To strew upon the floors, and came at length
To a great room.

SECOND MUSICIAN: Be silent; there are steps!
    [*Enter Fergus, an old man, who moves about from door to window*
    excitedly through what follows.]

FERGUS: I thought to find a message from the King.
You are musicians by these instruments,
And if as seems – for you are comely women –
You can praise love, you'll have the best of luck,
For there'll be two, before the night is in,
That bargained for their love, and paid for it
All that men value. You have but the time
To weigh a happy music with a sad,
To find what is most pleasing to a lover,
Before the son of Usna and his queen
Have passed this threshold!

FIRST MUSICIAN: Deirdre and her man!

FERGUS: I was to have found a message in this house,
And ran to meet it. Is there no messenger
From Conchubar to Fergus, son of Rogh?

FIRST MUSICIAN: Are Deirdre and her lover tired of life?

FERGUS: You are not of this country, or you'd know
That they are in my charge[4] and all forgiven.

FIRST MUSICIAN: We have no country but the roads of the world.

FERGUS: Then you should know that all things change in the world,
And hatred turns to love and love to hate,
And even kings forgive.

FIRST MUSICIAN: An old man's love
Who casts no second line is hard to cure;
His jealousy is like his love.

FERGUS: And that's but true.
You have learned something in your wanderings.
He was so hard to cure that the whole court,
But I alone, thought it impossible;
Yet after I had urged it at all seasons,

I had my way, and all's forgiven now;
And you shall speak the welcome and the joy
That I lack tongue for.

FIRST MUSICIAN: Yet old men are jealous.[5]

FERGUS [*going to door*]: I am Conchubar's near friend, and that
    weighed somewhat,
And it was policy to pardon them.
The need of some young, famous, popular man
To lead the troops, the murmur of the crowd,
And his own natural impulse, urged him to it.
They have been wandering half a dozen years.

FIRST MUSICIAN: And yet old men are jealous.

FERGUS [*coming from door*]:   Sing the more sweetly
Because, though age is arid as a bone,
This man has flowered. I've need of music, too;
If this grey head would suffer no reproach,
I'd dance and sing—
    [*Dark-faced men with strange, barbaric dress and arms begin to
    pass by the doors and windows. They pass one by one and in
    silence.*]
                  and dance till the hour ran out,
Because I have accomplished this good deed.

FIRST MUSICIAN: Look there – there at the window, those dark men,
With murderous and outlandish-looking arms –
They've been about the house all day.

FERGUS [*looking after them*]:   What are you?
Where do you come from, who is it sent you here?

FIRST MUSICIAN: They will not answer you.

FERGUS: They do not hear.

FIRST MUSICIAN: Forgive my open speech, but to these eyes
That have seen many lands they are such men
As kings will gather for a murderous task
That neither bribes, commands, nor promises
Can bring their people to.

FERGUS: And that is why
You harped upon an old man's jealousy.
A trifle sets you quaking. Conchubar's fame
Brings merchandise on every wind that blows.

They may have brought him Libyan dragon-skin,
Or the ivory of the fierce unicorn.

FIRST MUSICIAN: If these be merchants, I have seen the goods
   They have brought to Conchubar, and understood
   His murderous purpose.

FERGUS: Murderous, you say?
   Why, what new gossip of the roads is this?
   But I'll not hear.

FIRST MUSICIAN: It may be life or death.
   There is a room in Conchubar's house, and there—

FERGUS: Be silent, or I'll drive you from the door.
   There's many a one that would do more than that,
   And make it prison, or death, or banishment
   To slander the High King.
      [*Suddenly restraining himself and speaking gently.*]
                              He is my friend;
   I have his oath, and I am well content.
   I have known his mind as if it were my own
   These many years, and there is none alive
   Shall buzz against him, and I there to stop it.
   I know myself, and him, and your wild thought
   Fed on extravagant poetry, and lit
   By such a dazzle of old fabulous tales
   That common things are lost, and all that's strange
   Is true because 'twere pity if it were not.
      [*Going to the door again.*]
   Quick! quick! your instruments! they are coming now.
   I hear the hoofs a-clatter. Begin that song!
   But what is it to be? I'd have them hear
   A music foaming up out of the house
   Like wine out of a cup. Come now, a verse
   Of some old time not worth remembering,
   And all the lovelier because a bubble.
   Begin, begin, of some old king and queen,
   Of Lugaidh Redstripe or another; no, not him,
   He and his lady perished wretchedly.[6]

FIRST MUSICIAN [*singing*]:

                  'Why is it', Queen Edain[7] said,

'If I do but climb the stair . . .

FERGUS: Ah! that is better. . . . They are alighted now.
Shake all your cockscombs, children; these are lovers.
    [*Fergus goes out.*]

FIRST MUSICIAN:

> 'Why is it', Queen Edain said,
>   'If I do but climb the stair
> To the tower overhead,
>   When the winds are calling there,
> Or the gannets calling out
>   In waste places of the sky,
> There's so much to think about
>   That I cry, that I cry?'

SECOND MUSICIAN:

> But her goodman answered her:
>   'Love would be a thing of naught
> Had not all his limbs a stir
>   Born out of immoderate thought;
> Were he anything by half,
>   Were his measure running dry.
> Lovers, if they may not laugh,
>   Have to cry, have to cry.'

[*Deirdre, Naoise, and Fergus have been seen for a moment through
the windows, but now they have entered.*][8]

THE THREE MUSICIANS [*together*]:

> But is Edain worth a song
>   Now the hunt begins anew?
> Praise the beautiful and strong;
>   Praise the redness of the yew;
> Praise the blossoming apple-stem.
>   But our silence had been wise.
> What is all our praise to them
>   That have one another's eyes?

DEIRDRE: Silence your music, though I thank you for it;
    But the wind's blown upon my hair, and I
    Must set the jewels on my neck and head
    For one that's coming.

NAOISE: Your colour has all gone
　　As 'twere with fear, and there's no cause for that.

DEIRDRE: These women have the raddle[9] that they use
　　To make them brave and confident, although
　　Dread, toil, or cold may chill the blood o' their cheeks.
　　You'll help me, women. It is my husband's will
　　I show my trust in one that may be here
　　Before the mind can call the colour up.
　　My husband took these rubies from a king
　　Of Surracha[10] that was so murderous
　　He seemed all glittering dragon. Now wearing them
　　Myself wars on myself, for I myself –
　　That do my husband's will, yet fear to do it –
　　Grow dragonish to myself.

　　　　[*The women have gathered about her. Naoise has stood looking
　　　　at her, but Fergus brings him to the chess-table.*]

NAOISE: No messenger!
　　It's strange that there is none to welcome us.

FERGUS: King Conchubar has sent no messenger
　　That he may come himself.

NAOISE: And being himself,
　　Being High King, he cannot break his faith.
　　I have his word and I must take that word,
　　Or prove myself unworthy of my nurture
　　Under a great man's roof.

FERGUS: We'll play at chess[11]
　　Till the King comes. It is but natural
　　That she should doubt him, for her house has been
　　The hole of the badger and the den of the fox.

NAOISE: If I had not King Conchubar's word I'd think
　　That chess-board ominous.

FERGUS: How can a board
　　That has been lying there these many years
　　Be lucky or unlucky?

NAOISE: It is the board
　　Where Lugaidh Redstripe and that wife of his,
　　Who had a seamew's body half the year,
　　Played at the chess upon the night they died.

FERGUS: I can remember now, a tale of treachery,
   A broken promise and a journey's end –
   But it were best forgot.
      [*Deirdre has been standing with the women about her. They have
      been helping her to put on her jewels and to put the pigment on
      her cheeks and arrange her hair. She has gradually grown attentive
      to what Fergus is saying.*]

NAOISE: If the tale's true,
   When it was plain that they had been betrayed,
   They moved the men and waited for the end
   As it were bedtime, and had so quiet minds
   They hardly winked their eyes when the sword flashed.

FERGUS: She never could have played so, being a woman,
   If she had not the cold sea's blood in her.

DEIRDRE: The gods turn clouds and casual accidents
   Into omens.

NAOISE: It would but ill become us,
   Now that King Conchubar has pledged his word,
   Should we be startled by a cloud or a shadow.

DEIRDRE: There's none to welcome us.

NAOISE: Being his guest,
   Words that would wrong him can but wrong ourselves.

DEIRDRE: An empty house upon the journey's end!
   Is that the way a king that means no mischief
   Honours a guest?

FERGUS: He is but making ready
   A welcome in his house, arranging where
   The moorhen and the mallard go, and where
   The speckled heathcock on a golden dish.

DEIRDRE: Had he no messenger?[12]

NAOISE: Such words and fears
   Wrong this old man who's pledged his word to us.
   We must not speak or think as women do,
   That when the house is all abed sit up
   Marking among the ashes with a stick
   Till they are terrified. – Being what we are
   We must meet all things with an equal mind.
      [*To Fergus.*] Come, let us look if there's a messenger

From Conchubar. We cannot see from this
Because we are blinded by the leaves and twigs,
But it may be the wood will thin again.
It is but kind that when the lips we love
Speak words that are unfitting for kings' ears
Our ears be deaf.

FERGUS: But now I had to threaten
These wanderers because they would have weighed
Some crazy fantasy of their own brain
Or gossip of the road with Conchubar's word.
If I had thought so little of mankind
I never could have moved him to this pardon.
I have believed the best of every man,
And find that to believe it is enough
To make a bad man show him at his best,
Or even a good man swing his lantern higher.

[*Naoise and Fergus go out. The last words are spoken as they go
through the door. One can see them through part of what follows,
either through door or window. They move about, talking or
looking along the road towards Conchubar's house.*]

FIRST MUSICIAN: If anything lies heavy on your heart,
Speak freely of it, knowing it is certain
That you will never see my face again.

DEIRDRE: You've been in love?

FIRST MUSICIAN: If you would speak of love
Speak freely. There is nothing in the world
That has been friendly to us but the kisses
That were upon our lips, and when we are old
Their memory will be all the life we have.

DEIRDRE: There was a man that loved me. He was old:
I could not love him. Now I can but fear.
He has made promises, and brought me home;
But though I turn it over in my thoughts,
I cannot tell if they are sound and wholesome,
Or hackles on the hook.

FIRST MUSICIAN: I have heard he loved you
As some old miser loves the dragon-stone
He hides among the cobwebs near the roof.

DEIRDRE: You mean that when a man who has loved like that
  Is after crossed, love drowns in its own flood,
  And that love drowned and floating is but hate;
  And that a king who hates sleeps ill at night
  Till he has killed; and that, though the day laughs,
  We shall be dead at cock-crow.

FIRST MUSICIAN: You've not my thought.
  When I lost one I loved distractedly,
  I blamed my crafty rival and not him,
  And fancied, till my passion had run out,
  That could I carry him away with me,
  And tell him all my love, I'd keep him yet.

DEIRDRE: Ah! now I catch your meaning, that this king
  Will murder Naoise, and keep me alive.

FIRST MUSICIAN: 'Tis you that put that meaning upon words
  Spoken at random.

DEIRDRE: Wanderers like you,
  Who have their wit alone to keep their lives,
  Speak nothing that is bitter to the ear
  At random; if they hint at it at all
  Their eyes and ears have gathered it so lately
  That it is crying out in them for speech.

FIRST MUSICIAN: We have little that is certain.

DEIRDRE: Certain or not,
  Speak it out quickly, I beseech you to it;
  I never have met any of your kind
  But that I gave them money, food, and fire.

FIRST MUSICIAN: There are strange, miracle-working, wicked stones,
  Men tear out of the heart and the hot brain
  Of Libyan dragons.

DEIRDRE: The hot Istain stone,
  And the cold stone of Fanes, that have power
  To stir even those at enmity to love.

FIRST MUSICIAN: They have so great an influence, if but sewn
  In the embroideries that curtain in
  The bridal bed.

DEIRDRE: O Mover of the stars
  That made this delicate house of ivory,

And made my soul its mistress, keep it safe!

FIRST MUSICIAN: I have seen a bridal bed, so curtained in,
So decked for miracle in Conchubar's house,
And learned that a bride's coming.

DEIRDRE: And I the bride?
Here is worse treachery than the seamew suffered,
For she but died and mixed into the dust
Of her dear comrade, but I am to live
And lie in the one bed with him I hate.
Where is Naoise? I was not alone like this
When Conchubar first chose me for his wife;
I cried in sleeping or waking and he came,
But now there is worse need.

NAOISE [entering with Fergus]: Why have you called?
I was but standing there, without the door.

DEIRDRE: I have heard terrible mysterious things,
Magical horrors and the spells of wizards.

FERGUS: Why, that's no wonder. You have been listening
To singers of the roads that gather up
The stories of the world.

DEIRDRE: But I have one
To make the stories of the world but nothing.

NAOISE: Be silent if it is against the King
Whose guest you are.

FERGUS: No, let her speak it out.
I know the High King's heart as it were my own,
And can refute a slander, but already
I have warned these women that it may be death.

NAOISE: I will not weigh the gossip of the roads
With the King's word. I ask your pardon for her:
She has the heart of the wild birds that fear
The net of the fowler or the wicker cage.

DEIRDRE: Am I to see the fowler and the cage
And speak no word at all?

NAOISE: You would have known,
Had they not bred you in that mountainous place,
That when we give a word and take a word
Sorrow is put away, past wrong forgotten.

DEIRDRE: Though death may come of it?

NAOISE: Though death may come.

DEIRDRE: When first we came into this empty house
You had foreknowledge of our death,[13] and even
When speaking of the paleness of my cheek
Your own cheek blanched.

NAOISE: Listen to this old man.
He can remember all the promises
We trusted to.

DEIRDRE: You speak from the lips out,
And I am pleading for your life and mine.

NAOISE: Listen to this old man, for many think
He has a golden tongue.

DEIRDRE: Then I will say
What it were best to carry to the grave.
Look at my face where the leaf raddled it
And at these rubies on my hair and breast.
It was for him, to stir him to desire,
I put on beauty; yes, for Conchubar.

NAOISE: What frenzy put these words into your mouth?

DEIRDRE: No frenzy, for what need is there for frenzy
To change what shifts with every change of the wind,
Or else there is no truth in men's old sayings?
Was I not born a woman?

NAOISE: You're mocking me.

DEIRDRE: And is there mockery in this face and eyes,
Or in this body, in these limbs that brought
So many mischiefs? Look at me and say
If that that shakes my limbs be mockery.

NAOISE: What woman is there that a man can trust
But at the moment when he kisses her
At the first midnight?

DEIRDRE: Were it not most strange
That women should put evil in men's hearts
And lack it in themselves? And yet I think
That being half good I might change round again
Were we aboard our ship and on the sea.

NAOISE: We'll to the horses and take ship again.

FERGUS: Fool, she but seeks to rouse your jealousy
  With crafty words.

DEIRDRE: Were we not born to wander?
  These jewels have been reaped by the innocent sword
  Upon a mountain, and a mountain bred me;
  But who can tell what change can come to love
  Among the valleys? I speak no falsehood now.
  Away to windy summits, and there mock
  The night-jar and the valley-keeping bird!

FERGUS: Men blamed you that you stirred a quarrel up
  That has brought death to many. I have made peace,
  Poured water on the fire, but if you fly
  King Conchubar may think that he is mocked
  And the house blaze again: and in what quarter,
  If Conchubar were the treacherous man you think,
  Would you find safety now that you have come
  Into the very middle of his power,
  Under his very eyes?

DEIRDRE: Under his eyes
  And in the very middle of his power![14]
  Then there is but one way to make all safe:
  I'll spoil this beauty that brought misery
  And houseless wandering on the man I loved.
  These wanderers will show me how to do it;
  To clip this hair to baldness, blacken my skin
  With walnut juice, and tear my face with briars.
  O that the creatures of the woods had torn
  My body with their claws!

FERGUS: What, wilder yet!

DEIRDRE [to Naoise]: Whatever were to happen to my face
  I'd be myself, and there's not any way
  But this to bring all trouble to an end.

NAOISE: Leave the gods' handiwork unblotched, and wait
  For their decision, our decision is past.

  [A Dark-faced Messenger comes to the threshold.]

FERGUS: Peace, peace; the messenger is at the door;
  He stands upon the threshold; he stands there;

He stands, King Conchubar's purpose on his lips.

MESSENGER: Supper is on the table. Conchubar
Is waiting for his guests.

FERGUS: All's well again!
All's well! All's well! You cried your doubts so loud
That I had almost doubted.

NAOISE: We doubted him,
And he the while but busy in his house
For the more welcome.

DEIRDRE: The message is not finished.

FERGUS: Come quickly. Conchubar will laugh, that I –
Although I held out boldly in my speech –
That I, even I—

DEIRDRE: Wait, wait! He is not done.[15]

MESSENGER: Deirdre and Fergus, son of Rogh, are summoned;
But not the traitor that bore off the Queen.
It is enough that the King pardon her,
And call her to his table and his bed.

NAOISE: So, then, it's treachery.

FERGUS: I'll not believe it.

NAOISE: Lead on and I will follow at your heels
That I may challenge him before his court
To match me there, or match me in some place
Where none can come between us but our swords,
For I have found no truth on any tongue
That's not of iron.

MESSENGER: I am Conchubar's man,
I am content to serve an iron tongue:
That Tongue commands that Fergus, son of Rogh,
And Deirdre come this night into his house,
And none but they.

    [He goes, followed by Naoise.]

FERGUS: Some rogue, some enemy,
Has bribed him to embroil us with the King;
I know that he has lied because I know
King Conchubar's mind as if it were my own,
But I'll find out the truth.

[*He is about to follow Naoise, but Deirdre stops him.*]

DEIRDRE: No, no, old man.
You thought the best, and the worst came of it;
We listened to the counsel of the wise,
And so turned fools. But ride and bring your friends.
Go, and go quickly. Conchubar has not seen me;
It may be that his passion is asleep,
And that we may escape.

FERGUS: But I'll go first,
And follow up that Libyan heel, and send
Such words to Conchubar that he may know
At how great peril he lays hands upon you.
[*Naoise enters.*]

NAOISE: The Libyan, knowing that a servant's life
Is safe from hands like mine, but turned and mocked.

FERGUS: I'll call my friends, and call the reaping-hooks,[16]
And carry you in safety to the ships.
My name has still some power.[17] I will protect,
Or, if that is impossible, revenge.
[*Goes out by other door.*]

NAOISE [*who is calm, like a man who has passed beyond life*]:
The crib has fallen and the birds are in it;
There is not one of the great oaks about us
But shades a hundred men.

DEIRDRE: Let's out and die,
Or break away, if the chance favour us.

NAOISE: They would but drag you from me, stained with blood.
Their barbarous weapons would but mar that beauty,
And I would have you die as a queen should –
In a death-chamber. You are in my charge.
We will wait here, and when they come upon us,
I'll hold them from the doors, and when that's over,
Give you a cleanly death with this grey edge.

DEIRDRE: I will stay here; but you go out and fight.
Our way of life has brought no friends to us,
And if we do not buy them leaving it,
We shall be ever friendless.

NAOISE: What do they say?

That Lugaidh Redstripe and that wife of his
Sat at this chess-board, waiting for their end.
They knew that there was nothing that could save them,
And so played chess as they had any night
For years, and waited for the stroke of sword.
I never heard a death so out of reach
Of common hearts, a high and comely end.
What need have I, that gave up all for love,
To die like an old king out of a fable,
Fighting and passionate? What need is there
For all that ostentation at my setting?
I have loved truly and betrayed no man.
I need no lightning at the end, no beating
In a vain fury at the cage's door.
[*To Musicians.*] Had you been here when that man and his queen
Played at so high a game, could you have found
An ancient poem for the praise of it?
It should have set out plainly that those two,
Because no man and woman have loved better,
Might sit on there contentedly, and weigh
The joy comes after. I have heard the seamew
Sat there, with all the colour in her cheeks,
As though she'd say: 'There's nothing happening
But that a king and queen are playing chess.'

DEIRDRE: He's in the right, though I have not been born
Of the cold, haughty waves, my veins being hot,
And though I have loved better than that queen,
I'll have as quiet fingers on the board.
O, singing women, set it down in a book,
That love is all we need, even though it is
But the last drops we gather up like this;
And though the drops are all we have known of life,
For we have been most friendless – praise us for it,
And praise the double sunset, for naught's lacking
But a good end to the long, cloudy day.

NAOISE: Light torches there and drive the shadows out,
For day's grey end comes up.
[*A Musician lights a torch in the fire and then crosses before the
chess-players, and slowly lights the torches in the sconces. The*

light is almost gone from the wood, but there is a clear evening light in the sky, increasing the sense of solitude and loneliness.[18]]

DEIRDRE: Make no sad music.
What is it but a king and queen at chess?
They need a music that can mix itself
Into imagination, but not break
The steady thinking that the hard game needs.

[*During the chess, the Musicians sing this song.*]

> Love is an immoderate thing
>   And can never be content
> Till it dip an ageing wing
>   Where some laughing element
> Leaps and Time's old lanthorn dims.
>   What's the merit in love-play,
> In the tumult of the limbs
>   That dies out before 'tis day,
> Heart on heart, or mouth on mouth,
>   All that mingling of our breath,
> When love-longing is but drouth
>   For the things come after death?

[*During the last verses Deirdre rises from the board and kneels at Naoise's feet.*]

DEIRDRE: I cannot go on playing like that woman
    That had but the cold blood of the sea in her veins.

NAOISE: It is your move. Take up your man again.

DEIRDRE: Do you remember that first night in the woods
    We lay all night on leaves, and looking up,
    When the first grey of the dawn awoke the birds,
    Saw leaves above us? You thought that I still slept,
    And bending down to kiss me on the eyes,
    Found they were open. Bend and kiss me now,
    For it may be the last before our death.
    And when that's over, we'll be different;
    Imperishable things, a cloud or a fire.
    And I know nothing but this body, nothing
    But that old vehement, bewildering kiss.

[*Conchubar comes to the door.*[19]]

FIRST MUSICIAN: Children, beware!

NAOISE [*laughing*]: He has taken up my challenge;
   Whether I am a ghost or living man
   When day has broken, I'll forget the rest,
   And say that there is kingly stuff in him.
      [*Turns to fetch spear and shield, and then sees that Conchubar
      has gone.*]

FIRST MUSICIAN: He came to spy[20] upon you, not to fight.

NAOISE: A prudent hunter, therefore, but no king.
   He'd find if what has fallen in the pit
   Were worth the hunting, but has come too near,
   And I turn hunter. You're not man, but beast.
   Go scurry in the bushes, now, beast, beast,
   For now it's topsy-turvy, I upon you.
      [*He rushes out after Conchubar.*]

DEIRDRE: You have a knife there, thrust into your girdle.
   I'd have you give it me.

FIRST MUSICIAN: No, but I dare not.

DEIRDRE: No, but you must.

FIRST MUSICIAN: If harm should come to you,
   They'd know I gave it.

DEIRDRE [*snatching knife*]: There is no mark on this
   To make it different from any other
   Out of a common forge.
      [*Goes to the door and looks out.*]

FIRST MUSICIAN: You have taken it,
   I did not give it you; but there are times
   When such a thing is all the friend one has.

DEIRDRE: The leaves hide all, and there's no way to find
   What path to follow. Why is there no sound?
      [*She goes from door to window.*]

FIRST MUSICIAN: Where would you go?

DEIRDRE: To strike a blow for Naoise,
   If Conchubar call the Libyans to his aid.
   But why is there no clash? They have met by this!

FIRST MUSICIAN: Listen. I am called wise. If Conchubar win,
   You have a woman's wile that can do much,
   Even with men in pride of victory.

He is in love and old. What were one knife
Among a hundred?

DEIRDRE [*going towards them*]: Women, if I die,
If Naoise die this night, how will you praise?
What words seek out? for that will stand to you;
For being but dead we shall have many friends.
All through your wanderings, the doors of kings
Shall be thrown wider open, the poor man's hearth
Heaped with new turf, because you are wearing this
    [*Gives Musician a bracelet.*]
To show that you have Deirdre's story right.

FIRST MUSICIAN: Have you not been paid servants in love's house
To sweep the ashes out and keep the doors?
And though you have suffered all for mere love's sake
You'd live your lives again.

DEIRDRE: Even this last hour.
    [*Conchubar enters with dark-faced men.*]

CONCHUBAR: One woman and two men; that is the quarrel
That knows no mending. Bring in the man she chose
Because of his beauty and the strength of his youth.
    [*The dark-faced men drag in Naoise entangled in a net.*[21]]

NAOISE: I have been taken like a bird or a fish.

CONCHUBAR: He cried 'Beast, beast!' and in a blind-beast rage
He ran at me and fell into the nets,
But we were careful for your sake, and took him
With all the comeliness that woke desire
Unbroken in him. I being old and lenient,
I would not hurt a hair upon his head.

DEIRDRE: What do you say? Have you forgiven him?

NAOISE: He is but mocking us. What's left to say
Now that the seven years' hunt is at an end?

DEIRDRE: He never doubted you until I made him,
And therefore all the blame for what he says
Should fall on me.

CONCHUBAR: But his young blood is hot,
And if we're of one mind, he shall go free,
And I ask nothing for it, or, if something,
Nothing I could not take. There is no king

In the wide world that, being so greatly wronged,
Could copy me, and give all vengeance up.
Although her marriage-day had all but come,
You carried her away; but I'll show mercy.
Because you had the insolent strength of youth
You carried her away; but I've had time
To think it out through all these seven years.
I will show mercy.

NAOISE: You have many words.

CONCHUBAR: I will not make a bargain; I but ask
What is already mine.

[*Deirdre moves slowly towards Conchubar while he is speaking,
her eyes fixed upon him.*]
                                    You may go free
If Deirdre will but walk into my house
Before the people's eyes, that they may know,
When I have put the crown upon her head,
I have not taken her by force and guile.
The doors are open, and the floors are strewed
And in the bridal chamber curtains sewn
With all enchantments that give happiness
By races that are germane to the sun,
And nearest him, and have no blood in their veins –
For when they're wounded the wound drips with wine –
Nor speech but singing. At the bridal door
Two fair king's daughters carry in their hands
The crown and robe.

DEIRDRE: O no! Not that, not that!
Ask any other thing but that one thing.
Leave me with Naoise. We will go away
Into some country at the ends of the earth.
We'll trouble you no more; and there is no one
That will not praise you if you pardon us.
'He is good, he is good', they'll say to one another;
'There's nobody like him, for he forgave
Deirdre and Naoise.'

CONCHUBAR: Do you think that I
Shall let you go again, after seven years
Of longing and of planning here and there,

And trafficking with merchants for the stones
That make all sure, and watching my own face
That none might read it?

DEIRDRE [*to Naoise*]:   It's better to go with him.
Why should you die when one can bear it all?
My life is over; it's better to obey.
Why should you die? I will not live long, Naoise.
I'd not have you believe I'd long stay living;
O no, no, no! You will go far away.
You will forget me. Speak, speak, Naoise, speak,
And say that it is better that I go.
I will not ask it. Do not speak a word,
For I will take it all upon myself.
Conchubar, I will go.

NAOISE: And do you think
That, were I given life at such a price,
I would not cast it from me? O my eagle!
Why do you beat vain wings upon the rock
When hollow night's above?

DEIRDRE: It's better, Naoise.
It may be hard for you, but you'll forget.
For what am I, to be remembered always?
And there are other women. There was one,
The daughter of the King of Leodas;
I could not sleep because of her.[22] Speak to him;
Tell it out plain, and make him understand.
And if it be he thinks I shall stay living,
Say that I will not.

NAOISE: Would I had lost life
Among those Scottish kings that sought it of me
Because you were my wife, or that the worst
Had taken you before this bargaining!
O eagle! If you were to do this thing,
And buy my life of Conchubar with your body,
Love's law being broken, I would stand alone
Upon the eternal summits, and call out,
And you could never come there, being banished.

DEIRDRE [*kneeling to Conchubar*]: I would obey,
      but cannot. Pardon us.

I know that you are good. I have heard you praised
For giving gifts; and you will pardon us,
Although I cannot go into your house.
It was my fault. I only should be punished.
  [*Unseen by Deirdre, Naoise is gagged.*]
The very moment these eyes fell on him,
I told him; I held out my hands to him;
How could he refuse? At first he would not –
I am not lying – he remembered you.
What do I say? My hands? – No, no, my lips –
For I had pressed my lips upon his lips –
I swear it is not false – my breast to his;
  [*Conchubar motions; Naoise, unseen by Deirdre, is taken behind
  the curtain.*]
Until I woke the passion that's in all,
And how could he resist? I had my beauty.
You may have need of him, a brave, strong man,
Who is not foolish at the council-board,
Nor does he quarrel by the candle-light
And give hard blows to dogs. A cup of wine
Moves him to mirth, not madness.
  [*She stands up.*]
                              What am I saying?
You may have need of him, for you have none
Who is so good a sword, or so well loved
Among the common people. You may need him,
And what king knows when the hour of need may come?
You dream that you have men enough. You laugh.
Yes; you are laughing to yourself. You say,
'I am Conchubar – I have no need of him.'
You will cry out for him some day and say,
'If Naoise were but living'— [*she misses Naoise*]. Where is he?
Where have you sent him? Where is the son of Usna?
Where is he, O, where is he?
  [*She staggers over to the Musicians. The Executioner has come
  out with a sword on which there is blood; Conchubar points to
  it. The Musicians give a wail.*]
CONCHUBAR: The traitor who has carried off my wife
  No longer lives. Come to my house now, Deirdre,

For he that called himself your husband's dead.

DEIRDRE: O, do not touch me. Let me go to him.
    [*Pause.*[23]]
    King Conchubar is right. My husband's dead.
    A single woman is of no account,
    Lacking array of servants, linen cupboards,
    The bacon hanging – and King Conchubar's house
    All ready, too – I'll to King Conchubar's house.
    It is but wisdom to do willingly
    What has to be.

CONCHUBAR: But why are you so calm?
    I thought that you would curse me and cry out,
    And fall upon the ground and tear your hair.

DEIRDRE [*laughing*]: You know too much of women to think so;
    Though, if I were less worthy of desire,
    I would pretend as much; but, being myself,
    It is enough that you were master here.
    Although we are so delicately made,
    There's something brutal in us, and we are won
    By those who can shed blood. It was some woman
    That taught you how to woo: but do not touch me:
    I shall do all you bid me, but not yet,
    Because I have to do what's customary.
    We lay the dead out, folding up the hands,
    Closing the eyes, and stretching out the feet,
    And push a pillow underneath the head,
    Till all's in order; and all this I'll do
    For Naoise, son of Usna.[24]

CONCHUBAR: It is not fitting.
    You are not now a wanderer, but a queen,
    And there are plenty that can do these things.

DEIRDRE [*motioning Conchubar away*]: No, no. Not yet. I cannot
    be your queen
    Till the past's finished, and its debts are paid.
    When a man dies, and there are debts unpaid,
    He wanders by the debtor's bed and cries,
    'There's so much owing.'

CONCHUBAR: You are deceiving me.

You long to look upon his face again.
Why should I give you now to a dead man
That took you from a living?
    [*He makes a step towards her.*]

DEIRDRE: In good time.
You'll stir me to more passion than he could,
And yet, if you are wise, you'll grant me this:
That I go look upon him that was once
So strong and comely and held his head so high
That women envied me. For I will see him
All blood-bedabbled and his beauty gone.
It's better, when you're beside me in your strength,
That the mind's eye should call up the soiled body,
And not the shape I loved. Look at him, women.
He heard me pleading to be given up,
Although my lover was still living, and yet
He doubts my purpose. I will have you tell him
How changeable all women are; how soon
Even the best of lovers is forgot
When his day's finished.

CONCHUBAR: No; but I will trust
The strength that you have praised, and not your purpose.

DEIRDRE [*almost with a caress*]: It is so small a gift and you will
    grant it
Because it is the first that I have asked.
He has refused. There is no sap in him;
Nothing but empty veins. I thought as much.
He has refused me the first thing I have asked –
Me, me, his wife. I understand him now;
I know the sort of life I'll have with him;
But he must drag me to his house by force.
If he refuses [*she laughs*], he shall be mocked of all.
They'll say to one another, 'Look at him
That is so jealous that he lured a man
From over sea, and murdered him, and yet
He trembled at the thought of a dead face!'[25]
    [*She has her hand upon the curtain.*]

CONCHUBAR: How do I know that you have not some knife,
    And go to die upon his body?

DEIRDRE: Have me searched,
  If you would make so little of your queen.
  It may be that I have a knife hid here
  Under my dress. Bid one of these dark slaves
  To search me for it.
    [*Pause.*]

CONCHUBAR: Go to your farewells, Queen.

DEIRDRE: Now strike the wire, and sing to it a while,
  Knowing that all is happy, and that you know
  Within what bride-bed I shall lie this night,
  And by what man, and lie close up to him,
  For the bed's narrow, and there outsleep the cock-crow.[26]
    [*She goes behind the curtain.*]

FIRST MUSICIAN: They are gone, they are gone. The proud may lie
    by the proud.

SECOND MUSICIAN: Though we were bidden to sing, cry nothing
    loud.

FIRST MUSICIAN: They are gone, they are gone.

SECOND MUSICIAN: Whispering were enough.

FIRST MUSICIAN: Into the secret wilderness of their love.

SECOND MUSICIAN: A high, grey cairn. What more is to be said?

FIRST MUSICIAN: Eagles have gone into their cloudy bed.
    [*Shouting outside. Fergus enters. Many men with scythes and
    sickles and torches gather about the doors. The house is lit with
    the glare of their torches.*]

FERGUS: Where's Naoise, son of Usna, and his queen?
  I and a thousand reaping-hooks and scythes
  Demand him of you.

CONCHUBAR: You have come too late.
  I have accomplished all. Deirdre is mine;
  She is my queen, and no man now can rob me.
  I had to climb the topmost bough, and pull
  This apple among the winds. Open the curtain
  That Fergus learn my triumph from her lips.
    [*The curtain is drawn back. The Musicians begin to keen with
    low voices.*]
  No, no; I'll not believe it. She is not dead –
  She cannot have escaped a second time!

FERGUS: King, she is dead; but lay no hand upon her.
 What's this but empty cage and tangled wire,
 Now the bird's gone? But I'll not have you touch it.

CONCHUBAR: You are all traitors, all against me – all.
 And she has deceived me for a second time;
 And every common man can keep his wife,
 But not the King.
 [*Loud shouting outside: 'Death to Conchubar!' 'Where is Naoise?'
 etc. The dark-faced men gather round Conchubar and draw their
 swords; but he motions them away.*]
                     I have no need of weapons,
 There's not a traitor that dare stop my way.
 Howl, if you will; but I, being King, did right
 In choosing her most fitting to be Queen,
 And letting no boy lover take the sway.

THE END

AT THE HAWK'S WELL

Persons in the Play

THREE MUSICIANS (*their faces made up to resemble masks*)
THE GUARDIAN OF THE WELL (*with face made up to resemble a mask*)
AN OLD MAN (*wearing a mask*)
A YOUNG MAN (*wearing a mask*)

Time – the Irish Heroic Age.

The stage is any bare space before a wall[1] against which stands a patterned screen. A drum and a gong and a zither[2] have been laid close to the screen before the play begins. If necessary, they can be carried in, after the audience is seated, by the First Musician, who also can attend to the lights if there is any special lighting. We had two lanterns upon posts – designed by Mr. Dulac – at the outer corners of the stage, but they did not give enough light, and we found it better to play by the light of a large chandelier. Indeed, I think, so far as my present experience goes, that the most effective lighting is the lighting we are most accustomed to in our rooms. These masked players seem stranger when there is no mechanical means of separating them from us.[3] The First Musician[4] carries with him a folded black cloth[5] and goes to the centre of the stage towards the front and stands motionless, the folded cloth hanging from between his hands. The two other Musicians enter and, after standing a moment at either side of the stage, go towards him and slowly unfold the cloth, singing as they do so:

> I call to the eye of the mind
> A well long choked up and dry
> And boughs long stripped by the wind,
> And I call to the mind's eye
> Pallor of an ivory face,
> Its lofty dissolute air,
> A man climbing up to a place
> The salt sea wind has swept bare.

As they unfold the cloth, they go backward a little so that the stretched

*cloth and the wall make a triangle with the First Musician at the apex
supporting the centre of the cloth. On the black cloth is a gold pattern
suggesting a hawk.*[6] *The Second and Third Musicians now slowly fold
up the cloth again, pacing with a rhythmic movement of the arms
towards the First Musician and singing:*

> What were his life soon done!
> Would he lose by that or win?
> A mother that saw her son
> Doubled over a speckled shin,
> Cross-grained with ninety years,
> Would cry, 'How little worth
> Were all my hopes and fears
> And the hard pain of his birth!'[7]

*The words 'a speckled shin' are familiar to readers of Irish legendary
stories in descriptions of old men bent double over the fire. While the
cloth has been spread out, the Guardian of the Well has entered and is
now crouching upon the ground. She is entirely covered by a black
cloak; beside her lies a square blue cloth to represent a well.*[8] *The
three Musicians have taken their places against the wall beside their
instruments of music; they will accompany the movements of the players
with gong or drum or zither.*

FIRST MUSICIAN [*singing*]:

> The boughs of the hazel[9] shake,
> The sun goes down in the west.

SECOND MUSICIAN [*singing*]:

> The heart would be always awake,
> The heart would turn to its rest.

[*They now go to one side of the stage rolling up the cloth.*]

FIRST MUSICIAN [*speaking*]: Nights falls;
The mountain-side grows dark;
The withered leaves of the hazel
Half choke the dry bed of the well;
The guardian of the well is sitting
Upon the old grey stone at its side,
Worn out from raking its dry bed,
Worn out from gathering up the leaves.
Her heavy eyes
Know nothing, or but look upon stone.

The wind that blows out of the sea
Turns over the heaped-up leaves at her side;
They rustle and diminish.

SECOND MUSICIAN: I am afraid of this place.

BOTH MUSICIANS [*singing*]:

> 'Why should I sleep?' the heart cries,
> 'For the wind, the salt wind, the sea wind,
> Is beating a cloud through the skies;
> I would wander always like the wind.'

[*An Old Man*[10] *enters through the audience.*]

FIRST MUSICIAN [*speaking*]: That old man climbs up hither,
Who has been watching by his well
These fifty years.
He is all doubled up with age;
The old thorn-trees are doubled so
Among the rocks where he is climbing.

[*The Old Man stands for a moment motionless by the side of the
stage with bowed head. He lifts his head at the sound of a drum-tap.
He goes towards the front of the stage moving to the taps of the
drum. He crouches and moves his hands as if making a fire. His
movements, like those of the other persons of the play, suggest a
marionette.*[11]]

FIRST MUSICIAN [*speaking*]: He has made a little heap of leaves;
He lays the dry sticks on the leaves
And, shivering with cold, he has taken up
The fire-stick and socket from its hole.
He whirls it round to get a flame;
And now the dry sticks take the fire,
And now the fire leaps up and shines
Upon the hazels and the empty well.

MUSICIANS [*singing*]:

> 'O wind, O salt wind, O sea wind!'
> Cries the heart, 'it is time to sleep;
> Why wander and nothing to find?
> Better grow old and sleep.'

OLD MAN [*speaking*]: Why don't you speak to me? Why don't you
say:
'Are you not weary gathering those sticks?

Are not your fingers cold?' You have not one word,
While yesterday you spoke three times. You said:
'The well is full of hazel leaves.' You said:
'The wind is from the west.' And after that:
'If there is rain it's likely there'll be mud.'
To-day you are as stupid as a fish,
No, worse, worse, being less lively and as dumb.
  [*He goes nearer.*]
Your eyes are dazed and heavy. If the Sidhe[12]
Must have a guardian to clean out the well
And drive the cattle off, they might choose somebody
That can be pleasant and companionable
Once in the day. Why do you stare like that?
You had that glassy look about the eyes
Last time it happened. Do you know anything?
It is enough to drive an old man crazy
To look all day upon these broken rocks,
And ragged thorns, and that one stupid face,
And speak and get no answer.

YOUNG MAN [12] [*who has entered through the audience during the
    last speech*]:   Then speak to me,
For youth is not more patient than old age;
And though I have trod the rocks for half a day
I cannot find what I am looking for.

OLD MAN: Who speaks?
Who comes so suddenly into this place
Where nothing thrives? If I may judge by the gold
On head and feet and glittering in your coat,
You are not of those who hate the living world.

YOUNG MAN: I am named Cuchulain, I am Sualtim's son.

OLD MAN: I have never heard that name.

YOUNG MAN: It is not unknown.
I have an ancient house beyond the sea.

OLD MAN: What mischief brings you hither? – you are like those
Who are crazy for the shedding of men's blood,
And for the love of women.

YOUNG MAN: A rumour has led me,
A story told over the wine towards dawn.

I rose from table, found a boat, spread sail,
And with a lucky wind under the sail
Crossed waves that have seemed charmed, and found this shore.

OLD MAN: There is no house to sack among these hills
Nor beautiful woman to be carried off.

YOUNG MAN: You should be native here, for that rough tongue
Matches the barbarous spot. You can, it may be,
Lead me to what I seek, a well wherein
Three hazels drop their nuts and withered leaves,
And where a solitary girl keeps watch
Among grey boulders. He who drinks, they say,
Of that miraculous water[14] lives for ever.

OLD MAN: And are there not before your eyes at the instant
Grey boulders and a solitary girl
And three stripped hazels?

YOUNG MAN: But there is no well.

OLD MAN: Can you see nothing yonder?

YOUNG MAN: I but see
A hollow among stones half-full of leaves.

OLD MAN: And do you think so great a gift is found
By no more toil than spreading out a sail,
And climbing a steep hill? O, folly of youth,
Why should that hollow place fill up for you,
That will not fill for me? I have lain in wait
For more than fifty years, to find it empty,
Or but to find the stupid wind of the sea
Drive round the perishable leaves.

YOUNG MAN: So it seems
There is some moment when the water fills it.

OLD MAN: A secret moment that the holy shades
That dance upon the desolate mountain know,
And not a living man, and when it comes
The water has scarce plashed before it is gone.

YOUNG MAN: I will stand here and wait. Why should the luck
Of Sualtim's son desert him now? For never
Have I had long to wait for anything.

OLD MAN: No! Go from this accursed place! This place
Belongs to me, that girl there, and those others,

Deceivers of men.

YOUNG MAN: And who are you who rail
Upon those dancers[15] that all others bless?

OLD MAN: One whom the dancers cheat. I came like you
When young in body and in mind, and blown
By what had seemed to me a lucky sail.
The well was dry, I sat upon its edge,
I waited the miraculous flood, I waited
While the years passed and withered me away.
I have snared the birds for food and eaten grass
And drunk the rain, and neither in dark nor shine
Wandered too far away to have heard the plash,
And yet the dancers have deceived me. Thrice
I have awakened from a sudden sleep
To find the stones were wet.

YOUNG MAN: My luck is strong,
It will not leave me waiting, nor will they
That dance among the stones put me asleep;
If I grow drowsy I can pierce my foot.

OLD MAN: No, do not pierce it, for the foot is tender,
It feels pain much. But find your sail again
And leave the well to me, for it belongs
To all that's old and withered.

YOUNG MAN: No, I stay.
[*The Guardian of the Well gives the cry of the hawk.*[16]]
There is that bird again.

OLD MAN: There is no bird.

YOUNG MAN: It sounded like the sudden cry of a hawk,
But there's no wing in sight. As I came hither
A great grey hawk swept down out of the sky,
And though I have good hawks, the best in the world
I had fancied, I have not seen its like. It flew
As though it would have torn me with its beak,
Or blinded me, smiting with that great wing.
I had to draw my sword to drive it off,
And after that it flew from rock to rock.
I pelted it with stones, a good half-hour,
And just before I had turned the big rock there

And seen this place, it seemed to vanish away.
Could I but find a means to bring it down
I'd hood it.[17]

OLD MAN: The Woman of the Sidhe[18] herself,
The mountain witch, the unappeasable shadow.
She is always flitting upon this mountain-side,
To allure or to destroy. When she has shown
Herself to the fierce women of the hills
Under that shape they offer sacrifice
And arm for battle. There falls a curse
On all who have gazed in her unmoistened eyes;
So get you gone while you have that proud step
And confident voice, for not a man alive
Has so much luck that he can play with it.
Those that have long to live should fear her most,
The old are cursed already. That curse may be
Never to win a woman's love and keep it;
Or always to mix hatred in the love;
Or it may be that she will kill your children,
That you will find them, their throats torn and bloody,
Or you will be so maddened that you kill them
With your own hand.

YOUNG MAN: Have you been set down there
To threaten all who come, and scare them off?
You seem as dried up as the leaves and sticks,
As though you had no part in life.
     [The Guardian of the Well gives hawk cry again.]
                         That cry!
There is that cry again. That woman made it,
But why does she cry out as the hawk cries?

OLD MAN: It was her mouth, and yet not she, that cried.
It was that shadow cried behind her mouth;
And now I know why she has been so stupid
All the day through, and had such heavy eyes.
Look at her shivering now, the terrible life
Is slipping through her veins. She is possessed.
Who knows whom she will murder or betray
Before she awakes in ignorance of it all,
And gathers up the leaves? But they'll be wet;

The water will have come and gone again;
That shivering is the sign. O, get you gone,
At any moment now I shall hear it bubble.
If you are good you will leave it. I am old,
And if I do not drink it now, will never;
I have been watching all my life and maybe
Only a little cupful will bubble up.

YOUNG MAN: I'll take it in my hands. We shall both drink,
And even if there are but a few drops,
Share them.

OLD MAN: But swear that I may drink the first;
The young are greedy, and if you drink the first
You'll drink it all. Ah, you have looked at her;
She has felt your gaze and turned her eyes on us;
I cannot bear her eyes, they are not of this world,
Nor moist, nor faltering; they are no girl's eyes.

  [*He covers his head. The Guardian of the Well throws off her
  cloak and rises. Her dress under the cloak suggests a hawk.*[19]]

YOUNG MAN: Why do you fix those eyes of a hawk upon me?
I am not afraid of you, bird, woman, or witch.

  [*He goes to the side of the well, which the Guardian of the Well
  has left.*]

Do what you will, I shall not leave this place
Till I have grown immortal like yourself.

  [*He has sat down; the Guardian of the Well has begun to dance,
  moving like a hawk.*[20] *The Old Man sleeps. The dance goes on
  for some time.*]

FIRST MUSICIAN [*singing or half-singing*]:

          O God, protect me
          From a horrible deathless body
          Sliding through the veins of a sudden.

  [*The dance goes on for some time. The Young Man rises slowly.*]

FIRST MUSICIAN [*speaking*]: The madness has laid hold upon him
    now,
For he grows pale and staggers to his feet.

  [*The dance goes on.*]

YOUNG MAN: Run where you will,
Grey bird, you shall be perched upon my wrist.

Some were called queens and yet have been perched there.
   [*The dance goes on.*]

FIRST MUSICIAN [*speaking*]: I have heard water plash; it comes, it
     comes;
Look where it glitters. He has heard the plash;
Look, he has turned his head.
   [*The Guardian of the Well has gone out. The Young Man drops
   his spear as if in a dream and goes out.*]

MUSICIANS [*singing*]:

> He has lost what may not be found
> Till men heap his burial-mound
> And all the history ends.
> He might have lived at his ease,
> An old dog's head on his knees,
> Among his children and friends.

   [*The Old Man creeps up to the well.*]

OLD MAN: The accursed shadows have deluded me,
The stones are dark and yet the well is empty;
The water flowed and emptied while I slept.
You have deluded me my whole life through,
Accursed dancers, you have stolen my life.
That there should be such evil in a shadow!

YOUNG MAN [*entering*]: She has fled from me and hidden in the
     rocks.

OLD MAN: She has but led you from the fountain. Look!
Though stones and leaves are dark where it has flowed,
There's not a drop to drink.
   [*The Musicians cry 'Aoife!' 'Aoife!'* [21] *and strike gong.*]

YOUNG MAN: What are those cries?
What is that sound that runs along the hill?
Who are they that beat a sword upon a shield?

OLD MAN: She has roused up the fierce women of the hills,
Aoife, and all her troop, to take your life,
And never till you are lying in the earth
Can you know rest.

YOUNG MAN: The clash of arms again!

OLD MAN: O, do not go! The mountain is accursed;
Stay with me, I have nothing more to lose,

I do not now deceive you.

YOUNG MAN:　　　　　　I will face them.

[*He goes out, no longer as if in a dream, but shouldering his spear and calling:*]

He comes! Cuchulain, son of Sualtim, comes![22]

[*The Musicians stand up; one goes to centre with folded cloth. The others unfold it. While they do so they sing. During the singing, and while hidden by the cloth, the Old Man goes out. When the play is performed with Mr. Dulac's music, the Musicians do not rise or unfold the cloth till after they have sung the words 'a bitter life'.*]

[*Songs for the unfolding and folding of the cloth.*]

> Come to me, human faces,
> Familiar memories;
> I have found hateful eyes
> Among the desolate places,
> Unfaltering, unmoistened eyes.

> Folly alone I cherish,
> I choose it for my share;
> Being but a mouthful of air,
> I am content to perish;
> I am but a mouthful of sweet air.

> O lamentable shadows,
> Obscurity of strife!
> I choose a pleasant life
> Among indolent meadows;
> Wisdom must live a bitter life.

[*They then fold up the cloth, singing.*]

> 'The man that I praise',
> Cries out the empty well,
> 'Lives all his days
> Where a hand on the bell
> Can call the milch cows
> To the comfortable door of his house.
> Who but an idiot would praise
> Dry stones in a well?'

> 'The man that I praise',
> Cries out the leafless tree,

'Has married and stays
By an old hearth, and he
On naught has set store
But children and dogs on the floor.
Who but an idiot would praise
A withered tree?' [23]

[*They go out.*]

THE END

THE DREAMING OF THE BONES

Persons in the Play

THREE MUSICIANS (*their faces made up to resemble masks*)
A YOUNG MAN
A STRANGER (*wearing a mask*)
A YOUNG GIRL (*wearing a mask*)

Time – 1916

The stage is any bare place in a room close to the wall. A screen, with a pattern of mountain and sky, can stand against the wall, or a curtain with a like pattern hang upon it, but the pattern must only symbolise or suggest. One Musician enters and then two others; the first stands singing, as in preceding plays, while the others take their places. Then all three sit down against the wall by their instruments, which are already there – a drum, a zither, and a flute. Or they unfold a cloth as in 'At the Hawk's Well', while the instruments are carried in.

[*Song for the folding and unfolding of the cloth.*]

FIRST MUSICIAN [*or all three Musicians, singing*]:

> Why does my heart beat so?
> Did not a shadow pass?
> It passed but a moment ago.
> Who can have trod in the grass?
> What rogue is night-wandering?
> Have not old writers said
> That dizzy[1] dreams can spring
> From the dry bones of the dead?
> And many a night it seems
> That all the valley fills
> With those fantastic dreams.
> They overflow the hills,
> So passionate is a shade,
> Like wine that fills to the top

A grey-green cup of jade,
Or maybe an agate cup.[2]

[*The three Musicians are now seated by the drum, flute, and zither
at the back of the stage. The First Musician speaks.*]

The hour before dawn and the moon covered up;
The little village of Abbey is covered up;
The little narrow trodden way that runs
From the white road to the Abbey of Corcomroe
Is covered up; and all about the hills
Are like a circle of agate or of jade.[3]
Somewhere among great rocks on the scarce grass
Birds cry, they cry their loneliness.
Even the sunlight can be lonely here,
Even hot noon is lonely. I hear a footfall –
A young man with a lantern comes this way.
He seems an Aran fisher, for he wears
The flannel bawneen[4] and the cow-hide shoe.
He stumbles wearily, and stumbling prays.

[*A Young Man enters, praying in Irish.*]

Once more the birds cry in their loneliness,
But now they wheel about our heads; and now
They have dropped on the grey stone to the north-east.

[*A Stranger and a Young Girl, in the costume of a past time, come
in. They wear heroic[5] masks.*]

YOUNG MAN [*raising his lantern*]: Who is there? I cannot see what
        you are like.
    Come to the light.

STRANGER: But what have you to fear?

YOUNG MAN: And why have you come creeping through the dark?
    [*The Girl blows out lantern.*]
    The wind has blown my lantern out. Where are you?
    I saw a pair of heads against the sky
    And lost them after; but you are in the right,
    I should not be afraid in County Clare;
    And should be, or should not be, have no choice,
    I have to put myself into your hands,
    Now that my candle's out.

STRANGER: You have fought in Dublin?[6]

YOUNG MAN: I was in the Post Office,[7] and if taken
   I shall be put against a wall and shot.

STRANGER: You know some place of refuge, have some plan
   Or friend who will come to meet you?

YOUNG MAN: I am to lie
   At daybreak on the mountain and keep watch
   Until an Aran coracle puts in
   At Muckanish or at the rocky shore
   Under Finvara,[8] but would break my neck
   If I went stumbling there alone in the dark.

STRANGER: We know the pathways that the sheep tread out,
   And all the hiding-places of the hills,
   And that they had better hiding-places once.

YOUNG MAN: You'd say they had better before English robbers
   Cut down the trees or set them upon fire
   For fear their owners might find shelter there.
   What is that sound?

STRANGER: An old horse gone astray.
   He has been wandering on the road all night.

YOUNG MAN: I took him for a man and horse. Police
   Are out upon the roads. In the late Rising
   I think there was no man of us but hated
   To fire at soldiers who but did their duty
   And were not of our race, but when a man
   Is born in Ireland and of Irish stock,
   When he takes part against us—[9]

STRANGER: I will put you safe,
   No living man shall set his eyes upon you;
   I will not answer for the dead.

YOUNG MAN: The dead?

STRANGER: For certain days the stones where you must lie
   Have in the hour before the break of day
   Been haunted.

YOUNG MAN: But I was not born at midnight.[10]

STRANGER: Many a man that was born in the full daylight
   Can see them plain, will pass them on the high-road
   Or in the crowded market-place of the town,
   And never know that they have passed.

YOUNG MAN: My Grandam
  Would have it they did penance everywhere;
  Some lived through their old lives again.[11]

STRANGER: In a dream;
  And some for an old scruple must hang spitted
  Upon the swaying tops of lofty trees;
  Some are consumed in fire, some withered up
  By hail and sleet out of the wintry North,
  And some but live through their old lives again.

YOUNG MAN: Well, let them dream into what shape they please
  And fill waste mountains with the invisible tumult
  Of the fantastic conscience. I have no dread;
  They cannot put me into gaol or shoot me;
  And seeing that their blood has returned to fields
  That have grown red from drinking blood[12] like mine,
  They would not if they could betray.

STRANGER: This pathway
  Runs to the ruined Abbey of Corcomroe;
  The Abbey passed, we are soon among the stone
  And shall be at the ridge before the cocks
  Of Aughanish or Bailevelehan
  Or grey Aughtmana[13] shake their wings and cry.
    [*They go round the stage once.*[14]]

FIRST MUSICIAN [*speaking*]: They've passed the shallow well and
    the flat stone
  Fouled by the drinking cattle, the narrow lane
  Where mourners for five centuries have carried
  Noble or peasant to his burial;
  An owl is crying out above their heads.
    [*singing*]

> Why should the heart take fright?
> What sets it beating so?
> The bitter sweetness of the night
> Has made it but a lonely thing.
> Red bird of March,[15] begin to crow!
> Up with the neck and clap the wing,
> Red cock, and crow!

  [*They go round the stage once. The First Musician speaks.*]

And now they have climbed through the long grassy field
And passed the ragged thorn-trees and the gap
In the ancient hedge; and the tomb-nested owl
At the foot's level beats with a vague wing.

   [*singing*]

> My head is in a cloud;
> I'd let the whole world go;
> My rascal heart is proud
> Remembering and remembering.
> Red bird of March, begin to crow!
> Up with the neck and clap the wing,
> Red cock, and crow!

[*They go round the stage once. The First Musician speaks.*]
They are among the stones above the ash,
Above the briar and thorn and the scarce grass;
Hidden amid the shadow far below them
The cat-headed bird is crying out.

   [*singing*]

> The dreaming bones cry out
> Because the night winds blow
> And heaven's a cloudy blot.
> Calamity can have its fling.
> Red bird of March, begin to crow!
> Up with the neck and clap the wing,
> Red cock, and crow!

STRANGER: We're almost at the summit and can rest.
The road is a faint shadow there; and there
The Abbey lies amid its broken tombs.
In the old days we should have heard a bell
Calling the monks before day broke to pray;
And when the day had broken on the ridge,
The crowing of its cocks.

YOUNG MAN: Is there no house
Famous for sanctity or architectural beauty
In Clare or Kerry, or in all wide Connacht,
The enemy has not unroofed?

STRANGER: Close to the altar
Broken by wind and frost and worn by time

Donough O'Brien[16] has a tomb, a name in Latin.
He wore fine clothes and knew the secrets of women,
But he rebelled against the King of Thomond
And died in his youth.

YOUNG MAN: And why should he rebel?
The King of Thomond was his rightful master.
It was men like Donough who made Ireland weak –
My curse on all that troop, and when I die
I'll leave my body, if I have any choice,
Far from his ivy-tod and his owl. Have those
Who, if your tale is true, work out a penance
Upon the mountain-top where I am to hide,
Come from the Abbey graveyard?

YOUNG GIRL:[17]   They have not that luck,
But are more lonely; those that are buried there
Warred in the heat of the blood; if they were rebels
Some momentary impulse made them rebels,
Or the commandment of some petty king
Who hated Thomond. Being but common sinners,
No callers-in of the alien from oversea,
They and their enemies of Thomond's party
Mix in a brief dream-battle above their bones;
Or make one drove; or drift in amity;
Or in the hurry of the heavenly round
Forget their earthly names. These are alone,
Being accursed.

YOUNG MAN: But if what seems is true
And there are more upon the other side
Than on this side of death, many a ghost
Must meet them face to face and pass the word
Even upon this grey and desolate hill.

YOUNG GIRL: Until this hour no ghost or living man
Has spoken, though seven centuries have run
Since they, weary of life and of men's eyes,
Flung down their bones in some forgotten place,
Being accursed.

YOUNG MAN: I have heard that there are souls
Who, having sinned after a monstrous fashion,
Take on them, being dead, a monstrous image

    To drive the living, should they meet its face,
    Crazy, and be a terror to the dead.

YOUNG GIRL: But these
    Were comely even in their middle life
    And carry, now that they are dead, the image
    Of their first youth, for it was in that youth
    Their sin began.

YOUNG MAN: I have heard of angry ghosts
    Who wander in a wilful solitude.

YOUNG GIRL: These have no thought but love; nor any joy
    But that upon the instant when their penance
    Draws to its height, and when two hearts are wrung
    Nearest to breaking, if hearts of shadows break,
    His eyes can mix with hers; nor any pang
    That is so bitter as that double glance,
    Being accursed.

YOUNG MAN: But what is this strange penance –
    That when their eyes have met can wring them most?

YOUNG GIRL: Though eyes can meet, their lips can never meet.

YOUNG MAN: And yet it seems they wander side by side.
    But doubtless you would say that when lips meet
    And have not living nerves, it is no meeting.

YOUNG GIRL: Although they have no blood, or living nerves,
    Who once lay warm and live the live-long night
    In one another's arms, and know their part
    In life, being now but of the people of dreams,
    Is a dream's part; although they are but shadows,
    Hovering between a thorn-tree and a stone,
    Who have heaped up night on wingéd night; although
    No shade however harried and consumed
    Would change his own calamity for theirs,
    Their manner of life were blessed could their lips
    A moment meet; but when he has bent his head
    Close to her head, or hand would slip in hand,
    The memory of their crime flows up between
    And drives them apart.[18]

YOUNG MAN: The memory of a crime –
    He took her from a husband's house, it may be,

But does the penance for a passionate sin
Last for so many centuries?

YOUNG GIRL: No, no;
The man she chose, the man she was chosen by,
Cared little and cares little from whose house
They fled towards dawn amid the flights of arrows,
Or that it was a husband's and a king's;
And how, if that were all, could she lack friends,
On crowded roads or on the unpeopled hill?
Helen[19] herself had opened wide the door
Where night by night she dreams herself awake
And gathers to her breast a dreaming man.

YOUNG MAN: What crime can stay so in the memory?
What crime can keep apart the lips of lovers
Wandering and alone?

YOUNG GIRL: Her king and lover
Was overthrown in battle by her husband,
And for her sake and for his own, being blind
And bitter and bitterly in love, he brought
A foreign army from across the sea.

YOUNG MAN: You speak of Diarmuid and Dervorgilla[20]
Who brought the Norman in?

YOUNG GIRL: Yes, yes, I spoke
Of that most miserable, most accursed pair
Who sold their country into slavery; and yet
They were not wholly miserable and accursed
If somebody of their race at last would say,
'I have forgiven them'.

YOUNG MAN: O, never, never
Shall Diarmuid and Dervorgilla be forgiven.

YOUNG GIRL: If some one of their race forgave at last
Lip would be pressed on lip.

YOUNG MAN: O, never, never
Shall Diarmuid and Dervorgilla be forgiven.
You have told your story well,[21] so well indeed
I could not help but fall into the mood
And for a while believe that it was true,
Or half believe; but better push on now.[22]

The horizon to the east is growing bright.
 [*They go round stage once. The Musicians play.*]
So here we're on the summit. I can see
The Aran Islands, Connemara Hills,
And Galway in the breaking light; there too
The enemy has toppled roof and gable,
And torn the panelling from ancient rooms;
What generations of old men had known
Like their own hands, and children wondered at,
Has boiled a trooper's porridge. That town had lain,
But for the pair that you would have me pardon,
Amid its gables and its battlements
Like any old admired Italian town;
For though we have neither coal, nor iron ore,
To make us wealthy and corrupt the air,
Our country, if that crime were uncommitted,
Had been most beautiful.[23] Why do you dance?
Why do you gaze, and with so passionate eyes,
One on the other; and then turn away,
Covering your eyes, and weave it in a dance?
Who are you? what are you? you are not natural.

YOUNG GIRL: Seven hundred years our lips have never met.

YOUNG MAN: Why do you look so strangely at one another,
 So strangely and so sweetly?

YOUNG GIRL: Seven hundred years.

YOUNG MAN: So strangely and so sweetly. All the ruin,
 All, all their handiwork is blown away
 As though the mountain air had blown it away
 Because their eyes have met. They cannot hear,
 Being folded up and hidden in their dance.
 The dance is changing now. They have dropped their eyes,
 They have covered up their eyes as though their hearts
 Had suddenly been broken – never, never
 Shall Diarmuid and Dervorgilla be forgiven.
 They have drifted in the dance from rock to rock.
 They have raised their hands as though to snatch the sleep
 That lingers always in the abyss of the sky
 Though they can never reach it.[24] A cloud floats up
 And covers all the mountain-head in a moment;

And now it lifts and they are swept away.
   [*The Stranger and the Young Girl go out.*]
I had almost yielded[25] and forgiven it all –
Terrible the temptation and the place!
   [*The Musicians begin unfolding and folding a black cloth. The
   First Musician comes forward to the front of the stage, at the
   centre. He holds the cloth before him. The other two come one
   on either side and unfold it. They afterwards fold it up in the same
   way. While it is unfolded, the Young Man leaves the stage.*]

[*Songs for the unfolding and folding of the cloth.*]
THE MUSICIANS [*singing*]:

I

> At the grey round of the hill
> Music of a lost kingdom
> Runs, runs and is suddenly still.
> The winds out of Clare-Galway
> Carry it: suddenly it is still.
>
> I have heard in the night air
> A wandering airy music;
> And moidered in that snare
> A man is lost of a sudden,
> In that sweet wandering snare.
>
> What finger first began
> Music of a lost kingdom?
> They dream that laughed in the sun,
> Dry bones that dream are bitter,
> They dream and darken our sun.
>
> Those crazy fingers play
> A wandering airy music;
> Our luck is withered away,
> And wheat in the wheat-ear withered,
> And the wind blows it away.

II

> My heart ran wild when it heard
> The curlew cry before dawn
> And the eddying cat-headed bird;

But now the night is gone.
I have heard from far below
The strong March birds a-crow.
Stretch neck and clap the wing,
Red cocks, and crow![26]

THE END

THE CAT AND THE MOON

Persons in the Play

A BLIND BEGGAR
A LAME BEGGAR
THREE MUSICIANS

Scene. – The scene is any bare place before a wall against which stands a patterned screen, or hangs a patterned curtain suggesting Saint Colman's Well. Three Musicians are sitting close to the wall, with zither, drum, and flute.[1] Their faces are made up to resemble masks.

FIRST MUSICIAN [*singing*]:

> The cat went here and there
> And the moon spun round like a top,
> And the nearest kin of the moon,
> The creeping cat, looked up.
> Black Minnaloushe stared at the moon,
> For, wander and wail as he would,
> The pure cold light in the sky
> Troubled his animal blood.[2]

[*Two beggars enter – a blind man with a lame man on his back. They wear grotesque masks. The Blind Beggar is counting the paces.*]

BLIND BEGGAR: One thousand and six, one thousand and seven, one thousand and nine. Look well now, for we should be in sight of the holy well of Saint Colman. The beggar at the cross-roads said it was one thousand paces from where he stood and a few paces over. Look well now, can you see the big ash-tree that's above it?

LAME BEGGAR [*getting down*]: No, not yet.

BLIND BEGGAR: Then we must have taken a wrong turn; flighty you always were, and maybe before the day is over you will have me drowned in Kiltartan River[3] or maybe in the sea itself.

LAME BEGGAR: I have brought you the right way, but you are a lazy man, Blind Man, and you make very short strides.

BLIND BEGGAR: It's great daring you have, and how could I make a long stride and you on my back from the peep o' day?

LAME BEGGAR: And maybe the beggar of the cross-roads was only making it up when he said a thousand paces and a few paces more. You and I, being beggars, know the way of beggars, and maybe he never paced it at all, being a lazy man.

BLIND BEGGAR: Get up. It's too much talk you have.

LAME BEGGAR [getting up]: But as I was saying, he being a lazy man – O, O, O, stop pinching the calf of my leg and I'll not say another word till I'm spoken to.

    [They go round the stage once, moving to drum-taps,[4] and as they move the following song is sung.]

FIRST MUSICIAN [singing]:

> Minnaloushe runs in the grass
> Lifting his delicate feet.
> Do you dance, Minnaloushe, do you dance?
> When two close kindred meet
> What better than call a dance?
> Maybe the moon may learn,
> Tired of that courtly fashion,
> A new dance turn.

BLIND BEGGAR: Do you see the big ash-tree?

LAME BEGGAR: I do then, and the wall under it, and the flat stone, and the things upon the stone; and here is a good dry place to kneel in.

BLIND BEGGAR: You may get down so. [Lame Beggar gets down.] I begin to have it in my mind that I am a great fool, and it was you who egged me on with your flighty[5] talk.

LAME BEGGAR: How should you be a great fool to ask the saint to give you back your two eyes?

BLIND BEGGAR: There is many gives money to a blind man and would give nothing but a curse to a whole man,[6] and if it was not for one thing – but no matter anyway.

LAME BEGGAR: If I speak out all that's in my mind you won't take a blow at me at all?

BLIND BEGGAR: I will not this time.

LAME BEGGAR: Then I'll tell you why you are not a great fool. When you go out to pick up a chicken, or maybe a stray goose on the road, or a cabbage from a neighbour's garden, I have to go riding on your back; and if I want a goose, or a chicken, or a cabbage, I must have your two legs under me.

BLIND BEGGAR: That's true now, and if we were whole men and went different ways, there'd be as much again between us.

LAME BEGGAR: And your own goods keep going from you because you are blind.

BLIND BEGGAR: Rogues and thieves ye all are, but there are some I may have my eyes on yet.

LAME BEGGAR: Because there's no one to see a man slipping in at the door, or throwing a leg over the wall of a yard, you are a bitter temptation to many a poor man, and I say it's not right, it's not right at all. There are poor men that because you are blind will be delayed in Purgatory.

BLIND BEGGAR: Though you are a rogue, Lame Man, maybe you are in the right.

LAME BEGGAR: And maybe we'll see the blessed saint this day, for there's an odd one sees him, and maybe that will be a grander thing than having my two legs, though legs are a grand thing.

BLIND BEGGAR: You're getting flighty again, Lame Man; what could be better for you than to have your two legs?

LAME BEGGAR: Do you think now will the saint put an ear on him at all, and we without an Ave or a Paternoster to put before the prayer or after the prayer?

BLIND BEGGAR: Wise though you are and flighty though you are, and you throwing eyes to the right of you and eyes to the left of you, there's many a thing you don't know about the heart of man.

LAME BEGGAR: But it stands to reason that he'd be put out and he maybe with a great liking for the Latin.

BLIND BEGGAR: I have it in mind that the saint will be better pleased at us not knowing a prayer at all, and that we had best say what we want in plain language. What pleasure can he have in all that holy company kneeling at his well on holidays and Sundays, and they as innocent maybe as himself?

LAME BEGGAR: That's a strange thing to say, and do you say it as I or another might say it, or as a blind man?

BLIND BEGGAR: I say it as a blind man, I say it because since I went blind in the tenth year of my age, I have been hearing and remembering the knowledges of the world.

LAME BEGGAR: And you who are a blind man say that a saint, and he living in a pure well of water, would soonest be talking with a sinful man.

BLIND BEGGAR: Do you mind what the beggar told you about the holy man in the big house at Laban?

LAME BEGGAR: Nothing stays in my head, Blind Man.

BLIND BEGGAR: What does he do but go knocking about the roads with an old lecher from the county of Mayo,[7] and he a woman-hater from the day of his birth! And what do they talk of by candle-light and by daylight? The old lecher does be telling over all the sins he committed, or maybe never committed at all, and the man of Laban does be trying to head him off and quiet him down that he may quit telling them.

LAME BEGGAR: Maybe it is converting him he is.

BLIND BEGGAR: If you were a blind man you wouldn't say a foolish thing the like of that. He wouldn't have him different, no, not if he was to get all Ireland. If he was different, what would they find to talk about, will you answer me that now?

LAME BEGGAR: We have great wisdom between us, that's certain.

BLIND BEGGAR: Now the Church says that it is a good thought, and a sweet thought, and a comfortable thought, that every man may have a saint to look after him, and I, being blind, give it out to all the world that the bigger the sinner the better pleased is the saint. I am sure and certain that Saint Colman would not have us two different from what we are.

LAME BEGGAR: I'll not give in to that, for, as I was saying, he has a great liking maybe for the Latin.

BLIND BEGGAR: It is contradicting me you are? Are you in reach of my arm? [Swinging stick.]

LAME BEGGAR: I'm not, Blind Man, you couldn't touch me at all; but as I was saying—

FIRST MUSICIAN [speaking]: Will you be cured or will you be blessed?

LAME BEGGAR: Lord save us, that is the saint's voice and we not on our knees.

[*They kneel.*]

BLIND BEGGAR: Is he standing before us, Lame Man?

LAME BEGGAR: I cannot see him at all. It is in the ash-tree he is, or up in the air.

FIRST MUSICIAN: Will you be cured or will you be blessed?

LAME BEGGAR: There he is again.

BLIND BEGGAR: I'll be cured of my blindness.

FIRST MUSICIAN: I am a saint and lonely. Will you become blessed and stay blind and we will be together always?

BLIND BEGGAR: No, no, your Reverence, if I have to choose, I'll have the sight of my two eyes, for those that have their sight are always stealing my things and telling me lies, and some maybe that are near me. So don't take it bad of me, Holy Man, that I ask the sight of my two eyes.

LAME BEGGAR: No one robs him and no one tells him lies; it's all in his head, it is. He's had his tongue on me all day because he thinks I stole a sheep of his.

BLIND BEGGAR: It was the feel of his sheepskin coat put it into my head, but my sheep was black, they say, and he tells me, Holy Man, that his sheepskin is of the most lovely white wool so that it is a joy to be looking at it.

FIRST MUSICIAN: Lame Man, will you be cured or will you be blessed?

LAME BEGGAR: What would it be like to be blessed?

FIRST MUSICIAN: You would be of the kin of the blessed saints and of the martyrs.

LAME BEGGAR: Is it true now that they have a book and that they write the names of the blessed in that book?

FIRST MUSICIAN: Many a time I have seen the book, and your name would be in it.

LAME BEGGAR: It would be a grand thing to have two legs under me, but I have it in my mind that it would be a grander thing to have my name in that book.

FIRST MUSICIAN: It would be a grander thing.

LAME BEGGAR: I still stay lame, Holy Man, and I will be blessed.

FIRST MUSICIAN: In the name of the Father, the Son and the Holy Spirit I give this Blind Man sight and I make this Lame Man blessed.

BLIND BEGGAR: I see it all now, the blue sky and the big ash-tree and the well and the flat stone, – all as I have heard the people say – and the things the praying people put on the stone, the beads and the candles and the leaves torn out of prayer-books, and the hairpins and the buttons.[8] It is a great sight and a blessed sight, but I don't see yourself, Holy Man – is it up in the big tree you are?

LAME BEGGAR: Why, there he is in front of you and he laughing out of his wrinkled face.

BLIND BEGGAR: Where, where?

LAME BEGGAR: Why, there, between you and the ash-tree.

BLIND BEGGAR: There's nobody there – you're at your lies again.

LAME BEGGAR: I am blessed, and that is why I can see the holy saint.

BLIND BEGGAR: But if I don't see the saint, there's something else I can see.

LAME BEGGAR: The blue sky and green leaves are a great sight, and a strange sight to one that has been long blind.

BLIND BEGGAR: There is a stranger sight than that, and that is the skin of my own black sheep on your back.

LAME BEGGAR: Haven't I been telling you from the peep o' day that my sheepskin is that white it would dazzle you?

BLIND BEGGAR: Are you so swept with the words that you've never thought that when I had my own two eyes, I'd see what colour was on it?

LAME BEGGAR [very dejected]: I never thought of that.

BLIND BEGGAR: Are you that flighty?

LAME BEGGAR: I am that flighty. [Cheering up.] But am I not blessed, and it's a sin to speak against the blessed?

BLIND BEGGAR: Well, I'll speak against the blessed, and I'll tell you something more that I'll do. All the while you were telling me how, if I had my two eyes, I could pick up a chicken here and a goose there, while my neighbours were in bed, do you know what I was thinking?

LAME BEGGAR: Some wicked blind man's thought.

BLIND BEGGAR: It was, and it's not gone from me yet. I was saying to myself, I have a long arm and a strong arm and a very weighty arm, and when I get my own two eyes I shall know where to hit.

LAME BEGGAR: Don't lay a hand on me. Forty years we've been

knocking about the roads together, and I wouldn't have you bring your soul into mortal peril.

BLIND BEGGAR: I have been saying to myself, I shall know where to hit and how to hit and who to hit.

LAME BEGGAR: Do you not know that I am blessed? Would you be as bad as Caesar and as Herod and Nero and the other wicked emperors of antiquity?

BLIND BEGGAR: Where'll I hit him, for the love of God, where'll I hit him?

[*Blind Beggar beats Lame Beggar. The beating takes the form of a dance and is accompanied on drum and flute. The Blind Beggar goes out.*]

LAME BEGGAR: That is a soul lost, Holy Man.

FIRST MUSICIAN: Maybe so.

LAME BEGGAR: I'd better be going, Holy Man, for he'll rouse the whole country against me.[9]

FIRST MUSICIAN: He'll do that.

LAME BEGGAR: And I have it in my mind not to even myself again with the martyrs, and the holy confessors, till I am more used to being blessed.

FIRST MUSICIAN: Bend down your back.

LAME BEGGAR: What for, Holy Man?

FIRST MUSICIAN: That I may get up on it.

LAME BEGGAR: But my lame legs would never bear the weight of you.

FIRST MUSICIAN: I'm up now.

LAME BEGGAR: I don't feel you at all.

FIRST MUSICIAN: I don't weigh more than a grasshopper.

LAME BEGGAR: You do not.

FIRST MUSICIAN: Are you happy?

LAME BEGGAR: I would be if I was right sure I was blessed.

FIRST MUSICIAN: Haven't you got me for a friend?

LAME BEGGAR: I have so.

FIRST MUSICIAN: Then you're blessed.

LAME BEGGAR: Will you see that they put my name in the book?

FIRST MUSICIAN: I will then.

LAME BEGGAR: Let us be going, Holy Man.[10]

FIRST MUSICIAN: But you must bless the road.

LAME BEGGAR: I haven't the right words.

FIRST MUSICIAN: What do you want words for? Bow to what is before you, bow to what is behind you, bow to what is to the left of you, bow to what is to the right of you.

[*The Lame Beggar begins to bow.*]

FIRST MUSICIAN: That's no good.

LAME BEGGAR: No good, Holy Man?

FIRST MUSICIAN: No good at all. You must dance.

LAME BEGGAR: But how can I dance? Ain't I a lame man?

FIRST MUSICIAN: Aren't you blessed?

LAME BEGGAR: Maybe so.

FIRST MUSICIAN: Aren't you a miracle?

LAME BEGGAR: I am, Holy Man.

FIRST MUSICIAN: Then dance, and that'll be a miracle.

[*The Lame Beggar begins to dance, at first clumsily, moving about with his stick, then he throws away the stick and dances more and more quickly. Whenever he strikes the ground strongly with his lame foot the cymbals clash. He goes out dancing, after which follows the First Musician's song.*]

FIRST MUSICIAN [*singing*]:

> Minnaloushe creeps through the grass
> From moonlit place to place.
> The sacred moon overhead
> Has taken a new phase.
> Does Minnaloushe know that his pupils
> Will pass from change to change,
> And that from round to crescent,
> From crescent to round they range?
> Minnaloushe creeps through the grass
> Alone, important and wise,
> And lifts to the changing moon
> His changing eyes.

THE END

THE ONLY JEALOUSY OF EMER

Persons in the Play

THREE MUSICIANS (*their faces made up to resemble masks*[1])
THE GHOST OF CUCHULAIN (*wearing a mask*)
THE FIGURE OF CUCHULAIN (*wearing a mask*)
EMER
EITHNE INGUBA } (*masked, or their faces made up to resemble masks*)
WOMAN OF THE SIDHE (*wearing a mask*)

Enter Musicians, who are dressed and made up as in 'At the Hawk's Well'. They have the same musical instruments, which can either be already upon the stage or be brought in by the First Musician before he stands in the centre with the cloth between his hands, or by a player when the cloth has been unfolded. The stage as before can be against the wall of any room, and the same black cloth can be used as in 'At the Hawk's Well'.

[*Song for the folding and unfolding of the cloth.*]

FIRST MUSICIAN:

A woman's beauty is like a white
Frail bird, like a white sea-bird alone
At daybreak after stormy night
Between two furrows upon the ploughed land:
A sudden storm, and it was thrown
Between dark furrows upon the ploughed land.
How many centuries spent
The sedentary soul
In toils of measurement
Beyond eagle or mole,
Beyond hearing or seeing,
Or Archimedes' guess,
To raise into being
That loveliness?

*

A strange, unserviceable thing,
A fragile, exquisite, pale shell,
That the vast troubled waters bring
To the loud sands before day has broken.
The storm arose and suddenly fell
Amid the dark before day had broken.
What death? what discipline?
What bonds no man could unbind,
Being imagined within
The labyrinth of the mind,
What pursuing or fleeing,
What wounds, what bloody press,
Dragged into being
This loveliness?[2]

[*When the cloth is folded again the Musicians take their place
against the wall. The folding of the cloth shows on one side of
the stage the curtained bed or litter on which lies a man in his
grave-clothes. He wears an heroic mask. Another man with exactly
similar clothes and mask crouches near the front. Emer is sitting
beside the bed.*]

FIRST MUSICIAN [*speaking*]: I call before the eyes a roof
With cross-beams darkened by smoke;
A fisher's net hangs from a beam,
A long oar lies against the wall.
I call up a poor fisher's house;
A man lies dead or swooning,
That amorous man,
That amorous, violent man, renowned Cuchulain,
Queen Emer at his side.
At her own bidding all the rest have gone;[3]
But now one comes on hesitating feet,
Young Eithne Inguba, Cuchulain's mistress.
She stands a moment in the open door.
Beyond the open door the bitter sea,
The shining, bitter sea, is crying out,
[*singing*] White shell, white wing!
I will not choose for my friend
A frail, unserviceable thing
That drifts and dreams, and but knows

That waters are without end
And that wind blows.

EMER [*speaking*]: Come hither, come sit down beside the bed;
You need not be afraid, for I myself
Sent for you, Eithne Inguba.

EITHNE INGUBA: No, Madam,
I have too deeply wronged you to sit there.

EMER: Of all the people in the world we two,
And we alone, may watch together here,
Because we have loved him best.

EITHNE INGUBA: And is he dead?

EMER: Although they have dressed him out in his grave-clothes
And stretched his limbs, Cuchulain is not dead;
The very heavens when that day's at hand,
So that his death may not lack ceremony,
Will throw out fires, and the earth grow red with blood.
There shall not be a scullion but foreknows it
Like the world's end.

EITHNE INGUBA: How did he come to this?

EMER: Towards noon in the assembly of the kings
He met with one who seemed a while most dear.
The kings stood round; some quarrel was blown up;
He drove him out and killed him on the shore
At Baile's tree, and he who was so killed
Was his own son begot on some wild woman
When he was young, or so I have heard it said;
And thereupon, knowing what man he had killed,
And being mad with sorrow, he ran out;
And after, to his middle in the foam,
With shield before him and with sword in hand,
He fought the deathless sea. The kings looked on
And not a king dared stretch an arm, or even
Dared call his name, but all stood wondering
In that dumb stupor like cattle in a gale,
Until at last, as though he had fixed his eyes
On a new enemy, he waded out
Until the water had swept over him;
But the waves washed his senseless image up

And laid it at this door.[4]

EITHNE INGUBA: How pale he looks!

EMER: He is not dead.

EITHNE INGUBA: You have not kissed his lips
   Nor laid his head upon your breast.

EMER: It may be
   An image has been put into his place,
   A sea-borne log[5] bewitched into his likeness,
   Or some stark horseman grown too old to ride
   Among the troops of Manannan,[6] Son of the Sea,
   Now that his joints are stiff.

EITHNE INGUBA: Cry out his name.
   All that are taken from our sight, they say,
   Loiter amid the scenery of their lives
   For certain hours or days, and should he hear
   He might, being angry, drive the changeling out.

EMER: It is hard to make them hear amid their darkness,
   And it is long since I could call him home;
   I am but his wife, but if you cry aloud
   With the sweet voice that is so dear to him
   He cannot help but listen.

EITHNE INGUBA: He loves me best,
   Being his newest love, but in the end
   Will love the woman best who loved him first
   And loved him through the years when love seemed lost.

EMER: I have that hope,[7] the hope that some day somewhere
   We'll sit together at the hearth again.

EITHNE INGUBA: Women like me, the violent hour passed over,
   Are flung into some corner like old nut-shells.
   Cuchulain, listen.

EMER: No, not yet, for first
   I'll cover up his face to hide the sea;
   And throw new logs upon the hearth and stir
   The half-burnt logs until they break in flame.
   Old Manannan's unbridled horses come
   Out of the sea, and on their backs his horsemen;
   But all the enchantments of the dreaming foam
   Dread the hearth-fire.

[*She pulls the curtains of the bed so as to hide the sick man's face, that the actor may change his mask unseen. She goes to one side of the platform and moves her hand as though putting logs on a fire and stirring it into a blaze. While she makes these movements the Musicians play, marking the movements with drum and flute perhaps.*

Having finished she stands beside the imaginary fire at a distance from Cuchulain and Eithne Inguba.]

Call on Cuchulain now.

EITHNE INGUBA: Can you not hear my voice?

EMER: Bend over him;
Call out dear secrets till you have touched his heart,
If he lies there; and if he is not there,
Till you have made him jealous.

EITHNE INGUBA: Cuchulain, listen.

EMER: Those words sound timidly; to be afraid
Because his wife is but three paces off,
When there is so great need, were but to prove
The man that chose you made but a poor choice:
We're but two women struggling with the sea.

EITHNE INGUBA: O my beloved, pardon me, that I
Have been ashamed. I thrust my shame away.
I have never sent a message or called out,
Scarce had a longing for your company
But you have known and come; and if indeed
You are lying there, stretch out your arms and speak;
Open your mouth and speak, for to this hour
My company has made you talkative.
What ails your tongue, or what has closed your ears?
Our passion had not chilled when we were parted
On the pale shore under the breaking dawn.
He cannot speak: or else his ears are closed
And no sound reaches him.

EMER: Then kiss that image;
The pressure of your mouth upon his mouth
May reach him where he is.

EITHNE INGUBA [*starting back*]: It is no man.
I felt some evil thing that dried my heart

When my lips touched it.

EMER: No, his body stirs;
The pressure of your mouth has called him home;
He has thrown the changeling out.

EITHNE INGUBA [*going further off*]: Look at that arm;
That arm is withered to the very socket.

EMER [*going up to the bed*]: What do you come for; and from where?

FIGURE OF CUCHULAIN: I have come
From Manannan's court upon a bridleless horse.

EMER: What one among the Sidhe[8] has dared to lie
Upon Cuchulain's bed and take his image?

FIGURE OF CUCHULAIN: I am named Bricriu – not the man – that
      Bricriu,
Maker of discord among gods and men,
Called Bricriu of the Sidhe.[9]

EMER: Come for what purpose?

FIGURE OF CUCHULAIN [*sitting up, parting curtains and showing
      its distorted face, as Eithne Inguba goes out*]: I show my face,
      and everything he loves
Must fly away.

EMER: You people of the wind
Are full of lying speech and mockery:
I have not fled your face.

FIGURE OF CUCHULAIN: You are not loved.

EMER: And therefore have no dread to meet your eyes
And to demand him of you.

FIGURE OF CUCHULAIN: For that I have come.
You have but to pay the price and he is free.

EMER: Do the Sidhe bargain?

FIGURE OF CUCHULAIN: When they would free a captive
They take in ransom a less valued thing.
The fisher, when some knowledgeable man
Restores to him his wife, or son, or daughter,
Knows he must lose a boat or net, or it may be
The cow that gives his children milk; and some
Have offered their own lives. I do not ask
Your life, or any valuable thing;

You spoke but now of the mere chance that some day
You'd be the apple of his eye again
When old and ailing, but renounce that chance
And he shall live again.

EMER: I do not question
But you have brought ill-luck on all he loves;
And now, because I am thrown beyond your power
Unless your words are lies, you come to bargain.

FIGURE OF CUCHULAIN: You loved your mastery, when but newly
        married,
And I love mine for all my withered arm;
You have but to put yourself into that power
And he shall live again.

EMER: No, never, never.

FIGURE OF CUCHULAIN: You dare not be accursed, yet he has dared.

EMER: I have but two joyous thoughts, two things I prize,
A hope, a memory, and now you claim that hope.

FIGURE OF CUCHULAIN: He'll never sit beside you at the hearth
Or make old bones, but die of wounds and toil
On some far shore or mountain, a strange woman
Beside his mattress.

EMER: You ask for my one hope
That you may bring your curse on all about him.

FIGURE OF CUCHULAIN: You've watched his loves and you have
        not been jealous,
Knowing that he would tire, but do those tire
That love the Sidhe? Come closer to the bed
That I may touch your eyes and give them sight.
    [He touches her eyes with his left hand,¹⁰ the right being withered.]

EMER [seeing the crouching Ghost of Cuchulain]: My husband is
        there.

FIGURE OF CUCHULAIN: I have dissolved the dark
That hid him from your eyes, but not that other
That's hidden you from his.

EMER: O husband, husband!

FIGURE OF CUCHULAIN: He cannot hear – being shut off, a phantom
That can neither touch, nor hear, nor see;

The longing and the cries have drawn him hither.
He heard no sound, heard no articulate sound;
They could but banish rest, and make him dream,
And in that dream, as do all dreaming shades
Before they are accustomed to their freedom,
He has taken his familiar form; and yet
He crouches there not knowing where he is
Or at whose side he is crouched.

[*A Woman of the Sidhe has entered and stands a little inside the door.*]

EMER: Who is this woman?

FIGURE OF CUCHULAIN: She has hurried from the Country-
    under-Wave
And dreamed herself into that shape that he
May glitter in her basket; for the Sidhe
Are dexterous fishers and they fish for men
With dreams upon the hook.

EMER: And so that woman
Has hid herself in this disguise and made
Herself into a lie.

FIGURE OF CUCHULAIN: A dream is body;
The dead move ever towards a dreamless youth
And when they dream no more return no more;
And those more holy shades that never lived
But visit you in dreams.

EMER: I know her sort.
They find our men asleep, weary with war,
Lap them in cloudy hair or kiss their lips;
Our men awake in ignorance of it all,
But when we take them in our arms at night
We cannot break their solitude.

[*She draws a knife from her girdle.*]

FIGURE OF CUCHULAIN: No knife
Can wound that body of air. Be silent; listen;
I have not given you eyes and ears for nothing.

[*The Woman of the Sidhe moves round the crouching Ghost of
Cuchulain at front of stage in a dance that grows gradually quicker,
as he slowly awakes. At moments she may drop her hair upon his*

head, but she does not kiss him. She is accompanied by string and flute and drum. Her mask and clothes must suggest gold or bronze or brass or silver, so that she seems more an idol than a human being. This suggestion may be repeated in her movements. Her hair, too, must keep the metallic suggestion.[11]]

GHOST OF CUCHULAIN: Who is it stands before me there
   Shedding such light from limb and hair
   As when the moon, complete at last
   With every labouring crescent past,
   And lonely with extreme delight,
   Flings out upon the fifteenth night?[12]

WOMAN OF THE SIDHE: Because I long I am not complete.
   What pulled your hands about your feet,
   Pulled down your head upon your knees,
   And hid your face?

GHOST OF CUCHULAIN: Old memories:
   A woman in her happy youth
   Before her man had broken troth,
   Dead men and women. Memories
   Have pulled my head upon my knees.[13]

WOMAN OF THE SIDHE: Could you that have loved many a woman
   That did not reach beyond the human,
   Lacking a day to be complete,
   Love one that, though her heart can beat,
   Lacks it but by an hour or so?

GHOST OF CUCHULAIN: I know you now, for long ago
   I met you on a cloudy hill
   Beside old thorn-trees and a well.
   A woman danced and a hawk flew,
   I held out arms and hands; but you,
   That now seem friendly, fled away,
   Half woman and half bird of prey.[14]

WOMAN OF THE SIDHE: Hold out your arms and hands again;
   You were not so dumbfounded when
   I was that bird of prey, and yet
   I am all woman now.

GHOST OF CUCHULAIN: I am not
   The young and passionate man I was,

And though that brilliant light surpass
All crescent forms, my memories
Weigh down my hands, abash my eyes.

WOMAN OF THE SIDHE: Then kiss my mouth. Though memory
Be beauty's bitterest enemy
I have no dread, for at my kiss
Memory on the moment vanishes:
Nothing but beauty can remain.

GHOST OF CUCHULAIN: And shall I never know again
Intricacies of blind remorse?

WOMAN OF THE SIDHE: Time shall seem to stay his course;
When your mouth and my mouth meet
All my round shall be complete
Imagining all its circles run;
And there shall be oblivion[15]
Even to quench Cuchulain's drouth,
Even to still that heart.

GHOST OF CUCHULAIN: Your mouth!
   [*They are about to kiss, he turns away.*]
O Emer, Emer!

WOMAN OF THE SIDHE: So then it is she
Made you impure with memory.

GHOST OF CUCHULAIN: O Emer, Emer, there we stand;
Side by side and hand in hand
Tread the threshold of the house
As when our parents married us.[16]

WOMAN OF THE SIDHE: Being among the dead you love her
That valued every slut above her
While you still lived.

GHOST OF CUCHULAIN: O my lost Emer!

WOMAN OF THE SIDHE: And there is not a loose-tongued schemer
But could draw you, if not dead,
From her table and her bed.
But what could make you fit to wive
With flesh and blood, being born to live
Where no one speaks of broken troth,
For all have washed out of their eyes
Wind-blown dirt of their memories

To improve their sight?

GHOST OF CUCHULAIN: Your mouth, your mouth!
 [*She goes out followed by Ghost of Cuchulain.*]

FIGURE OF CUCHULAIN: Cry out that you renounce his love; make haste
And cry that you renounce his love for ever.

EMER: No, never will I give that cry.[17]

FIGURE OF CUCHULAIN: Fool, fool!
I am Fand's enemy come to thwart her will,
And you stand gaping there. There is still time.
Hear how the horses trample on the shore,
Hear how they trample! She has mounted up.
Cuchulain's not beside her in the chariot.
There is still a moment left; cry out, cry out!
Renounce him, and her power is at an end.
Cuchulain's foot is on the chariot-step.
Cry—

EMER: I renounce Cuchulain's love for ever.
 [*The Figure of Cuchulain sinks back upon the bed, half-drawing the curtain. Eithne Inguba comes in and kneels by bed.*]

EITHNE INGUBA: Come to me, my beloved, it is I.
I, Eithne Inguba. Look! He is there.
He has come back and moved upon the bed.
And it is I that won him from the sea,
That brought him back to life.

EMER: Cuchulain wakes.
 [*The figure turns round. It once more wears the heroic mask.*]

CUCHULAIN: Your arms, your arms! O Eithne Inguba,
I have been in some strange place and am afraid.
 [*The First Musician comes to the front of stage, the others from each side, and unfold the cloth singing.*]
 [*Song for the unfolding and folding of the cloth.*]

THE MUSICIANS:
    Why does your heart beat thus?
    Plain to be understood,
    I have met in a man's house
    A statue of solitude,
    Moving there and walking;

Its strange heart beating fast
For all our talking.
O still that heart at last.

O bitter reward
Of many a tragic tomb!
And we though astonished are dumb
Or give but a sigh and a word,
A passing word.

Although the door be shut
And all seem well enough,
Although wide world hold not
A man but will give you his love
The moment he has looked at you,
He that has loved the best
May turn from a statue
His too human breast.

O bitter reward
Of many a tragic tomb!
And we though astonished are dumb
Or give but a sigh and a word,
A passing word.

What makes your heart so beat?
What man is at your side?
When beauty is complete
Your own thought will have died
And danger not be diminished;
Dimmed at three-quarter light,
When moon's round is finished
The stars are out of sight.

O bitter reward
Of many a tragic tomb!
And we though astonished are dumb
Or give but a sigh and a word,
A passing word.

[*When the cloth is folded again the stage is bare.*[18]]

THE END

CALVARY

Persons in the Play

THREE MUSICIANS (*their faces made up to resemble masks*)
CHRIST (*wearing a mask*)
LAZARUS (*wearing a mask*)
JUDAS (*wearing a mask*)
THREE ROMAN SOLDIERS (*their faces masked or made up to resemble masks*)

At the beginning of the play the First Musician comes to the front of the bare place, round three sides of which the audience are seated,[1] with a folded cloth hanging from his joined hands. Two other Musicians come, as in the preceding play, one from either side, and unfold the cloth so that it shuts out the stage, and then fold it again, singing and moving rhythmically. They do the same at the end of the play, which enables the players to leave the stage unseen.

[*Song for the folding and unfolding of the cloth.*]

FIRST MUSICIAN:

> Motionless under the moon-beam,
> Up to his feathers in the stream;
> Although fish leap, the white heron
> Shivers in a dumbfounded dream.[2]

SECOND MUSICIAN:

> God has not died for the white heron.

THIRD MUSICIAN:

> Although half famished he'll not dare
> Dip or do anything but stare
> Upon the glittering image of a heron,
> That now is lost and now is there.

SECOND MUSICIAN:

> God has not died for the white heron.

FIRST MUSICIAN:

> But that the full is shortly gone
> And after that is crescent moon,
> It's certain that the moon-crazed heron
> Would be but fishes' diet soon.

SECOND MUSICIAN:

> God has not died for the white heron.

[*The three Musicians are now seated by the drum, flute, and zither at the back of stage.*]

FIRST MUSICIAN: The road to Calvary, and I beside it
Upon an ancient stone. Good Friday's come,
The day whereon Christ dreams His passion through.
He climbs up hither but as a dreamer climbs.
The cross that but exists because He dreams it
Shortens His breath and wears away His strength.
And now He stands amid a mocking crowd,
Heavily breathing.

[*A player with the mask of Christ and carrying a cross has entered and now stands leaning upon the cross.*]

Those that are behind
Climb on the shoulders of the men in front
To shout their mockery: 'Work a miracle',
Cries one, 'and save yourself'; another cries,
'Call on your father now before your bones
Have been picked bare by the great desert birds';
Another cries, 'Call out with a loud voice
And tell him that his son is cast away
Amid the mockery of his enemies'.

[*singing*]

> O, but the mockers' cry
> Makes my heart afraid,
> As though a flute of bone
> Taken from a heron's thigh,
> A heron crazed by the moon,
> Were cleverly, softly played.

[*speaking*]
Who is this from whom the crowd has shrunk,
As though he had some look that terrified?

He has a deathly face, and yet he moves
Like a young foal that sees the hunt go by
And races in the field.[3]
    [*A player with the mask of Lazarus has entered.*]

LAZARUS: He raised me up.
I am the man that died and was raised up;
I am called Lazarus.

CHRIST: Seeing that you died,
Lay in the tomb four days and were raised up,
You will not mock at me.

LAZARUS: For four whole days
I had been dead and I was lying still
In an old comfortable mountain cavern
When you came climbing there with a great crowd
And dragged me to the light.

CHRIST: I called your name:
'Lazarus, come out', I said, and you came out
Bound up in cloths, your face bound in a cloth.

LAZARUS: You took my death, give me your death instead.

CHRIST: I gave you life.

LAZARUS: But death is what I ask.
Alive I never could escape your love,
And when I sickened towards my death I thought,
'I'll to the desert, or chuckle[4] in a corner,
Mere ghost, a solitary thing.' I died
And saw no more until I saw you stand
In the opening of the tomb; 'Come out!' you called;
You dragged me to the light as boys drag out
A rabbit when they have dug its hole away;
And now with all the shouting at your heels
You travel towards the death I am denied.
And that is why I have hurried to this road
And claimed your death.

CHRIST: But I have conquered death,
And all the dead shall be raised up again.

LAZARUS: Then what I heard is true. I thought to die
When my allotted years ran out again;
And that, being gone, you could not hinder it;

But now you will blind with light the solitude
That death has made; you will disturb that corner
Where I had thought I might lie safe for ever.

CHRIST: I do my Father's will.

LAZARUS: And not your own;
And I was free four days, four days being dead.
Climb up to Calvary, but turn your eyes
From Lazarus that cannot find a tomb
Although he search all height and depth: make way,
Make way for Lazarus that must go search
Among the desert places where there is nothing
But howling wind and solitary birds.
    [*He goes out.*]

FIRST MUSICIAN: The crowd shrinks backward from the face that
        seems
Death-stricken and death-hungry still; and now
Martha, and those three Marys,[5] and the rest
That live but in His love are gathered round Him.
He holds His right arm out, and on His arm
Their lips are pressed and their tears fall; and now
They cast them on the ground before His dirty
Blood-dabbled feet and clean them with their hair.
    [*sings*]

                    Take but His love away,
                    Their love becomes a feather
                    Of eagle, swan or gull,
                    Or a drowned heron's feather
                    Tossed hither and thither
                    Upon the bitter spray
                    And the moon at the full.

CHRIST: I felt their hair upon my feet a moment
And then they fled away – why have they fled?
Why has the street grown empty of a sudden
As though all fled in terror?

JUDAS [*who has just entered*]: I am Judas[6]
That sold you for the thirty pieces of silver.

CHRIST: You were beside me every day, and saw
The dead raised up and blind men given their sight,

And all that I have said and taught you have known,
Yet doubt that I am God.

JUDAS: I have not doubted;
I knew it from the first moment that I saw you;
I had no need of miracles to prove it.

CHRIST: And yet you have betrayed me.

JUDAS: I have betrayed you
Because you seemed all-powerful.

CHRIST: My Father
Even now, if I were but to whisper it,
Would break the world in His miraculous fury
To set me free.

JUDAS: And is there not one man
In the wide world that is not in your power?

CHRIST: My Father put all men into my hands.

JUDAS: That was the very thought that drove me wild.
I could not bear to think you had but to whistle
And I must do; but after that I thought,
'Whatever man betrays Him will be free';
And life grew bearable again. And now
Is there a secret left I do not know,
Knowing that if a man betrays a God
He is the stronger of the two?

CHRIST: But if
'Twere the commandment of that God Himself,
That God were still the stronger.

JUDAS: When I planned it
There was no live thing near me but a heron
So full of itself that it seemed terrified.

CHRIST: But my betrayal was decreed that hour
When the foundations of the world were laid.

JUDAS: It was decreed that somebody betray you –
I'd thought of that – but not that I should do it,
I the man Judas, born on such a day,
In such a village, such and such his parents;
Nor that I'd go with my old coat upon me
To the High Priest, and chuckle to myself
As people chuckle when alone, and do it

For thirty pieces and no more, no less,
And neither with a nod nor a sent message,
But with a kiss upon your cheek. I did it,
I, Judas, and no other man, and now
You cannot even save me.

CHRIST: Begone from me.
 [*Three Roman Soldiers have entered.*]

FIRST ROMAN SOLDIER: He has been chosen to hold up the cross.[7]
 [*During what follows, Judas holds up the cross while Christ stands
 with His arms stretched out upon it.*]

SECOND ROMAN SOLDIER: We'll keep the rest away; they are too
     persistent;
 They are always wanting something.

THIRD ROMAN SOLDIER: Die in peace.
 There's no one here but Judas and ourselves.

CHRIST: And who are you that ask your God for nothing?

THIRD ROMAN SOLDIER: We are the gamblers, and when you are
     dead
 We'll settle who is to have that cloak of yours
 By throwing dice.

SECOND ROMAN SOLDIER: Our dice were carved
 Out of an old sheep's thigh at Ephesus.[8]

FIRST ROMAN SOLDIER: Although but one of us can win the cloak
 That will not make us quarrel; what does it matter?
 One day one loses and the next day wins.

SECOND ROMAN SOLDIER: Whatever happens is the best, we say,
 So that it's unexpected.

THIRD ROMAN SOLDIER: Had you sent
 A crier through the world you had not found
 More comfortable companions for a death-bed
 Than three old gamblers that have asked for nothing.

FIRST ROMAN SOLDIER: They say you're good and that you made
     the world,
 But it's no matter.

SECOND ROMAN SOLDIER: Come now; let us dance
 The dance of the dice-throwers, for it may be
 He cannot live much longer and has not seen it.

THIRD ROMAN SOLDIER: If he were but the God of dice he'd know
   it,
But he is not that God.

FIRST ROMAN SOLDIER: One thing is plain,
   To know that he has nothing that we need
   Must be a comfort to him.

SECOND ROMAN SOLDIER: In the dance
   We quarrel for a while, but settle it
   By throwing dice, and after that, being friends,
   Join hand to hand and wheel about the cross.
      [*They dance.*⁹]

CHRIST: My Father, why hast Thou forsaken Me?
      [*Song for the folding and unfolding of the cloth.*]

FIRST MUSICIAN:

> Lonely the sea-bird lies at her rest,
> Blown like a dawn-blenched parcel of spray
> Upon the wind, or follows her prey
> Under a great wave's hollowing crest.

SECOND MUSICIAN:

> God has not appeared to the birds.

THIRD MUSICIAN:

> The ger-eagle has chosen his part
> In blue deep of the upper air
> Where one-eyed day can meet his stare;
> He is content with his savage heart.

SECOND MUSICIAN:

> God has not appeared to the birds.

FIRST MUSICIAN:

> But where have last year's cygnets gone?
> The lake is empty; why do they fling
> White wing out beside white wing?
> What can a swan need but a swan?

SECOND MUSICIAN:

> God has not appeared to the birds.

THE END

SOPHOCLES' KING OEDIPUS

A VERSION FOR THE MODERN STAGE

Persons in the Play

OEDIPUS, *King of Thebes*
JOCASTA, *wife of Oedipus*
ANTIGONE, *daughter of Oedipus*
ISMENE, *daughter of Oedipus*
CREON, *brother-in-law of Oedipus*
TIRESIAS, *a seer*
A PRIEST
MESSENGERS
A HERDSMAN
CHORUS

Scene. – The Palace of King Oedipus at Thebes.

OEDIPUS: Children, descendants of old Cadmus,[1] why do you come before me, why do you carry the branches of suppliants, while the city smokes with incense and murmurs with prayer and lamentation? I would not learn from any mouth but yours, old man, therefore I question you myself. Do you know of anything that I can do and have not done? How can I, being the man I am, being King Oedipus, do other than all I know? I were indeed hard of heart did I not pity such suppliants.

PRIEST: Oedipus, King of my country, we who stand before your door are of all ages, some too young to have walked so many miles, some – priests of Zeus[2] such as I – too old. Among us stand the pick of the young men, and behind in the market-places the people throng, carrying suppliant branches. We all stand here because the city stumbles towards death, hardly able to raise up its head. A blight has fallen upon the fruitful blossoms of the land, a blight upon flock and field and upon the bed of marriage – plague ravages the city. Oedipus, King, not God but foremost of living men, seeing that when you first came to this town of Thebes you freed us from that harsh

165

singer, the riddling Sphinx,[3] we beseech you, all we suppliants, to find some help; whether you find it by your power as a man, or because, being near the Gods, a God has whispered you. Uplift our State; think upon your fame; your coming brought us luck, be lucky to us still; remember that it is better to rule over men than over a waste place, since neither walled town nor ship is anything if it be empty and no man within it.

OEDIPUS: My unhappy children! I know well what need has brought you, what suffering you endure; yet, sufferers though you be, there is not a single one whose suffering is as mine – each mourns himself, but my soul mourns the city, myself, and you. It is not therefore as if you came to arouse a sleeping man. No! Be certain that I have wept many tears and searched hither and thither for some remedy. I have already done the only thing that came into my head for all my search. I have sent the son of Menoeceus, Creon, my own wife's brother, to the Pythian House of Phoebus,[4] to hear if deed or word of mine may yet deliver this town. I am troubled, for he is a long time away – a longer time than should be – but when he comes I shall not be an honest man unless I do whatever the God commands.

PRIEST: You have spoken at the right time. They have just signalled to us that Creon has arrived.

OEDIPUS: O King Apollo, may he bring brighter fortune, for his face is shining!

PRIEST: He brings good news, for he is crowned with bay.

OEDIPUS: We shall know soon. Brother-in-law, Menoeceus' son, what news from the God?

CREON: Good news; for pain turns to pleasure when we have set the crooked straight.

OEDIPUS: But what is the oracle? – so far the news is neither good nor bad.

CREON: If you would hear it with all these about you, I am ready to speak. Or do we go within?

OEDIPUS: Speak before all.[5] The sorrow I endure is less for my own life than these.

CREON: Then, with your leave, I speak. Our lord Phoebus bids us drive out a defiling thing that has been cherished in this land.

OEDIPUS: By what purification?

CREON: King Laius was our King before you came to pilot us.

OEDIPUS: I know – but not of my own knowledge, for I never saw him.

CREON: He was killed; and the God now bids us revenge it on his murderers, whoever they be.

OEDIPUS: Where shall we come upon their track after all these years? Did he meet his death in house or field, at home or in some foreign land?

CREON: In a foreign land: he was journeying to Delphi.

OEDIPUS: Did no fellow-traveller see the deed? Was there none there who could be questioned?

CREON: All perished but one man who fled in terror and could tell for certain but one thing of all he had seen.

OEDIPUS: One thing might be a clue to many things.

CREON: He said that they were fallen upon by a great troop of robbers.

OEDIPUS: What robbers would be so daring unless bribed from here?

CREON: Such things were indeed guessed at, but Laius once dead no avenger arose. We were amid our troubles.

OEDIPUS: But when royalty had fallen what troubles could have hindered search?

CREON: The riddling Sphinx put those dark things out of our thoughts – we thought of what had come to our own doors.

OEDIPUS: But I will start afresh and make the dark things plain.[6] In doing right by Laius I protect myself, for whoever slew Laius might turn a hand against me. Come, my children, rise up from the altar steps; lift up these suppliant boughs and let all the children of Cadmus be called hither that I may search out everything and find for all happiness or misery as God wills.

PRIEST: May Phoebus, sender of the oracle, come with it and be our saviour and deliverer!

[The Chorus[7] enter.]

Chorus

What message comes to famous Thebes from the Golden House?[8]
What message of disaster from that sweet-throated Zeus?
What monstrous thing our fathers saw do the seasons bring?
Or what that no man ever saw, what new monstrous thing?
Trembling in every limb I raise my loud importunate cry,

And in a sacred terror wait the Delian God's[9] reply.

Apollo chase the God of Death that leads no shouting men,
Bears no rattling shield and yet consumes this form with pain.
Famine takes what the plague spares, and all the crops are lost;
No new life fills the empty place – ghost flits after ghost
To that God-trodden western shore,[10] as flit benighted birds.
Sorrow speaks to sorrow, but no comfort finds in words.

Hurry him from the land of Thebes with a fair wind behind
Out on to that formless deep where not a man can find
Hold for an anchor-fluke, for all is world-enfolding sea;
Master of the thunder-cloud,[11] set the lightning free,
And add the thunder-stone to that and fling them on his head,
For death is all the fashion now, till even Death be dead.

We call against the pallid face of this God-hated God
The springing heel of Artemis[12] in the hunting sandal shod,
The tousle-headed Maenads,[13] blown torch and drunken sound,
The stately Lysian king himself with golden fillet crowned,
And in his hands the golden bow and the stretched golden string,
And Bacchus' wine-ensanguined face[14] that all the Maenads sing.

OEDIPUS: You are praying, and it may be that your prayer will be
answered; that if you hear my words and do my bidding you may
find help out of all your trouble. This is my proclamation, children
of Cadmus. Whoever among you knows by what man Laius, son of
Labdacus, was killed, must tell all he knows. If he fear for himself
and being guilty denounce himself, he shall be in the less danger,
suffering no worse thing than banishment. If on the other hand there
be one that knows that a foreigner did the deed, let him speak, and
I shall give him a reward and my thanks: but if any man keep silent
from fear or to screen a friend, hear all what I will do to that man.
No one in this land shall speak to him, nor offer sacrifice beside him;
but he shall be driven from their homes as if he himself had done
the deed. And in this I am the ally of the Pythian God and of the
murdered man, and I pray that the murderer's life may, should he
be so hidden and screened, drop from him and perish away, whoever
he may be, whether he did the deed with others or by himself alone:
and on you I lay it to make – so far as man may – these words good,
for my sake, and for the God's sake, and for the sake of this land.
And even if the God had not spurred us to it, it were a wrong to

leave the guilt unpurged, when one so noble, and he your King, had perished; and all have sinned that could have searched it out and did not: and now since it is I who hold the power which he held once, and have his wife for wife – she who would have borne him heirs had he but lived – I take up this cause even as I would were it that of my own father. And if there be any who do not obey me in it, I pray that the Gods send them neither harvest of the earth nor fruit of the womb; but let them be wasted by this plague, or by one more dreadful still. But may all be blessed for ever who hear my words and do my will!

CHORUS: We do not know the murderer, and it were indeed more fitting that Phoebus, who laid the task upon us, should name the man.

OEDIPUS: No man can make the Gods speak against their will.

CHORUS: Then I will say what seems the next best thing.

OEDIPUS: If there is a third course, show it.

CHORUS: I know that our lord Tiresias[15] is the seer most like to our lord Phoebus, and through him we may unravel all.

OEDIPUS: So I was advised by Creon, and twice already have I sent to bring him.

CHORUS: If we lack his help we have nothing but vague and ancient rumours.

OEDIPUS: What rumours are they? I would examine every story.

CHORUS: Certain wayfarers were said to have killed the King.

OEDIPUS: I know, I know. But who was there that saw it?

CHORUS: If there is such a man, and terror can move him, he will not keep silence when they have told him of your curses.

OEDIPUS: He that such a deed did not terrify will not be terrified because of a word.

CHORUS: But there is one who shall convict him. For the blind prophet comes at last – in whom alone of all men the truth lives.

[*Enter Tiresias, led by a boy.*]

OEDIPUS: Tiresias, master of all knowledge, whatever may be spoken, whatever is unspeakable, whatever omens of earth and sky reveal, the plague is among us, and from that plague, Great Prophet, protect us and save us. Phoebus in answer to our question says that it will not leave us till we have found the murderers of Laius, and driven them into exile or put them to death. Do you therefore neglect neither the voice of birds, nor any other sort of wisdom, but rescue yourself, rescue the State, rescue me, rescue all that are defiled by the deed. For we are in your hands, and what greater task falls to a man than to help other men with all he knows and has?

TIRESIAS: Aye, and what worse task than to be wise and suffer for it?[16] I know this well; it slipped out of mind, or I would never have come.

OEDIPUS: What now?

TIRESIAS: Let me go home. You will bear your burden to the end more easily, and I bear mine – if you but give me leave for that.

OEDIPUS: Your words are strange and unkind to the State that bred you.

TIRESIAS: I see that you, on your part, keep your lips tight shut, and therefore I have shut mine that I may come to no misfortune.

OEDIPUS: For God's love do not turn away – if you have knowledge. We suppliants implore you on our knees.

TIRESIAS: You are fools – I will bring misfortune neither upon you nor upon myself.

OEDIPUS: What is this? You know all and will say nothing? You are minded to betray me and Thebes?

TIRESIAS: Why do you ask these things? You will not learn them from me.

OEDIPUS: What! Basest of the base! You would enrage the very stones. Will you never speak out? Cannot anything touch you?

TIRESIAS: The future will come of itself though I keep silent.

OEDIPUS: Then seeing that come it must, you had best speak out.

TIRESIAS: I will speak no further. Rage if you have a mind to; bring out all the fierceness that is in your heart.

OEDIPUS: That will I. I will not spare to speak my thoughts. Listen to what I have to say. It seems to me that you have helped to plot the deed; and, short of doing it with your own hands, have done the deed yourself. Had you eyesight I would declare that you alone had done it.

TIRESIAS: So that is what you say? I charge you to obey the decree that you yourself have made, and from this day out to speak neither to these nor to me. You are the defiler of this land.

OEDIPUS: So brazen in your impudence? How do you hope to escape punishment?

TIRESIAS: I have escaped; my strength is in my truth.

OEDIPUS: Who taught you this? You never got it by your art.

TIRESIAS: You, because you have spurred me to speech against my will.

OEDIPUS: What speech? Speak it again that I may learn it better.

TIRESIAS: You are but tempting me – you understood me well enough.

OEDIPUS: No; not so that I can say I know it; speak it again.

TIRESIAS: I say that you are yourself the murderer that you seek.

OEDIPUS: You shall rue it for having spoken twice such outrageous words.

TIRESIAS: Would you that I say more that you may be still angrier?

OEDIPUS: Say what you will. I will not let it move me.

TIRESIAS: I say that you are living with your next of kin in unimagined shame.

OEDIPUS: Do you think you can say such things and never smart for it?

TIRESIAS: Yes, if there be strength in truth.

OEDIPUS: There is; yes – for everyone but you. But not for you that are maimed in ear and in eye and in wit.

TIRESIAS: You are but a poor wretch flinging taunts that in a little while everyone shall fling at you.

OEDIPUS: Night, endless night has covered you up so that you can neither hurt me nor any man that looks upon the sun.

TIRESIAS: Your doom is not to fall by me. Apollo is enough: it is his business to work out your doom.

OEDIPUS: Was it Creon that planned this or you yourself?

TIRESIAS: Creon is not your enemy; you are your own enemy.

OEDIPUS: Power, ability, position, you bear all burdens, and yet what envy you create! Great must that envy be if envy of my power in this town – a power put into my hands unsought – has made trusty Creon, my old friend Creon, secretly long to take that power from me; if he has suborned this scheming juggler, this quack and trickster, this man with eyes for his gains and blindness in his art. Come, come, where did you prove yourself a seer? Why did you say nothing to set the townsmen free when the riddling Sphinx was here? Yet that riddle was not for the first-comer to read; it needed the skill of a seer. And none such had you! Neither found by help of birds, nor straight from any God. No, I came; I silenced her, I the ignorant Oedipus, it was I that found the answer in my mother-wit, untaught by any birds.[17] And it is I that you would pluck out of my place, thinking to stand close to Creon's throne. But you and the plotter of all this shall mourn despite your zeal to purge the land. Were you not an old man, you had already learnt how bold you are and learnt it to your cost.

CHORUS: Both this man's words and yours, Oedipus, have been said in anger. Such words cannot help us here, nor any but those that teach us to obey the oracle.

TIRESIAS: King though you are, the right to answer when attacked belongs to both alike. I am not subject to you, but to Loxias;[18] and therefore I shall never be Creon's subject. And I tell you, since you have taunted me with blindness, that though you have your sight, you cannot see in what misery you stand, nor where you are living, nor with whom, unknowing what you do – for you do not know the stock you come of – you have been your own kin's enemy be they living or be they dead. And one day a mother's curse and father's curse alike shall drive you from this land in dreadful haste with darkness upon those eyes. Therefore, heap your scorn on Creon and on my message if you have a mind to; for no one of living men shall be crushed as you shall be crushed.

OEDIPUS: Begone this instant! Away, away! Get you from these doors!

TIRESIAS: I had never come but that you sent for me.

OEDIPUS: I did not know you were mad.

TIRESIAS: I may seem mad to you, but your parents thought me sane.

OEDIPUS: My parents! Stop! Who was my father?

TIRESIAS: This day shall you know your birth; and it will ruin you.

OEDIPUS: What dark words you always speak!

TIRESIAS: But are you not most skilful in the unravelling of dark words?

OEDIPUS: You mock me for that which made me great?

TIRESIAS: It was that fortune that undid you.

OEDIPUS: What do I care? For I delivered all this town.

TIRESIAS: Then I will go: boy, lead me out of this.

OEDIPUS: Yes, let him lead you. You take vexation with you.

TIRESIAS: I will go: but first I will do my errand. For frown though you may you cannot destroy me. The man for whom you look, the man you have been threatening in all the proclamations about the death of Laius, that man is here. He seems, so far as looks go, an alien;[19] yet he shall be found a native Theban and shall nowise be glad of that fortune. A blind man, though now he has his sight; a beggar, though now he is most rich; he shall go forth feeling the ground before him with his stick; so you go in and think on that, and if you find I am in fault say that I have no skill in prophecy.

[*Tiresias is led out by the boy. Oedipus enters the palace.*]

Chorus

The Delphian rock[20] has spoken out, now must a wicked mind,
Planner of things I dare not speak and of this bloody wrack,
Pray for feet that are as fast as the four hoofs of the wind:
Cloudy Parnassus[21] and the Fates[22] thunder at his back.

That sacred crossing-place of lines upon Parnassus' head,
Lines that have run through North and South, and run through West
       and East,
That navel of the world[23] bids all men search the mountain wood,
The solitary cavern, till they have found that infamous beast.

[*Creon enters from the house.*]

CREON: Fellow-citizens, having heard that King Oedipus accuses me of dreadful things, I come in my indignation. Does he think that he has suffered wrong from me in these present troubles, or anything that could lead to wrong, whether in word or deed? How can I live under blame like that? What life would be worth having if by you here, and by my nearest friends, called a traitor through the town?

CHORUS: He said it in anger, and not from his heart out.

CREON: He said it was I put up the seer to speak those falsehoods.

CHORUS: Such things were said.

CREON: And had he his right mind saying it?

CHORUS: I do not know – I do not know what my masters do.

[*Oedipus enters.*]

OEDIPUS: What brought you here? Have you a face so brazen that you come to my house – you, the proved assassin of its master – the certain robber of my crown? Come, tell me in the face of the Gods what cowardice, or folly, did you discover in me that you plotted this? Did you think that I would not see what you were at till you had crept upon me, or seeing it would not ward it off? What madness to seek a throne, having neither friends nor followers!

CREON: Now, listen, hear my answer, and then you may with knowledge judge between us.

OEDIPUS: You are plausible, but waste words now that I know you.

CREON: Hear what I have to say. I can explain it all.

OEDIPUS: One thing you will not explain away – that you are my enemy.

CREON: You are a fool to imagine that senseless stubbornness sits well upon you.

OEDIPUS: And you to imagine that you can wrong a kinsman and escape the penalty.

CREON: That is justly said,[24] I grant you; but what is this wrong that you complain of?

OEDIPUS: Did you advise, or not, that I should send for that notorious prophet?

CREON: And I am of the same mind still.

OEDIPUS: How long is it, then, since Laius –

CREON: What, what about him?

OEDIPUS: Since Laius was killed by an unknown hand?

CREON: That was many years ago.

OEDIPUS: Was this prophet at his trade in those days?

CREON: Yes; skilled as now and in equal honour.

OEDIPUS: Did he ever speak of me?

CREON: Never certainly when I was within earshot.

OEDIPUS: And did you enquire into the murder?

CREON: We did enquire but learnt nothing.

OEDIPUS: And why did he not tell out his story then?

CREON: I do not know. When I know nothing I say nothing.

OEDIPUS: This much at least you know and can say out.

CREON: What is that? If I know it I will say it.

OEDIPUS: That if he had not consulted you he would never have said that it was I who killed Laius.

CREON: You know best what he said; but now, question for question.

OEDIPUS: Question your fill – I cannot be proved guilty of that blood.

CREON: Answer me then. Are you not married to my sister?

OEDIPUS: That cannot be denied.

CREON: And do you not rule as she does? And with a like power?

OEDIPUS: I give her all she asks for.

CREON: And am not I the equal of you both?

OEDIPUS: Yes: and that is why you are so false a friend.

CREON: Not so; reason this out as I reason it, and first weigh this: who would prefer to lie awake amid terrors rather than to sleep in peace, granting that his power is equal in both cases? Neither I nor any sober-minded man. You give me what I ask and let me do what I want, but were I King I would have to do things I did not want to do. Is not influence and no trouble with it better than any throne, am I such a fool as to hunger after unprofitable honours? Now all are glad to see me, every one wishes me well, all that want a favour from you ask speech of me – finding in that their hope. Why should I give up these thngs and take those? No wise mind is treacherous. I am no contriver of plots, and if another took to them he would not come to me for help. And in proof of this go to the Pythian Oracle, and ask if I have truly told what the Gods said: and after that, if you have found that I have plotted with the Soothsayer, take me and kill me; not by the sentence of one mouth only – but of two mouths, yours and my own. But do not condemn me in a corner, upon some fancy and without proof. What right have you to declare a good man bad or a bad good? It is as bad a thing to cast off a true friend as it is for a man to cast away his own life – but you will learn these things with certainty when the time comes; for time alone shows a just man; though a day can show a knave.

CHORUS: King! He has spoken well, he gives himself time to think; a headlong talker does not know what he is saying.

OEDIPUS: The plotter is at his work, and I must counterplot headlong, or he will get his ends and I miss mine.

CREON: What will you do then? Drive me from the land?

OEDIPUS: Not so; I do not desire your banishment – but your death.

CREON: You are not sane.

OEDIPUS: I am sane at least in my own interest.

CREON: You should be in mine also.

OEDIPUS: No, for you are false.

CREON: But if you understand nothing?

OEDIPUS: Yet I must rule.

CREON: Not if you rule badly.

OEDIPUS: Hear him, O Thebes!

CREON: Thebes is for me also, not for you alone.

CHORUS: Cease, princes: I see Jocasta coming out of the house; she comes just in time to quench the quarrel.

    [*Jocasta enters.*]

JOCASTA: Unhappy men! Why have you made this crazy uproar? Are you not ashamed to quarrel about your own affairs when the whole country is in trouble? Go back into the palace, Oepidus, and you, Creon, to your own house. Stop making all this noise about some petty thing.

CREON: Your husband is about to kill me – or to drive me from the land of my fathers.

OEDIPUS: Yes: for I have convicted him of treachery against me.

CREON: Now may I perish accursed if I have done such a thing!

JOCASTA: For God's love believe it, Oedipus. First, for the sake of his oath, and then for my sake, and for the sake of these people here.

CHORUS [*all*]: King, do what she asks.

OEDIPUS: What would you have me do?

CHORUS: Not to make a dishonourable charge, with no more evidence than rumour, against a friend who has bound himself with an oath.

OEDIPUS: Do you desire my exile or my death?

CHORUS: No, by Helios,[25] by the first of all the Gods, may I die abandoned by Heaven and earth if I have that thought! What breaks my heart is that our public griefs should be increased by your quarrels.

OEDIPUS: Then let him go, though I am doomed thereby to death or to be thrust dishonoured from the land; it is your lips, not his, that move me to compassion; wherever he goes my hatred follows him.

CREON: You are as sullen in yielding as you were vehement in anger, but such natures are their own heaviest burden.

OEDIPUS: Why will you not leave me in peace and begone?

CREON: I will go away; what is your hatred to me? In the eyes of all here I am a just man.

[*He goes.*]

CHORUS: Lady, why do you not take your man into the house?

JOCASTA: I will do so when I have learned what has happened.

CHORUS: The half of it was blind suspicion bred of talk; the rest the wounds left by injustice.

JOCASTA: It was on both sides?

CHORUS: Yes.

JOCASTA: What was it?

CHORUS: Our land is vexed enough. Let the thing alone now that it is over.[26]

JOCASTA: In the name of the Gods, King, what put you in this anger?

OEDIPUS: I will tell you; for I honour you more than these men do. The cause is Creon and his plots against me.

JOCASTA: Speak on, if you can tell clearly how this quarrel arose.

OEDIPUS: He says that I am guilty of the blood of Laius.

JOCASTA: On his own knowledge, or on hearsay?

OEDIPUS: He has made a rascal of a seer his mouthpiece.

JOCASTA: Do not fear that there is truth in what he says. Listen to me, and learn to your comfort that nothing born of woman can know what is to come. I will give you proof of that. An oracle came to Laius once, I will not say from Phoebus, but from his ministers, that he was doomed to die by the hand of his own child sprung from him and me. When his child was but three days old, Laius bound its feet together[27] and had it thrown by sure hands upon a trackless mountain; and when Laius was murdered at the place where three highways meet, it was, or so at least the rumour says, by foreign robbers. So Apollo did not bring it about that the child should kill its father, nor did Laius die in the dreadful way he feared by his child's hand. Yet that was how the message of the seers mapped out the future. Pay no attention to such things. What the God would show[28] he will need no help to show it, but bring it to light himself.

OEDIPUS: What restlessness of soul, lady, has come upon me since I heard you speak, what a tumult of the mind![29]

JOCASTA: What is this new anxiety? What has startled you?

OEDIPUS: You said that Laius was killed where three highways meet.

JOCASTA: Yes: that was the story.

OEDIPUS: And where is the place?

JOCASTA: In Phocis where the road divides branching off to Delphi and to Daulia.

OEDIPUS: And when did it happen? How many years ago?

JOCASTA: News was published in this town just before you came into power.

OEDIPUS: O Zeus! What have you planned to do unto me?

JOCASTA: He was tall; the silver had just come into his hair; and in shape not greatly unlike to you.[30]

OEDIPUS: Unhappy that I am! It seems that I have laid a dreadful curse upon myself, and did not know it.

JOCASTA: What do you say? I tremble when I look on you, my King.

OEDIPUS: And I have a misgiving that the seer can see indeed. But I will know it all more clearly, if you tell me one thing more.

JOCASTA: Indeed, though I tremble I will answer whatever you ask.

OEDIPUS: Had he but a small troop with him; or did he travel like a great man with many followers?

JOCASTA: There were but five in all – one of them a herald; and there was one carriage with Laius in it.

OEDIPUS: Alas! It is now clear indeed. Who was it brought the news, lady?

JOCASTA: A servant – the one survivor.

OEDIPUS: Is he by chance in the house now?

JOCASTA: No; for when he found you reigning instead of Laius he besought me, his hand clasped in mine, to send him to the fields among the cattle that he might be far from the sight of this town; and I sent him. He was a worthy man for a slave and might have asked a bigger thing.

OEDIPUS: I would have him return to us without delay.

JOCASTA: Oedipus, it is easy. But why do you ask this?

OEDIPUS: I fear that I have said too much, and therefore I would question him.[31]

JOCASTA: He shall come, but I too have a right to know what lies so heavy upon your heart, my King.

OEDIPUS: Yes: and it shall not be kept from you now that my fear has grown so heavy. Nobody is more to me than you, nobody has the same right to learn my good or evil luck.[32] My father was Polybus of Corinth, my mother the Dorian Merope, and I was held the foremost man in all that town until a thing happened – a thing to startle a man, though not to make him angry as it made me. We were sitting at the table, and a man who had drunk too much cried out that I was not my father's son – and I, though angry, restrained my anger for that day; but the next day went to my father and my mother and questioned them. They were indignant at the taunt and that comforted me – and yet the man's words rankled, for they had spread a rumour through the town. Without consulting my father or my mother I went to Delphi, but Phoebus told me nothing of the thing for which I came, but much of other things – things of sorrow and of terror: that I should live in incest with my mother, and beget a brood that men would shudder to look upon; that I should be my father's murderer. Hearing those words I fled out of Corinth, and from that day have but known where it lies when I have found its direction by the stars. I sought where I might escape those infamous things – the doom that was laid upon me. I came in my flight to that very spot where you tell me this king perished. Now, lady, I will tell you the truth. When I had come close up to those three roads, I came upon a herald, and a man like him you have described seated in a carriage. The man who held the reins and the old man himself would not give me room, but thought to force me from the path, and I struck the driver in my anger. The old man, seeing what I had done, waited till I was passing him and then struck me upon the head. I paid him back in full, for I knocked him out of the carriage with a blow of my stick. He rolled on his back, and after that I killed them all. If this stranger were indeed Laius, is there a more miserable man in the world than the man before you? Is there a man more hated of Heaven? No stranger, no citizen, may receive him into his house, not a soul may speak to him, and no mouth but my own mouth has laid this curse upon me. Am I not wretched? May I be swept from this world before I have endured this doom!

CHORUS: These things, O King, fill us with terror; yet hope till you speak with him that saw the deed, and have learnt all.

OEDIPUS: Till I have learnt all, I may hope. I await the man that is coming from the pastures.

JOCASTA: What is it that you hope to learn?

OEDIPUS: I will tell you. If his tale agrees with yours, then I am clear.

JOCASTA: What tale of mine?

OEDIPUS: He told you that Laius met his death from robbers; if he keeps to that tale now and speaks of several slayers, I am not the slayer. But if he says one lonely wayfarer, then beyond a doubt the scale dips to me.

JOCASTA: Be certain of this much at least, his first tale was of robbers. He cannot revoke that tale – the city heard it and not I alone. Yet, if he should somewhat change his story, King, at least he cannot make the murder of Laius square with prophecy; for Loxias plainly said of Laius that he would die by the hand of my child. That poor innocent did not kill him, for it died before him. Therefore from this out I would not, for all divination can do, so much as look to my right hand or to my left hand, or fear at all.

OEDIPUS: You have judged well; and yet for all that, send and bring this peasant to me.

JOCASTA: I will send without delay. I will do all that you would have of me – but let us come into the house. ·
    [*They go into the house.*]

Chorus

For this one thing above all I would be praised as a man,
That in my words and my deeds I have kept those laws in mind
Olympian Zeus, and that high clear Empyrean,
Fashioned, and not some man or people of mankind,
Even those sacred laws nor age nor sleep can blind.

A man becomes a tyrant out of insolence,
He climbs and climbs, until all people call him great,
He seems upon the summit, and God flings him thence;
Yet an ambitious man may lift up a whole State,
And in his death be blessed, in his life fortunate.

And all men honour such; but should a man forget
The holy images, the Delphian Sibyl's[33] trance,
And the world's navel-stone, and not be punished for it
And seem most fortunate, or even blessed perchance,
Why should we honour the Gods, or join the sacred dance?[34]
    [*Jocasta enters from the palace.*]

JOCASTA: It has come into my head, citizens of Thebes, to visit every altar of the Gods, a wreath in my hand and a dish of incense. For all manner of alarms trouble the soul of Oedipus, who instead of weighing new oracles by old, like a man of sense, is at the mercy of every mouth that speaks terror. Seeing that my words are nothing to him, I cry to you, Lysian Apollo, whose altar is the first I meet: I come, a suppliant, bearing symbols of prayer; O, make us clean, for now we are all afraid, seeing him afraid, even as they who see the helmsman afraid.

[*Enter Messenger.*]

MESSENGER: May I learn from you, strangers, where is the home of King Oedipus? Or better still, tell me where he himself is, if you know.

CHORUS: This is his house, and he himself, stranger, is within it, and this lady is the mother of his children.

MESSENGER: Then I call a blessing upon her, seeing what man she has married.

JOCASTA: May God reward those words with a like blessing, stranger! But what have you come to seek or to tell?

MESSENGER: Good news for your house, lady, and for your husband.

JOCASTA: What news? From whence have you come?

MESSENGER: From Corinth, and you will rejoice at the message I am about to give you; yet, maybe, it will grieve you.

JOCASTA: What is it? How can it have this double power?

MESSENGER: The people of Corinth, they say, will take him for king.

JOCASTA: How then? Is old Polybus no longer on the throne?

MESSENGER: No. He is in his tomb.

JOCASTA: What do you say? Is Polybus dead, old man?

MESSENGER: May I drop dead if it is not the truth.

JOCASTA: Away! Hurry to your master with this news. O oracle of the Gods, where are you now? This is the man whom Oedipus feared and shunned lest he should murder him, and now this man has died a natural death, and not by the hand of Oedipus.

[*Enter Oedipus.*]

OEDIPUS: Jocasta, dearest wife, why have you called me from the house?

JOCASTA: Listen to this man, and judge to what the oracles of the Gods have come.

OEDIPUS: And he – who may he be? And what news has he?

JOCASTA: He has come from Corinth to tell you that your father, Polybus, is dead.[35]

OEDIPUS: How, stranger? Let me have it from your own mouth.

MESSENGER: If I am to tell the story, the first thing is that he is dead and gone.

OEDIPUS: By some sickness or by treachery?

MESSENGER: A little thing can bring the aged to their rest.

OEDIPUS: Ah! He died, it seems, from sickness?

MESSENGER: Yes; and of old age.

OEDIPUS: Alas! Alas! Why, indeed, my wife, should one look to that Pythian seer, or to the birds that scream above our heads? For they would have it that I was doomed to kill my father. And now he is dead – hid already beneath the earth. And here am I – who had no part in it, unless indeed he died from longing for me. If that were so, I may have caused his death; but Polybus has carried the oracles with him into Hades[36] – the oracles as men have understood them – and they are worth nothing.

JOCASTA: Did I not tell you so, long since?

OEDIPUS: You did, but fear misled me.

JOCASTA: Put this trouble from you.

OEDIPUS: Those bold words[37] would sound better, were not my mother living. But as it is – I have some grounds for fear; yet you have said well.

JOCASTA: Yet your father's death is a sign that all is well.

OEDIPUS: I know that: but I fear because of her who lives.

MESSENGER: Who is this woman who makes you afraid?

OEDIPUS: Merope, old man, the wife of Polybus.

MESSENGER: What is there in her to make you afraid?

OEDIPUS: A dreadful oracle sent from Heaven, stranger.

MESSENGER: Is it a secret, or can you speak it out?

OEDIPUS: Loxias said that I was doomed to marry my own mother, and to shed my father's blood. For that reason I fled from my house in Corinth; and I did right, though there is great comfort in familiar faces.

MESSENGER: Was it indeed for that reason that you went into exile?

OEDIPUS: I did not wish, old man, to shed my father's blood.

MESSENGER: King, have I not freed you from that fear?

OEDIPUS: You shall be fittingly rewarded.

MESSENGER: Indeed, to tell the truth, it was for that I came; to bring you home and be the better for it—

OEDIPUS: No! I will never go to my parents' home.

MESSENGER: Ah, my son, it is plain enough, you do not know what you do.

OEDIPUS: How, old man? For God's love, tell me.

MESSENGER: If for these reasons you shrink from going home.

OEDIPUS: I am afraid lest Phoebus has spoken true.

MESSENGER: You are afraid of being made guilty through Merope?

OEDIPUS: That is my constant fear.

MESSENGER: A vain fear.

OEDIPUS: How so, if I was born of that father and mother?

MESSENGER: Because they were nothing to you in blood.

OEDIPUS: What do you say? Was Polybus not my father?

MESSENGER: No more nor less than myself.

OEDIPUS: How can my father be no more to me than you who are nothing to me?

MESSENGER: He did not beget you any more than I.

OEDIPUS: No? Then why did he call me his son?

MESSENGER: He took you as a gift from these hands of mine.

OEDIPUS: How could he love so dearly what came from another's hands?

MESSENGER: He had been childless.

OEDIPUS: If I am not your son, where did you get me?

MESSENGER: In a wooded valley of Cithaeron.[38]

OEDIPUS: What brought you wandering there?

MESSENGER: I was in charge of mountain sheep.

OEDIPUS: A shepherd – a wandering, hired man.

MESSENGER: A hired man who came just in time.

OEDIPUS: Just in time – had it come to that?

MESSENGER: Have not the cords left their marks upon your ankles?

OEDIPUS: Yes, that is an old trouble.

MESSENGER: I took your feet out of the spancel.

OEDIPUS: I have had those marks from the cradle.

MESSENGER: They have given you the name you bear.[39]

OEDIPUS: Tell me, for God's sake, was that deed my mother's or my father's?

MESSENGER: I do not know – he who gave you to me knows more of that than I.

OEDIPUS: What? You had me from another? You did not chance on me yourself?

MESSENGER: No. Another shepherd gave you to me.

OEDIPUS: Who was he? Can you tell me who he was?

MESSENGER: I think that he was said to be of Laius' household.

OEDIPUS: The king who ruled this country long ago?

MESSENGER: The same – the man was herdsman in his service.

OEDIPUS: Is he alive, that I might speak with him?

MESSENGER: You people of this country should know that.

OEDIPUS: Is there any one here present who knows the herd he speaks of? Any one who has seen him in the town pastures? The hour has come when all must be made clear.

CHORUS: I think he is the very herd you sent for but now; Jocasta can tell you better than I.

JOCASTA: Why ask about that man? Why think about him? Why waste a thought on what this man has said? What he has said is of no account.

OEDIPUS: What, with a clue like that in my hands and fail to find out my birth?

JOCASTA: For God's sake, if you set any value upon your life, give up this search – my misery is enough.

OEDIPUS: Though I be proved the son of a slave, yes, even of three generations of slaves, you cannot be made base-born.

JOCASTA: Yet, hear me, I implore you. Give up this search.

OEDIPUS: I will not hear of anything but searching the whole thing out.

JOCASTA: I am only thinking of your good – I have advised you for the best.

OEDIPUS: Your advice makes me impatient.

JOCASTA: May you never come to know who you are, unhappy man!

OEDIPUS: Go, some one, bring the herdsman here – and let that woman glory in her noble blood.

JOCASTA: Alas, alas, miserable man! Miserable! That is all that I can call you now or for ever.

[*She goes out.*]

CHORUS: Why has the lady gone, Oedipus, in such a transport of despair? Out of this silence will burst a storm of sorrows.

OEDIPUS: Let come what will. However lowly my origin I will discover it. That woman, with all a woman's pride, grows red with shame at my base birth. I think myself the child of Good Luck, and that the years are my foster-brothers. Sometimes they have set me up, and sometimes thrown me down, but he that has Good Luck for mother can suffer no dishonour. That is my origin, nothing can change it, so why should I renounce this search into my birth?

Chorus

Oedipus' nurse, mountain of many a hidden glen,
Be honoured among men;
A famous man, deep-thoughted, and his body strong;
Be honoured in dance and song.

Who met in the hidden glen? Who let his fancy run
Upon nymph of Helicon?
Lord Pan or Lord Apollo or the mountain Lord
By the Bacchantes adored?[40]

OEDIPUS: If I, who have never met the man, may venture to say so, I think that the herdsman we await approaches; his venerable age matches with this stranger's, and I recognise as servants of mine those who bring him. But you, if you have seen the man before, will know the man better than I.

CHORUS: Yes, I know the man who is coming; he was indeed in Laius' service, and is still the most trusted of the herdsmen.

OEDIPUS: I ask you first, Corinthian stranger, is this the man you mean?

MESSENGER: He is the very man.

OEDIPUS: Look at me, old man! Answer my questions. Were you once in Laius' service?

HERDSMAN: I was: not a bought slave, but reared up in the house.

OEDIPUS: What was your work – your manner of life?

HERDSMAN: For the best part of my life I have tended flocks.

OEDIPUS: Where, mainly?

HERDSMAN: Cithaeron or its neighbourhood.

OEDIPUS: Do you remember meeting with this man there?

HERDSMAN: What man do you mean?

OEDIPUS: This man. Did you ever meet him?

HERDSMAN: I cannot recall him to mind.

MESSENGER: No wonder in that, master; but I will bring back his memory. He and I lived side by side upon Cithaeron. I had but one flock and he had two. Three full half-years we lived there, from spring to autumn, and every winter I drove my flock to my own fold, while he drove his to the fold of Laius. Is that right? Was it not so?

HERDSMAN: True enough; though it was long ago.

MESSENGER: Come, tell me now – do you remember giving me a boy to rear as my own foster-son?

HERDSMAN: What are you saying? Why do you ask me that?

MESSENGER: Look at that man, my friend, he is the child you gave me.

HERDSMAN: A plague upon you! Cannot you hold your tongue?

OEDIPUS: Do not blame him, old man; your own words are more blameable.

HERDSMAN: And how have I offended, master?

OEDIPUS: In not telling of that boy he asks of.

HERDSMAN: He speaks from ignorance, and does not know what he is saying.

OEDIPUS: If you will not speak with a good grace you shall be made to speak.

HERDSMAN: Do not hurt me for the love of God, I am an old man.

OEDIPUS: Some one there, tie his hands behind his back.

HERDSMAN: Alas! Wherefore! What more would you learn?

OEDIPUS: Did you give this man the child he speaks of?

HERDSMAN: I did: would I had died that day!

OEDIPUS: Well, you may come to that unless you speak the truth.

HERDSMAN: Much more am I lost if I speak it.

OEDIPUS: What! Would the fellow make more delay?

HERDSMAN: No, no. I said before that I gave it to him.

OEDIPUS: Where did you come by it? Your own child, or another?

HERDSMAN: It was not my own child – I had it from another.

OEDIPUS: From any of those here? From what house?

HERDSMAN: Do not ask any more, master; for the love of God do not ask.

OEDIPUS: You are lost if I have to question you again.

HERDSMAN: It was a child from the house of Laius.

OEDIPUS: A slave? Or one of his own race?

HERDSMAN: Alas! I am on the edge of dreadful words.

OEDIPUS: And I of hearing: yet hear I must.

HERDSMAN: It was said to have been his own child. But your lady within can tell you of these things best.

OEDIPUS: How? It was she who gave it to you?

HERDSMAN: Yes, King.

OEDIPUS: To what end?

HERDSMAN: That I should make away with it.

OEDIPUS: Her own child?

HERDSMAN: Yes: from fear of evil prophecies.

OEDIPUS: What prophecies?

HERDSMAN: That he should kill his father.

OEDIPUS: Why, then, did you give him up to this old man?

HERDSMAN: Through pity, master, believing that he would carry him to whatever land he had himself come from – but he saved him for dreadful misery; for if you are what this man says, you are the most miserable of all men.

OEDIPUS: O! O! All brought to pass! All truth! Now, O light, may I look my last upon you, having been found accursed in bloodshed, accursed in marriage, and in my coming into the world accursed!

[*He rushes into the palace.*]

Chorus

What can the shadow-like generations of man attain
But build up a dazzling mockery of delight that under their touch
    dissolves again?

Oedipus seemed blessed, but there is no man blessed amongst men.

Oedipus overcame the woman-breasted[41] Fate;
He seemed like a strong tower against Death and first among the
    fortunate;
He sat upon the ancient throne of Thebes, and all men called him
    great.

But, looking for a marriage-bed, he found the bed of his birth,
Tilled the field his father had tilled, cast seed into the same abounding
    earth;
Entered through the door that had sent him wailing forth.

Begetter and begot as one! How could that be hid?
What darkness cover up that marriage-bed? Time watches, he is
    eagle-eyed,
And all the works of man are known and every soul is tried.

Would you had never come to Thebes, nor to this house,
Nor riddled with the woman-breasted Fate, beaten off Death and
    succoured us,
That I had never raised this song, heartbroken Oedipus![42]

SECOND MESSENGER [*coming from the house*]: Friends and kinsmen
of this house! What deeds must you look upon, what burden of
sorrow bear, if true to race you still love the House of Labdacus.
For not Ister nor Phasis[43] could wash this house clean, so many
misfortunes have been brought upon it, so many has it brought upon
itself, and those misfortunes are always the worst that a man brings
upon himself.

CHORUS: Great already are the misfortunes of this house, and you
bring us a new tale.

SECOND MESSENGER: A short tale in the telling: Jocasta, our Queen,
is dead.

CHORUS: Alas, miserable woman, how did she die?

SECOND MESSENGER: By her own hand. It cannot be as terrible to
you as to one that saw it with his eyes, yet so far as words can serve,
you shall see it. When she had come into the vestibule, she ran half
crazed towards her marriage-bed, clutching at her hair with the
fingers of both hands, and once within the chamber dashed the doors
together behind her. Then called upon the name of Laius, long since
dead, remembering that son who killed the father and upon the

mother begot an accursed race. And wailed because of that marriage wherein she had borne a two-fold race – husband by husband, children by her child. Then Oedipus with a shriek burst in and running here and there asked for a sword, asked where he would find the wife that was no wife but a mother who had borne his children and himself. Nobody answered him, we all stood dumb; but supernatural power helped him, for, with a dreadful shriek, as though beckoned, he sprang at the double doors, drove them in, burst the bolts out of their sockets, and ran into the room. There we saw the woman hanging in a swinging halter, and with a terrible cry he loosened the halter from her neck. When that unhappiest woman lay stretched upon the ground, we saw another dreadful sight. He dragged the golden brooches from her dress and lifting them struck them upon his eyeballs, crying out, 'You have looked enough upon those you ought never to have looked upon, failed long enough to know those that you should have known; henceforth you shall be dark'. He struck his eyes, not once, but many times, lifting his hands and speaking such or like words. The blood poured down and not with a few slow drops, but all at once over his beard in a dark shower as it were hail.

[*The Chorus wails and he steps further on to the stage.*]

Such evils have come forth from the deeds of those two and fallen not on one alone but upon husband and wife. They inherited much happiness, much good fortune; but to-day, ruin, shame, death, and loud crying, all evils that can be counted up, all, all are theirs.

CHORUS: Is he any quieter?

SECOND MESSENGER: He cries for some one to unbar the gates and to show to all the men of Thebes his father's murderer, his mother's – the unholy word must not be spoken. It is his purpose to cast himself out of the land that he may not bring all this house under his curse. But he has not the strength to do it. He must be supported and led away. The curtain is parting,[44] you are going to look upon a sight which even those who shudder must pity.

[*Enter Oedipus.*[45]]

OEDIPUS: Woe, woe is me! Miserable, miserable that I am! Where am I? Where am I going? Where am I cast away? Who hears my words?

CHORUS: Cast away indeed, dreadful to the sight of the eye, dreadful to the ear.

OEDIPUS: Ah, friend, the only friend left to me, friend still faithful to the blind man! I know that you are there; blind though I am, I recognise your voice.

CHORUS: Where did you get the courage to put out your eyes? What unearthly power drove you to that?

OEDIPUS: Apollo, friends, Apollo, but it was my own hand alone, wretched that I am, that quenched these eyes.

CHORUS: You were better dead than blind.

OEDIPUS: No, it is better to be blind. What sight is there that could give me joy? How could I have looked into the face of my father when I came among the dead, aye, or on my miserable mother, since against them both I sinned such things that no halter can punish? And what to me this spectacle, town, statue, wall, and what to me this people, since I, thrice wretched, I, noblest of Theban men, have doomed myself to banishment, doomed myself when I commanded all to thrust out the unclean thing?

CHORUS: It had indeed been better if that herdsman had never taken your feet out of the spancel or brought you back to life.

OEDIPUS: O three roads, O secret glen; O coppice and narrow way where three roads met; you that drank up the blood I spilt, the blood that was my own, my father's blood: remember what deeds I wrought for you to look upon, and then, when I had come hither, the new deeds that I wrought. O marriage-bed that gave me birth and after that gave children to your child, creating an incestuous kindred of fathers, brothers, sons, wives, and mothers. Yes, all the shame and the uncleanness that I have wrought among men.

CHORUS: For all my pity I shudder and turn away.

OEDIPUS: Come near, condescend to lay your hands upon a wretched man; listen, do not fear. My plague can touch no man but me. Hide me somewhere out of this land for God's sake, or kill me, or throw me into the sea where you shall never look upon me more.

[*Enter Creon and attendants.*]

CHORUS: Here Creon comes at a fit moment; you can ask of him what you will, help or counsel, for he is now in your place. He is King.

OEDIPUS: What can I say to him? What can I claim, having been altogether unjust to him?

CREON: I have not come in mockery, Oedipus, nor to reproach you. Lead him into the house as quickly as you can. Do not let him display his misery before strangers.

OEDIPUS: I must obey, but first, since you have come in so noble a spirit, you will hear me.

CREON: Say what you will.

OEDIPUS: I know that you will give her that lies within such a tomb as befits your own blood, but there is something more, Creon. My sons are men and can take care of themselves, but my daughters, my two unhappy daughters, that have ever eaten at my own table and shared my food, watch over my daughters, Creon. If it is lawful, let me touch them with my hands. Grant it, Prince, grant it, noble heart. I would believe, could I touch them, that I still saw them.

[Ismene and Antigone are led in by attendants.]

But do I hear them sobbing? Has Creon pitied me and sent my children, my darlings? Has he done this?

CREON: Yes, I ordered it, for I know how greatly you have always loved them.

OEDIPUS: Then may you be blessed, and may Heaven be kinder to you than it has been to me! My children, where are you? Come hither – hither – come to the hands of him whose mother was your mother; the hands that put out your father's eyes, eyes once as bright as your own; his who, understanding nothing, seeing nothing, became your father by her that bore him. I weep when I think of the bitter life that men will make you live, and the days that are to come. Into what company dare you go, to what festival, but that you shall return home from it not sharing in the joys, but bathed in tears? When you are old enough to be married, what man dare face the reproach that must cling to you and to your children? What misery is there lacking? Your father killed his father, he begat you at the spring of his own being, offspring of her that bore him. That is the taunt that would be cast upon you and on the man that you should marry. That man is not alive; my children, you must wither away in barrenness. Ah, son of Menoeceus, listen. Seeing that you are the only father now left to them, for we their parents are lost, both of us lost, do not let them wander in beggary – are they not your own kindred? – do not let them sink down into my misery. No, pity them, seeing them utterly wretched in helpless childhood if you do not protect them. Show me that you promise, generous man, by touching me with your hand. *[Creon touches him.]* My children, there is much advice that I would give you were you but old enough to understand, but all I can do now is bid you pray that you may live wherever you are let live, and that your life be happier than your father's.

CREON: Enough of tears. Pass into the house.

OEDIPUS: I will obey, though upon conditions.

CREON: Conditions?

OEDIPUS: Banish me from this country. I know that nothing can destroy me, for I wait some incredible fate; yet cast me upon Cithaeron, chosen by my father and my mother for my tomb.

CREON: Only the Gods can say yes or no to that.

OEDIPUS: No, for I am hateful to the Gods.

CREON: If that be so you will get your wish the quicker. They will banish that which they hate.

OEDIPUS: Are you certain of that?

CREON: I would not say it if I did not mean it.

OEDIPUS: Then it is time to lead me within.

CREON: Come, but let your children go.

OEDIPUS: No, do not take them from me.

CREON: Do not seek to be master; you won the mastery but could not keep it to the end.

[*He leads Oedipus into the palace, followed by Ismene, Antigone, and attendants.*]

Chorus

Make way for Oedipus. All people said,
'That is a fortunate man';
And now what storms are beating on his head!
Call no man fortunate that is not dead.
The dead are free from pain.

THE END

THE RESURRECTION

Persons in the Play

THE HEBREW
THE GREEK
THE SYRIAN
CHRIST
THREE MUSICIANS

Before I had finished this play I saw that its subject-matter might make it unsuited for the public stage in England or in Ireland. I had begun it with an ordinary stage scene in the mind's eye, curtained walls, a window and door at back, a curtained door at left.[1] I now changed the stage directions and wrote songs for the unfolding and folding of the curtain that it might be played in a studio or a drawing-room like my dance plays,[2] or at the Peacock Theatre[3] before a specially chosen audience. If it is played at the Peacock Theatre the Musicians may sing the opening and closing songs, as they pull apart or pull together the proscenium curtains; the whole stage may be hung with curtains with an opening at the left. While the play is in progress the Musicians will sit towards the right of the audience; if at the Peacock, on the step which separates the stage from the audience, or one on either side of the proscenium.

[*Song for the unfolding and folding of the curtain.*]

I

I saw a staring virgin stand
Where holy Dionysus died,
And tear the heart out of his side,
And lay the heart upon her hand
And bear that beating heart away;
And then did all the Muses sing
Of Magnus Annus at the spring,
As though God's death were but a play.

II

Another Troy must rise and set,

> Another lineage feed the crow,
> Another Argo's painted prow
> Drive to a flashier bauble yet.
> The Roman Empire stood appalled:
> It dropped the reins of peace and war
> When that fierce virgin and her Star
> Out of the fabulous darkness called.[4]

[*The Hebrew is discovered alone upon the stage; he has a sword or spear. The Musicians make faint drum-taps, or sound a rattle; the Greek enters through the audience from the left.*]

THE HEBREW: Did you find out what the noise was?

THE GREEK: Yes, I asked a Rabbi.

THE HEBREW: Were you not afraid?

THE GREEK: How could he know that I am called a Christian? I wore the cap I brought from Alexandria. He said the followers of Dionysus were parading the streets with rattles and drums; that such a thing had never happened in this city before; that the Roman authorities were afraid to interfere. The followers of Dionysus have been out among the fields tearing a goat to pieces and drinking its blood, and are now wandering through the streets like a pack of wolves. The mob was so terrified of their frenzy that it left them alone, or, as seemed more likely, so busy hunting Christians it had time for nothing else. I turned to go, but he called me back and asked where I lived. When I said outside the gates, he asked if it was true that the dead had broken out of the cemeteries.[5]

THE HEBREW: We can keep the mob off for some minutes, long enough for the Eleven[6] to escape over the roofs. I shall defend the narrow stair between this and the street until I am killed, then you will take my place. Why is not the Syrian here?

THE GREEK: I met him at the door and sent him on a message; he will be back before long.

THE HEBREW: The three of us will be few enough for the work in hand.

THE GREEK [*glancing towards the opening at the left*]: What are they doing now?

THE HEBREW: While you were down below, James brought a loaf out of a bag, and Nathanael found a skin of wine. They put them on the table. It was a long time since they had eaten anything. Then they began to speak in low voices, and John spoke of the last time they had eaten in that room.

THE GREEK: They were thirteen then.

THE HEBREW: He said that Jesus divided bread and wine amongst them.[7] When John had spoken they sat still, nobody eating or drinking. If you stand here you will see them. That is Peter close to the window. He has been quite motionless for a long time, his head upon his breast.

THE GREEK: Is it true that when the soldier asked him if he were a follower of Jesus he denied it?[8]

THE HEBREW: Yes, it is true. James told me. Peter told the others what he had done. But when the moment came they were all afraid. I must not blame. I might have been no braver. What are we all but dogs who have lost their master?

THE GREEK: Yet you and I if the mob come will die rather than let it up that stair.

THE HEBREW: Ah! That is different. I am going to draw that curtain; they must not hear what I am going to say.

[He draws curtain.]

THE GREEK: I know what is in your mind.

THE HEBREW: They are afraid because they do not know what to think. When Jesus was taken they could no longer believe him the Messiah. We can find consolation, but for the Eleven it was always complete light or complete darkness.

THE GREEK: Because they are so much older.

THE HEBREW: No, no. You have only to look into their faces to see they were intended to be saints. They are unfitted for anything else. What makes you laugh?[9]

THE GREEK: Something I can see through the window. There, where I am pointing. There, at the end of the street.

[They stand together looking out over the heads of the audience.]

THE HEBREW: I cannot see anything.

THE GREEK: The hill.

THE HEBREW: That is Calvary.

THE GREEK: And the three crosses on the top of it. [He laughs again.]

THE HEBREW: Be quiet. You do not know what you are doing. You have gone out of your mind. You are laughing at Calvary.

THE GREEK: No, no. I am laughing because they thought they were nailing the hands of a living man upon the Cross, and all the time there was nothing there but a phantom.

THE HEBREW: I saw him buried.

THE GREEK: We Greeks understand these things. No god has ever been buried; no god has ever suffered. Christ only seemed to be born, only seemed to eat, seemed to sleep, seemed to walk, seemed to die. I did not mean to tell you until I had proof.

THE HEBREW: Proof?

THE GREEK: I shall have proof before nightfall.

THE HEBREW: You talk wildly, but a masterless dog can bay the moon.

THE GREEK: No Jew can understand these things.

THE HEBREW: It is you who do not understand. It is I and those men in there, perhaps, who begin to understand at last. He was nothing more than a man, the best man who ever lived. Nobody before him had so pitied human misery. He preached the coming of the Messiah because he thought the Messiah would take it all upon himself. Then some day when he was very tired, after a long journey perhaps, he thought that he himself was the Messiah. He thought it because of all destinies it seemed the most terrible.

THE GREEK: How could a man think himself the Messiah?

THE HEBREW: It was always foretold that he would be born of a woman.

THE GREEK: To say that a god can be born of a woman, carried in her womb, fed upon her breast, washed as children are washed, is the most terrible blasphemy.

THE HEBREW: If the Messiah were not born of a woman he could not take away the sins of man. Every sin starts a stream of suffering, but the Messiah takes it all away.

THE GREEK: Every man's sins are his property. Nobody else has a right to them.

THE HEBREW: The Messiah is able to exhaust human suffering as though it were all gathered together in the spot of a burning-glass.

THE GREEK: That makes me shudder. The utmost possible suffering as an object of worship! You are morbid because your nation has no statues.[10]

THE HEBREW: What I have described is what I thought until three days ago.[11]

THE GREEK: I say that there is nothing in the tomb.

THE HEBREW: I saw him carried up the mountain and the tomb shut upon him.

THE GREEK: I have sent the Syrian to the tomb to prove that there is nothing there.

THE HEBREW: You knew the danger we were all in and yet you weakened our guard?

THE GREEK: I have risked the apostles' lives and our own. What I have sent the Syrian to find out is more important.

THE HEBREW: None of us are in our right mind to-day. I have got something in my own head that shocks me.

THE GREEK: Something you do not want to speak about?

THE HEBREW: I am glad that he was not the Messiah; we might all have been deceived to our lives' end, or learnt the truth too late. One had to sacrifice everything that the divine suffering might, as it were, descend into one's mind and soul and make them pure. [*A sound of rattles and drums, at first in short bursts that come between sentences, but gradually growing continuous.*[12]] One had to give up all worldly knowledge, all ambition, do nothing of one's own will. Only the divine could have any reality. God had to take complete possession. It must be a terrible thing when one is old, and the tomb round the corner, to think of all the ambitions one has put aside; to think, perhaps, a great deal about women. I want to marry and have children.

THE GREEK [*who is standing facing the audience, and looking out over their heads*]: It is the worshippers of Dionysus. They are under the window now. There is a group of women who carry upon their shoulders a bier with an image of the dead god upon it. No, they are not women. They are men dressed as women. I have seen something like it in Alexandria. They are all silent, as if something were going to happen. My God! What a spectacle! In Alexandria a few men paint their lips vermilion. They imitate women that they may attain in worship a woman's self-abandonment. No great harm comes of it – but here! Come and look for yourself.

THE HEBREW: I will not look at such madmen.

THE GREEK: Though the music has stopped, some men are still dancing, and some of the dancers have gashed themselves with knives, imagining themselves, I suppose, at once the god and the Titans that murdered him. A little further off a man and woman are coupling in the middle of the street. She thinks the surrender to some man the dance threw into her arms may bring her god back to life. All are from the foreign quarter, to judge by face and costume, and are the most ignorant and excitable class of Asiatic Greeks, the dregs of the population. Such people suffer terribly and seek forgetfulness in monstrous ceremonies. Ah, that is what they were waiting for. The crowd has parted to make way for a singer. It is a girl. No, not a girl; a boy from the theatre. I know him. He acts girls' parts. He is dressed as a girl, but his finger-nails are gilded and his wig is made of gilded cords. He looks like a statue out of some temple. I remember something of the kind in Alexandria. Three days after the full moon, a full moon in March,[13] they sing the death of the god and pray for his resurrection.

[*One of the Musicians sings the following song.*]

> Astrea's[14] holy child!
> A rattle in the wood
> Where a Titan strode!
> His rattle drew the child
> Into that solitude.

Barrum, barrum, barrum [*Drum-taps accompany and follow the words*].

> We wandering women,
> Wives for all that come,
> Tried to draw him home;
> And every wandering woman
> Beat upon a drum.

Barrum, barrum, barrum [*Drum-taps as before*].

> But the murderous Titans
> Where the woods grow dim
> Stood and waited him.
> The great hands of those Titans
> Tore limb from limb.

Barrum, barrum, barrum [*Drum-taps as before*].

> On virgin Astrea
> That can succour all
> Wandering women call;
> Call out to Astrea

That the moon stood at the full.

Barrum, barrum, barrum [*Drum-taps as before*].

THE GREEK: I cannot think all that self-surrender and self-abasement is Greek, despite the Greek name of its god. When the goddess came to Achilles in the battle she did not interfere with his soul, she took him by his yellow hair.[15] Lucretius[16] thinks that the gods appear in the visions of the day and night but are indifferent to human fate; that, however, is the exaggeration of a Roman rhetorician. They can be discovered by contemplation, in their faces a high keen joy like the cry of a bat, and the man who lives heroically gives them the only earthly body that they covet. He, as it were, copies their gestures and their acts. What seems their indifference is but their eternal possession of themselves. Man, too, remains separate. He does not surrender his soul. He keeps his privacy.[17]

[*Drum-taps to represent knocking at the door.*]

THE HEBREW: There is someone at the door, but I dare not open with that crowd in the street.

THE GREEK: You need not be afraid. The crowd has begun to move away. [*The Hebrew goes down into the audience towards the left.*] I deduce from our great philosophers that a god can overwhelm man with disaster, take health and wealth away, but man keeps his privacy. If that is the Syrian he may bring such confirmation that mankind will never forget his words.

THE HEBREW [*from amongst the audience*]: It is the Syrian. There is something wrong. He is ill or drunk.

[*He helps the Syrian on to the stage.*]

THE SYRIAN: I am like a drunken man. I can hardly stand upon my feet. Something incredible has happened.[18] I have run all the way.

THE HEBREW: Well?

THE SYRIAN: I must tell the Eleven at once. Are they still in there? Everybody must be told.

THE HEBREW: What is it? Get your breath and speak.

THE SYRIAN: I was on my way to the tomb. I met the Galilean women, Mary the mother of Jesus, Mary the mother of James, and the other women. The younger women were pale with excitement and began to speak all together. I did not know what they were saying; but Mary the mother of James said that they had been to the tomb at daybreak and found that it was empty.

THE GREEK: Ah!

THE HEBREW: The tomb cannot be empty. I will not believe it.

THE SYRIAN: At the door stood a man all shining, and cried out that Christ had arisen. [*Faint drum-taps and the faint sound of a rattle.*] As they came down the mountain a man stood suddenly at their side; that man was Christ himself. They stooped down and kissed his feet.[19] Now stand out of my way that I may tell Peter and James and John.

THE HEBREW [*standing before the curtained entrance of the inner room*]: I will not stand out of the way.

THE SYRIAN: Did you hear what I said? Our master has arisen.

THE HEBREW: I will not have the Eleven disturbed for the dreams of women.

THE GREEK: The women were not dreaming. They told you the truth, and yet this man is in the right. He is in charge here. We must all be convinced before we speak to the Eleven.

THE SYRIAN: The Eleven will be able to judge better than we.

THE GREEK: Though we are so much younger we know more of the world than they do.

THE HEBREW: If you told your story they would no more believe it than I do, but Peter's misery would be increased. I know him longer than you do and I know what would happen. Peter would remember that the women did not flinch; that not one amongst them denied her master; that the dream proved their love and faith. Then he would remember that he had lacked both, and imagine that John was looking at him. He would turn away and bury his head in his hands.

THE GREEK: I said that we must all be convinced, but there is another reason why you must not tell them anything. Somebody else is coming. I am certain that Jesus never had a human body; that he is a phantom and can pass through that wall; that he will so pass; that he will pass through this room; that he himself will speak to the apostles.

THE SYRIAN: He is no phantom. We put a great stone over the mouth of the tomb, and the women say that it has been rolled back.

THE HEBREW: The Romans heard yesterday that some of our people planned to steal the body, and to put abroad a story that Christ had arisen; and so escape the shame of our defeat. They probably stole it in the night.

THE SYRIAN: The Romans put sentries at the tomb. The women found the sentries asleep. Christ had put them asleep that they might not see him move the stone.

THE GREEK: A hand without bones, without sinews, cannot move a stone.

THE SYRIAN: What matter if it contradicts all human knowledge? – another Argo seeks another fleece, another Troy is sacked.

THE GREEK: Why are you laughing?[20]

THE SYRIAN: What is human knowledge?

THE GREEK: The knowledge that keeps the road from here to Persia free from robbers, that has built the beautiful humane cities, that has made the modern world, that stands between us and the barbarian.

THE SYRIAN: But what if there is something it cannot explain, something more important than anything else?

THE GREEK: You talk as if you wanted the barbarian back.

THE SYRIAN: What if there is always something that lies outside knowledge, outside order? What if at the moment when knowledge and order seem complete that something appears?

[He has begun to laugh.]

THE HEBREW: Stop laughing.

THE SYRIAN: What if the irrational return? What if the circle begin again?

THE HEBREW: Stop! He laughed when he saw Calvary through the window, and now you laugh.

THE GREEK: He too has lost control of himself.

THE HEBREW: Stop, I tell you. [Drums and rattles.]

THE SYRIAN: But I am not laughing. It is the people out there who are laughing.

THE HEBREW: No, they are shaking rattles and beating drums.

THE SYRIAN: I thought they were laughing. How horrible!

THE GREEK [looking out over heads of audience]: The worshippers of Dionysus are coming this way again. They have hidden their image of the dead god, and have begun their lunatic cry, 'God has arisen! God has arisen!'

[*The Musicians who have been saying 'God has arisen!' fall silent.*]
They will cry 'God has arisen!' through all the streets of the city.
They can make their god live and die at their pleasure; but why are
they silent? They are dancing silently. They are coming nearer and
nearer, dancing all the while, using some kind of ancient step unlike
anything I have seen in Alexandria. They are almost under the
window now.

THE HEBREW: They have come back to mock us, because their god
arises every year, whereas our god is dead for ever.

THE GREEK: How they roll their painted eyes as the dance grows
quicker and quicker! They are under the window. Why are they all
suddenly motionless? Why are all those unseeing eyes turned upon
this house? Is there anything strange about this house?

THE HEBREW: Somebody has come into the room.

THE GREEK: Where?

THE HEBREW: I do not know; but I thought I heard a step.

THE GREEK: I knew that he would come.

THE HEBREW: There is no one here. I shut the door at the foot of the
steps.

THE GREEK: The curtain over there is moving.

THE HEBREW: No, it is quite still, and besides there is nothing behind
it but a blank wall.

THE GREEK: Look, look!

THE HEBREW: Yes, it has begun to move.
[*During what follows he backs in terror towards the left-hand
corner of the stage.*]

THE GREEK: There is someone coming through it.
[*The figure of Christ wearing a recognisable but stylistic mask
enters through the curtain. The Syrian slowly draws back the
curtain that shuts off the inner room where the apostles are. The
three young men are towards the left of the stage, the figure of
Christ is at the back towards the right.*]

THE GREEK: It is the phantom of our master. Why are you afraid? He
has been crucified and buried, but only in semblance, and is among
us once more. [*The Hebrew kneels.*] There is nothing here but a

phantom, it has no flesh and blood. Because I know the truth I am not afraid. Look, I will touch it. It may be hard under my hand like a statue – I have heard of such things – or my hand may pass through it – but there is no flesh and blood. [*He goes slowly up to the figure and passes his hand over its side.*] The heart of a phantom is beating! The heart of a phantom is beating![21]

[*He screams. The figure of Christ crosses the stage and passes into the inner room.*]

THE SYRIAN: He is standing in the midst of them. Some are afraid. He looks at Peter and James and John. He smiles. He has parted the clothes at his side. He shows them his side. There is a great wound there. Thomas has put his hand into the wound. He has put his hand where the heart is.[22]

THE GREEK: O Athens, Alexandria, Rome,[23] something has come to destroy you. The heart of a phantom is beating. Man has begun to die. Your words are clear at last, O Heraclitus.[24] God and man die each other's life, live each other's death.

[*The Musicians rise, one or more singing the following words. If the performance is in a private room or studio, they unfold and fold a curtain as in my dance plays; if at the Peacock Theatre, they draw the proscenium curtain across.*]

I

In pity for man's darkening thought
He walked that room and issued thence
In Galilean turbulence;
The Babylonian starlight brought
A fabulous, formless darkness in;
Odour of blood when Christ was slain
Made all Platonic tolerance vain
And vain all Doric discipline.

II

Everything that man esteems
Endures a moment or a day:
Love's pleasure drives his love away,
The painter's brush consumes his dreams;
The herald's cry, the soldier's tread
Exhaust his glory and his might:

Whatever flames upon the night
Man's own resinous heart has fed.[25]

THE END

THE WORDS UPON THE WINDOW-PANE

IN MEMORY OF
LADY GREGORY
IN WHOSE HOUSE IT WAS WRITTEN

Persons in the Play

DR. TRENCH
MISS MACKENNA
JOHN CORBET
CORNELIUS PATTERSON
ABRAHAM JOHNSON
MRS. MALLET
MRS. HENDERSON

A lodging-house room, an armchair, a little table in front of it, chairs on either side. A fireplace and window. A kettle on the hob and some tea-things on a dresser. A door to back and towards the right. Through the door one can see an entrance hall. The sound of a knocker. Miss Mackenna passes through and then she re-enters hall together with John Corbet, a man of twenty-two or twenty-three, and Dr. Trench, a man of between sixty and seventy.

DR. TRENCH [*in hall*]: May I introduce John Corbet, one of the Corbets of Ballymoney, but at present a Cambridge student? This is Miss Mackenna, our energetic secretary.

   [*They come into room, take off their coats.*]

MISS MACKENNA: I thought it better to let you in myself. This country is still sufficiently medieval to make spiritualism an undesirable theme for gossip. Give me your coats and hats, I will put them in my own room. It is just across the hall. Better sit down; your watches must be fast. Mrs. Henderson is lying down, as she always does before a séance. We won't begin for ten minutes yet.

[*She goes out with hats and coats.*]

DR. TRENCH: Miss Mackenna does all the real work of the Dublin Spiritualists' Association. She did all the correspondence with Mrs. Henderson, and persuaded the landlady to let her this big room and a small room upstairs. We are a poor society and could not guarantee anything in advance. Mrs. Henderson has come from London at her own risk. She was born in Dublin and wants to spread the movement here. She lives very economically and does not expect a great deal. We all give what we can. A poor woman with the soul of an apostle.

JOHN CORBET: Have there been many séances?

DR. TRENCH: Only three so far.

JOHN CORBET: I hope she will not mind my scepticism. I have looked into Myers' *Human Personality* and a wild book by Conan Doyle,[1] but am unconvinced.

DR. TRENCH: We all have to find the truth for ourselves. Lord Dunraven, then Lord Adare, introduced my father to the famous David Home.[2] My father often told me that he saw David Home floating in the air in broad daylight, but I did not believe a word of it. I had to investigate for myself, and I was very hard to convince. Mrs. Piper,[3] an American trance medium, not unlike Mrs. Henderson, convinced me.

JOHN CORBET: A state of somnambulism and voices coming through her lips that purport to be those of dead persons?[4]

DR. TRENCH: Exactly: quite the best kind of mediumship if you want to establish the identity of a spirit. But do not expect too much. There has been a hostile influence.

JOHN CORBET: You mean an evil spirit?

DR. TRENCH: The poet Blake[5] said that he never knew a bad man that had not something very good about him. I say a hostile influence, an influence that disturbed the last séance very seriously. I cannot tell you what happened, for I have not been at any of Mrs. Henderson's séances. Trance mediumship has nothing new to show me – I told the young people when they made me their President that I would probably stay at home, that I could get more out of Emanuel Swedenborg[6] than out of any séance. [*A knock.*] That is probably old Cornelius Patterson; he thinks they race horses and whippets in the other world, and is, so they tell me, so anxious to find out if he is right that he is always punctual. Miss Mackenna will keep him to herself for some minutes. He gives her tips for Harold's Cross.[7]

[*Miss Mackenna crosses to hall[8] door and admits Cornelius Patterson. She brings him to her room across the hall.*]

JOHN CORBET [*who has been wandering about*]: This is a wonderful room for a lodging-house.

DR. TRENCH: It was a private house until about fifty years ago. It was not so near the town in those days, and there are large stables at the back. Quite a number of notable people lived her. Grattan was born upstairs; no, not Grattan,[9] Curran[10] perhaps – I forget – but I do know that this house in the early part of the eighteenth century belonged to friends of Jonathan Swift,[11] or rather of Stella.[12] Swift chaffed her in the *Journal to Stella*[13] because of certain small sums of money she lost at cards probably in this very room. That was before Vanessa[14] appeared upon the scene. It was a country-house in those days, surrounded by trees and gardens. Somebody cut some lines from a poem of hers upon the window-pane – tradition says Stella herself. [*A knock.*] Here they are, but you will hardly make them out in this light.

[*They stand in the window. Corbet stoops down to see better. Miss Mackenna and Abraham Johnson enter and stand near door.*]

ABRAHAM JOHNSON: Where is Mrs. Henderson?

MISS MACKENNA: She is upstairs; she always rests before a séance.

ABRAHAM JOHNSON: I must see her before the séance. I know exactly what to do to get rid of this evil influence.

MISS MACKENNA: If you go up to see her there will be no séance at all. She says it is dangerous even to think, much less to speak, of an evil influence.

ABRAHAM JOHNSON: Then I shall speak to the President.

MISS MACKENNA: Better talk the whole thing over first in my room. Mrs. Henderson says that there must be perfect harmony.

ABRAHAM JOHNSON: Something must be done. The last séance was completely spoiled.

[*A knock.*]

MISS MACKENNA: That may be Mrs. Mallet; she is a very experienced spiritualist. Come to my room, old Patterson and some others are there already.

[*She brings him to the other room and later crosses to hall door to admit Mrs. Mallet.*]

JOHN CORBET: I know those lines well – they are part of a poem Stella wrote for Swift's fifty-fourth birthday.[15] Only three poems of hers – and some lines she added to a poem of Swift's – have come down to us, but they are enough to prove her a better poet than Swift. Even those few words on the window make me think of a seventeenth-century poet, Donne[16] or Crashaw.[17] [*He quotes.*]

> 'You taught how I might youth prolong
> By knowing what is right and wrong;
> How from my heart to bring supplies
> Of lustre to my fading eyes.'

How strange that a celibate scholar, well on in life, should keep the love of two such women! He met Vanessa in London at the height of his political power. She followed him to Dublin. She loved him for nine years, perhaps died of love, but Stella loved him all her life.

DR. TRENCH: I have shown that writing to several persons, and you are the first who has recognised the lines.

JOHN CORBET: I am writing an essay on Swift and Stella for my doctorate at Cambridge. I hope to prove that in Swift's day men of intellect reached the height of their power – the greatest position they ever attained in society and the State, that everything great in Ireland and in our character, in what remains of our architecture, comes from that day; that we have kept its seal longer than England.[18]

DR. TRENCH: A tragic life: Bolingbroke, Harley, Ormonde,[19] all those great Ministers that were his friends, banished and broken.

JOHN CORBET: I do not think you can explain him in that way – his tragedy had deeper foundations. His ideal order was the Roman Senate, his ideal men Brutus and Cato.[20] Such an order and such men had seemed possible once more, but the movement passed and he foresaw the ruin to come, Democracy, Rousseau, the French Revolution;[21] that is why he hated the common run of men, – 'I hate lawyers, I hate doctors,' he said, 'though I love Dr. So-and-so and Judge So-and-so' – that is why he wrote *Gulliver*,[22] that is why he wore out his brain, that is why he felt *saeva indignatio*,[23] that is why he sleeps under the greatest epitaph in history. You remember how it goes? It is almost finer in English than in Latin: 'He has gone where fierce indignation can lacerate his heart no more.'

[*Abraham Johnson comes in, followed by Mrs. Mallet and Cornelius Patterson.*]

ABRAHAM JOHNSON: Something must be done, Dr. Trench, to drive away the influence that has destroyed our séances. I have come here week after week at considerable expense. I am from Belfast. I am by profession a minister of the Gospel, I do a great deal of work among the poor and ignorant. I produce considerable effect by singing and preaching, but I know that my effect should be much greater than it is. My hope is that I shall be able to communicate with the great Evangelist Moody. I want to ask him to stand invisible beside me when I speak or sing, and lay his hands upon my head and give me such a portion of his power that my work may be blessed as the work of Moody and Sankey[24] was blessed.

MRS. MALLET: What Mr. Johnson says about the hostile influence is quite true. The last two séances were completely spoilt. I am thinking of starting a tea-shop in Folkestone. I followed Mrs. Henderson to Dublin to get my husband's advice, but two spirits kept talking and would not let any other spirit say a word.

DR. TRENCH: Did the spirits say the same thing and go through the same drama at both séances?

MRS. MALLET: Yes – just as if they were characters in some kind of horrible play.

DR. TRENCH: That is what I was afraid of.

MRS. MALLET: My husband was drowned at sea ten years ago, but constantly speaks to me through Mrs. Henderson as if he were still alive. He advises me about everything I do, and I am utterly lost if I cannot question him.

CORNELIUS PATTERSON: I never did like the Heaven they talk about in churches: but when somebody told me that Mrs. Mallet's husband ate and drank and went about with his favourite dog, I said to myself, 'That is the place for Corney Patterson'. I came here to find out if it was true, and I declare to God I have not heard one word about it.

ABRAHAM JOHNSON: I ask you, Dr. Trench, as President of the Dublin Spiritualists' Association, to permit me to read the ritual of exorcism appointed for such occasions. After the last séance I copied it out of an old book in the library of Belfast University. I have it here. [He takes paper out of his pocket.]

DR. TRENCH: The spirits are people like ourselves, we treat them as our guests and protect them from discourtesy and violence, and every exorcism is a curse or a threatened curse. We do not admit that there are evil spirits. Some spirits are earth-bound – they think they are still living and go over and over some action of their past lives, just as we go over and over some painful thought, except that where they are thought is reality. For instance, when a spirit which has died a violent death comes to a medium for the first time, it re-lives all the pains of death.

MRS. MALLET: When my husband came for the first time the medium gasped and struggled as if she was drowning. It was terrible to watch.

DR. TRENCH: Sometimes a spirit re-lives not the pain of death but some passionate or tragic moment of life. Swedenborg describes this and gives the reason for it.[25] There is an incident of the kind in the *Odyssey*,[26] and many in Eastern literature; the murderer repeats his murder, the robber his robbery, the lover his serenade, the soldier hears the trumpet once again. If I were a Catholic I would say that such spirits were in Purgatory. In vain do we write *requiescat in pace*[27] upon the tomb, for they must suffer, and we in our turn must suffer until God gives peace. Such spirits do not often come to séances unless those séances are held in houses where those spirits lived, or where the event took place. This spirit which speaks those incomprehensible words and does not answer when spoken to is of such a nature. The more patient we are, the more quickly will it pass out of its passion and its remorse.

ABRAHAM JOHNSON: I am still convinced that the spirit which disturbed the last séance is evil. If I may not exorcise it I will certainly pray for protection.

DR. TRENCH: Mrs. Henderson's control, Lulu, is able and experienced and can protect both medium and sitters, but it may help Lulu if you pray that the spirit find rest.

[*Abraham Johnson sits down and prays silently, moving his lips. Mrs. Henderson comes in with Miss Mackenna and others. Miss Mackenna shuts the door.*]

DR. TRENCH: Mrs. Henderson, may I introduce to you Mr. Corbet, a young man from Cambridge and a sceptic, who hopes that you will be able to convince him?

MRS. HENDERSON: We were all sceptics once. He must not expect too much from a first séance. He must persevere.

[*She sits in the armchair, and the others begin to seat themselves. Miss Mackenna goes to John Corbet and they remain standing.*]

MISS MACKENNA: I am glad that you are a sceptic.

JOHN CORBET: I thought you were a spiritualist.

MISS MACKENNA: I have seen a good many séances, and sometimes think it is all coincidence and thought-transference. [*She says this in a low voice.*] Then at other times I think as Mr. Trench does, and then I feel like Job – you know the quotation[28] – the hair of my head stands up. A spirit passes before my face.

MRS. MALLET: Turn the key, Dr. Trench, we don't want anybody blundering in here. [*Dr. Trench locks door.*] Come and sit here, Miss Mackenna.

MISS MACKENNA: No, I am going to sit beside Mr. Corbet.
  [*Corbet and Miss Mackenna sit down.*]

JOHN CORBET: You feel like Job to-night?

MISS MACKENNA: I feel that something is going to happen, that is why I am glad that you are a sceptic.

JOHN CORBET: You feel safer?

MISS MACKENNA: Yes, safer.

MRS. HENDERSON: I am glad to meet all my dear friends again and to welcome Mr. Corbet amongst us. As he is a stranger I must explain that we do not call up spirits, we make the right conditions and they come. I do not know who is going to come; sometimes there are a great many and the guides choose between them. The guides try to send somebody for everybody but do not always succeed. If you want to speak to some dear friend who has passed over, do not be discouraged. If your friend cannot come this time, maybe he can next time. My control is a dear little girl called Lulu who died when she was five or six years old. She describes the spirits present and tells us what spirit wants to speak. Miss Mackenna, a verse of a hymn, please, the same we had last time, and will everyone join in the singing.
  [*They sing the following lines from Hymn 564,[29] Irish Church Hymnal.*]

> 'Sun of my soul, Thou Saviour dear,
> It is not night if Thou be near:
> O may no earth-born cloud arise
> To hide Thee from Thy servant's eyes.'

  [*Mrs. Henderson is leaning back in her chair asleep.*]

MISS MACKENNA [*to John Corbet*]: She always snores like that when she is going off.

MRS. HENDERSON [*in a child's voice*[30]]: Lulu so glad to see all her friends.

MRS. MALLET: And we are glad you have come, Lulu.

MRS. HENDERSON [*in a child's voice*]: Lulu glad to see new friend.

MISS MACKENNA [*to John Corbet*]: She is speaking to you.

JOHN CORBET: Thank you, Lulu.

MRS. HENDERSON [*in a child's voice*]: You mustn't laugh at the way I talk.

JOHN CORBET: I am not laughing, Lulu.

MRS. HENDERSON [*in a child's voice*]: Nobody must laugh. Lulu does her best but can't say big long words. Lulu sees a tall man here, lots of hair on face [*Mrs. Henderson passes her hands over her cheeks and chin*], not much on the top of his head [*Mrs. Henderson passes her hand over the top of her head*], red necktie, and such a funny sort of pin.

MRS. MALLET: Yes. . . . Yes. . . .

MRS. HENDERSON [*in a child's voice*]: Pin like a horseshoe.

MRS. MALLET: It's my husband.

MRS. HENDERSON [*in a child's voice*]: He has a message.

MRS. MALLET: Yes.

MRS. HENDERSON [*in a child's voice*]: Lulu cannot hear. He is too far off. He has come near. Lulu can hear now. He says . . . he says, 'Drive that man away!' He is pointing to somebody in the corner, that corner over there. He says it is the bad man who spoilt everything last time. If they won't drive him away, Lulu will scream.

MISS MACKENNA: That horrible spirit again.

ABRAHAM JOHNSON: Last time he monopolised the séance.

MRS. MALLET: He would not let anybody speak but himself.

MRS. HENDERSON [*in a child's voice*]: They have driven that bad man away. Lulu sees a young lady.

MRS. MALLET: Is not my husband here?

MRS. HENDERSON [*in a child's voice*]: Man with funny pin gone away. Young girl here – Lulu thinks she must be at a fancy dress party, such funny clothes, hair all in curls – all bent down on floor near that old man with glasses.

DR. TRENCH: No, I do not recognize her.[31]

MRS. HENDERSON [*in a child's voice*]: That bad man, that bad old man in the corner, they have let him come back. Lulu is going to scream. O. ... O. ... [*In a man's voice.*] How dare you write to her? How dare you ask if we were married? How dare you question her?

DR. TRENCH: A soul in its agony – it cannot see us or hear us.

MRS. HENDERSON [*upright and rigid, only her lips moving, and still in a man's voice*]: You sit crouching there. Did you not hear what I said? How dared you question her? I found you an ignorant little girl without intellect, without moral ambition. How many times did I not stay away from great men's houses, how many times forsake the Lord Treasurer,[32] how many times neglect the business of the State that we might read Plutarch[33] together!

[*Abraham Johnson half rises. Dr. Trench motions him to remain seated.*]

DR. TRENCH: Silence!

ABRAHAM JOHNSON: But, Dr. Trench ...

DR. TRENCH: Hush – we can do nothing.

MRS. HENDERSON [*speaking as before*]: I taught you to think in every situation of life not as Hester Vanhomrigh would think in that situation, but as Cato or Brutus would, and now you behave like some common slut with her ear against the keyhole.

JOHN CORBET [*to Miss Mackenna*]: It is Swift, Jonathan Swift, talking to the woman he called Vanessa. She was christened Hester Vanhomrigh.

MRS. HENDERSON [*in Vanessa's voice*]: I questioned her, Jonathan, because I love. Why have you let me spend hours in your company if you did not want me to love you? [*In Swift's voice.*] When I rebuilt Rome in your mind it was as though I walked its streets. [*In Vanessa's voice.*] Was that all, Jonathan? Was I nothing but a painter's canvas? [*In Swift's voice.*] My God, do you think it was easy? I was a man of strong passions and I had sworn never to marry. [*In Vanessa's voice.*] If you and she are not married, why should we not marry like other men and women? I loved you from the first moment when you came to my mother's house and began to teach me. I thought it would be enough to look at you, to speak to you, to hear you speak. I followed you to Ireland five years ago and I can bear it no longer.

It is not enough to look, to speak, to hear. Jonathan, Jonathan, I am a woman, the women Brutus and Cato loved were not different. [*In Swift's voice.*] I have something in my blood that no child must inherit. I have constant attacks of dizziness; I pretend they come from a surfeit of fruit[34] when I was a child. I had them in London.[35] ... There was a great doctor there, Dr. Arbuthnot;[36] I told him of those attacks of dizziness, I told him of worse things. It was he who explained. There is a line of Dryden's.[37] ... [*In Vanessa's voice.*] O, I know – 'Great wits are sure to madness near allied'. If you had children, Jonathan, my blood would make them healthy. I will take your hand, I will lay it upon my heart – upon the Vanhomrigh blood that has been healthy for generations. [*Mrs. Henderson slowly raises her left hand.*] That is the first time you have touched my body, Jonathan. [*Mrs. Henderson stands up and remains rigid. In Swift's voice.*] What do I care if it be healthy? What do I care if it could make mine healthy? Am I to add another to the healthy rascaldom and knavery of the world? [*In Vanessa's voice.*] Look at me, Jonathan. Your arrogant intellect separates us. Give me both your hands. I will put them upon my breast. [*Mrs. Henderson raises her right hand to the level of her left and then raises both to her breast.*] O, it is white – white as the gambler's dice – white ivory dice. Think of the uncertainty. Perhaps a mad child – perhaps a rascal – perhaps a knave – perhaps not, Jonathan. The dice of the intellect are loaded, but I am the common ivory dice. [*Her hands are stretched out as though drawing somebody towards her.*] It is not my hands that draw you back. My hands are weak, they could not draw you back if you did not love as I love. You said that you have strong passions; that is true, Jonathan – no man in Ireland is so passionate. That is why you need me, that is why you need children, nobody has greater need. You are growing old. An old man without children is very solitary. Even his friends, men as old as he, turn away, they turn towards the young, their children or their children's children. They cannot endure an old man like themselves. [*Mrs. Henderson moves away from the chair, her movements gradually growing convulsive.*] You are not too old for the dice, Jonathan, but a few years if you turn away will make you an old miserable childless man. [*In Swift's voice.*] O God, hear the prayer of Jonathan Swift, that afflicted man, and grant that he may leave to posterity nothing but his intellect that came to him from Heaven. [*In Vanessa's voice.*] Can you face solitude with that mind, Jonathan? [*Mrs. Henderson goes to the door, finds*

that it is closed.] Dice, white ivory dice. [*In Swift's voice.*] My God,
I am left alone with my enemy. Who locked the door, who locked
me in with my enemy? [*Mrs. Henderson beats upon the door, sinks
to the floor and then speaks as Lulu.*] Bad old man! Do not let him
come back. Bad old man does not know he is dead. Lulu cannot find
fathers, mothers, sons that have passed over. Power almost gone.
[*Mrs. Mallet leads Mrs. Henderson, who seems very exhausted, back
to her chair. She is still asleep. She speaks again as Lulu.*] Another
verse of hymn. Everybody sing. Hymn will bring good influence.
  [*They sing.*]

> 'If some poor wandering child of Thine
> Have spurned to-day the voice divine,
> Now, Lord, the gracious work begin;
> Let him no more lie down in sin.'[38]

[*During the hymn Mrs. Henderson has been murmuring 'Stella',
but the singing has almost drowned her voice. The singers draw
one another's attention to the fact that she is speaking. The singing
stops.*]

DR. TRENCH: I thought she was speaking.

MRS. MALLET: I saw her lips move.

DR. TRENCH: She would be more comfortable with a cushion, but we
  might wake her.

MRS. MALLET: Nothing can wake her out of a trance like that until
  she wakes up herself.
  [*She brings a cushion and she and Dr. Trench put Mrs. Henderson
  into a more comfortable position.*]

MRS. HENDERSON [*in Swift's voice*]: Stella.

MISS MACKENNA [*to John Corbet*]: Did you hear that? She said 'Stella'.

JOHN CORBET: Vanessa has gone, Stella has taken her place.

MISS MACKENNA: Did you notice the change while we were singing?
  The new influence in the room?

JOHN CORBET: I thought I did, but it must have been fancy.

MRS. MALLET: Hush!

MRS. HENDERSON [*in Swift's voice*]: Have I wronged you, beloved
  Stella? Are you unhappy? You have no children, you have no lover,
  you have no husband. A cross and ageing man for friend – nothing
  but that. But no, do not answer – you have answered already in that

poem you wrote for my last birthday. With what scorn you speak
of the common lot of women 'with no endowments but a face –'

> 'Before the thirtieth year of life
> A maid forlorn or hated wife.'

It is the thought of the great Chrysostom[39] who wrote in a famous
passage that women loved according to the soul, loved as saints can
love, keep their beauty longer, have greater happiness than women
loved according to the flesh. That thought has comforted me, but it
is a terrible thing to be responsible for another's happiness. There
are moments when I doubt, when I think Chrysostom may have been
wrong. But now I have your poem to drive doubt away. You have
addressed me in these noble words:

> 'You taught how I might youth prolong
> By knowing what is right and wrong;
> How from my heart to bring supplies
> Of lustre to my fading eyes;[40]
> How soon a beauteous mind repairs
> The loss of chang'd or falling hairs;
> How wit and virtue from within
> Can spread a smoothness o'er the skin.'

JOHN CORBET: The words upon the window-pane!

MRS. HENDERSON [*in Swift's voice*]: Then, because you understand
that I am afraid of solitude, afraid of outliving my friends – and
myself – you comfort me in that last verse – you overpraise my moral
nature when you attribute to it a rich mantle, but O how touching
those words which describe your love:

> 'Late dying may you cast a shred
> Of that rich mantle o'er my head;
> To bear with dignity my sorrow,
> One day alone, then die to-morrow.'

Yes, you will close my eyes, Stella. O, you will live long after me,[41]
dear Stella, for you are still a young woman, but you will close my
eyes. [*Mrs. Henderson sinks back in chair and speaks as Lulu.*] Bad
old man gone. Power all used up. Lulu can do no more. Good-bye,
friends. [*Mrs. Henderson, speaking in her own voice.*] Go away, go
away! [*She wakes.*] I saw him a moment ago, has he spoilt the séance
again?

MRS. MALLET: Yes, Mrs. Henderson, my husband came, but he was
driven away.

DR. TRENCH: Mrs. Henderson is very tired. We must leave her to rest. [*To Mrs. Henderston.*] You did your best and nobody can do more than that. [*He takes out money.*]

MRS. HENDERSON: No.... No.... I cannot take any money, not after a séance like that.

DR. TRENCH: Of course you must take it, Mrs. Henderson.
[*He puts money on table, and Mrs. Henderson gives a furtive glance to see how much it is. She does the same as each sitter lays down his or her money.*]

MRS. MALLET: A bad séance is just as exhausting as a good séance, and you must be paid.

MRS. HENDERSON: No.... No.... Please don't. It is very wrong to take money for such a failure.
[*Mrs. Mallet lays down money.*]

CORNELIUS PATTERSON: A jockey is paid whether he wins or not. [*He lays down money.*]

MISS MACKENNA: That spirit rather thrilled me. [*She lays down money.*]

MRS. HENDERSON: If you insist, I must take it.

ABRAHAM JOHNSON: I shall pray for you to-night. I shall ask God to bless and protect your séances. [*He lays down money.*]
[*All go out except John Corbet and Mrs. Henderson.*]

JOHN CORBET: I know you are tired, Mrs. Henderson, but I must speak to you. I have been deeply moved by what I have heard. This is my contribution to prove that I am satisfied, completely satisfied. [*He puts a note on the table.*]

MRS. HENDERSON: A pound note – nobody ever gives me more than ten shillings, and yet the séance was a failure.

JOHN CORBET [*sitting down near Mrs. Henderson*]: When I say I am satisfied I do not mean that I am convinced it was the work of spirits. I prefer to think that you created it all, that you are an accomplished actress and scholar. In my essay for my Cambridge doctorate I examine all the explanations of Swift's celibacy offered by his biographers and prove that the explanation you selected was the only plausible one. But there is something I must ask you. Swift was the chief representative of the intellect of his epoch, that arrogant intellect free at last from superstition. He foresaw its collapse. He foresaw Democracy, he must have dreaded the future. Did he refuse to beget children because of that dread? Was Swift mad? Or was it the intellect itself that was mad?

MRS. HENDERSON: Who are you talking of, sir?

JOHN CORBET: Swift, of course.

MRS. HENDERSON: Swift? I do not know anybody called Swift.

JOHN CORBET: Jonathan Swift, whose spirit seemed to be present to-night.

MRS. HENDERSON: What? That dirty old man?

JOHN CORBET: He was neither old nor dirty when Stella and Vanessa loved him.

MRS. HENDERSON: I saw him very clearly just as I woke up. His clothes were dirty, his face covered with boils. Some disease had made one of his eyes swell up, it stood out from his face like a hen's egg.

JOHN CORBET: He looked like that in his old age. Stella had been dead a long time. His brain had gone,[42] his friends had deserted him. The man appointed to take care of him beat him to keep him quiet.

MRS. HENDERSON: Now they are old, now they are young. They change all in a moment as their thought changes. It is sometimes a terrible thing to be out of the body, God help us all.

DR. TRENCH [at doorway]: Come along, Corbet, Mrs. Henderson is tired out.

JOHN CORBET: Good-bye, Mrs. Henderson.

[He goes out with Dr. Trench. All the sitters except Miss Mackenna, who has returned to her room, pass along the passage on their way to the front door. Mrs. Henderson counts the money, finds her purse, which is in a vase on the mantelpiece, and puts the money in it.]

MRS. HENDERSON: How tired I am! I'd be the better of a cup of tea. [She finds the teapot and puts kettle on fire, and then as she crouches down by the hearth suddenly lifts up her hands and counts her fingers, speaking in Swift's voice.]

Five great Ministers that were my friends are gone, ten great Ministers that were my friends are gone. I have not fingers enough to count the great Ministers that were my friends and that are gone.

[She wakes with a start and speaks in her own voice.]

Where did I put that tea-caddy? Ah! there it is. And there should be a cup and saucer.

[*She finds the saucer.*]

But where's the cup?

[*She moves aimlessly about the stage and then, letting the saucer fall and break, speaks in Swift's voice.*]

Perish the day on which I was born![43]

THE END

THE KING OF THE GREAT CLOCK TOWER

NINETTE DE VALOIS
ASKING PARDON FOR COVERING
HER EXPRESSIVE FACE WITH A MASK

Persons in the Play

FIRST ATTENDANT
SECOND ATTENDANT
THE KING
THE QUEEN
THE STROLLER

*When the stage curtain rises it shows an inner curtain whereon is
perhaps a stencilled pattern of dancers. At the right and left sides of
the proscenium are a drum and gong. The Queen should wear a beautiful
impassive mask; the Stroller a wild half-savage mask. It should cover
the upper part of his face, the lower part being hidden by his red beard.
The Attendants stand by drum and gong; they slowly part the curtains,
singing.*

SECOND ATTENDANT: They dance all day that dance in Tir-nan-oge.[1]

FIRST ATTENDANT: There every lover is a happy rogue;
   And should he speak, it is the speech of birds.
   No thought has he, and therefore has no words,
   No thought because no clock, no clock because
   If I consider deeply, lad and lass,
   Nerve touching nerve upon that happy ground,
   Are bobbins where all time is bound and wound.

SECOND ATTENDANT: O never may that dismal thread run loose;

FIRST ATTENDANT: For there the hound that Oisin saw pursues

221

The hornless deer that runs in such a fright;
And there the woman clasps an apple tight
For all the clamour of a famished man.
They run in foam, and there in foam they ran,
Nor can they stop to take a breath that still
Hear in the foam the beating of a bell.[2]

[*When the curtains are parted one sees to left the King and Queen upon two thrones, which may be two cubes. There should be two cubes upon the opposite side to balance them. The background may be a curtain hung in a semicircle, or a semicircle of one-foot Craig screens.[3]*

The two Attendants sit down by drum and gong. They remain facing the audience at either side of the stage, but a little in the shadow.]

THE KING: A year ago you walked into this house,
A year ago to-night. Though neither I
Nor any man could tell your family,
Country or name, I put you on that throne.
And now before the assembled court, before
Neighbours, attendants, courtiers, men-at-arms,
I ask your country, name and family,
And not for the first time. Why sit you there
Dumb as an image made of wood or metal,
A screen between the living and the dead?
All persons here assembled, and because
They think that silence unendurable,
Fix eyes upon you.

[*There is a pause. The Queen neither speaks nor moves. First Attendant strikes the drum three times.*]
                    Captain of the Guard!
Some traveller strikes a blow upon the gate.
Open. Admit him.

FIRST ATTENDANT [*speaking as Captain of the Guard, without turning his head*]: I admit him, King.
[*The Stroller enters.*]

THE KING: What is your name?

THE STROLLER: Enough that I am called
A stroller and a fool, that you are called
King of the Great Clock Tower.

THE KING: What do you want?

THE STROLLER: A year ago I heard a brawler say
   That you had married with a woman called
   Most beautiful of her sex. I am a poet.
   From that day out I put her in my songs,
   And day by day she grew more beautiful.
   Hard-hearted men that plough the earth and sea
   Sing what I sing, yet I that sang her first
   Have never seen her face.

THE KING: Have you no wife,
   Mistress or friend to put into a song?

THE STROLLER: I had a wife. The image in my head
   Made her appear fat, slow, thick of the limbs,
   In all her movements like a Michaelmas goose.
   I left her, but a night or two ago
   I ate my sausage at a tavern table –
   A stroller and a man of no account
   I dine among the ganders – a gander scoffed,
   Said I would drink myself to sleep, or cry
   My head among the dishes on the table,
   Because of a woman I had never seen.

THE KING: But what have I to do with it?

THE STROLLER: Send for the Queen.
   The ganders cannot scoff when I have seen her.

THE KING: He seems a most audacious brazen man,
   Not caring what he speaks of, nor to whom,
   Nor where he stands.

THE STROLLER: But never have I said
   Brazen, audacious, disrespectful words
   Of the image in my head. Summon her in
   That I may look on its original.

THE KING: She is at my side.

THE STROLLER: The Queen of the Great Clock Tower?

THE KING: The Queen of the Great Clock Tower is at my side.

THE STROLLER: Neither so red, nor white, nor full in the breast
   As I had thought. What matter for all that
   So long as I proclaim her everywhere
   Most beautiful!

THE KING: Go now that you have seen!

THE STROLLER: Not yet, for on the night the gander gabbed
I swore that I would see the Queen, and that –
My God, but I was drunk – the Queen would dance
And dance to me alone.

THE KING: What?

THE STROLLER: Dance, and dance
Till I grow grateful, and grown grateful sing.

THE KING: Sing out you may, but not from gratitude.
Guard, flog this man!

THE STROLLER: What, flog a sacred man?

THE KING: A sacred man?

THE STROLLER: I ran to the Boyne Water[4]
And where a sea-mew and the salt sea wind
Yelled Godhead, on a round green hillock lay;
Nine days I fasted there – but that's a secret
Between us three – then Aengus[5] and the Gods
Appeared, and when I said what I had sworn
Shouted approval. Then great Aengus spoke –
O listen, for I speak his very words –
'On stroke of midnight when the old year dies,[6]
Upon that stroke, the tolling of that bell,
The Queen shall kiss your mouth,' – his very words –
Your Queen, my mouth, the Queen shall kiss my mouth.

THE KING: Come, Captain of the Guard.

FIRST ATTENDANT [speaking as Captain of the Guard]: King, I am
here.

THE KING: This man insults me and insults the Queen.
Take him and bring me his head.

FIRST ATTENDANT [speaking as Captain of the Guard]: I take him,
King.

THE STROLLER: I go; but this must happen:

          [Counting on his fingers] First the Queen
Will dance before me, second I shall sing.

THE KING: What, sing without a head?

THE STROLLER: Grateful I sing,
Then, grateful in her turn, the Queen will kiss

My mouth because it sang.

THE KING: Stand where you are!
Stand! All from the beginning has been lies,
Extravagance and lies. Who is this man?
Perhaps if you will speak, and speak the truth,
I may not kill him. What? You will not speak?
Then take him, Captain of the Guard.

FIRST ATTENDANT [*speaking as Captain of the Guard*]: I take him.

THE KING: And bring his head as evidence of his death.
If he was not your lover in that place
You come from, if the nothing that he seems,
A stroller and a fool, a rambling rogue
That has insulted you, laugh, dance or sing,
Do something, anything, I care not what
So that you move – but why those staring eyes?

SECOND ATTENDANT [*singing as Queen in a low voice*]:

> O, what may come
> Into my womb?

THE KING: Ah! That is better. Let the voice ring out.
Let everybody hear that song of joy.

SECOND ATTENDANT [*singing as Queen*]:

> He longs to kill
> My body, until
> That sudden shudder
> And limbs lie still.
>
> O, what may come
> Into my womb,
> What caterpillar
> My beauty consume?

THE KING: I do not know the meaning of those words
That have a scornful sound.
    [*The King goes to right and returns with the head of the Stroller,
    and lays it upon the cubical throne to the right nearest audience.*]
                     Sing, Stroller and fool.
Open that mouth, my Queen awaits a song.
    [*The Queen begins to dance.*[7]]
Dance, turn him into mockery with a dance!

No woman ever had a better thought.
All here applaud that thought. Dance, woman, dance!
Neither so red, nor white, nor full in the breast,
That's what he said! Dance, give him scorn for scorn,
Display your beauty, spread your peacock tail.

[*The Queen dances, then takes up the severed head and stands in centre of the stage facing audience, the severed head upon her shoulder.*]

THE KING: His eyelids tremble, his lips begin to move.

FIRST ATTENDANT [*singing as Head in a low voice*]:

    Clip and lip and long for more –

THE KING: O, O, they have begun to sing.

FIRST ATTENDANT [*singing as Head*]:

    Clip and lip and long for more,
    Mortal men our abstracts are.[8]
    What of the hands on the Great Clock face?
    All those living wretches crave
    Prerogatives of the dead that have
    Sprung heroic from the grave.
    A moment more and it tolls midnight.

    Crossed fingers there in pleasure can
    Exceed the nuptial bed of man;
    What of the hands on the Great Clock face?
    A nuptial bed exceed all that
    Boys at puberty have thought,
    Or sibyls in a frenzy sought.
    A moment more and it tolls midnight.

    What's prophesied? What marvel is
    Where the dead and living kiss?
    What of the hands on the Great Clock face?
    Sacred Virgil[9] never sang
    All the marvel there begun,
    But there's a stone upon my tongue.
    A moment more and it tolls midnight.

[*When the song has finished, the dance begins again, the Clock strikes. The strokes are represented by blows on a gong struck by Second Attendant. The Queen dances to the sound, and at the last stroke presses her lips to the lips of the head. The King has risen and drawn his sword. The Queen lays the head upon her breast, and fixes her eyes upon him. He appears about to strike, but kneels, laying the sword at her feet. The two Attendants rise singing, and slowly close the inner curtain.*]

FIRST ATTENDANT:

O, but I saw a solemn sight;
Said the rambling, shambling travelling-man;
Castle Dargan's ruin all lit,[10]
Lovely ladies dancing in it.

SECOND ATTENDANT:

What though they danced! Those days are gone.
Said the wicked, crooked, hawthorn tree;
Lovely lady or gallant man
Are blown cold dust or a bit of bone.

FIRST ATTENDANT:

O, what is life but a mouthful of air?
Said the rambling, shambling travelling-man;
Yet all the lovely things that were
Live, for I saw them dancing there.

[*The Queen has come down stage and now stands framed in the half-closed curtains.*]

SECOND ATTENDANT:

Nobody knows what may befall,
Said the wicked, crooked, hawthorn tree.
I have stood so long by a gap in the wall
Maybe I shall not die at all.

[*The outer curtain descends.*]

THE END

THE HERNE'S EGG

Persons in the Play

CONGAL, *King of Connacht*
AEDH, *King of Tara*
CORNEY, *Attracta's servant*
MIKE, PAT, MALACHI, MATHIAS, JAMES, JOHN, *Connacht soldiers*
ATTRACTA, *A Priestess*
KATE, AGNES, MARY, *Friends of Attracta*
A FOOL
Soldiers of Tara

SCENE I

Mist and rocks; high up on backcloth a rock, its base hidden in mist; on this rock stands a great herne.[1] All should be suggested, not painted realistically.[2] Many men fighting with swords and shields, but sword and sword, shield and sword, never meet. The men move rhythmically as if in a dance; when swords approach one another cymbals clash; when swords and shields approach drums boom. The battle[3] *flows out at one side; two Kings are left fighting in the centre of the stage; the battle returns and flows out at the other side. The two Kings remain, but are now face to face and motionless. They are Congal, King of Connacht, and Aedh, King of Tara.*

CONGAL: How many men have you lost?
AEDH: Some five-and-twenty men.
CONGAL: No need to ask my losses.
AEDH: Your losses equal mine.
CONGAL: They always have and must.
AEDH: Skill, strength, arms matched.
CONGAL: Where is the wound this time?
AEDH: There, left shoulder-blade.
CONGAL: Here, right shoulder-blade.

229

AEDH: Yet we have fought all day.

CONGAL: This is our fiftieth battle.

AEDH: And all were perfect battles.

CONGAL: Come, sit upon this stone.
    Come and take breath awhile.

AEDH: From daybreak until noon,
    Hopping among these rocks.

CONGAL: Nothing to eat or drink.

AEDH: A story is running round
    Concerning two rich fleas.

CONGAL: We hop like fleas, but war
    Has taken all our riches.

AEDH: Rich, and rich, so rich that they
    Retired and bought a dog.

CONGAL: Finish the tale and say
    What kind of dog they bought.

AEDH: Heaven knows.

CONGAL: You must have thought
What kind of dog they bought.

AEDH: Heaven knows.

CONGAL: Unless you say,
    I'll up and fight all day.

AEDH: A fat, square, lazy dog,
    No sort of scratching dog.

SCENE II

The same place as in previous scene. Corney enters, leading a donkey on wheels like a child's toy, but life-size.

CORNEY: A tough, rough mane, a tougher skin,
    Strong legs though somewhat thin,
    A strong body, a level line
    Up to the neck along the spine.
    All good points, and all are spoilt
    By that rapscallion Clareman's eye!

What if before your present shape[4]
You could slit purses and break hearts,
You are a donkey now, a chattel,
A taker of blows, not a giver of blows.
No tricks, you're not in County Clare,
No, not one kick upon the shin.
    [*Congal, Pat, Mike, James, Mathias, Malachi, John, enter, in the
    dress and arms of the previous scene but without shields.*]

CONGAL: I have learned of a great hernery
    Among these rocks, and that a woman,
    Prophetess or priestess, named Attracta,
    Owns it – take this donkey and man,
    Look for the creels, pack them with eggs.

MIKE: Manners!

CONGAL: This man is in the right.
I will ask Attracta for the eggs
If you will tell how to summon her.

CORNEY: A flute lies there upon the rock
    Carved out of a herne's thigh.
    Go pick it up and play the tune
    My mother calls 'The Great Herne's Feather'.
    If she has a mind to come, she will come.

CONGAL: That's a queer way of summoning.

CORNEY: This is a holy place and queer;
    But if you do not know that tune,
    Custom permits that I should play it,
    But you must cross my hand with silver.
    [*Congal gives money, and Corney plays flute.*]

CONGAL: Go pack the donkey creels with eggs.[5]
    [*All go out except Congal and Mike. Attracta enters.*]

ATTRACTA: For a thousand or ten thousand years,
    For who can count so many years,
    Some woman has lived among these rocks,
    The Great Herne's bride, or promised bride,
    And when a visitor has played the flute
    Has come or not. What would you ask?

CONGAL: Tara and I have made a peace;
    Our fiftieth battle fought, there is need

Of preparation for the next;
He and all his principal men,
I and all my principal men,
Take supper at his principal house
This night, in his principal city, Tara,
And we have set our minds upon
A certain novelty or relish.

MIKE: Herne's eggs.

CONGAL: This man declares our need;
A donkey, both creels packed with eggs,
Somebody that knows the mind of a donkey
For donkey-boy.

ATTRACTA: Custom forbids:
Only the women of these rocks,
Betrothed or married to the Herne,
The god or ancestor of hernes,
Can eat, handle, or look upon those eggs.

CONGAL: Refused! Must old campaigners lack
The one sole dish that takes their fancy,
My cooks what might have proved their skill,
Because a woman thinks that she
Is promised or married to a bird?

MIKE: Mad!

CONGAL: Mad! This man is right,
But you are not to blame for that.
Women thrown into despair
By the winter of their virginity
Take its abominable snow,
As boys take common snow, and make
An image of god or bird or beast
To feed their sensuality:
Ovid had a literal mind,
And though he sang it neither knew
What lonely lust dragged down the gold
That crept on Danae's lap, nor knew
What rose against the moony feathers
When Leda lay upon the grass.[6]

ATTRACTA: There is no reality but the Great Herne.

MIKE: The cure.

CONGAL: Why, that is easy said;
An old campaigner is the cure
For everything that woman dreams –
Even I myself, had I but time.

MIKE: Seven men.[7]

CONGAL: This man of learning means
That not a weather-stained, war-battered
Old campaigner such as I, –
But seven men packed into a day
Or dawdled out through seven years –
Are needed to melt down the snow
That's fallen among these wintry rocks.

ATTRACTA: There is no happiness but the Great Herne.

CONGAL: It may be that life is suffering,
But youth that has not yet known pleasure
Has not the right to say so; pick,
Or be picked by seven men,
And we shall talk it out again.

ATTRACTA: Being betrothed to the Great Herne
I know what may be known: I burn
Not in the flesh but in the mind;
Chosen out of all my kind
That I may lie in a blazing bed
And a bird take my maidenhead,
To the unbegotten I return,
All a womb and a funeral urn.

   [Enter Corney, Pat, James, Mathias, etc., with Donkey. A creel
   packed with eggs is painted upon the side of the Donkey.]

CORNEY: Think of yourself; think of the songs:
Bride of the Herne, and the Great Herne's bride,
Grow terrible: go into a trance.

ATTRACTA: Stop!

CORNEY: Bring the god out of your gut;
Stand there asleep until the rascals
Wriggle upon his beak like eels.

ATTRACTA: Stop!

CORNEY: The country calls them rascals,
  I, sacrilegious rascals that have taken
  Every new-laid egg in the hernery.

ATTRACTA: Stop! When have I permitted you
  To say what I may, or may not do?
  But you and your donkey must obey
  All big men who can say their say.

CONGAL: And bid him keep a civil tongue.

ATTRACTA: Those eggs are stolen from the god.
  It is but right that you hear said
  A curse so ancient that no man
  Can say who made it, or any thing at all
  But that it was nailed upon a post
  Before a herne had stood on one leg.

CORNEY: Hernes must stand on one leg when they fish
  In honour of the bird who made it.

            'This they nailed upon a post,
            On the night my leg was lost,'
            Said the old, old herne that had but one leg.

            'He that a herne's egg dare steal
            Shall be changed into a fool,'
            Said the old, old herne that had but one leg.

            'And to end his fool breath
            At a fool's hand meet his death,'
            Said the old, old herne that had but one leg.

  I think it was the Great Herne made it,
  Pretending that he had but the one leg
  To fool us all; but Great Herne or another
  It has not failed these thousand years.

CONGAL: That I shall live and die a fool,
  And die upon some battlefield
  At some fool's hand, is but natural,
  And needs no curse to bring it.

MIKE: Pickled!

CONGAL: He says that I am an old campaigner,
  Robber of sheepfolds and cattle trucks,
  So cursed from morning until midnight

There is not a quarter of an inch
To plaster a new curse upon.

MIKE: Luck!

CONGAL: Adds that your luck begins when you
Recall that though we took those eggs
We paid with good advice; and then
Take to your bosom seven men.
   [*Congal, Mike, Corney, Pat, Malachi, John, Mathias, James, and
   Donkey go out. Enter timidly three girls, Kate, Agnes, Mary.*]

MARY: Have all those fierce men gone?

ATTRACTA: All those fierce men have gone.

AGNES: But they will come again?

ATTRACTA: No, never again.

KATE: We bring three presents.
   [*All except Attracta kneel.*]

MARY: This is a jug of cream.

AGNES: This is a bowl of butter.

KATE: This is a basket of eggs.
   [*They lay jug, bowl and basket on the ground.*]

ATTRACTA: I know what you would ask.
Sit round upon these stones.
Children, why do you fear
A woman but little older,
A child yesterday?
All, when I am married,
Shall have good husbands. Kate
Shall marry a black-headed lad.

AGNES: She swore but yesterday
That she would marry black.

ATTRACTA: But Agnes there shall marry
A honey-coloured lad.

AGNES: O!

ATTRACTA: Mary shall be married
When I myself am married
To the lad that is in her mind.

MARY: Are you not married yet?

ATTRACTA: No. But it is almost come,

May come this very night.

MARY: And must he be all feathers?

AGNES: Have a terrible beak?

KATE: Great terrible claws?

ATTRACTA: Whatever shape he choose,
Though that be terrible,
Will best express his love.

AGNES: When he comes – will he? –

ATTRACTA: Child, ask what you please.

AGNES: Do all that a man does?

ATTRACTA: Strong sinew and soft flesh
Are foliage round the shaft
Before the arrowsmith
Has stripped it, and I pray
That I, all foliage gone,
May shoot into my joy –
[*Sound of a flute, playing 'The Great Herne's Feather'.*]

MARY: Who plays upon that flute?

AGNES: Her god is calling her.

KATE: Look, look, she takes
An egg out of the basket.
My white hen laid it,
My favourite white hen.

MARY: Her eyes grow glassy, she moves
According to the notes of the flute.

AGNES: Her limbs grow rigid, she seems
A doll upon a wire.

MARY: Her human life is gone
And that is why she seems
A doll upon a wire.[8]

AGNES: You mean that when she looks so
She is but a puppet?

MARY: How do I know? And yet
Twice have I seen her so,
She will move for certain minutes
As though her god were there
Thinking how best to move

A doll upon a wire.
Then she will move away
In long leaps as though
He had remembered his skill.
She has still my little egg.[9]

AGNES: Who knows but your little egg
Comes into some mystery?

KATE: Some mystery to make
Love-loneliness more sweet.

AGNES: She has moved. She has moved away.

KATE: Travelling fast asleep
In long loops like a dancer.

MARY: Like a dancer, like a hare.

AGNES: The last time she went away
The moon was full[10] – she returned
Before its side had flattened.

KATE: This time she will not return.

AGNES: Because she is called to her marriage?

KATE: Those leaps may carry her where
No woman has gone, and he
Extinguish sun, moon, star.
No bridal torch can burn
When his black midnight is there.

AGNES: I have heard her claim that they couple
In the blazing heart of the sun.

KATE: But you have heard it wrong!
In blue-black midnight they couple.

AGNES: No, in the sun.

KATE: Blue-black!

AGNES: In the sun!

KATE: Blue-black, blue-black!

MARY: All I know is that she
Shall lie there in his bed.
Nor shall it end until
She lies there full of his might,
His thunderbolts in her hand.

SCENE III

Before the Gates of Tara, Congal, Mike, Pat, Malachi, James, Mathias, etc., soldiers of Congal, Corney, and the Donkey.

CONGAL: This is Tara; in a moment
　　Men must come out of the gate
　　With a great basket between them
　　And we give up our arms;
　　No armed man can enter.

CORNEY: And here is that great bird
　　Over our heads again.

PAT: The Great Herne himself
　　And he in a red rage.

MIKE: Stones.

CONGAL:　　This man is right.
Beat him to death with stones.

　　　　[*All go through the motion of picking up and throwing stones.
　　　　There are no stones except in so far as their gestures can suggest
　　　　them.*[11]]

PAT: All those stones fell wide.

CORNEY: He has come down so low
　　His legs are sweeping the grass.

MIKE: Swords.

CONGAL:　　This man is right.
Cut him up with swords.

PAT: I have him within my reach.

CONGAL: No, no, he is here at my side.

CORNEY: His wing has touched my shoulder.

CONGAL: We missed him again and he
　　Rises again and sinks
　　Behind the wall of Tara.

　　　　[*Two men come in carrying a large basket slung between two
　　　　poles. One is whistling. All except Corney, who is unarmed, drop
　　　　their swords and helmets into the basket. Each soldier when he
　　　　takes off his helmet shows that he wears a skull-cap of soft cloth.*]

CONGAL: Where have I heard that tune?

MIKE: This morning.

CONGAL: I know it now,
The tune of 'The Great Herne's Feather'.
It puts my teeth on edge.

SCENE IV

*Banqueting hall. A throne painted on the backcloth. Enter Congal,
alone, drunk, and shouting.*

CONGAL: To arms, to arms! Connacht to arms!
  Insulted and betrayed, betrayed and insulted.
  Who has insulted me? Tara has insulted.
  To arms, to arms! Connacht to arms!
  To arms – but if you have not got any
  Take a table-leg or a candlestick,
  A boot or a stool or any odd thing.
  Who has betrayed me? Tara has betrayed!
  To arms, to arms! Connacht to arms!
    [*He goes out to one side. Music, perhaps drum and concertina,*[12]
    *to suggest breaking of wood. Enter, at the other side, the King of
    Tara, drunk.*]

AEDH: Where is that beastly drunken liar
  That says I have insulted him?
    [*Congal enters with two table-legs.*]

CONGAL: I say it!

AEDH: What insult?

CONGAL: How dare you ask?
When I have had a common egg,
A common hen's egg put before me,
An egg dropped in the dirty straw
And crowed for by a cross-bred gangling cock,
And every other man at the table
A herne's egg. [*Throws a table-leg on the floor.*]
                There is your weapon. Take it!
Take it up, defend yourself.
An egg that some half-witted slattern

Spat upon and wiped on her apron!

AEDH: A servant put the wrong egg there.[13]

CONGAL: But at whose orders?

AEDH: At your own.
A murderous drunken plot, a plot
To put a weapon that I do not know
Into my hands.

CONGAL: Take up that weapon.
If I am as drunken as you say,
And you as sober as you think,
A coward and a drunkard are well matched.

> [*Aedh takes up the table-leg. Connacht and Tara soldiers come
> in, they fight, and the fight sways to and fro. The weapons,
> table-legs, candlesticks, etc., do not touch. Drum-taps represent
> blows. All go out fighting.*[14] *Enter Pat, drunk, with bottle.*]

PAT: Herne's egg, hen's egg, great difference.
  There's insult in that difference.
  What do hens eat? Hens live upon mash,
  Upon slop, upon kitchen odds and ends.
  What do hernes eat? Hernes live on eels,
  On things that must always run about.
  Man's a high animal and runs about,
  But mash is low, O, very low.
  Or, to speak like a philosopher,
  When a man expects the movable
  But gets the immovable, he is insulted.

> [*Enter Congal, James, Malachi, Mathias, etc.*[15]]

CONGAL: Tara knew that he was overmatched;
  Knew from the start he had no chance;
  Died of a broken head; died drunk;
  Accused me with his dying breath
  Of secretly practising with a table-leg,
  Practising at midnight until I
  Became a perfect master with the weapon.
  But that is all lies.

PAT: Let all men know
  He was a noble character
  And I must weep at his funeral.

CONGAL: He insulted me with a hen's egg,
  Said I had practised with a table-leg,
  But I have taken kingdom and throne
  And that has made all level again
  And I can weep at his funeral.
  I would not have had him die that way
  Or die at all, he should have been immortal.
  Our fifty battles had made us friends;
  And there are fifty more to come.
  New weapons, a new leader will be found
  And everything begin again.

MIKE: Much bloodier.

CONGAL: They had, we had
Forgotten what we fought about,
So fought like gentlemen, but now
Knowing the truth must fight like the beasts.
Maybe the Great Herne's curse has done it.[16]
Why not? Answer me that; why not?

MIKE: Horror henceforth.

CONGAL: This wise man means
We fought so long like gentlemen
That we grew blind.
    [*Attracta enters, walking in her sleep, a herne's egg in her hand.
    She stands near the throne and holds her egg towards it for a
    moment.*]

MATHIAS: Look! Look!
  She offers that egg. Who is to take it?

CONGAL: She walks with open eyes but in her sleep.

MATHIAS: I can see it all in a flash.
  She found that herne's egg on the table
  And left the hen's egg there instead.

JAMES: She brought the hen's egg on purpose
  Walking in her wicked sleep.

CONGAL: And if I take that egg, she wakes,
  Completes her task, her circle;
  We all complete a task or circle,
  Want a woman, then all goes – pff.
    [*He goes to take the egg.*]

MIKE: Not now.

CONGAL: This wise man says 'not now'.
    There must be something to consider first.

JAMES: By changing one egg for another
    She has brought bloodshed on us all.

PAT: He was a noble character,
    And I must weep at his funeral.

JAMES: I say that she must die, I say;
    According to what my mother said,
    All that have done what she did must die,
    But, in a manner of speaking, pleasantly,
    Because legally, certainly not
    By beating with a table-leg
    As though she were a mere Tara man,
    Nor yet by beating with a stone
    As though she were the Great Herne himself.

MIKE: The Great Herne's bride.

CONGAL: I had forgotten
    That all she does he makes her do,
    But he is god and out of reach;
    Nor stone can bruise, nor a sword pierce him,
    And yet through his betrothed, his bride,
    I have the power to make him suffer;
    His curse has given me the right,
    I am to play the fool and die
    At a fool's hands.

MIKE: Seven men.
    [*He begins to count, seeming to strike the table with the table-leg,
    but table and table-leg must not meet, the blow is represented by
    the sound of the drum.*[17]]
    One, two, three, four,
    Five, six, seven men.

PAT: Seven that are present in this room,
    Seven that must weep at his funeral.

CONGAL: This man who struck those seven blows
    Means that we seven in the name of the law
    Must handle, penetrate, and possess her,
    And do her a great good by that action,

Melting out the virgin snow,
And that snow image, the Great Herne;
For nothing less than seven men
Can melt that snow, but when it melts
She may, being free from all obsession,
Live as every woman should.[18]
I am the Court; judgement has been given.
I name the seven:[19] Congal of Tara,
Patrick, Malachi, Mike, John, James,
And that coarse hulk of clay, Mathias.

MATHIAS: I dare not lay a hand upon that woman.
The people say that she is holy
And carries a great devil in her gut.

PAT: What mischief can a Munster devil
Do to a man that was born in Connacht?

MALACHI: I made a promise to my mother
When we set out on this campaign
To keep from women.

JOHN: I have a wife that's jealous
If I but look the moon in the face.

JAMES: I am promised to an educated girl.
Her family are most particular,
What would they say – O my God!

CONGAL: Whoever disobeys the Court
Is an unmannerly, disloyal lout,
And no good citizen.

PAT: Here is my bottle.
Pass it along, a long, long pull;
Although it's round like a woman carrying,
No unmannerly, disloyal bottle,
An affable, most loyal bottle.
    [*All drink.*]

MATHIAS: I first.

CONGAL: That's for the Court to say.
A Court of Law is a blessed thing,
Logic, Mathematics, ground in one,
And everything out of balance accursed.
When the Court decides on a decree

Men carry it out with dignity.[20]
Here where I put down my hand
I will put a mark, then all must stand
Over there in a level row.
And all take off their caps and throw.
The nearest cap shall take her first,
The next shall take her next, so on
Till all is in good order done.
I need a mark and so must take
The herne's egg, and let her wake.

[*He takes egg and lays it upon the ground. Attracta stands motion-less, looking straight in front of her. She sings. The seven standing in a row throw their caps one after another.*]

ATTRACTA:

When I take a beast to my joyful breast,
Though beak and claw I must endure,
Sang the bride of the Herne, and the Great Herne's bride,
No lesser life, man, bird or beast,
Can make unblessed what a beast made blessed,
Can make impure what a beast made pure.

Where is he gone, where is that other,
He that shall take my maidenhead?
Sang the bride of the Herne, and the Great Herne's bride,
Out of the moon came my pale brother,
The blue-black midnight is my mother.
Who will turn down the sheets of the bed?

When beak and claw their work begin
Shall horror stir in the roots of my hair?
Sang the bride of the Herne, and the Great Herne's bride,
And who lie there in the cold dawn
When all that terror has come and gone?
Shall I be the woman lying there?

SCENE V

Before the Gates of Tara. Corney enters with Donkey.

CORNEY: You thought to go on sleeping though dawn was up,

Rapscallion of a beast, old highwayman.
That light in the eastern sky is dawn,
You cannot deny it; many a time
You looked upon it following your trade.
Cheer up, we shall be home before sunset.
   [*Attracta comes in.*]

ATTRACTA: I have packed all the uneaten or unbroken eggs
   Into the creels. Help carry them
   And hang them on the donkey's back.

CORNEY: We could boil them hard and keep them in the larder,
   But Congal has had them all boiled soft.

ATTRACTA: Such eggs are holy. Many pure souls,
   Especially among the country-people,
   Would shudder if herne's eggs were left
   For foul-tongued, bloody-minded men.
   [*Congal, Malachi, Mike, etc., enter.*[21]]

CONGAL: A sensible woman; you gather up what's left,
   Your thoughts upon the cupboard and the larder.
   No more a herne's bride – a crazed loony
   Waiting to be trodden by a bird—
   But all woman, all sensible woman.

MIKE: Manners.

CONGAL: This man who is always right
Desires that I should add these words,
The seven that held you in their arms last night
Wish you good luck.

ATTRACTA: What do you say?
My husband came to me in the night.

CONGAL: Seven men lay with you in the night.
   Go home desiring and desirable,
   And look for a man.

ATTRACTA: The Herne is my husband,
   I lay beside him, his pure bride.

CONGAL: Pure in the embrace of seven men?

MIKE: She slept.

CONGAL: You say that though I thought,
Because I took the egg out of her hand,

That she awoke, she did not wake
Until day broke upon her sleep –
Her sleep and ours – did she wake pure?
Seven men can answer that.

CORNEY: King though you are, I will not hear
The bride of the Great Herne defamed—
Seven times a liar.[22]

MIKE: Seven men.

CONGAL: I, Congal, lay with her last night.

MATHIAS: And I, Mathias.

MIKE: And I.

JAMES: And I.

MALACHI: And I.

JOHN: And I.

PAT: And I; swear it;
And not a drop of drink since dawn.

CORNEY: One plain liar, six men bribed to lie.

ATTRACTA: Great Herne, Great Herne, Great Herne,
Your darling is crying out,
Great Herne, declare her pure,
Pure as that beak and claw,
Great Herne, Great Herne, Great Herne,
Let the round heaven declare it.
   [*Silence. Then low thunder growing louder. All except Attracta
   and Congal kneel.*]

JAMES: Great Herne, I swear that she is pure;
I never laid a hand upon her.

MATHIAS: I was a fool to believe myself
When everybody knows that I am a liar.

PAT: Even when it seemed that I covered her
I swear that I knew it was the drink.

ATTRACTA: I lay in the bride-bed,
His thunderbolts in my hand,
But gave them back, for he,
My lover, the Great Herne,
Knows everything that is said

And every man's intent,
And every man's deed; and he
Shall give these seven that say
That they upon me lay
A most memorable punishment.
  [*It thunders. All prostrate themselves except Attracta and Congal.
  Congal had half knelt, but he has stood up again.*]

ATTRACTA: I share his knowledge, and I know
  Every punishment decreed.
  He will come when you are dead,
  Push you down a step or two
  Into cat or rat or bat,
  Into dog or wolf or goose.
  Everybody in his new shape I can see,
  But Congal there stands in a cloud
  Because his fate is not yet settled.
  Speak out, Great Herne, and make it known
  That everything I have said is true.[23]

  [*Thunder. All now, except Attracta, have prostrated themselves.*]

ATTRACTA: What has made you kneel?

CONGAL: This man
  That's prostrate at my side would say,
  Could he say anything at all,
  That I am terrified by thunder.

ATTRACTA: Why did you stand up so long?

CONGAL: I held you in my arms last night,
  We seven held you in our arms.

ATTRACTA: You were under the curse, in all
  You did, in all you seemed to do.

CONGAL: If I must die at a fool's hand,
  When must I die?

ATTRACTA: When the moon is full.

CONGAL: And where?

ATTRACTA: Upon the holy mountain,
  Upon Slieve Fuadh,[24] there we meet again
  Just as the moon comes round the hill.
  There all the gods must visit me,
  Acknowledging my marriage to a god;

One man will I have among the gods.[25]

CONGAL: I know the place and I will come,
  Although it be my death, I will come.
  Because I am terrified, I will come.

SCENE VI

*A mountain-top, the moon has just risen; the moon of comic tradition,
a round smiling face.[26] A cauldron lid, a cooking-pot, and a spit lie
together at one side of the stage. The Fool, a man in ragged clothes,
enters carrying a large stone; he lays it down at one side and goes out.
Congal enters carrying a wine-skin, and stands at the other side of the
stage. The Fool re-enters with a second large stone which he places
beside the first.*

CONGAL: What is your name, boy?

FOOL: Poor Tom Fool.
Everybody knows Tom Fool.

CONGAL: I saw something in the mist,
  There lower down upon the slope,
  I went up close to it and saw
  A donkey, somebody's stray donkey.
  A donkey and a Fool – I don't like it at all.

FOOL: I won't be Tom the Fool after to-night.
  I have made a level patch out there,
  Clearing away the stones, and there
  I shall fight a man and kill a man
  And get great glory.

CONGAL: Where did you get
  The cauldron lid, the pot and the spit?

FOOL: I sat in Widow Rooney's kitchen,
  Somebody said, 'King Congal's on the mountain
  Cursed to die at the hands of a fool'.
  Somebody else said 'Kill him, Tom'.
  And everybody began to laugh
  And said I should kill him at the full moon,
  And that is to-night.

CONGAL: I too have heard

That Congal is to die to-night.
Take a drink.

FOOL: I took this lid,
And all the women screamed at me.
I took the spit, and all screamed worse.
A shoulder of lamb stood ready for the roasting –
I put the pot upon my head.
They did not scream but stood and gaped.
  [*Fool arms himself with spit, cauldron lid and pot, whistling 'The
  Great Herne's Feather'.*]

CONGAL: Hush, that is an unlucky tune!
And why must you kill Congal, Fool?
What harm has he done you?

FOOL: None at all.
But there's a Fool called Johnny from Meath,
We are great rivals and we hate each other,
But I can get the pennies if I kill Congal,
And Johnny nothing.

CONGAL: I am King Congal,
And is not that a thing to laugh at, Fool?

FOOL: Very nice, O very nice indeed,
For I can kill you now, and I
Am tired of walking.

CONGAL: Both need rest.
Another drink apiece – that is done –
Lead to the place you have cleared of stones.

FOOL: But where is your sword? You have not got a sword.

CONGAL: I lost it, or I never had it,
Or threw it at the strange donkey below,
But that's no matter – I have hands.
  [*They go out at one side. Attracta, Corney and Donkey come in.
  Attracta sings.*]

ATTRACTA:
      When beak and claw their work began
      What horror stirred in the roots of my hair?
      Sang the bride of the Herne, and the Great Herne's bride.
      But who lay there in the cold dawn,
      When all that terror had come and gone?

Was I the woman lying there?[27]

[*They go out. Congal and Tom the Fool come. Congal is carrying the cauldron lid, pot and spit. He lays them down.*]

CONGAL: I was sent to die at the hands of a Fool.
There must be another Fool on the mountain.

FOOL: That must be Johnny from Meath.
But that's a thing I could not endure,
For Johnny would get all the pennies.

CONGAL: Here, take a drink and have no fear;
All's plain at last; though I shall die
I shall not die at a Fool's hand.
I have thought out a better plan.
I and the Herne have had three bouts,
He won the first, I won the second,[28]
Six men and I possessed his wife.

FOOL: I ran after a woman once.
I had seen two donkeys in a field.

CONGAL: And did you get her, did you get her, Fool?

FOOL: I almost had my hand upon her.
She screamed, and somebody came and beat me.
Were you beaten?

CONGAL: No, no, Fool.
But she said that nobody had touched her,
And after that the thunder said the same,
Yet I had won that bout, and now
I know that I shall win the third.

FOOL: If Johnny from Meath comes, kill him!

CONGAL: Maybe I will, maybe I will not.

FOOL: You let me off, but don't let him off.

CONGAL: I could not do you any harm,
For you and I are friends.

FOOL: Kill Johnny!

CONGAL: Because you have asked me to, I will do it,
For you and I are friends.

FOOL: Kill Johnny!
Kill with the spear, but give it to me
That I may see if it is sharp enough.

[*Fool takes spit.*]

CONGAL: And is it, Fool?

FOOL: I spent an hour
Sharpening it upon a stone.
Could I kill you now?

CONGAL: Maybe you could.

FOOL: I will get all the pennies for myself.
  [*He wounds Congal. The wounding is symbolised by a movement
  of the spit towards or over Congal's body.*]

CONGAL: It passed out of your mind for a moment
  That we are friends, but that is natural.

FOOL [*dropping spit*]: I must see it, I never saw a wound.

CONGAL: The Herne has got the first blow in;
  A scratch, a scratch, a mere nothing.
  But had it been a little deeper and higher
  It would have gone through the heart, and maybe
  That would have left me better off,
  For the Great Herne may beat me in the end.
  Here I must sit through the full moon,
  And he will send up Fools against me,
  Meandering, roaring, yelling,
  Whispering Fools, then chattering Fools,
  And after that morose, melancholy,
  Sluggish, fat, silent Fools;
  And I, moon-crazed, moon-blind,
  Fighting and wounded, wounded and fighting.
  I never thought of such an end.
  Never be a soldier, Tom;
  Though it begins well, is this a life?
  If this is a man's life, is there any life
  But a dog's life?

FOOL: That's it, that's it;
  Many a time they have put a dog at me.

CONGAL: If I should give myself a wound,
  Let life run away, I'd win the bout.
  He said I must die at the hands of a Fool
  And sent you hither. Give me that spit!
  I put it in this crevice of the rock,

That I may fall upon the point.
These stones will keep it sticking upright.
  [*They arrange stones, he puts the spit in.*[29]]

CONGAL [*almost screaming in his excitement*]: Fool! Am I myself a
    Fool?
For if I am a Fool, he wins the bout.

FOOL: You are King of Connacht. If you were a Fool
  They would have chased you with their dogs.

CONGAL: I am King Congal of Connacht and of Tara,
  That wise, victorious, voluble, unlucky,
  Blasphemous, famous, infamous man.
  Fool, take this spit when red with blood,
  Show it to the people and get all the pennies;
  What does it matter what they think?
  The Great Herne knows that I have won.
    [*He falls symbolically upon the spit. It does not touch him. Fool
    takes the spit and wine-skin and goes out.*]
  It seems that I am hard to kill,
  But the wound is deep. Are you up there?
  Your chosen kitchen spit has killed me,
  But killed me at my own will, not yours.
    [*Attracta and Corney enter.*]

ATTRACTA: Will the knot hold?

CORNEY: There was a look
  About the old highwayman's eye of him
  That warned me, so I made him fast
  To that old stump among the rocks
  With a great knot that he can neither
  Break, nor pull apart with his teeth.

CONGAL: Attracta!

ATTRACTA: I called you to this place,
You came, and now the story is finished.

CONGAL: You have great powers, even the thunder
  Does whatever you bid it do.
  Protect me, I have won my bout,
  But I am afraid of what the Herne
  May do with me when I am dead.
  I am afraid that he may put me

Into the shape of a brute beast.

ATTRACTA: I will protect you if, as I think,
Your shape is not yet fixed upon.

CONGAL: I am slipping now, and you up there
With your long leg and your long beak.
But I have beaten you, Great Herne,
In spite of your kitchen spit – seven men –[30]
    [*He dies.*]

ATTRACTA: Come lie with me upon the ground,
Come quickly into my arms, come quickly, come
Before his body has had time to cool.[31]

CORNEY: What? Lie with you?

ATTRACTA: Lie and beget.
If you are afraid of the Great Herne,
Put that away, for if I do his will,
You are his instrument or himself.

CORNEY: The thunder has me terrified.

ATTRACTA: I lay with the Great Herne, and he,
Being all a spirit, but begot
His image in the mirror of my spirit,
Being all sufficient to himself
Begot himself; but there's a work
That should be done, and that work needs
No bird's beak nor claw, but a man,
The imperfection of a man.
    [*The sound of a donkey braying.*]

CORNEY: The donkey is braying.
He has some wickedness in his mind.

ATTRACTA: Too late, too late, he broke that knot,
And there, down there among the rocks
He couples with another donkey.
That donkey has conceived. I thought that I
Could give a human form to Congal,
But now he must be born a donkey.

CORNEY: King Congal must be born a donkey!

ATTRACTA: Because we were not quick enough.

CORNEY: I have heard that a donkey carries its young

Longer than any other beast,
Thirteen months it must carry it.
   [*He laughs.*]
All that trouble and nothing to show for it,
Nothing but just another donkey.[32]

THE END

PURGATORY

Persons in the Play

A BOY
AN OLD MAN

Scene. – A ruined house and a bare tree in the background.

BOY: Half-door, hall door,
   Hither and thither day and night,
   Hill or hollow, shouldering this pack,
   Hearing you talk.[1]

OLD MAN: Study that house.
   I think about its jokes and stories;
   I try to remember what the butler
   Said to a drunken gamekeeper
   In mid-October, but I cannot.
   If I cannot, none living can.
   Where are the jokes and stories of a house,
   Its threshold gone to patch a pig-sty?

BOY: So you have come this path before?

OLD MAN: The moonlight falls upon the path,
   The shadow of a cloud upon the house,
   And that's symbolical; study that tree,
   What is it like?

BOY: A silly old man.

OLD MAN: It's like – no matter what it's like.
   I saw it a year ago stripped bare as now,
   So I chose a better trade.
   I saw it fifty years ago
   Before the thunderbolt had riven it,
   Green leaves, ripe leaves, leaves thick as butter,
   Fat, greasy life. Stand there and look,
   Because there is somebody in that house.

[*The Boy puts down pack and stands in the doorway.*]

BOY: There's nobody here.

OLD MAN: There's somebody there.

BOY: The floor is gone, the windows gone,
And where there should be roof there's sky,
And here's a bit of an egg-shell thrown
Out of a jackdaw's nest.

OLD MAN: But there are some
That do not care what's gone, what's left:
The souls in Purgatory that come back
To habitations and familiar spots.

BOY: Your wits are out again.

OLD MAN: Re-live
Their transgressions, and that not once
But many times; they know at last
The consequence of those transgressions
Whether upon others or upon themselves;
Upon others, others may bring help,[2]
For when the consequence is at an end
The dream must end; if upon themselves,
There is no help but in themselves
And in the mercy of God.

BOY: I have had enough!
Talk to the jackdaws, if talk you must.

OLD MAN: Stop! Sit there upon that stone.
That is the house where I was born.

BOY: The big old house that was burnt down?

OLD MAN: My mother that was your grand-dam owned it,
This scenery and this countryside,
Kennel and stable, horse and hound –
She had a horse at the Curragh,[3] and there met
My father, a groom in a training stable,
Looked at him and married him.
Her mother never spoke to her again,
And she did right.

BOY: What's right and wrong?
My grand-dad got the girl and the money.

OLD MAN: Looked at him and married him,
   And he squandered everything she had.
   She never knew the worst, because
   She died in giving birth to me,
   But now she knows it all, being dead.
   Great people lived and died in this house;[4]
   Magistrates, colonels, members of Parliament,
   Captains and Governors, and long ago
   Men that had fought at Aughrim and the Boyne.[5]
   Some that had gone on Government work
   To London or to India came home to die,
   Or came from London every spring
   To look at the may-blossom in the park.[6]
   They had loved the trees that he cut down
   To pay what he had lost at cards
   Or spent on horses, drink and women;
   Had loved the house, had loved all
   The intricate passages of the house,
   But he killed the house; to kill a house
   Where great men grew up, married, died,
   I here declare a capital offence.

BOY: My God, but you had luck! Grand clothes,
   And maybe a grand horse to ride.

OLD MAN: That he might keep me upon his level
   He never sent me to school, but some
   Half-loved me for my half of her:
   A gamekeeper's wife taught me to read,
   A Catholic curate taught me Latin.
   There were old books and books made fine
   By eighteenth-century French binding, books
   Modern and ancient, books by the ton.[7]

BOY: What education have you given me?

OLD MAN: I gave the education that befits
   A bastard that a pedlar got
   Upon a tinker's daughter in a ditch.
   When I had come to sixteen years old
   My father burned down the house when drunk.

BOY: But that is my age, sixteen years old,
   At the Puck Fair.[8]

OLD MAN: And everything was burnt;
    Books, library, all were burnt.

BOY: Is what I have heard upon the road the truth,
    That you killed him in the burning house?

OLD MAN: There's nobody here but our two selves?

BOY: Nobody, Father.

OLD MAN: I stuck him with a knife,[9]
    That knife that cuts my dinner now,
    And after that I left him in the fire.
    They dragged him out, somebody saw
    The knife-wound but could not be certain
    Because the body was all black and charred.
    Then some that were his drunken friends
    Swore they would put me upon trial,
    Spoke of quarrels, a threat I had made.
    The gamekeeper gave me some old clothes,
    I ran away, worked here and there
    Till I became a pedlar on the roads,
    No good trade, but good enough
    Because I am my father's son,
    Because of what I did or may do.
    Listen to the hoof-beats![10] Listen, listen!

BOY: I cannot hear a sound.

OLD MAN: Beat! Beat!
    This night is the anniversary
    Of my mother's wedding night,
    Or of the night wherein I was begotten.
    My father is riding from the public-house,
    A whiskey-bottle under his arm.
        [*A window is lit showing a young girl.*[11]]
    Look at the window; she stands there
    Listening, the servants are all in bed,
    She is alone, he has stayed late
    Bragging and drinking in the public-house.

BOY: There's nothing but an empty gap in the wall.
    You have made it up. No, you are mad!
    You are getting madder every day.

OLD MAN: It's louder now because he rides

Upon a gravelled avenue
All grass to-day. The hoof-beat stops,
He has gone to the other side of the house,
Gone to the stable, put the horse up.
She has gone down to open the door.
This night she is no better than her man
And does not mind that he is half drunk,
She is mad about him. They mount the stairs.
She brings him into her own chamber.
And that is the marriage-chamber now.
The window is dimly lit again.

Do not let him touch you! It is not true
That drunken men cannot beget,
And if he touch he must beget
And you must bear his murderer.
Deaf! Both deaf! If I should throw
A stick or a stone they would not hear;
And that's a proof my wits are out.
But there's a problem: she must live
Through everything in exact detail,
Driven to it by remorse, and yet
Can she renew the sexual act
And find no pleasure in it, and if not,
If pleasure and remorse must both be there,
Which is the greater?
                              I lack schooling.
Go fetch Tertullian;[12] he and I
Will ravel all that problem out
Whilst those two lie upon the mattress
Begetting me.
                    Come back! Come back!
And so you thought to slip away,
My bag of money between your fingers,
And that I could not talk and see!
You have been rummaging in the pack.
   [*The light in the window has faded out.*]

BOY: You never gave me my right share.

OLD MAN: And had I given it, young as you are,
     You would have spent it upon drink.

BOY: What if I did? I had a right
  To get it and spend it as I chose.

OLD MAN: Give me that bag and no more words.

BOY: I will not.

OLD MAN: I will break your fingers.
  [*They struggle for the bag. In the struggle it drops, scattering the
  money. The Old Man staggers but does not fall. They stand
  looking at each other.*]

BOY: What if I killed you? You killed my grand-dad,
  Because you were young and he was old.
  Now I am young and you are old.
  [*The window is lit up. A man is seen pouring whiskey into a
  glass.*[13]]

OLD MAN [*staring at window*]: Better-looking, those sixteen years –

BOY: What are you muttering?

OLD MAN: Younger – and yet
  She should have known he was not her kind.

BOY: What are you saying? Out with it!
  [*Old Man points to window.*]
  My God! The window is lit up
  And somebody stands there, although
  The floorboards are all burnt away.

OLD MAN: The window is lit up because my father
  Has come to find a glass for his whiskey.
  He leans there like some tired beast.

BOY: A dead, living, murdered man!

OLD MAN: 'Then the bride-sleep fell upon Adam':[14]
  Where did I read those words?
                              And yet
  There's nothing leaning in the window
  But the impression upon my mother's mind;
  Being dead she is alone in her remorse.

BOY: A body that was a bundle of old bones
  Before I was born. Horrible! Horrible!
  [*He covers his eyes.*]

OLD MAN: That beast there would know nothing, being nothing,
   If I should kill a man under the window
   He would not even turn his head.
      [*He stabs the Boy.*]
   My father and my son on the same jack-knife!
   That finishes – there – there – there –
      [*He stabs again and again. The window grows dark.*]
   'Hush-a-bye baby, thy father's a knight,
   Thy mother a lady, lovely and bright.'[15]
   No, that is something that I read in a book,
   And if I sing it must be to my mother,
   And I lack rhyme.
      [*The stage has grown dark except where the tree stands in white
      light.*]
                              Study that tree.
   It stands there like a purified soul,
   All cold, sweet, glistening light.
   Dear mother, the window is dark again,
   But you are in the light because
   I finished all that consequence.
   I killed that lad because had he grown up
   He would have struck a woman's fancy,
   Begot, and passed pollution on.
   I am a wretched foul old man
   And therefore harmless.[16] When I have stuck
   This old jack-knife into a sod
   And pulled it out all bright again,
   And picked up all the money that he dropped,
   I'll to a distant place, and there
   Tell my old jokes among new men.
      [*He cleans the knife and begins to pick up money.*]
   Hoof-beats! Dear God,
   How quickly it returns – beat – beat – !

   Her mind cannot hold up that dream.
   Twice a murderer and all for nothing,
   And she must animate that dead night
   Not once but many times!

                              *

O God,

Release my mother's soul from its dream![17]
Mankind can do no more. Appease
The misery of the living and the remorse of the dead.

THE END

THE DEATH OF CUCHULAIN

Persons in the Play

CUCHULAIN

EITHNE INGUBA

AOIFE

EMER

THE MORRIGU, *Goddess of War*

AN OLD MAN

A BLIND MAN

A SERVANT

A SINGER, A PIPER, AND A DRUMMER

Scene. – A bare stage of any period. A very old man looking like something out of mythology.[1]

OLD MAN: I have been asked to produce a play called *The Death of Cuchulain*. It is the last of a series of plays which has for theme his life and death. I have been selected because I am out of fashion and out of date like the antiquated romantic stuff the thing is made of. I am so old that I have forgotten the name of my father and mother, unless indeed I am, as I affirm, the son of Talma,[2] and he was so old that his friends and acquaintances still read Virgil and Homer. When they told me that I could have my own way, I wrote certain guiding principles on a bit of newspaper. I wanted an audience of fifty or a hundred,[3] and if there are more, I beg them not to shuffle their feet or talk when the actors are speaking. I am sure that as I am producing a play for people I like, it is not probable, in this vile age, that they will be more in number than those who listened to the first performance of Milton's *Comus*.[4] On the present occasion they must know the old epics and Mr. Yeats' plays about them; such people, however poor, have libraries of their own. If there are more than a hundred I won't be able to escape people who are educating themselves out of the Book Societies and the like, sciolists[5] all, pickpockets and opinionated bitches. Why pickpockets? I will explain that, I will make it all quite clear.

[*Drum and pipe behind the scene, then silence.*][6]
That's from the musicians; I asked them to do that if I was getting
excited. If you were as old you would find it easy to get excited.
Before the night ends you will meet the music. There is a singer, a
piper, and a drummer. I have picked them up here and there about
the streets, and I will teach them, if I live, the music of the beggar-man,
Homer's music.[7] I promise a dance. I wanted a dance because where
there are no words there is less to spoil. Emer must dance, there
must be severed heads – I am old, I belong to mythology – severed
heads for her to dance before. I had thought to have had those heads
carved,[8] but no, if the dancer can dance properly no wood-carving
can look as well as a parallelogram of painted wood. But I was at
my wit's end to find a good dancer; I could have got such a dancer
once, but she has gone;[9] the tragi-comedian dancer, the tragic dancer,
upon the same neck love and loathing, life and death.[10] I spit three
times. I spit upon the dancers painted by Degas.[11] I spit upon their
short bodices, their stiff stays, their toes whereupon they spin like
peg-tops, above all upon that chambermaid face. They might have
looked timeless, Rameses the Great,[12] but not the chambermaid, that
old maid history. I spit! I spit! I spit![13]

[*The stage is darkened, the curtain falls. Pipe and drum begin and
continue until the curtain rises on a bare stage. Half a minute later
Eithne Inguba[14] enters.*]

EITHNE: Cuchulain! Cuchulain!

[*Cuchulain enters from back.*]

                        I am Emer's messenger,
I am your wife's messenger, she has bid me say
You must not linger here in sloth, for Maeve[15]
With all those Connacht ruffians at her back
Burns barns and houses up at Emain Macha:[16]
Your house at Muirthemne[17] already burns.
No matter what's the odds, no matter though
Your death may come of it, ride out and fight.
The scene is set and you must out and fight.

CUCHULAIN: You have told me nothing. I am already armed,
I have sent a messenger to gather men,
And wait for his return. What have you there?

EITHNE: I have nothing.

CUCHULAIN: There is something in your hand.

EITHNE: No.

CUCHULAIN: Have you a letter in your hand?

EITHNE: I do not know how it got into my hand.
  I am straight from Emer. We were in some place.
  She spoke. She saw.

CUCHULAIN: This letter is from Emer,
  It tells a different story. I am not to move
  Until to-morrow morning, for, if now,
  I must face odds no man can face and live.
  To-morrow morning Conall Caernach[18] comes
  With a great host.

EITHNE: I do not understand.
  Who can have put that letter in my hand?

CUCHULAIN: And there is something more to make it certain
  I shall not stir till morning; you are sent
  To be my bedfellow, but have no fear,
  All that is written, but I much prefer
  Your own unwritten words. I am for the fight,
  I and my handful are set upon the fight;
  We have faced great odds before, a straw decided.

  [*The Morrigu*[19] *enters and stands between them.*]

EITHNE: I know that somebody or something is there,
  Yet nobody that I can see.

CUCHULAIN: There is nobody.

EITHNE: Who among the gods of the air and upper air
  Has a bird's head?

CUCHULAIN: Morrigu is headed like a crow.

EITHNE [*dazed*]: Morrigu, war goddess, stands between.
  Her black wing touched me upon the shoulder, and
  All is intelligible.

  [*The Morrigu goes out.*]

                     Maeve put me in a trance.
  Though when Cuchulain slept with her as a boy
  She seemed as pretty as a bird, she has changed,
  She has an eye in the middle of her forehead.

CUCHULAIN: A woman that has an eye in the middle of her forehead!
  A woman that is headed like a crow!
  But she that put those words into your mouth

Had nothing monstrous; you put them there yourself;
You need a younger man, a friendlier man,
But, fearing what my violence might do,
Thought out these words to send me to my death,
And were in such excitement you forgot
The letter in your hand.

EITHNE: Now that I wake
I say that Maeve did nothing out of reason;
What mouth could you believe if not my mouth?

CUCHULAIN: When I went mad at my son's death and drew
My sword against the sea, it was my wife
That brought me back.

EITHNE: Better women than I
Have served you well, but 'twas to me you turned.[20]

CUCHULAIN: You thought that if you changed I'd kill you for it,
When everything sublunary must change,
And if I have not changed that goes to prove
That I am monstrous.

EITHNE: You're not the man I loved,
That violent man forgave no treachery.
If, thinking what you think, you can forgive,
It is because you are about to die.

CUCHULAIN: Spoken too loudly and too near the door;
Speak low if you would speak about my death,
Or not in that strange voice exulting in it.
Who knows what ears listen behind the door?

EITHNE: Some that would not forgive a traitor, some
That have the passion necessary to life,
Some not about to die. When you are gone
I shall denounce myself to all your cooks,
Scullions, armourers, bed-makers and messengers,
Until they hammer me with a ladle, cut me with a knife,
Impale me upon a spit, put me to death
By what foul way best please their fancy,
So that my shade can stand among the shades
And greet your shade and prove it is no traitor.

CUCHULAIN: Women have spoken so, plotting a man's death.[21]
    [*Enter a Servant.*]

SERVANT: Your great horse is bitted. All wait the word.

CUCHULAIN: I come to give it, but must ask a question.
  This woman, wild with grief, declares that she
  Out of pure treachery has told me lies
  That should have brought my death. What can I do?
  How can I save her from her own wild words?

SERVANT: Is her confession true?

CUCHULAIN: I make the truth!
  I say she brings a message from my wife.

SERVANT: What if I make her swallow poppy-juice?

CUCHULAIN: What herbs seem suitable, but protect her life
  As if it were your own, and should I not return
  Give her to Conall Caernach because the women
  Have called him a good lover.

EITHNE: I might have peace that know
  The Morrigu, the woman like a crow,
  Stands to my defence and cannot lie,
  But that Cuchulain is about to die.

> [*Pipe and drum. The stage grows dark for a moment. When it lights up again, it is empty. Cuchulain enters wounded. He tries to fasten himself to a pillar-stone with his belt. Aoife,*[22] *an erect white-haired woman, enters.*]

AOIFE: Am I recognised, Cuchulain?

CUCHULAIN: You fought with a sword,
  It seemed that we should kill each other, then
  Your body wearied and I took your sword.

AOIFE: But look again, Cuchulain! Look again!

CUCHULAIN: Your hair is white.

AOIFE: That time was long ago,
  And now it is my time. I have come to kill you.

CUCHULAIN: Where am I? Why am I here?

AOIFE: You asked their leave,
  When certain that you had six mortal wounds,
  To drink out of the pool.[23]

CUCHULAIN: I have put my belt
  About this stone and want to fasten it
  And die upon my feet, but am too weak.

Fasten this belt.
   [*She helps him to do so.*]
                And now I know your name,
Aoife, the mother of my son. We met
At the Hawk's Well under the withered trees.
I killed him upon Baile's Strand, that is why
Maeve parted ranks that she might let you through.
You have a right to kill me.

AOIFE: Though I have,
  Her army did not part to let me through.
  The grey of Macha, that great horse of yours
  Killed in the battle, came out of the pool
  As though it were alive, and went three times
  In a great circle round you and that stone,
  Then leaped into the pool; and not a man
  Of all that terrified army dare approach,
  But I approach.

CUCHULAIN: Because you have the right.

AOIFE: But I am an old woman now, and that
  Your strength may not start up when the time comes
  I wind my veil about this ancient stone
  And fasten you to it.

CUCHULAIN: But do not spoil your veil.
  Your veils are beautiful, some with threads of gold.

AOIFE: I am too old to care for such things now.
  [*She has wound the veil about him.*[24]]

CUCHULAIN: There was no reason so to spoil to your veil:
  I am weak from loss of blood.

AOIFE: I was afraid,
  But now that I have wound you in the veil
  I am not afraid. But – how did my son fight?

CUCHULAIN: Age makes more skilful but not better men.

AOIFE: I have been told you did not know his name
  And wanted, because he had a look of me,
  To be his friend, but Conchubar forbade it.

CUCHULAIN: Forbade it and commanded me to fight;
  That very day I had sworn to do his will,
  Yet refused him, and spoke about a look;

But somebody spoke of witchcraft and I said
Witchcraft had made the look, and fought and killed him.
Then I went mad, I fought against the sea.

AOIFE: I seemed invulnerable; you took my sword,
You threw me on the ground and left me there.
I searched the mountain for your sleeping-place
And laid my virgin body at your side,
And yet, because you had left me, hated you,
And thought that I would kill you in your sleep,
And yet begot a son that night between
Two black thorn-trees.

CUCHULAIN: I cannot understand.

AOIFE: Because about to die!

                              Somebody comes,
Some countryman, and when he finds you here,
And none to protect him, will be terrified.
I will keep out of his sight, for I have things
That I must ask questions on before I kill you.[25]
    [*She goes. The Blind Man of 'On Baile's Strand' comes in. He
    moves his stick about until he finds the standing stone; he lays his
    stick down, stoops and touches Cuchulain's feet. He feels the legs.*]

BLIND MAN: Ah! Ah!

CUCHULAIN: I think you are a blind old man.

BLIND MAN: A blind old beggar-man. What is your name?

CUCHULAIN: Cuchulain.

BLIND MAN: They say that you are weak with wounds.
I stood between a Fool and the sea at Baile's Strand
When you went mad. What's bound about your hands
So that they cannot move? Some womanish stuff.
I have been fumbling with my stick since dawn
And then heard many voices. I began to beg.
Somebody said that I was in Maeve's tent,
And somebody else, a big man by his voice,
That if I brought Cuchulain's head in a bag
I would be given twelve pennies; I had the bag
To carry what I get at kitchen doors,
Somebody told me how to find the place;
I thought it would have taken till the night,

But this has been my lucky day.

CUCHULAIN: Twelve pennies!

BLIND MAN: I would not promise anything until the woman,
The great Queen Maeve herself, repeated the words.

CUCHULAIN: Twelve pennies![26] What better reason for killing a man?
You have a knife, but have you sharpened it?

BLIND MAN: I keep it sharp because it cuts my food.
[He lays bag on ground and begins feeling Cuchulain's body, his
hands mounting upward.]

CUCHULAIN: I think that you know everything, Blind Man.
My mother or my nurse said that the blind
Know everything.

BLIND MAN: No, but they have good sense.
How could I have got twelve pennies for your head
If I had not good sense?

CUCHULAIN: There floats out there
The shape that I shall take when I am dead,
My soul's first shape, a soft feathery shape,
And is not that a strange shape for the soul
Of a great fighting-man?

BLIND MAN: Your shoulder is there,
This is your neck. Ah! Ah! Are you ready, Cuchulain!

CUCHULAIN: I say it is about to sing.[27]
[The stage darkens.]

BLIND MAN: Ah! Ah!
[Music of pipe and drum, the curtain falls. The music ceases as
the curtain rises upon a bare stage. There is nobody upon the stage
except a woman with a crow's head. She is the Morrigu.[28] She
stands towards the back. She holds a black parallelogram, the size
of a man's head. There are six other parallelograms near the
backcloth.]

THE MORRIGU: The dead can hear me, and to the dead I speak.
This head is great Cuchulain's, those other six
Gave him six mortal wounds. This man came first;
Youth lingered though the years ran on, that season
A woman loves the best. Maeve's latest lover,[29]
This man, had given him the second wound,
He had possessed her once; these were her sons,

Two valiant men that gave the third and fourth:
These other men were men of no account,
They saw that he was weakening and crept in;
One gave him the sixth wound and one the fifth;
Conall avenged him. I arranged the dance.

[*Emer enters. The Morrigu places the head of Cuchulain upon the
ground and goes out. Emer runs in and begins to dance. She so
moves that she seems to rage against the heads of those that had
wounded Cuchulain, perhaps makes movements as though to
strike them, going three times round the circle of the heads. She
then moves towards the head of Cuchulain; it may, if need be, be
raised above the others on a pedestal. She moves as if in adoration
or triumph. She is about to prostrate herself before it, perhaps
does so, then rises, looking up as if listening; she seems to hesitate
between the head and what she hears. Then she stands motionless.
There is silence, and in the silence a few faint bird notes.*[30]

The stage darkens slowly. Then comes loud music,[31] *but now
it is quite different. It is the music of some Irish Fair of our day.
The stage brightens.*[32] *Emer and the head are gone. . . . There is no
one there but the three musicians. They are in ragged street-singers'
clothes; two of them begin to pipe and drum. They cease. The
Street-Singer begins to sing.*]

SINGER:

> The harlot sang to the beggar-man.
> I meet them face to face,
> Conall, Cuchulain, Usna's boys,[33]
> All that most ancient race;
> Maeve had three in an hour, they say.
> I adore those clever eyes,
> Those muscular bodies, but can get
> No grip upon their thighs.
> I meet those long pale faces,
> Hear their great horses,[34] then
> Recall what centuries have passed
> Since they were living men.
> That there are still some living
> That do my limbs unclothe,
> But that the flesh my flesh has gripped
> I both adore and loathe.[35]

[*Pipe and drum music.*]

> Are those things that men adore and loathe
> Their sole reality?
> What stood in the Post Office[36]
> With Pearse and Connolly?[37]
> What comes out of the mountain
> Where men first shed their blood?
> Who thought Cuchulain till it seemed
> He stood where they had stood?
>
> No body like his body
> Has modern woman borne,
> But an old man looking back on life
> Imagines it in scorn.
> A statue's there to mark the place,
> By Oliver Sheppard[38] done.
> So ends the tale that the harlot
> Sang to the beggar-man.

[*Music from pipe and drum.*]

THE END

COMMENTARIES AND NOTES

The Shadowy Waters

It is appropriate that *The Shadowy Waters* should appear first in this volume, since Yeats had been working on the play since the late 1880s. Performances of earlier versions of the text at the Abbey in 1904 and 1906 resulted in his making large-scale revisions, and Yeats did not realize an acting version of the play that satisfied him until 1907. Including collaborations with George Moore and Lady Gregory, ten plays for the stage had been completed by the date that *The Shadowy Waters* was published in its final revised form; but its long genesis involving continual restructurings of the action, reshapings of the symbolic ramifications of the work, and redraftings of the dialogue to achieve a proper degree of characterization through speech cannot disguise the fact that the thematic preoccupations and fundamental dramatic method of the piece make it very much a *fin de siècle* conception and product of Yeats's interest in Wagner and Nietzsche, Maeterlinck and Villiers de l'Isle Adam.

Conceived initially as a dramatized poem, *The Shadowy Waters* had been subjected to periodic bursts of intense revision, especially after Yeats had seen a performance of Villiers' *Axël* in Paris in 1894, when he was profoundly moved by the dream-like self-absorption of the actors. When his first-performed play, *The Land of Heart's Desire*, proved successful in Florence Farr's production at the Avenue Theatre the same year, he had hopes that she would subsequently stage *The Shadowy Waters*, but the scheme came to nothing; so too did his plans for performances by the Irish Literary Theatre around 1900. The problem was the intractably convoluted symbolism. (Lady Gregory records being startled to learn from Yeats that half the characters in one version were eagle-headed; and Moore in *Hail and Farewell* tells of long sessions in which he tried to help Yeats break the threads of the 'knotted and entangled skein' that the plot of the play had become and opines that the work failed as drama, whatever its virtues as poetry, for 'lack of human sympathy'.) A version published in 1900 supports Moore's criticism: the persons of the drama are not distinguished from each other; the dialogue is overly poetical in a way that would quickly rob a performance of tension; and much of the symbolic reference carries a significance too private for it to engage an audience imaginatively.

Frank Fay regularly used this version for verse-speaking exercises with his actors in the Irish National Theatre Society and (without consulting Yeats who was on a lecture-tour in America) decided to stage it at the Molesworth Hall on 14 January 1904, with himself as Forgael and Maire nic Shiubhlaigh as Dectora. Joseph Holloway at a first viewing found it 'weird, puzzling, melancholy and depressingly gloomy'; but he attended all three performances and finally expressed in his diary a sense of pity 'that such a precious thing should thus leave itself open to ridicule' because of 'the dense obscurity of the text'. The reviewer for the *United Irishman* considered that the obscurity affected 'the psychological development' of both characters and action. Yeats ever responded creatively to criticism. He saw a private performance of Fay's production on his return to Dublin and again tackled the text. By the summer of 1905, when Florence Farr requested permission to direct the play at the Court Theatre for a Theosophical Convention during July, Yeats had a 'strong simple' version ready for her. Despite the specialist audience for this occasion, the esoteric qualities of the piece were sizably cut, colourful idiomatic speech, especially for the sailors, now permeated the dialogue and the motivation was altogether clearer.

Yeats was still not wholly satisfied and revised the play quite extensively before allowing a revival at the Abbey on 8 December 1906, when Fay again played Forgael to the Dectora of Florence Darragh. The sailors now spoke a vigorous prose; Aibric had lost none of his deep-seated loyalty to Forgael but had become decidedly blunter in expressing his viewpoint; Dectora's characterization had increased in subtlety so that the progress of her commitment to share in Forgael's visionary ambitions was clearer, because better paced in its development; and Forgael's authority as poet, magus and lover was throughout more credible. The play had lost none of its dream-like quality but its method in no way denied an audience imaginative access now.

The intense but vaguely defined yearnings for a transcendent experience, for a love that exceeds all mortal imagining, which motivate Forgael's quest over the Northern seas remain the constant focus of the play in all its versions and these, together with the recommended colour-scheme for the design and the prescription that the actors sustain a kind of rapt stillness throughout the performance, root *The Shadowy Waters* firmly in the symbolist tradition as it was manifest in nineteenth-century theatre. Forgael and Dectora have a closer kinship with Tristan and Isolde, Pelléas and Mélisande, or Axël and Sara than with Yeats's Cuchulain and Emer or his Deirdre and Naoise, whose conception is altogether harder-edged, psychologically tauter and explicitly Irish. Yeats was perhaps right to describe *The Shadowy Waters* to Frank Fay as 'more a ritual than a human story'. However, judged *as* a symbolist drama, the play has an undeniable power in performance, with its rising arc of emotional intensity, its bold juxtaposing of visionary and transcendental speech with earthy, ribald diction and its use of music and effects with stage lighting to instil an eerie but compelling supernatural atmosphere.

Simply to describe the play as 'symbolist' is, however, to risk undervaluing its distinctively Yeatsian theatricality and tone. Interestingly, though Yeats knew little at this stage of his career about Japanese theatre, his concern that the chief performers should adopt a prevailing stillness except where the text calls for specific gestures, which take on an icon-like profundity of significance by virtue of the sudden contrast (such as Dectora's cutting of the rope that binds the two ships together or her final covering of Forgael within the dense tresses of her hair), makes for an effect in performance that is very akin to the use of ritualized movement in Noh. *The Shadowy Waters* is an excellent yardstick against which to measure the extent of Yeats's subsequent innovations in dramatic technique: because of its strangely protracted composition, it is poised between an old style of theatre and a new.

Setting: The opening stage directions were considerably modified in subsequent print-ings of the acting text, those for *Collected Plays* being the tersest; dating from 1906 to 1907, they most closely evoke the look of the initial production at the Abbey. The colour-scheme had first been mooted in a letter of March 1903 from Yeats to Thomas Sturge Moore concerning a possible setting for the play: 'The play is dreamy and dim and the colours should be the same – (say) a blue-green sail against an indigo-blue backcloth, and the mast and bulwark indigo blue. The persons in blue and green with some copper ornaments. By making one colour predominate only slightly in backcloth and one only slightly in persons the whole will be kept dim and mysterious, like the waters themselves.' Yeats included the following two designs in his letter: a floor-plan showing how the stage should be arranged for his ideal setting and a sketch of how this would all appear to an audience.

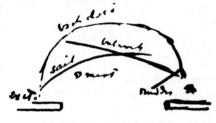 

1. Yeats's sketch of a floor-plan for a production of *The Shadowy Waters*.

2. Yeats's sketch of how that setting for *The Shadowy Waters* would appear when realized.

This setting was eventually realized by Robert Gregory, who also undertook the design of the lighting, which, inspired by Charles Ricketts's recent production of Wilde's *Salome*, made great use of blue and green lamps to achieve remote, dream-like effects without resorting to the then standard practice when staging dream scenes of playing the action behind a gauze scrim (this had been Sturge Moore's initial recommendation). Some printings of the text give specific, practical details about the Abbey production: 'The sea or sky is represented by a semicircular cloth of which nothing can be seen except a dark abyss, for the stage is lighted by arclights so placed upon a bridge over the proscenium as to throw a perpendicular light upon the stage. The light is dim, and there are deep shadows which waver as if with the passage of clouds over the moon.' Particularly of note here is Yeats's use of a curving cloth about the rear of the stage in the manner of a cyclorama; such a device was not commonly in use at this date and attests to Yeats's developed awareness of experimental theatre practice on the continent and his concern that the Abbey be in the vanguard of the new movement for minimalist staging methods. It was rare for play texts at this period (even by avowedly symbolist dramatists such as Maeterlinck) to give quite as many directions as here for effects with lighting, which enforces one's sense with *The Shadowy Waters* that gradually changing relations on stage between pools of darkness and of light are intimately bound up in performance with the creation of meaning.

1. *waste places of the great sea*: In *The Wind Among the Reeds* Yeats refers to the Neoplatonic conception of the sea 'as a symbol of the drifting indefinite bitterness of life' and suggests that a 'like symbolism' is intended in many old Irish stories about 'voyages to the islands of enchantment'.

2. *out*: Off course and out of luck.

3. *hair that is the colour of burning*: Note that on her appearance, Dectora's hair is described as 'dull red' in the edition of 1907.

4. *man-headed bird*: References by Lady Gregory and George Moore to these characters – called (inaccurately) by the latter, the Fomorians – suggest that at one stage of composition they were actually to be seen on stage, forming a kind of chorus to the action. Yeats seemed unsure whether to depict them as man-headed birds or eagle-headed men.

5. *women . . . no shadow*: The women of the Sidhe, being immortal, exist outside the normal constrictions and effects of time and mutability as marked by the movement of the sun.

6. *dread of his harp . . . mad as himself*: This was an esoteric belief about the potency of song and music that is celebrated in the classical legend of Orpheus; he and those who inherited his gift had the power to enthral animals, trees and spirits with their harp-playing. At several points in the play Forgael is shown to have such mastery over the will and actions of others, which gives his seeming passivity an edge of danger. Though a dreamer, he is steadily invested with a dynamic self-possession as a consequence of being totally committed to the pursuit of his vision.

7. *I have but images . . . Impossible truths?*: Forgael's quest is more clearly defined here as longing for an amatory union that will bring him to a state where all oppositions and antinomies will be transcended and he will know what Yeats termed 'unity of being'. Much of the imagery in this speech recurs within Yeats's *The Rose* (1893) and *The Wind Among the Reeds* (1899), which afford an illuminating commentary on Forgael's state of mind here.

8. *Look there!*: This moment shows Yeats's expert control of tone as he shifts from Forgael's metaphysical despair to the sailors' tense excitement, changing from a style replete with searching rhetorical questions to one tense with ecstatic exclamations. Ironically the arrival of the strange boat presages the fulfilment of both the sailors' ambitions and their captain's, as Forgael quickly realizes. The episode is one of several Wagnerian sequences in the play, recalling in this instance the sudden appearance of the phantom ship looming through the mists in Act One of *The Flying Dutchman*.

9. *Stage direction*: A major revision here excised a number of speeches for sailors dying in the battle; this was felicitous since the (off-stage) sounds of battle and of death-throes now provide an ironic and disturbing counterpoint to Forgael's joyous counting of the souls transformed to birds as they gather at the masthead in ever greater numbers. That Forgael never considers the cost of perfecting his quest in terms of the human life expended for his sake contributes an ominous quality to his characterization. He is the first of a line of Yeatsian protagonists who choose to deny the demands of the ego in pursuit of an ideal; Yeats invariably finds ways of presenting such depersonalized individuals within contexts that allow audiences to register a critical perspective, even when as here the mode of the drama is verging on the allegorical. It is equally ironic that Dectora, when she arrives at the conclusion of this speech, promptly asserts her human status, anger and pride, and dismisses Forgael's authority and other-worldliness as 'mad'. The love they find together is the more powerful dramatically for growing out of shocked antipathy, distrust and naked hate.

10. *Stage direction*: Repeatedly Yeats deploys a simple but graphic body-language to characterize Dectora and the range of conflicting emotions she passes through before she finds peace with Forgael. Till now her statuesque deportment has intimated an

iron self-control but she is suddenly impelled into a movement that indicates she has apprehended the unearthly power invested in his harp. She promptly suppresses the intuition by reasserting an aristocratic disdain and clings to her sense of selfhood. In production these passages of silent mime should be paced to allow the audience time to register their full psychological complexity.

11. *My husband . . . talk of love*: There are strong verbal and situational echoes in this scene with the wooing of Lady Anne by Richard of Gloucester, the murderer of her husband and her father-in-law, in Shakespeare's *Richard III* (I.ii). Whether Yeats wished audiences to consider the parallel while experiencing his play is debatable, but the two characters afford contrasting studies of demonic (Richard) and daemonic (Forgael) possession.

12. *cold women of the sea*: Such as Fand, the Woman of the Sidhe, in *The Only Jealousy of Emer*.

13. *I'll strike at him*: Earlier versions have stage directions indicating considerable movement at this point about the still figure of Forgael: Aibric places himself in Forgael's defence with drawn sword but is thrown to the deck by the sailors as they advance to the attack. This makes sense of the later stage direction (p. 12).

14. *O! O! O! . . . killed*: Aibric begins a formal keening here which is a traditional part of the ceremony of the wake for a deceased person, along with the feasting, drinking and lengthy reminiscing. The sailors take up the keen off stage and this provides an ironic counterpoint to Dectora's growing commitment to Forgael, her former love seemingly forgotten. The ensuing scene has Wagnerian overtones: the harp music as it changes its tune becomes analogous with the potent love philtre that allays Tristan and Isolde's inhibitions and makes them forget her betrothal to King Mark.

15. *I will end . . . instant*: Another echo of Shakespeare's *Richard III*, where Lady Anne also ponders whether to stab Richard when she has possession of his sword.

16. *To win . . . despite*: See *Richard III*, I.ii.215 – 19:

> Was ever woman in this humour wooed?
> Was ever woman in this humour won? . . .
> To take her in her heart's extremest hate . . .

17. *Aengus*: The Celtic god of love, youth, beauty and poetry; his kingdom was the land of Tir-nan-oge: see n. 1 to *The King of the Great Clock Tower*; an account of his 'islands' and dancing 'children' can be found in Yeats's narrative poem *The Wanderings of Oisin* (1889) and in the Attendants' speeches at the opening of *The King of the Great Clock Tower*

18. *a burning coal*: The stage-picture affords a fine correlative for this important image. Forgael's confident self-possession begins to waver in the face of a new-found conscience and honesty; but, as his control of the situation falters, Dectora takes charge, her assurance (so different from her earlier cold disdain) being inspired by her passion. The stage has grown increasingly dark since the sailors threatened violence; what little light has remained would be caught and reflected in Dectora's dress with its copper ornaments (Yeats's prescriptions are always meticulously thought out). Forgael moves steadily out of the darkness of uncertainty towards her, for she has become his radiant guide. As they move towards their final embrace, so Yeats requires the lighting, confined now to a single 'ray', to consolidate in a sharply focused brilliance about them on a

stage that is otherwise a black void. This image magnificently realizes Dectora's wish (p. 16) that there be 'nothing in the world /But my beloved – that night and day had perished'. The lovers' compatibility is defined by the way the flame of inspiration passes between them before finally embracing them both. By contrast with this steady intensity, the flickering torches carried by the departing sailors (p. 17) would make them seem dim and strangely unreal for all their talk of plunder. In *Per Amica Silentia Lunae* (1918) Yeats was to write: 'There are two realities, the terrestrial and the condition of fire', which he subsequently glossed as 'the antithesis between man and Daimon'. The play dramatizes that distinction through the dialogue and the stagecraft.

19. *Speak to him, lady . . . contradict me*: Revisions in 1904 had greatly extended Aibric's part in the drama; Yeats summarized these for Florence Farr: 'Aibric is jealous of Forgael's absorption in his dream at the outset and ends by being jealous of Dectora.' This development was cut from the acting version, presumably lest it distract attention from Dectora's momentous choice whether to remain with Forgael or leave with the sailors. Aibric is characterized now as a model of loyalty and common sense.

20. *O ancient worm . . . no longer*: The central idea is of severing the cords that bind the lovers to the world to begin a new life elsewhere and of rapturously embracing the unknown that lies beyond material experience. Much of the imagery in the speech will carry resonances for readers of Yeats's poetry and essays ('bird', 'silver fish', 'morning star' and 'white fawn' recur in his early poems as objects of quests or as images of the joyful, transfigured soul). The terms are close to the traditional hyperboles of love poetry and can in performance be acceptably interpreted as expressions of passionate fulfilment.

21. *Stage direction*: The final stage-picture recalls the scene in Maeterlinck's play where Pelléas envelops himself in Mélisande's hair and, relishing its profusion and sheen, playfully imagines being able to bathe in it like the sea. Maeterlinck's lovers are more innocent than Yeats's, their union more fragile; ecstasy in Maeterlinck's play is quickly circumscribed by dread, whereas here it brings both physical and metaphysical release.

Cathleen ni Houlihan

The play was first performed by W. G. Fay's Irish National Dramatic Society in Dublin on 2 April 1902, with a cast that included Maire T. Quinn as Bridget, Dudley Digges as Michael, Fay himself as Peter and Maud Gonne as Cathleen, a part she realized with 'creepy realism' (Joseph Holloway) since her 'great height made Cathleen seem a divine being fallen into our mortal infirmity' (Yeats). Subsequent performers of the role include Maire nic Shiubhlaigh, Sara Allgood and Lady Gregory. The text was published first in *Samhain* in October 1902; it underwent little revision of substance in its many reprintings during Yeats's lifetime.

Yeats's inspiration for the drama came in a dream but, finding during the composition that he 'could not get down out of that high window of dramatic verse', he turned to Lady Gregory for help with the 'peasant dialogue'. It remains a vexed question how much of the finished play is hers. A first draft of the work in her hand, edited by James Pethica (*Yeats Annual 6*), contains a significant annotation immediately after the arrival of Cathleen into the Gillanes' cottage: 'All this mine alone. A.G.' The remainder of the manuscript, covering all Cathleen's involvement in the action, follows after a further pencilled insertion: 'This with W.B.Y.' The dialect of all the characters except Cathleen (whose speech register noticeably prompts the Gillanes to refer to her as 'ma'am') is in the 'Kiltartan' style that Lady Gregory subsequently perfected for her own peasant comedies. The play would appear to be the fruit of independent invention on her part as well as of close collaboration with Yeats.

Despite the apparent simplicity of the piece, it requires quite sophisticated acting because of the way a prevailing style of comic stage realism is intersected by a different, portentously symbolic mode. As Yeats himself opined, even the realism requires a degree of careful observation and insight to be fully effective; he could not imagine the play acted 'by players with no knowledge . . . of the awkwardness and stillness of bodies that have followed the plough, or too lacking in humility to copy these things without convention or caricature'. Holloway illuminates this point further in his comments on Sara Allgood's performance as Bridget in a 1903 revival: 'her eyes lit up with the true love-light of motherly idolatry as she looked at her big-framed boy, and he stood before her, his head to one side half bashful-like, beaming with delight at his mother's praise . . . The industrious way she knitted as the strange old woman rambled on at the fireside, and the natural way she now and again questioned her husband, without allowing her busy fingers to cease for an instant, ceased to be acting and became nature.' It is equally important in the context of this realism that a proper sense of the period (1798) be observed; Yeats was particularly scathing about an American actress who played Bridget in a 'becoming dress of the time of Louis the Fourteenth'.

Cathleen poses technical problems for the actress in that her speeches need to be carefully pitched tonally so as to be credible as answers to the Gillanes' inquiries on the level of realism while intimating a more profound significance for those spiritually attuned to her metaphorical expression. Again Yeats was critical of actresses who insisted 'on keeping their young faces' (Maud Gonne ' "made up" centuries old') and so destroyed the mythical pattern that underlies the action, of the hag who magically transfigures into a beautiful maiden for the warrior with the courage to give himself to her. He thought it equally important that the symbolic significance of the role should not be forced on an audience but should steadily suffuse their imaginations (Yeats considered banal the trick he saw one actress perform: she parted her cloak on making her entrance to reveal beneath a white satin dress decorated with shamrocks).

Setting: A force of a thousand French soldiers commanded by General Humbert landed at Killala in Co. Mayo on 22 August 1798. Swelled by numerous unarmed peasants the like of Michael Gillane, the army defeated government forces after marching inland to Castlebar, before being surrounded by Lord Cornwallis's troops at Ballinamuck on 8 September. A great deal of revolutionary activity after 1795, based on hopes of French republican support against the English, centred on Wolfe Tone. He was arrested bringing a second French force into Lough Swilly on 3 November 1798 and imprisoned; he committed suicide there on 19 November.

1. *hurling*: A traditional Irish field-game akin to hockey.

2. *Maurteen . . . shearing sheep*: This and the Old Woman's reference (p. 23) to the shearers who ignored her appeals would appear to be an addition to the text made between the first performances and the first printing. Yeats wrote to Lady Gregory

after the opening night: 'I have an idea of revising it before I put it in a book and of making Kathleen pass the door at the start. They can call her over and ask her some question and she can say she is going to old "so and so's" and pass on . . . When she came in the second time she might say that old so and so was shearing his sheep or the like and would not attend to her.' A brief appearance so early in the action would rob Cathleen's later intrusion into the house of a proper sense of dramatic climax; but reference here to the Old Woman and her 'strangeness' creates expectation and tension, which is amplified later when she talks of being rejected by Maurteen's family.

3. *Enniscrone*: Inishcrone, a coastal town in Sligo, is almost due east of Killala across the bay.

4. *Too many strangers . . . taken from me*: Coded reference to the English invasion of Ireland and its 'plantation' by the conquerors with English and Scottish settlers.

5. *four beautiful green fields*: The provinces (Connaught, Ulster, Leinster and Munster) that formerly made up the Gaelic kingdom of Ireland.

6. *I will go cry . . . Enniscrone*: Lady Gregory published a variant translation of this popular folk-song in the article 'West Irish Folk Ballads' in the same month that the play was first printed. The full lyric tells of the hanging of a Connaughtman for a political crime against the English and of his lover, who grieves that the 'marriage portion coming home for Donagh' will not be animals to stock his farm but tokens of a funeral wake, 'tobacco and pipes and white candles'. The ballad prefigures Michael's likely fate.

7. *a red man . . . the north*: 'Red' Hugh Roe O'Donnell, one of the last of the old Gaelic kings (inaugurated 1592), failed to withstand the forces of Mountjoy, the English Lord Deputy, at the Battle of Kinsale in December 1601; he escaped to Spain in the hope of enlisting the support of Philip III and was poisoned at Salamanca in 1602.

8. *a man . . . from the south*: The reference is believed to be to Donal O'Sullivan Beare (1560–1618). His fort at Dunbay was the only castle to resist the English after the Irish defeat at Kinsale. He contrived to escape to London but King James refused him restitution; he was subsequently murdered in Spain.

9. *Brian . . . Clontarf*: Brian Boru, High-King of Ireland, was killed at the Battle of Clontarf in 1014, though his armies defeated the invading Danes. He was the subject of Lady Gregory's first tragedy, *Kincora*, staged in 1905.

10. *the upper hand to-morrow*: This was Yeats's most fervently nationalist play; in later life he was troubled lest it might have inspired men to revolutionary action which cost them their lives:

> Did that play of mine send out
> Certain men the English shot?
> – 'The Man and the Echo'

11. *Poor Old Woman*: The Shan Van Vocht was another iconic representation of Ireland.

12. *Cathleen, the daughter of Houlihan*: See 'Red Hanrahan's Song about Ireland'.

13. *sent to walk . . . far countries*: Deportation to Australia or exile on the continent were the usual sentences passed on Irish revolutionaries by English judges, particularly in the nineteenth century. Such had been the fate of Yeats's mentor, the one-time Fenian leader John O'Leary.

14. *It is a hard service . . . well paid*: This final speech seems traditionally to have been delivered with the actress playing the Old Woman standing framed in the doorway (significantly on the threshold) with arm upraised. In time this tableau acquired the status of an icon, as one by one the various performers of the role were photographed in the pose. For some years it was the preferred image to advertise the Abbey players when on tour, as the following poster demonstrates:

3. Abbey Theatre poster for *Cathleen
ni Houlihan*.

15. *got the touch*: Disturbed mentally, acting as if in a trance.

16. *the walk of a queen*: Yeats's works give frequent instances of his fascination with body language long before he began consciously to explore the expressive power of movement, stance, mime and dance in his theories about acting and as a central feature of his plays.

The Hour-Glass

After seeing the first performance of *The Hour-Glass* produced for the Irish National Theatre Society by Frank Fay at the Molesworth Hall, Dublin, on 14 March 1903, Lady Gregory described it as 'a very strong acting play'. It proved to be a staple item in the Abbey's repertory for many years to come, being restaged in 1911 and randomly revised until Yeats found a version that totally satisfied him (the text printed here was first published in 1922). Like much of his early drama in prose, it was initially a collaboration with Lady Gregory, though as early as January 1903 Yeats wrote apologetically to her intimating the wish 'to put certain parts of "The Hour Glass" into verse – only the part with the Angel & the soliloquies'. In time a much more radical reshaping of the action was undertaken.

Yeats's inspiration had been a tale, 'The Priest's Soul', by Speranza (Lady Wilde) in her *Ancient Legends of Ireland* (1887) but from the first he made significant changes to the narrative. She tells the whole life of the Wise Priest and Teacher from childhood to death; his encounter with the Angel who offers not (as in the play) one hour's respite from damnation but twenty-four; his search and discovery of a child who, uncontaminated by his atheistic teaching, has faith and works the priest's conversion, brings about his death and watches 'a beautiful living creature, with four snow-white wings, mount from the dead man's body into the air and go fluttering round his head'. Yeats achieves dramatic intensity by confining the action to the climax of the story and thematic richness by contrasting his Wise Man with the Fool, Teigue, so that the opposition being explored is not simply about faith with unbelief or corrupt and corrupting experience with innocence, but about different qualities of knowledge and modes of perception: cerebral, materialist thinking as distinct from intuition and vision.

Speranza's story concludes with a definite moral and Yeats conceived his play in the tradition of the Morality drama (William Poel's revival of *Everyman* had occurred in July 1901). There was clearly another potent influence on the writing and structuring of the play: Marlowe's *Doctor Faustus* (also revived by Poel in 1896). Like the Elizabethan tragedy, *The Hour-Glass* is framed (in the first prose version) between two great speeches for the central character; but, as often with Yeats, inspiration transcended influence and it is the differences that impress rather than the similarities. Where *Faustus* opens with the Doctor's doubting God's existence and ends with his agony in the face of certain damnation, *The Hour-Glass* starts with the Wise Man's confident rationalism being unsettled by persistent dreams and concludes with his gesture of trust in God's mercy. The 1903 version of the play worked towards the climactic stage-picture of the Wise Man humbly kneeling before the Fool, desperately begging for the assurance he now knows Teigue alone can give him: 'Is there a Heaven? . . . Have pity upon me, Fool, and tell me!' Yeats grew to dislike this, feeling it made the Wise Man seem a coward. It is much more powerful and ironic in the revised version dating from 1912 that the Wise Man silences the Fool when he offers his assurance and chooses finally to submit to the divine will, whatever the outcome. Here there is no loss of tragic dignity.

There were two other major revisions in 1912. The whole play was restructured to a form that Yeats was to redeploy in later works such as *The Words upon the Window-Pane* and which may have been influenced by his increasing interest in Ben Jonson's masques, in which an anarchic, frequently comic rout (termed by Jonson an 'anti-masque') precedes the arrival of the serious figures of the drama, challenging their serenity, beneficence and poise. *The Hour-Glass* now started with the Wise Man's pupils and, instead of his self-communings, we watch their absurd preparations to ingratiate themselves in his favour out of fear of his authority and corrosive intellect. They next reveal him to the audience on an inner stage isolated in his cell; that his isolation, socially and intellectually, is absolute becomes poignantly clear as his earnest desperation is offset in the ensuing sequences by the ironic comedy of their mindless chatter, horseplay and evasiveness, which unsettle him as much as Teigue's vagaries. The new structure brilliantly intensifies the drama; so too does the other notable revision, whereby most of the Wise Man's and the Angel's speeches were rewritten as verse; they are sensed in consequence as belonging to a world apart, which Teigue clearly apprehends but cannot find the necessary decorum of language to express. Though the main outline of the morality remains, the play has grown much richer in the implications of its new stagecraft: an intensely personal crisis of conscience in the

Wise Man is explored within a social context that has a direct relation to his inner being.

The 1903 production was designed by Robert Gregory and Thomas Sturge Moore, who devised a mathematically precise box setting with stark doorways reflecting the proportions of a high desk and chair; the only decorations were the hour-glass and a bell, appropriate images of time and annunciation.

4. Thomas Sturge Moore's suggested
setting for *The Hour-Glass*.

Yeats offers more details about how this setting appeared to the first audiences: 'We always played . . . in front of an olive-green curtain, and dressed the Wise Man and his Pupils in various shades of purple (with a little green here and there); and because in all these decorative schemes, which are based on colour, one needs, I think, a third colour subordinate to the other two, we dressed the Fool in red-brown, and put touches of red-brown in the Wife's dress and painted the chair and desk the same colour.' In 1911 Edward Gordon Craig, who always admired this particular play, suggested a way of arranging his screens (a set of which he was allowing the Abbey to use) to create the effect less of a logician's study than a dark, private sanctum, withdrawn down a curving passageway from a door that admits radiant daylight. It is a setting that can be read realistically and metaphorically: as a deliberately chosen, lonely retreat and as the spatial representation of the state of mind of a benighted soul needing the light of redemption.

Craig also designed costumes for this production and recommended that Teigue, and perhaps the Angel, should wear a mask; Craig, Yeats wrote, 'evidently wants to keep what is supernatural from being inhuman'. In his notes to a printing of the text in 1922 Yeats observes that Teigue now wears a mask in Abbey performances, 'which makes him seem less a human being than a principle of the mind'. The concept of wearing a mask to denote that the actor is representing a being from a different moral order or dimension of reality and has a symbolic rather than a realistic function in the drama fired Yeats's imagination, preparing him for his discovery of Noh.

5. Edward Gordon Craig's suggested
setting for *The Hour-Glass*, deploying
his system of screens.

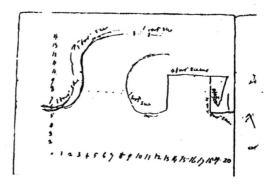

6. Yeats's sketch of a floor-plan
showing how Craig's screens would be
placed to realize his suggested setting
for *The Hour-Glass*.

Setting: This use of a forestage and stage curtain adds crucially to an audience's
sense of retreating inwards as the action develops.

1. *Teigue the Fool*: Teigue or Taig was the conventional name given (rather patroniz-
ingly) to comic, lower-class characters in English and Anglo-Irish comedies till around
1800. Yeats envisaged the Fool as being 'the Fat Fool of folklore who is "as wide and
wild as a hill" and not the Thin Fool of modern romance'.

2. *eagle in a church*: This is traditionally the design for lecterns; the eagle was
considered appropriate since it is the emblem of St John the Evangelist.

7. Edward Gordon Craig's design for
the Fool in *The Hour-Glass*.

3. *Diem . . . labuntur*: The passages in medieval Latin were translated by Alan Porter; they add considerably to the initial characterization of the Wise Man as remote and overly cerebral. Yeats observed accurately: 'Nothing said in Latin, necessary to the understanding of the play, cannot be inferred from who speaks and who is spoken to.' This passage translates as 'Day and night I argue, but those whom I have loved and have chosen, even they are wavering in their efforts.'

4. *beggar . . . Babylon*: Babylon with its celebrated astronomers came increasingly to signify for Yeats a largely scientific, logically ordered and fatalistic culture that spared little concern for the individual and his personal vision (see the final lyric in *The Resurrection* and 'The Dawn' in *The Wild Swans at Coole*). It is noticeably an outsider in that society, even as it is Teigue within the play, who upholds belief in a spiritual life. Hence the irony of the Wise Man's ensuing speech.

5. *Virgas . . . nugas*: 'Birds gather twigs together [to make nests] in order to rear their young, but the mind of man gathers rubbish.'

6. *all that we have done . . . the wind*: Such anarchy does afflict him by the end of the play, calling his life's work into question, even as he has dreamt it.

7. *Reason . . . dance in the dream*: Images and ideas in this passage anticipate many developments in Yeats's later plays concerned with the fears of rationally trained minds lest their concept of order be overthrown (Swift in *The Words upon the Window-Pane*, the Greek in *The Resurrection*, the King in *The King of the Great Clock Tower* and the whole action of *The Herne's Egg*). Notable too is the image of dance as the body's expression of its sense of being attuned to the world of the spirit (an idea Yeats culled from Castiglione's *The Book of the Courtier*); this belief motivated Yeats's quest for a form of dance-drama as the ideal vehicle for dramatizing modes of metaphysical awareness.

8. *coming through the door . . . own floor*: The dread is realized with the appearance of

the angel even as it is talked of – a powerful dramatic irony (not present in the early version) that may have been influenced by the final sequence of Synge's *Riders to the Sea*, where the villagers arrive with the corpse of Bartley and begin to keen his death even as Maurya speaks of her fear of her door being opened to admit such a tragic assembly. In *Memoirs* Yeats writes that *The Hour-Glass* was always 'played in full light except for a slight . . . dimming where the angel enters'; the performer then assumed a pose and 'stood immoveable'. To suggest a voice which is 'immortal and passionless', Yeats thought it desirable 'for the player to speak always upon pure musical notes, written out before-hand and carefully rehearsed' so there would be a marked contrast between 'the crystal-line quality of the pure notes and the more confused and passionate speaking of the Wise Man' (*Samhain*). Once the player wore a mask as Craig suggested, the lines about the angel's strange staring gaze would gain greater poignancy.

9. *that flowery branch*: In the 1903 text the Angel is described as 'carrying a blossoming apple bough in her hand' and is so drawn in Craig's costume sketch. See p. 287.

The branch is a suggestive stage-property: the blossom connotes rebirth and resurrec-tion; the apple, the fall of Adam as a consequence of eating the fruit of the Tree of Knowledge.

10. *crafty*: There is nothing sentimental about an angel who possesses such a sharply sardonic wit. See too the nicely positioned 'arguing' (p. 36).

11. *last grain . . . this glass*: The change from twenty-four hours (as in Yeats's source) to one as the Wise Man's period of grace makes for great tension and that quality in drama that Yeats always admired: implacability.

12. *You carry . . . pardon*: Angelic messengers have traditionally been pictured as bearing simple gifts as tokens of their visitation (Gabriel is usually depicted giving a lily to the Virgin at the Annunciation). The Wise Man significantly chooses to interpret the branch as an emblem of the promise of resurrection, not of humankind's lapse from grace. The carefully selected stage-properties – the book, the hour-glass, the branch – are steadily invested with a rich symbolic function.

13. *Enter . . . with Fool*: It is easy in simply reading the text to forget that the Fool is present throughout the ensuing scene, though he is largely a silent, watching presence (but for his two requests for a penny) once the pupils cease to pester him. The scholars may dismiss him as witless, but he readily understands the Wise Man's anguish here. The actor is faced with a difficult choice over how to play this silence: does he show malicious glee over the Wise Man's discomfiture (which would be in line with his later teasing refusal to confirm that he actually believes); does he express care and sympathy; or remain utterly impassive? The provision of a mask greatly helps the actor here: it allows him to leave the audience to interpret his silence how they will.

14. *Nullum esse . . . dei mater*: 'I have said that God and the Mother of God are nothing: but I have lied: for God and the Mother of God exist for the right-thinking individual.'

15. *Argumentis . . . particeps*: 'Now give proofs; for he who is a friend to reason demands proofs.'

16. *Pro certo . . . vidisse*: 'I am certain that one of you has persevered in his faith, one who has perceived more profoundly than I.'

17. *Quae destruxi . . . reaedificem*: 'It is necessary that all I have destroyed should be rebuilt.'

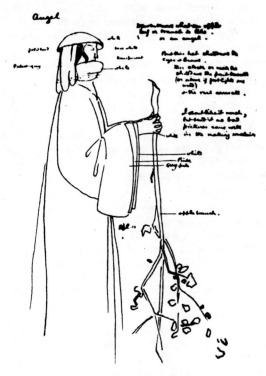

8. Edward Gordon Craig's design for
the Angel in *The Hour-Glass*.

18. *Haec rationibus . . . incunabula*: 'Such things were not in our thinking as children: now we are truly mature: we have abandoned our cradles.'

19. *Non iam . . . fictum est*: 'We are boys no more; only the body is modelled after the mother.'

20. *Docuisti . . . persuadetur*: 'You have taught and it has convinced us.'

21. *Mendaciis . . . simulacris*: 'I have steeped you in lies and filled your minds with shadows.'

22. *Nulli non persuasisti . . . nulli*: 'There is no one you have not convinced. No one, no one, no one.'

23. *beside those three . . . fourth*: See Daniel 3. Nebuchadnezzar threw three men, Shadrach, Meshach and Abednego, who refused to worship a golden idol of his making, into a fiery furnace; looking in, he found them unharmed and saw a further figure, an angel sent to protect them.

24. *mummer*: The Wise Man is experiencing a Hell of his own creating: his sincere remorse is being viewed by his pupils as comic acting, yet to add to his agony is the

awareness that he has himself conditioned their mode of perception. This sequence is a magnificent challenge to an actor's skill to make the pupils' response quite plausible while encouraging the audience to sense the man's horror as his every gesture of despair is appraised as clever parody.

25. *Argumentum . . . profer*: 'Master, cite the proof.'

26. *Credo . . . sanctum*: 'I believe in the Father, the Son and the Holy Ghost.'

27. *a mustard-grain of faith*: The reference is to Matthew 13:31 and a parable which tells of such a grain that fell among the seed sown in a field and how it grew to be 'the greatest among herbs' and a tree where birds lodged. This image was a late and highly felicitous addition to the revised text: the threatening image voiced by the Angel of the last grain of sand (p. 35) is indeed transformed into a mustard-grain of faith in the Wise Man's dying moment.

28. *He drives them out*: The Fool must leave at this point too to enable him to return on stage with Bridget (p. 43).

29. *bodach*: A tramp, cunning beggarman.

30. *Yes, I remember . . . would starve*: This is where Yeats made a major change (even after the revised text of 1912 had seen three printings) which considerably affects an audience's perception of the Wise Man's tragic status. The Cuala text of 1914 reads:

> WISE MAN [*seizing him*] I kneel to you – you are the man I have sought
> You alone can save me.
>
> FOOL No, no what should poor Teigue know, Teigue that is out in all weathers,
> Teigue that sleeps in the fishers' loft, poor Teague the Fool.
> [*He breaks away and goes out.*]

31. *Be silent*: The wish *not* to know is not stoic bravado but a deliberate moral choice: in consequence, the Wise Man's acceptance and trust in God's will are absolute, because wholly unaided.

32. *The stream . . . as the wind*: The Wise Man dies embracing the anarchy he formerly (p. 31) scorned, and does so without loss of human dignity. His final speech shows Yeats shaping a verse for tragic effect that owes nothing to the rhythm or music of Shakespeare's, Marlowe's or Milton's dramatic verse. T. S. Eliot argued that Yeats achieved this distinction with the verse for *Purgatory*, but he had in fact mastered a highly flexible style of dramatic blank verse that was wholly his own long before his late plays.

33. *the white butterfly!*: Fay was troubled by this in preparing the first production and wrote to Yeats: 'The butterfly is impossible and would have to be left to the imagination.' A delicate *mime* of capturing and releasing a butterfly into the casket can be powerfully effective: mime after all requires of its audience a kind of inspired belief and therefore is wholly apt at this moment. Joseph Holloway records that after the first performance 'the gentleman beside me inquired, "if a white flame really did appear at the end? For," he assured me, "I saw one. My imagination was so worked up by what had gone before!"' That, for Holloway, 'was a great tribute alike to the power of the poet and the players'.

On Baile's Strand

This play gave Yeats continuing pleasure throughout his life; revivals at the Abbey several times revitalized his inspiration. The satisfaction was not misplaced: in its final form *On Baile's Strand* has a perfect structure, exemplifying Yeats's dictum that a playwright must 'arrange much complicated life into a single action', if the work is to 'hold the attention or linger in the memory'. From the first, audiences perceived a new quality in the writing: early reviewers commented how there was 'less of the mystical and more of the human element in the composition', finding the characters 'virile and actual'; Yeats described his conception and style as 'masculine' through having 'more salt in it'. As with *The Shadowy Waters*, the subject – Cuchulain's killing of his son and ensuing madness – had originally been treated by Yeats in a narrative poem, 'Cuchulain's Fight with the Sea' (first printed in 1892), where much of the story is advanced by tense, pithy dialogue. Considerable emphasis in the poem is placed on the motivation of the mother (in this version wrongly identified as Emer, the wife of Cuchulain's maturity, rather than as Aoife, his lover in youth) in sending out her son as a stranger to challenge the champion; this theme is intimated rather than explored in the later play, where the focus is entirely on father and unknown son and the tragic irony that both are constrained by oaths which prevent them discovering till too late their actual relationship.

In 1902 Lady Gregory published *Cuchulain of Muirthemne*, a collated edition of the old Gaelic saga-epic, the *Táin Bó Cuailnge* (*The Cattle Raid of Cooley*), which she had translated into dialect English. Some months previously Yeats, fresh from the comparative success with Dublin audiences of his collaboration with George Moore in dramatizing another saga narrative, *Diarmuid and Grania* (staged 21 October 1901), began a play based on the story that Lady Gregory had entitled 'The Only Son of Aoife'. The result, *On Baile's Strand*, was first staged on 27 December 1904; the performance marked the inauguration of the Abbey Theatre as the permanent home of the Irish National Theatre Society. The roles of Cuchulain and the Fool were played by Frank and Willie Fay respectively and George Roberts was Conchubar.

Yeats's drama is in no way constrained by the narrative structure of the saga as rendered by Lady Gregory, where again attention is given to the mother's consuming hatred in training her son to fulfil her evil designs against his father. In the saga it is the dying Connla who reveals his identity to Cuchulain and both men roundly curse Aoife, 'the woman that is full of treachery', before Cuchulain voices a great lamentation over the body of his lost son. Conchubar is barely mentioned in the tale till Cuchulain rises from his mourning and faces the army of Ulstermen, when fear makes the king instruct Cathbad the Druid to 'put an enchantment' on the champion, binding him 'to go down to Baile's Strand and to give three days fighting against the waves of the sea'. Where malice, self-pity and complaint are the dominant traits exhibited by the characters as the story unfolds in the saga, magnanimity, absolute fearlessness and self-possession are the qualities that characterize Cuchulain and his son in the play. Malice, evil scheming and an indifference to human suffering are invested by Yeats instead in the two characters, the Blind Man and the Fool, which he invented to frame his heroic action. The Blind Man knows the secret of Connla's parentage and takes sadistic pleasure in timing its revelation to augment Cuchulain's misery. Despair at that knowledge, not magic, is what drives Yeats's Cuchulain to vengeful madness; and the Fool in his 'innocence' can see only the physical manifestation of that insanity, lacking the sensitivity and insight to interpret the spiritual and emotional breakdown that Cuchulain's fighting the waves betokens. Out of the plot-line of the saga, Yeats has created a tragedy investigating the nature of heroism.

Despite its popularity, Yeats quickly grew dissatisfied with the play in performance; after attempting some minor revisions, Yeats determined completely to rewrite *On Baile's Strand* 'up to the entrance of the Young Man'. The new version was staged and published in 1906; this is the text printed here. While Yeats was content that the climax of the play achieved the intensity which he believed essential to tragedy, he presumably thought the opening half devoid of the quality that he admired in Shakespeare and Sophocles: implacability.

The first version does rather meander. The knowing Blind Man bluntly expounds the background of the action to the largely uncomprehending Fool: teasingly he withholds salient bits of information to excite interest but finally admits that the Young Man 'is Cuchulain's son'. Cuchulain enters with a gang of young kings talking in buccaneering fashion about their ways with women; he proceeds largely to ignore Conchubar, who, in earnest discourse with older courtiers, is endeavouring to outline his plans to rebuild his capital city, Emain. It is impossible to attract Cuchulain's attention till a fanfare of trumpets announces the arrival of the Young Man. The manner in which Cuchulain's self-possession is dramatized here smacks of insubordination but hardly poses a threat to Conchubar's authority, and there is little dramatic conflict between them; the stage is just casually divided between two points of interest until later, when Cuchulain's growing fondness for the strange youth isolates him from a now united court. Though somewhat crudely done, the Blind Man's exposition does generate suspense, but this is rapidly dissipated by the leisurely episode that follows, despite Cuchulain's passing mention of the fierce Aoife as his ideal among women. Though all the material that Yeats will use in his revision is latent within this version, its dramatic and theatrical potential has yet to be fully realized.

A letter of January 1904 to Frank Fay who was to play Cuchulain offers a detailed account of Yeats's conception of the hero's nature: there is in it, he writes, 'a shadow of something a little proud, barren and restless, as if out of sheer strength of heart or from accident he had put affection away ... Probably his very strength of character ... made him become early in life a deliberate lover, a man of pleasure who can never really surrender himself. He is a little hard, and leaves the people about him a little repelled.' This hardness shows more like insolence in the early version, because the state of mind that occasions it is not really explored. A major revision of 1906 was to introduce Cuchulain and Conchubar alone together and not in full public council, and to define this psychological complexity in the hero through Conchubar's criticisms of him as disruptive of the well-being of a settled community. Conchubar must tame Cuchulain's wildness to safeguard his throne for his heirs; reference to the king's sons sparks off a mocking scorn in Cuchulain which the astute Conchubar uses to manipulate his champion into a confession of his desperate longing for a son as image of himself, and a lyrical memory of the passionate Aoife as the ideal mother for such a model son. This makes Cuchulain's intuitive attraction to the young stranger later more profoundly moving and his magnanimity the more compelling. The play now has a psychological through-line of gathering intricacy.

The change also gives greater weight to the character of Conchubar, who is nicely realized as a wily, though sensitive, politician. We know from the Blind Man's initial talk that there is to be a planned public ceremony requiring the subsidiary, tribal kings to offer total allegiance to Conchubar, and the Fool, not at all impressed, questions innocently whether anyone can 'master' Cuchulain. The High-King, however, comes to settle the matter quietly with his champion behind the scenes to ensure there is no antagonism in public that might cause division and conflict; he uses every means to curb Cuchulain's will, even emotional blackmail, to undermine the man's absolute self-possession. Conchubar's motives are not cruel, nor his strategies sadistic; his ambition for a settled kingdom is altruistic; but he lacks Cuchulain's heroic stature, wanting both his fierceness and his generosity. Conchubar is Yeats's means of effecting a deepening of the tragic ironies in the action: the king's insistence that Cuchulain take the oath for the protection of the hearthstone and family values and that he subsequently fight the stranger as proof of his allegiance unwittingly robs Cuchulain of fulfilment as a father and, condemning him to the terrible isolation of madness, destroys his self-possession entirely. All that is ultimately left Cuchulain is an ungovernable ferocity.

This new scene makes quite redundant an observation voiced ironically by Cuchulain in the earlier version: 'the blind man /Has need of the fool's eyesight and strong body, / While the poor fool has need of the other's wit'. Now the parallels between the heroic and mundane characters are fully sensed. In Shakespearean fashion the sub-plot mirrors the main action in a distorting glass, intensifying the ironies through points of likeness and difference: and the parallels are clear to an audience from the moment that the Blind Man rests on Conchubar's throne and, guessing the reasons for the formal lay-out of the hall, stages the forthcoming ceremony in his imagination, clearly relishing the king's authoritarian role, while leaving Cuchulain's part to the unthinking Fool. (The echoes are of King Lear and Henry IV, Part One but Yeats's handling wholly transcends any suggestion of direct influence.) The Blind Man's tales of Aoife and Scotland in the opening scene are now more plausibly designed to distract the Fool's mind from his hunger, while his genuine terror at voicing his suspicions about the identity of the father of Aoife's son provokes a sudden suspense that is sustained rather than diminished by the immediate arrival on stage of an irate Cuchulain shouting down an unmoved Conchubar.

The other major addition in 1906 was the ritual of the oath-taking, with its deployment of chanting women seers and the potent symbol of the great bowl of fire. The ceremony instils a mood of uneasy resolution till the incantatory tone is rudely disrupted by 'a loud knocking at the door' (so much more ominous than the trumpet-calls of the earlier version) which announces the arrival of the Young Man. Yeats's control of dramatic pace, of juxtapositions and transitions of tone in the revised version is masterly; so too is his use of a rich variety of modes of speech and of distinctive vocabularies and styles (prose, blank verse, short-lined rhymed couplets). With the revisions of 1906 Yeats came to his maturity as a dramatist: he had created a drama of intense psychological exploration that is a direct consequence of pitting his characters against actualized circumstance and imagining their bitterness and bewilderment. Also with the framing device of the Blind Man and the Fool he had found a way of endorsing his presentation of heroism by setting it in sharp contrast with its spiritual and emotional antithesis: the grotesque. On Baile's Strand was the most frequently revived of Yeats's

Cuchulain plays at the Abbey; he was rightly proud of it, since it was a milestone in his theatrical career: his playwriting knew a far greater freedom and innovatory daring thereafter.

Dedication: William Fay (1872–1947) was a founder member of the Irish National Theatre Society and an actor who built a considerable reputation in comedy and farce, especially in Synge's plays. He had a gift for playing fey or simple men (*The Freeman's Journal* wrote of his performance in *On Baile's Strand*, 'a more unstrained "natural" could not be imagined'). In *Dramatis Personae* Yeats recalled that Fay 'could play dirty tramp, stupid countryman, legendary fool, insist on dirt and imbecility, yet play – paradox of the stage – with indescribable personal distinction'.

Persons in the Play: The Fool and Blind Man were originally given the names Barach and Fintain respectively; these were omitted in the 1906 version, presumably to heighten the characters' symbolic status.

   Muirthemne was Cuchulain's fortress near Dundealgan (the modern Dundalk).
   Uladh was the ancient high-kingdom of Ulster, the region of north-eastern Ireland.

Setting: The setting originally focused on two thrones of equal height for Conchubar and Cuchulain, but the revised text offers a stage-picture that gives Conchubar supreme authority. The earliest printings of the 1906 version contain a further direction: 'An elaborate cloak lies on a chair at the other side' in opposition to the throne. Later this was cut as presumably too distracting a symbol; also in the ensuing dialogue, though the Blind Man touches and identifies Conchubar's throne, no reference is made to the brilliant cloak. Dramatically it is far more effective if the cloak is not drawn to the audience's attention till it becomes the token of the growing bond of affection between Cuchulain and the Young Man. Where the central doorway formally opened on an expanse of sea, it now reveals a more mysterious 'beyond' where mist swirls in an uncertain light. Robert Gregory's design for the Abbey productions adapted the scheme for a curtained box set first used for *The Hour-Glass*: undyed jute was used for the hangings on to which were projected amber floods. The doorway of the 1906 version was made a commanding image: two panels, nine feet in height, of studded gold were hung with six large round shields. With great economy Gregory evoked all the simplicity and grandeur of a setting for Greek tragedy.

their features . . . masks: This detail was included only in the 1922 edition of *Plays in Prose and Verse*, though the idea of defining the symbolic 'otherness' of the Blind Man and the Fool through the use of masks had occurred to Yeats during 1911 when Edward Gordon Craig included a woodcut of a mask for a Fool amongst his designs for *The Hour-Glass*. In *Plays for an Irish Theatre* of that year Yeats opined that the same mask could be worn by the Fool in *On Baile's Strand*, ideally to 'go with a masked Blind Man'. Craig took the hint and complied with the design shown here:

9. Edward Gordon Craig's design for the mask for the Fool in *The Hour-Glass* and *On Baile's Strand*.

10. Edward Gordon Craig's design for the mask for the Blind Man in *On Baile's Strand*.

There is no record that either mask was made, or that masks of any kind were used in Abbey productions of the play during Yeats's lifetime. However, Terence Gray staged the play in Cambridge in 1927 following Yeats's full prescriptions for masks, which clearly proved the theatrical validity of the dramatist's intended scheme. Several photographs of the two masked performers, whose stylized poses and movement work were choreographed by Ninette de Valois, were found amongst Yeats's private papers at his death.

1. *Boann*: The river deity who presides over the Boyne.

2. *Fand*: Wife of the sea-god, Manannan MacLir. She appears as the Woman of the Sidhe in *The Only Jealousy of Emer*.

3. *Aoife*: In his youth Cuchulain was sent to Scotland to study the art of fighting with the enchantress-queen Scathach, whose authority was challenged by the younger Aoife, leader of a local tribe of warriors (in *At the Hawk's Well* these are described as chiefly a troop of 'fierce women of the hills'). Cuchulain fought in single combat with her and, though she destroyed all his weapons, he defeated her ultimately by cunning: Scathach told him how much Aoife prized her chariot and horses; when she came to attack him for the last time, he shouted that they had plunged into a ravine; Aoife turned, Cuchulain seized her and carried her to Scathach's camp, where he held her at sword point till she begged her life before agreeing to make bonds of peace with her enemy. Subsequently she became Cuchulain's lover and, in Lady Gregory's account, was already pregnant with his child, when he was required to return to Ireland. Yeats changes this last detail to make Cuchulain totally ignorant of the fact that he is a father, thereby intensifying the tragic climax of the play.

4. *to a tune*: Florence Farr composed the following setting for this song in 1904:

THE FOOL'S SONG   FLORENCE FARR

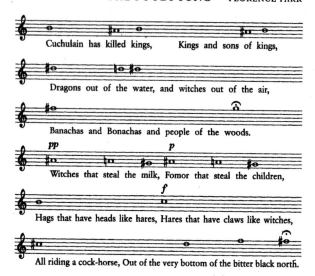

Cuchulain has killed kings, Kings and sons of kings,

Dragons out of the water, and witches out of the air,

Banachas and Bonachas and people of the woods.

Witches that steal the milk, Fomor that steal the children,

Hags that have heads like hares, Hares that have claws like witches,

All riding a cock-horse, Out of the very bottom of the bitter black north.

As this fell largely outside Willie Fay's range, Herbert Hughes composed an alternative for the early performances. Yeats wrote: 'These songs . . . are sung so as to preserve as far as possible the intonation and speed of ordinary passionate speech.'

5. *Banachas . . . Bonachas*: Goblin-like creatures of Gaelic folklore.

6. *Fomor*: Malign, misshapen spirits of death and night; often called the Firbolg, they had, according to Yeats, 'now the heads of goats and bulls, and now but one leg, and one arm'.

7. *What a mix-up . . . like a gate*: Joseph Holloway, veteran Dublin theatre-goer of conservative tastes, thought the 1906 version confusing for anyone unfamiliar with the saga; but this reiteration of the salient points of the exposition in the comic mode is a first-rate structural device, which sharply differentiates it from the tonal contrast that immediately follows of the Blind Man's fear of revealing the most crucial detail of the story.

8. *Maeve*: Queen of Connaught, whose capital was Cruachan in Roscommon; she was an implacable enemy of Cuchulain and of Ulster.

9. *northern pirates*: Norsemen who repeatedly attacked the coastal communities in the north and east of Ireland.

10. *Sorcha . . . World*: Countries in the Other-world of Gaelic lore.

11. *burns the earth*: When angry, a reddish 'hero-light' shone out of Cuchulain. In this state he was invincible.

12. *your father . . . sun*: The version of Cuchulain's birth recounted by Lady Gregory tells how Lugh, the god of light, fell in the form of a mayfly into a drink being

consumed by Dechtire, Conchubar's sister, at the time of her marriage to Sualtim, son of Roig. She went into a deep sleep and was abducted by the god with fifty of her maidens to the Land of the Sidhe, where she subsequently gave birth to the hero. Cuchulain was adopted by Sualtim when Dechtire was discovered and brought back to Ulster.

13. *names upon the harp*: Their lives will be the subject of epic poems sung to a musical accompaniment.

14. *clean hawk . . . air*: This is how Lugh appeared to Dechtire in another version of the story of Cuchulain's birth.

15. *Country-under-Wave*: One of the Celtic conceptions of the Other-world, peopled by the Sidhe, the ever-living ones.

16. *high . . . head*: The epithets applied here to Aoife are significantly ones often used by Yeats to describe Maud Gonne, the object of his unrequited passion for much of his early manhood.

17. *No wonder . . . ground*: This is the only substantial speech that Yeats (with but slight emendations) incorporated into his revised text from the 1904 version. There it was but a generalized statement to justify Cuchulain's claim to prefer fierce women as lovers; here in its new context the images acquire far greater density of psychological implication. What was descriptive has achieved a resonant dramatic life.

18. *I'll take . . . binding*: The agreement has an air of impetuous defiance, the only tone in which Cuchulain could submit and not seem to lose face. But there is also a note of despair in being pressured and isolated like this within the community, which nicely prepares the ground for his later upsurge of fellow-feeling for the Young Man as sharing a like-minded independence.

19. *oath-bound*: Oath-taking, being held under *geasa*, was absolutely sacrosanct within Celtic and old Irish societies; conflict between the claims of different fealties required of an individual is often the cause of tragic circumstance in Gaelic legend.

20. *Shape-Changers*: All the deities and supernatural figures of Celtic folklore, and most especially those associated with the elements, practise transformation and metamorphosis to the confusion of their enemies and humankind.

21. *May this fire . . . hearthstone*: The haunting seven-syllable line of these incantatory couplets carries strong echoes of the verse for the Witches in *Macbeth*, a resonance that Yeats seems deliberately to invite. This became an increasingly favourite metre for Yeats, who used it with consummate versatility in his later works. Some editions of the play carry a further stage direction at the conclusion of the song: '*After "Memory and Mind" their words die away to a murmur, but are loud again at "Therefore in". The others do not speak when these words are loud.*' This indicates how the episode was orchestrated in performance at the Abbey in relation to Cuchulain's ensuing speech.

22. *a loud knocking*: There is an echo here of the knocking at the gate that so disturbs the Macbeths after their murder of King Duncan. The situations are not parallel, but, as with the foregoing song, perhaps Yeats wished subliminally to touch the memory of his audiences to evoke in them a sense of tense unease. The use of music and ritual disrupted by sudden, aggressive sound shows an assured command of the arts of the theatre and control of audience-response.

23. *The door . . . sword enters*: This entrance was particularly memorable in the 1906 production. While the doors were closed for the oath-taking ceremony, Robert Gregory, who designed the lighting as well as the set, changed the grey-blue light on the rear sky-cloth used to evoke the sea-mist at the start of the play; when they opened again, according to Willie Fay, 'Aoife's son . . . stood silhouetted against a background of topaz blue giving an effect of sea and sky with an atmosphere that could never be obtained by paint.' This lighting state was sustained till the end of the play; the brilliant hue framed by the golden doorway would serve as an emblematic reminder of the youth, his high spirits and fearlessness during the tragic climax of Cuchulain's process of discovery.

24. *Looks . . . shoulder*: I have deleted a redundant detail in the stage direction here. Usually the passage reads: 'comes down steps and grasps Young Man by shoulder', but the reference to the steps is an oversight on Yeats's part. From the arrival of the Young Man onwards the 1904 and 1906 texts are virtually identical but for minor emendations. The early version includes a direction (subsequently cut in 1906) after 'And you speak highly, too' (see p. 62), requiring Cuchulain to '*come down from his great chair. He remains standing on the steps of the chair. The young kings gather about him and begin to arm him.*' This refers to the original stage-setting with its complementary thrones for Conchubar and Cuchulain. For the actor playing Cuchulain to move within a short amount of stage-time from the centre of the sword-ritual to fending off his friends from attacking the youth, then from sitting on his throne to descending to arm himself, must have been distractingly fussy. After the violent activity surrounding the Young Man's arrival, a degree of stillness is required for the actor to register the growth of Cuchulain's impulse to befriend the youth. It is in keeping with the greater psychological clarity of the 1906 version that the pattern of movement is more controlled. Without the presence of a throne for Cuchulain on stage, the reference to 'steps' is pointless.

25. *You will stop . . . this day out*: To compare this speech with its equivalent in the 1904 text is to see how much tauter and more precise Yeats's dramatic verse had become:

> You'll stop with us
> And we will hunt the deer and the wild bulls
> And, when we have grown weary, light our fires
> In sandy places where the wool-white foam
> Is murmuring and breaking, and it may be
> That long-haired women will come out of the dunes
> To dance in the yellow fire-light. You hang your head,
> Young man, as if it was not a good life;
> And yet what's better than to hurl the spear,
> And hear the long-remembering harp, and dance?
> Friendship grows quicker in the murmuring dark;
> But I can see there's no more need for words
> And that you'll be my friend now.

By 1906 the decorative and literary have given place to imaginatively sensed experience. The world of the play may be remote but the revised verse ensures that it has immediacy and credibility.

26. *Laegaire*: Leary was one of Conchubar's Red Branch warriors; for the source of his rivalry with Cuchulain, see *The Green Helmet*.

27. *four provinces*: Ulster, Connaught, Munster and Leinster made up the ancient kingdom of Ireland.

28. *Spreading out cloak.* The cloak with its designs evoking the powers of the sea is opposed at this moment on stage to the emblematic fire, which at Conchubar's command has been contained and reduced to a symbol of the hearth. Originally the costumes for the play had been designed and made by Yeats's patron Annie Horniman, through whose generosity the National Theatre Society had acquired the Abbey; they were sumptuous but ungainly to Yeats's eye. In 1915 Charles Ricketts redesigned the costumes to accompany Robert Gregory's set and lighting. For Cuchulain he produced a simple tunic and trousers to complement the lines of the actor's body but surmounted these with a vast cloak covered with stylized patterns suggestive of eddying water in blues and greens on a white and gold ground. The design was a felicitous response to the implications of Yeats's text.

11. Charles Ricketts's design for a costume for Cuchulain in *On Baile's Strand*.

29. *I have seen ... all finished*: This sequence was added to the 1906 version; earlier Barach, the Fool, dragged in Fintain, the Blind Man, and the text continued with 'You have eaten it, you have eaten it!' The new scene greatly enhances the pattern of ironic reversals that concludes the play. The flames in the women's bowl have died away and the element of fire is now envisioned as a force of devastation; the women read the future 'in the ashes', a pursuit which formerly called forth the reckless Cuchulain's scorn (see p. 55). The women are right in foretelling of doom; but the First Woman's

enigmatic utterances are misinterpreted by her two over-emotional companions so that the suspense mounts as to the precise outcome of the fight, which the audience can hear taking place without. Again this shows a wonderful command of different dimensions of reality on and off stage. The scene also requires expert orchestration in performance: Yeats is now writing confidently for good ensemble players, which the Abbey company had become by 1906. There is no surviving record showing how the women appeared in performance at that date, but a design for them by Charles Ricketts of 1915 found amongst Yeats's papers shows he invested them with a dignified but frightening strangeness that calls to mind the three Norns, shapers of human destiny, in Wagner's *Ring of the Niebelung*, which was a wholly apt analogy.

12. Charles Ricketts's design for costumes for the women in *On Baile's Strand*.

30. *crubeen*: A pig's foot used to flavour a stew.

31. *He has taken . . . country*: This short passage is another instance of the greater psychological tautness of the 1906 version. Originally in response to the Fool's reference to the blood on the sword, the Blind Man asked gleefully, 'Whose blood? Whose blood?', to which Cuchulain replied, 'That young champion's.' And seeking complete assurance, the Blind Man further questioned: 'He that came out of Aoife's country?' In the later version, the Blind Man is all-knowing and speaks with a quiet satisfaction that events are developing exactly as he foresaw. The contrasting tones here between two kinds of innocence and an evil, because emotionally detached, insight are superbly differentiated.

32. *He was about . . . died*: Yeats departs here from his saga sources, where it is the dying Connla who names his mother, to build towards a more terrible instant of recognition for Cuchulain.

33. *Scathach*: See n. 3 on *Aoife*, above.

34. *Uathach*: Scathach's daughter, who fell passionately in love with the hero when she saw him devising a means of crossing the magic bridge that gained admission to Scathach's island-fortress.

35. *Alba*: The Celtic name for Scotland.

36. *It is his own . . . slain*: This is a significant revision of the 1904 text, where Cuchulain himself voiced his realization of the truth. It is dramatically more powerful to deploy silence and a purely physical response at first, contrasting with Cuchulain's next sudden outpouring of confused words as his mind seeks to retreat from its terrible perception.

37. *Dubthach*: This warrior, called the Black Beetle of Ulster, was renowned for his satirical or chafing tongue. In *Cuchulain of Muirthemne* he is described as joining with Fergus in burning Emain Macha, Conchubar's city, in revenge for the king's treachery against the Sons of Usnach (see *Deirdre*). Subsequently he and Fergus joined the forces of Conchubar's enemy, Queen Maeve of Connaught.

38. *He is going . . . mastered him*: This is a taxing episode on the resources of the actor playing the Fool's role, since it is made up of short, flat, repeated sentences full of tragic import that the character in his innocence does not comprehend until the final moment ('the waves have mastered him'); the tone is one of childlike exhilaration in a fight, beyond which the audience must sense a more terrifying reality. Text and performer (Willie Fay) were perfectly matched in 1906: in *On the Boiler* (1939) Yeats was to write: 'I have aimed at tragic ecstasy, and here and there in my own work and in the work of my friends I have seen it greatly played'; he continues, 'I am haunted by certain moments' and gives but six instances, including 'William Fay at the end of *On Baile's Strand*'.

The Green Helmet

What impresses is the sheer variety of styles Yeats mastered once he turned regularly to professional playwriting. Though the dominant mode of his early work is tragic, he often deployed styles of comedy to deepen its poignant impact. That comedy had grown darker, crueller of late with the portrayal of the Blind Man and the Fool of *On Baile's Strand* and of Conchubar in *Deirdre*, with his self-satisfying malice and games of deception. These characters provoke a mirthless laughter in performance, near-allied to shocked outrage, as the comedy approaches the satirical in its depiction of predatory evil. In *The Green Helmet* satire took control and the effect is uproarious. Yeats had recently been studying Jonson, Marston and Byron, and the savagery of their work clearly made its mark on his inspiration. Originally a prose version of the play was staged with the title *The Golden Helmet* at the Abbey in March 1908; almost immediately Yeats began transposing it into verse with a rollicking ballad metre in irregular, rhyming fourteeners; the new version, now called *The Green Helmet*, was mounted in February 1910 with a virtually identical cast. J. M. Kerrigan, Arthur Sinclair and Fred O'Donovan played Cuchulain, Conall and Laegaire respectively; Sara Allgood appeared as Emer, her sister Molly as Conall's Wife, and Ambrose Power as the Red Man. A. E. Malone defined the wit of the play as Shavian in the way Yeats stripped the world of myth of its semi-divine attributes, exposing it as vulnerably human, and effortlessly invested legend with modern relevance.

Malone was not being wholly fair to Yeats's source material: as recounted by Lady Gregory in *Cuchulain of Muirthemne*, the saga-stories of 'Bricriu's Feast and the War of Words of the Women of Ulster' and 'The Championship of Ulster', on which the play is based, both subject the epic heroes and their wives to sustained mockery for their self-assertion and gross vanity. In the sagas Cuchulain is included in the satire along with the rest of Conchubar's court when the trickster, Bricriu, sows discord there as a joke. In Yeats's play, however, there is a significant change in the story: his Cuchulain stands apart from the madness that afflicts everyone else and is the only one capable of restoring order in the community. Yeats cleverly conflates two of Lady Gregory's tales: in the sagas Bricriu tricks Cuchulain, Conall and Laegaire into contesting who is the true champion of Ulster deserving the 'hero's portion' at the feast; Conchubar sends the trio to Maeve in Connaught for her to judge who is the superior warrior and then to the Druid-magician Curoi for absolute confirmation of the fact; Curoi as a final test stages the decapitating game to see which of the three men will keep his word; and here Cuchulain proves himself the victor. Whereas in the sagas Cuchulain's heroism ultimately transcends his vainglory and bombast, in the play he never succumbs to the temptation of pride or loses his compelling dignity. All the other characters in turn become the objects of our laughter to some degree, but Cuchulain is a source always of genial humour that voices a level-headed common sense. His ambition is to keep folly in check and save others from their own absurdity; in terms of the movement-patterning of the play in performance, he is the still point in a very giddy world.

The change from 'golden' to 'green' in the title is characteristic of the sharper satirical edge of the revision: it is a specifically *Irish* championship that is being contested. Joseph Holloway records Yeats saying (26 April 1905) that 'he had Charles Stewart Parnell' in his mind when he wrote *On Baile's Strand*. 'People who do aught for Ireland,' he said, 'ever and always have to fight with the waves in the end.' Such had in some measure been Yeats's lot throughout 1907 during the riots over Synge's *The Playboy of the Western World* and the secession of the Fay brothers from the Abbey (partly through a dispute over policy and programming) with all the public gossip and recriminations that inevitably accompanied their departure; he had in consequence to learn how to cope with others' animosity and venom and stay composed. His new poems of this date became pithily satirical, being epigrammatic in form; and that precision is carried over into the revised play where the ballad metre allows for a greater forcefulness of expression on account of the rhythmic pulse. It required confidence to write of Ireland as 'this unlucky country that was made when the Devil spat' (p. 75).

The plot and characterizations, dramatic method, scheme for staging and thematic intention were all clear in the first version, but the second has the greater verbal daring and punch. The rollicking verse immediately evokes a world that is under a strange enchantment and no longer true to itself: a once settled community is a prey to continued wrangling that now gets wholly out of control; verbal gives place to physical violence and words to sheer noise in a mad quest for a means to assert a properly heroic stature. The stage becomes a riot of movement and colour at the climax as the space fills with servants blasting away on weird horns, the women shriek and attack each other with daggers and the heroes snatch at the fatal helmet. One of Yeats's favourites amongst Jonson's plays was *Epicoene, or The Silent Woman*, where a man who loves silence, Morose, finds his home invaded on the day of his wedding by streams of visitors bringing caterers, trumpeters, dance-bands and the like to celebrate the occasion till stage and theatre are overwhelmed by a mounting tide of noise. If

Jonson was an influence here, Yeats transformed the inspiration by making his image of total chaos decidedly political in its significance.

Cuchulain, when he first encounters the Red Man, asks why he does not choose to play his tricks on his own sort:

> . . . if the waves have vexed you and you would find a sport
> Of a more Irish fashion, go fight without a rest
> A caterwauling phantom among the winds of the West.

This is a profoundly satirical thrust: being quintessentially 'Irish' is here associated with futile aggression, mindless brawling ('caterwauling') and delusion (a 'phantom'). These together with drunkenness are the stock qualities of the stage-Irishman, that racial and racist stereotype devised by the English as an expression of colonial superiority. Cuchulain's sarcasm runs deep: to be Irish on such terms is to betray one's fundamental humanity and one's nationhood. (Noticeably the imagery in which much human activity is described in the play is reductive, referring to 'cats' and 'cocks'.) The ensuing mayhem that the Red Man stage-manages by leaving the *green* helmet for the bravest to take up is a test of how staunchly Cuchulain can stand by the principles he voices here and so promote a more life-enhancing concept of Irishness. With considerable patience and insight he works to defuse all the provocations to violence that the Red Man initiates and finally is prepared even to sacrifice his life if it will end the strife and pettiness that afflict his community. He is fearless, not in the foolhardy way of the swashbuckler but in independently asserting (while anarchy prevails all around him) the value of peace, concord, trust, honesty and truth to one's word; and so defines a new style of heroism which ultimately wins him the prize of champion. Cuchulain has the courage to be true to himself. Repeatedly throughout the plays concerning Cuchulain, Yeats defines heroism as virtually synonymous with magnanimity. As is implied in the Red Man's final eulogy of his newly elected champion, heroism is less a matter of deeds than a habit of mind:

> . . . I choose the laughing lip
> That shall not turn from laughing, whatever rise or fall;
> The heart that grows no bitterer although betrayed by all;
> The hand that loves to scatter; the life like a gambler's throw;
> And these things I make prosper . . .

Yeats has in fact completely subverted the underlying values of his source material in the sagas by the highly accomplished technical feat of creating a hilarious farce in which the central character resists the belittling tendencies of that particular dramatic form.

Setting: This was certainly the boldest of the stylized colour-schemes Yeats devised along the principles he laid down in 1904, where one colour was to predominate in the setting and another in the costumes. In a note on the staging of the play, he observed:

> One . . . gets also much more effect out of concerted movements – above all, if there are many players – when all the clothes are the same colour. No breadth of treatment gives monotony when there is movement and change of lighting. It concentrates attention on every new effect and makes every change of outline or of light and shadow surprising and delightful . . . One wishes to make the movement of the action

as important as possible, and the simplicity which gives depth of colour does this, just as, for precisely similar reasons, the lack of colour in a statue fixes the attention upon the form.

That he should write here of 'concerted movements' in relation to the design indicates Yeats's wish that an audience should be made conscious that the movement patterns of the actors about the stage in this particular play have a near choreographic quality, essential in the faster paced sequences of farce, that has a symbolic rather than a realistic intent. Holloway recounts an amusing anecdote about the play in rehearsal that substantiates the point: he tells of

> Yeats . . . speaking to one of the supers . . . and telling him he did not come on right; he should walk on as if he were taking part in some great ritual, as if inspired by some great religious emotion. The super couldn't understand the poet . . . so Yeats turned to Wilson [the Company Manager] with, 'Let you explain'. Wilson merely said, 'Walk on and pause a moment; then proceed as if you were attending your grandfather's funeral!' The super understood and Yeats had got the effect he in vain had sought to explain.

The incongruity of the green helmet on the Red Man who is otherwise 'altogether in red' immediately invests the property with significance and interest; ultimately, of course, it completes the all-green attire of Cuchulain, giving him now a lofty appearance. Green and orange were at this time the traditional colours in the Irish nationalist flag; the staging visually alerted the initial audiences to the political implications of the action.

1. *the moon's at the full*: Always in Celtic lore a time when magic and the supernatural will be most likely to occur. See, for example, the final scene of *The Herne's Egg*.

2. *Scotland*: Emer's father disliked Cuchulain's wooing of his daughter, so in disguise he told the hero how the finest fighting skills were only to be learned from Scathach in Scotland. Fogall hoped that Cuchulain would be killed while travelling abroad, leaving Emer a widow. *At the Hawk's Well* is set in Scotland and there is reference to the time Cuchulain spent with Scathach in *On Baile's Strand*.

3. *long green cloak*: The colour symbolism is repeatedly emphasized in the revision; the 1908 text reads 'wrapped in a cloak'.

4. *Does anything . . . sea?*: 'Continually, as so often in Yeats's plays, the audience's attention is drawn to what lies beyond the stage-space that occasions fear and expectancy in those waiting within.

5. *rath*: Fortress or stronghold, often used as here in reference to the home of some fairy or supernatural beings.

6. *Old herring*: Throughout his scenes with the Red Man, Cuchulain adopts a line in genial banter that suggests a complete nonchalance in the face of danger, markedly contrasting with Conall and Laegaire's fear. The Red Man comments on this (p. 79) to provoke their jealousy of Cuchulain; they are as subject to mean-spiritedness as the court they have just been criticizing.

7. *Manannan*: The god of the sea, greatest shape-changer of all in Celtic myth.

8. *Irish*: See prefatory note above.

9. *Sualtim's son*: Sualtim, the son of Roig, was married to Dechtire, Conchubar's sister. According to some versions of the sagas, she was carried off by Lugh, the god of light, and bore him a son, Cuchulain, whom Sualtim adopted as his own.

10. *bravest*: The 1908 text here reads 'strongest', but it is strength of mind rather than of sinew that is being tested, which the revision more aptly intimates.

11. *ladles . . . like*: The 1908 text reads 'with great horns of many fantastic shapes'; the revision to include ladles and other kitchen utensils gives the servants' entrance more the quality of a traditional skimmington or skimmity (a low-class, Bacchic rout, generally accompanied by much banging of household objects, designed to express distaste for some member of the community).

12. *wrestle . . . struggling*: In Lady Gregory's account of the tale, the wives meet some way from the hall and proceed in a level row for a while, but the nearer they approach, the faster they try to stride, lifting up their skirts 'nearly to their knees' to speed their movement. In the 1908 version each wife had a song as she first appeared in the doorway, only to be thrust aside by the other two.

13. *Nothing . . . that fire*: Emer's song originally took for theme simply 'My man is the best'; the revision is emotionally and sensually more explicit, evoking the magnitude of Emer's passion for Cuchulain.

14. *three black hands . . . torches*: At the Abbey this detail had to be abandoned, according to Yeats: 'In performance we left the black hands to the imagination, and probably when there is so much noise and movement on the stage they would always fail to produce any effect. Our stage is too small to try the experiment, for they would be hidden by the figures of the players.'

15. *A light . . . sword*: From 1906, when Yeats saw Charles Ricketts's highly atmospheric use of electric lighting for his production of Wilde's *Salome*, Yeats, with Robert Gregory's help, had been experimenting with this new aspect of stage design. The productions of *The Shadowy Waters*, *On Baile's Strand* and *Deirdre* had realized some notable effects; now Yeats was actually writing such effects into his plays. This adventurous sequence stretched the Abbey's resources to the limit: darkness suddenly falls over a stage radiant with light and colour; then faint glimmerings show the mass of characters in silhouette, while only the Red Man and Cuchulain are caught in a shaft of light. The lighting changes skilfully effect a powerful tonal shift from outrageous farce to the high seriousness of the concluding episode: Cuchulain's rite of passage ends with his spiritual election, and the political strategy shaping the drama, concerned with restoring a proper dignity to Ireland, becomes clear. This is purposeful theatricality of a high order.

16. *no faithful man . . . dare?*: A confessional honesty in the presence of likely death. Both Uathach, Scathach's daughter, and Aoife had been Cuchulain's lovers in Scotland (see *On Baile's Strand*). This passage and the ensuing scene with Emer were additions to the revised text, demonstrating her heroism and his tender care of her. Some editions of the 1910 text have an exclamation mark after 'do you dare', but framing the remark as a question suffuses it with genuine wonder at Emer's courage. His last words to her ('Bear children and sweep the house') are not as a result cruelly reductive or intemperate, but an expression of his anxiety that she should live free from risk.

Deirdre

This is the most perfectly crafted of Yeats's early plays. Although it underwent revisions at various times (between 1906 and 1911, and again in 1922 and 1934), these were related to the texture of the verse and the pacing of episodes; the structure remained unchanged from its first conception. Yeats's first public announcement in *Samhain* (1904) that he was drafting *Deirdre* described the play as having 'choruses somewhat in the Greek manner'. The Musicians do certainly have that function at times, but the remark reveals that from the first Yeats was conceiving a drama along neoclassical lines. As Malone observed, Yeats's handling of the saga material 'concentrated its essence into a single act of great dramatic intensity'. Maud Gonne, comparing Yeats's version with Synge's *Deirdre of the Sorrows* (where over three acts the full story is told of Deirdre's elopement with Naoise on the eve of her marriage to Conchubar, the lovers' exile in Scotland and their tragic return to Emain), remarked wickedly that 'those first two acts are so difficult to make living . . . you were not interested enough in them to try and only began at the third'. But Yeats's motive was seemingly very different: his letters about Abbey policy and programming to Synge and Lady Gregory at this time often mention Racine and Sophocles; Robert Gregory thought of staging *Antigone* with Sara Allgood in the title role; and Yeats mused with Frank Fay, a great admirer of French classical theatre, about an Irish production of a play such as *Phèdre*. After his decidedly Irish reworking in *On Baile's Strand* of the Shakespearean model for tragedy, one can appreciate Yeats's wish to experiment with a different tradition and a more concentrated form. The story of Deirdre is the one saga that looks hard at extremes of emotion; it was the ideal subject for a neoclassical treatment.

Choice of form necessitated a very free handling of the legend generally known as 'The Fate of the Sons of Usnach': several characters of importance in the saga are omitted (Naoise's two brothers, Ainnle and Ardan; Deirdre's nurse, Levarcham; Cuchulain and Conall, who refuse Conchubar's request to bring back the lovers from Scotland, which Fergus is then prevailed on to take up; and Fergus's sons, Iollan and Buinne, who protect the lovers while returning to Emain when their father is prevented from accompanying them). More important, perhaps, are Yeats's introduction of the three wandering musicians as a chorus commenting on the action and his two major changes to the story: he brings Fergus back with the lovers to Emain, whereas in the saga Conchubar places him under bonds to feast with a warrior called Borach, so that he has to abandon Deirdre and Naoise to the king's mercy after their arrival in Ireland; and he unites the lovers in death, whereas in the saga a near crazed Deirdre wanders the countryside after Naoise's burial, lamenting her loss, before killing herself on the sea-shore. These changes deserve further comment.

In the saga Deirdre has the gift of prophecy and knows the tragedy that awaits her and Naoise if they return to Emain, but, Cassandra-like, she is relentlessly disbelieved and overruled by her lover and Fergus. Much of the tale is taken up with her increasingly poignant lamentations; indeed the end of the story is foretold by Cathbad the Druid even before Deirdre's birth; the effect is of a pattern inexorably completing itself. To transpose this directly into drama would make for a tonal monotony. Yeats changes Deirdre's skill in prophecy into intuition: she is at a pitch of nervous apprehension, but is less secure in her perceptions than her prototype. It is the shrewd spectators of the action, the Musicians, who here are confident of a tragic outcome: they observe the signs, engage imaginatively with their knowledge and await the completion of the pattern that they sense as shaping the characters' movements; they expect tragedy but are unsure how it will unfold. A terrific pressure in consequence is imposed on the characters to create an appropriate ending for their situation: Fergus and Naoise hope absurdly for a tragicomic resolution with past tensions eased as Conchubar shows a kingly chivalry to his one-time enemies; the aged king plans to wed the young Deirdre after murdering her lover out of jealous revenge, which would be a kind of black farce; Deirdre wishes to flee with Naoise out of Conchubar's trap, which would leave the situation permanently unresolved; and, when that proves impossible, she asserts her will to create a decorum appropriate to tragedy. She begins by dreading that ending but comes steadily to accept its necessity.

The metatheatrical modernity of this is carried further by the inclusion of Fergus in the drama. If the suspicions that the Musicians and Deirdre voice about Conchubar's treachery are true, then Fergus has been the king's pawn in a strategy designed to bring the lovers to play set roles in a scenario of Conchubar's clever devising. Conchubar himself is revealed to be the most accomplished of actors, feigning a generosity and mercy he does not feel. Fergus refuses to believe this ('I have known his mind as if it were my own /These many years . . . I know myself, and him . . .') until the arrival of the Messenger convinces him that he is the dupe of a wily trickster who, as we later learn, takes pride in having spent 'seven years /Of longing and of planning here and there . . . and watching my own face /That none might read it'.

Shape-changing was thought in Irish lore to be the property of supernatural beings; but it is also the stock-in-trade of actors and the essence of theatre. Shape-changing is transformation of the self; in *Deirdre* the transformations are deeply psychological and the token of them is the subtly changing timbres of the human voice. Yeats alerts us to the importance that the idea of acting has in this play from the moment of Deirdre's arrival on stage: a weary, frightened traveller, she is immediately required to dress, bedeck herself with jewels and make-up, and assume a confidence and vivacity at odds with her real mood. We watch her try first to play the wanton to excite Naoise's jealousy so that he will flee with her back into exile, and then to play the serene chess-player, her attention focused wholly on the game. In both roles she is miscast and her true self emerges despite her efforts to conceal it. Faced with Conchubar, she finds that speaking with sincerity to him about her feelings provokes not forgiveness of her but the command for Naoise's death. She is alone now with an unscrupulous politician, who is a self-confessed actor of consummate skill; and Deirdre realizes that she herself must act in earnest if she is to protect her integrity and be true to her passion for Naoise. She feigns being an alluring woman enamoured of Conchubar, playing the type through a range of moods to flatter his sense of power and sexual conquest; but it is all a strategy to gain her desired end. The irony of her predicament – having to act as the only means of proving the constancy of her love for Naoise – gives Deirdre's words an increasingly intricate wit as she comes under the pressure of death. Yeats's changes to the plot-line of the traditional story are what give the play its potent theatricality: in the theatre the play provokes a rapt attention from audiences as the games of deception become ever more complex.

Yeats's frequent revisions of the play have led some commentators, particularly Bushrui, to suppose he outgrew his early delight in *Deirdre* and was troubled by the verbal texture and idiom he created for it. There is another interpretation that can be put on Yeats's rewriting which links the verbal artistry with the chosen structure of the play. The nature of neoclassical dramatic form is to present us with an entrenched complex situation that is already realized; we do not watch the process of its coming into being; rather we focus on the fluctuating emotions of the characters as they understand the extent of their entrapment. The problem for the dramatist lies in sustaining and heightening the emotional pitch while avoiding monotony. (Yeats's advice to actresses playing Deirdre was, apparently, 'Red heat up to Naoise's death, white heat after he is dead.')

Yeats's earliest major changes were to include Deirdre's first scene of dressing to meet Conchubar, which more clearly introduced the image of acting as a shaping symbol within the dramatic action; and to make more pointed reference to the lack of any messenger to welcome Fergus and the lovers, which builds up suspense over the king's motives. Subsequent revisions were more concerned with getting the pacing and duration of episodes exactly right and with clarifying the motivation for Deirdre's endlessly fluctuating moods. The danger with this fine-tuned focus on the emotions is that analysis will replace evocation of feeling, which will tend to distance an audience when their imaginative engagement is what is required. Yeats himself wrote of the difficulty of matching a rigorously logical form with a passionate subject in these terms: 'if one have not patience to wait for the mood, or to rewrite again and again till it comes, there is rhetoric and logic and dry circumstances where there should be life'. Revisions, often in the wake of performances, were to remove all traces of 'dry', purely functional speech in preference for nuance and suggestion.

'I require for Deirdre,' Yeats wrote to Synge, 'an emotional actress of great experience.' The role of Deirdre indeed requires an actress with a virtuoso technique, if the symbol of acting with its range of psychological implications in the drama is not to seem forced or crude. The first actress to attempt the part (24 November 1906), Florence Darragh, was according to Joseph Holloway 'consistent and beautiful, with an undercurrent of intense subdued emotionalism underlying her outwardly seeming calm'; though clearly skilful, he thought she wanted 'the exquisite poetic touch'. On further viewing, as he grew more familiar with the play, he decided she lacked 'sincerity and charm'. Frank Fay as Noise was 'vigorous' or 'impressively subdued when occasion required'; J. M. Kerrigan 'made a promising debut as the love-tormented king'; but Arthur Sinclair as Fergus 'began to rant and fume almost from the first, instead of gently and gradually leading up to . . . his rage at the king's treachery'. The one voice he considered 'a joy to the ear . . . thrilling in its purity of tone and pathetic significance' was Sara Allgood's as the First Musician. This led Holloway to make a shrewd comment about the special attention actors should pay to their speaking in this particular play: it is 'like a symphony in which the voices are the instruments employed and if one or more is harsh or over-loudly employed the harmony is slain'. Mrs Patrick Campbell had toyed with playing the role when Yeats, urged by Annie Horniman, showed her the prose scenario, and did eventually do so in Dublin and London during November 1908. Though Yeats admired Mona Limerick, Sara Allgood, Maire O'Neill and Jean Forbes-Robertson as Deirdre in subsequent revivals, Stella Campbell's remained the performance he most treasured as 'passionate and solitary'.

The role remains a great test of an actress's skills and not only for its vocal and interpretative demands: around the time Yeats was completing and first staging *Deirdre* in 1906 he was also drafting *Discoveries*, where, in 'Personality and the Intellectual Essences', he expressed the belief that there was no great or popular drama that 'did not use, or seem to use, the bodily energies of its principal actor to the full'; *Deirdre* was the first of his plays to employ the 'speaking' body of a woman to such a powerful degree.

Dedication: Mrs Patrick Campbell (1865–1940), a close friend of George Bernard Shaw, had made her reputation with the title role in Pinero's *The Second Mrs Tanqueray* (1893), Sudermann's *Magda* (1896) and as Eliza Doolittle in *Pygmalion* (1914). In 1904 she had played Mélisande to Sarah Bernhardt's Pelléas in Maeterlinck's play in a performance which Yeats treasured for its acute presentation of innocence. By 1899 she had gone into management, and Ibsen's plays, especially *Ghosts*, regularly featured in her repertoire. After her success in *Deirdre*, Yeats began devising *The Player Queen* as a companion-piece to exploit her comic talents. Her company for the London performances of *Deirdre* at the New Theatre included Henry Ainley, who played Noise and Orestes in Hofmannsthal's version of Sophocles' *Electra*, which aptly shared the double bill with Yeats's play.

Robert Gregory (1881–1918), Lady Gregory's son, had trained as an artist at the Slade in London and at Blanche's atelier in Paris after leaving New College, Oxford. From 1903, when he helped with Sturge Moore to devise a setting for *The Hour-Glass*, Gregory, as designer, had been closely associated with staging and lighting the plays of Yeats (*On Baile's Strand*, *The Shadowy Waters*, *Deirdre*), Lady Gregory (*Kincora*, *The White Cockade*, *The Image*, *The Deliverer*), Douglas Hyde (*The Nativity*) and Synge (*Deirdre of the Sorrows*). He concentrated increasingly on easel-painting after his marriage in 1907. A pilot during the First World War, Gregory was killed on 23 January 1918: Yeats wrote four great elegies celebrating his achievements. Till Mrs Campbell played Deirdre for Yeats, the dedication was exclusively to Gregory.

Setting: Surviving photographs of Mrs Campbell's London performances show that Gregory's setting exactly followed Yeats's prescriptions; the brazier was situated to the audience's left and a low table with chessboard and two simple curved stools to their right. As a designer, Gregory always responded sensitively to the implications of the text of a play; that was notably the case here. The directions do not mention one felicitous detail in the realized design: the curtained inner room, approached up three steps, was seen dimly to contain hunting gear, animal skins and weapons. The emblematic connotations of cruelty and sport these suggested augmented the growing sense of danger. It is to be the place of death where Naoise will be dragged entangled like a boar in a net to be gutted at the king's command and where Deirdre will choose to go, proud and absolute, to find peace and revenge in suicide. From the opening of the play the chamber waits, a focus of attention, an embodiment of fate and inevitability to which the lovers *must* come for all the pathos of their struggles to resist. Gregory's design through this one detail subtly complemented the tragic inexorability of the play's structure.

During 1910 to 1911 Gordon Craig devised an alternative design using his system of screens as shown on p. 308:

13. Edward Gordon Craig's suggested setting for *Deirdre*.

There is no record of this scheme being used at the Abbey, though in *Plays for an Irish Theatre* (where the design first appeared) Yeats suggests some textual alterations to accommodate this setting and considers the dramatic effectiveness of projecting shadows of the 'barbarous dark-faced men' over the screens to create an ominous atmosphere. Craig gave Yeats a miniature theatre and set of screens to work with while composing plays, and he devised a number of floor-plans with other arrangements of the screens for *Deirdre*. Though none was implemented, it is interesting to see Yeats attempting to get away from a centralized placing of the inner room by turning the design to the diagonal, giving the actors a greater depth of usable stage-space for the earlier half of the play.

1. *First Musician*: This role was originally conceived for Florence Farr (Yeats told her: 'I always saw your face as I wrote') but was never played by her. Sara Allgood took the part at the Abbey and was invited by Mrs Campbell to play it in London, even though Florence Farr was in her company playing Clytemnestra in the *Electra* which shared the bill with *Deirdre*.

2. *royal house*: Situated at Armagh.

3. *old witch*: The saga account states that, on hearing Cathbad the Druid's terrible prophecy about Deirdre at her birth (that she would bring ruin on all Ireland on account of her beauty), her father, Fedlimid, hid her away in a secluded cottage in the forest to be reared by a nurse called Levarcham. At fourteen Deirdre was seen by a wandering soldier, who brought word of her to Conchubar. The king sought out the cottage and decided to make Deirdre his queen.

4. *in my charge*: Fergus pledged his protection, if the lovers would end their exile and return to Conchubar's court.

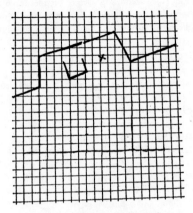

14. Yeats's sketch of a floor-plan showing a possible arrangement of Craig's screens to realize a setting for *Deirdre* (as re-created by Liam Miller).

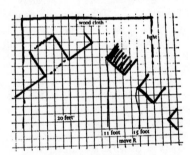

15. A further sketch by Yeats for an arrangement of screens to create a setting for *Deirdre* which approximates the setting designed by Craig (as re-created by Liam Miller).

5. *Yet . . . jealous*: Yeats had used repetition to characterize the mindless chatter of the Fool in *On Baile's Strand*; in *Deirdre* he began to experiment with the device to create a sense of the ominous; it was a technique he continued to explore in later plays for a wide variety of effects.

6. *Lugaidh Redstripe . . . wretchedly*: Lugaidh Riab nDerg was called 'of the Redstripes' on account of the circumstances of his conception. His mother, Clothra, had affairs with each of her three brothers in turn and the body of Lugaidh, the child of these

unions, was divided into three sections by two red stripes; each part resembled that same portion of one father's person. Lugaidh, who was High-King from A D 65 to 73, also had a son by Clothra, Crimthann Nia Nair, whose reign, succeeding his father–brother's, lasted till A D 90.

7. *Queen Edain*: The legend of Midhir and Etain is included in Lady Gregory's *Gods and Fighting Men* (1904). Etain was the second wife of Midhir, King of the Immortals, and object of jealousy to his first wife, Fuamach. Fuamach drove her rival out of Midhir's kingdom; Angus Og, the god of love and song, pitying Etain, took her into his keeping and refused to return her when Midhir requested it. While the two immortals met to discuss the matter, Fuamach transformed Etain into a fly and created a great wind that blew her around the world for seven years before she fell into a wine-cup and was drunk by Etar's wife, who subsequently gave birth to her as a human child. When a woman again Etain married Eochaid, High-King of Ireland; Midhir came and tried to win her back by making her the prize in a series of games of chess. At the third game he succeeded and took her back to his fairy kingdom for some years, but Eochaid made war on Midhir and eventually recovered her. This haunting song evokes the sadness that overwhelms the human Etain when in some deep of the mind she remembers her fairy existence – an inexplicable pain that not even the joys of sexual fulfilment can wholly assuage. The lyric also tells of a sensitive compatibility between two lovers, a union of sensibilities like that once known by Deirdre and Naoise but which has been jeopardized by their return to Emain. The story of Etain was dramatized by 'Fiona Macleod' (William Sharp) in *The Immortal Hour* (1900).

8. *Deirdre . . . entered*: Originally the direction for the lovers' entrance came at the close of the song and was extended to include details about the lighting design for the early half of the play: '*The sky outside is still bright so that the room is dim in the midst of a wood full of evening light, but gradually during what follows the light fades out of the sky; and except during a short time before the lighting of the torches, and at the end of all, the room is either dark amid light or light amid the darkness.*' This would have been a most atmospheric effect to have achieved (one closely akin to the symbolic use of light, gloom and total darkness in Maeterlinck's plays), but it would have been difficult to control such meticulous slow fades with the equipment available at the Abbey in 1906, even with Gregory's growing expertise. Editions from 1908 omit this direction and insert instead the simpler directions about changes in the lighting on pp. 102–103.

9. *raddle*: A red powder generally used with water as a dye in rural communities but here applied as facial make-up like rouge.

10. *Surracha*: Sorcha, the Celtic Other-world.

11. *We'll play at chess*: References to games of chess abound in the sagas and occur on two significant occasions in 'The Fate of the Sons of Usnach'. In Scotland the lovers are playing together at chess when Fergus arrives to persuade them to return to Ireland. They are at play together again in Conchubar's guest-house when a messenger from the king comes to spy on them to see if Deirdre has lost her beauty; Deirdre senses they are being watched and tells Naoise, who throws a chessman at the window, blinding the spy.

The image of chess accrues symbolic connotations as the action of the play advances: Conchubar's manoeuvring of Fergus and the lovers into exactly the positions he wants them in to pursue his revenge requires a series of cunningly planned and executed moves. Yeats does not force the analogy but allows it to resonate in an audience's mind sufficiently to build up an impression of Conchubar as possessing a prodigious intelligence. His long-delayed entrance into the action comes at precisely the moment that he moves to checkmate his rival's queen.

12. *Silence . . . no messenger*: This scene was first included by way of an appendix to the text of *Deirdre* printed in the *Collected Works* of 1908. Yeats, in an introductory note, explains his constant dissatisfaction with his first staging of Deirdre's entrance; it was Mrs Campbell's offer to play the role at the Abbey that 'so stirred [his] imagination that the scene came right in a moment'. The new scene introduces the all-important theme of acting as a mask to disguise one's true feelings. The dialogue has a nervous restlessness that generates great tension in performance.

13. *When first . . . death*: The first editions of 1907 and 1908 include a stage direction concerning Naoise after the lovers' entrance on p. 92 (it was subsequently cut) which carefully prepares for Deirdre's observation: '*Naoise lays down shield and spear and helmet, as if weary. He goes to the door opposite to the door he entered by. He looks out on to the road that leads to Conchubar's house. If he is anxious, he would not have Fergus or Deirdre notice it.*'

14. *Under his eyes . . . power*: Deirdre's studied repetition of Fergus's words was an addition first included in *Plays in Prose and Verse* (1922); it makes Deirdre's line of thought clearer and enhances one's sense of the irony that Fergus's attempt to defend his position serves only to strengthen Deirdre's anxiety, as she begins fully to apprehend the extent of the trap sprung about her.

15. *The message . . . done*: Another instance of repetition that cuts through Fergus's and Naoise's relief showing Deirdre's more acute perception. She reasons always out of her emotions but with unerring accuracy; this is steadily characterizing Deirdre as possessing an intelligence which, though differently formed, is as penetrating as Conchubar's. By the time they meet we are prepared for a battle of equally matched minds and wills.

16. *reaping-hooks*: Farmers.

17. *My name . . . power*: Fergus had formerly been King of Ulster but was persuaded by his wife, Ness, to let Conchubar, her son by her first marriage, reign for a year, 'so that his children after him may be called the children of a king'. During that year she bribed the chieftains of Ulster to vote that Conchubar should keep the throne. There is considerable pathos in the way Yeats shows the old man struggling to retain a little dignity: he has been tricked a second time and made to look a fool.

18. *A Musician . . . loneliness*: This was a change from Yeats's initial prescriptions for the lighting effects in the opening half of the play (see note 8 above). It is still a powerful moment in the performance when the gathering darkness (in which we hear only the lovers' voices as they attempt to get control of their fear) suddenly gives place with the lighting of the torches to a stage-picture of them already seated at chess, exactly mirroring what they have said about their counterparts, Lugaidh and his wife.

19. *Conchubar . . . door*: A powerfully enigmatic moment, which the actor playing Conchubar must decide how to motivate. Does Conchubar make an entrance expecting

to triumph over a pair of lovers transfixed by fear, only to be frustrated at finding them not, as they intended, playing chess with an imperturbable calm but lost to each other in a passionate embrace? Or does he appear simply to tease them with a show of strength, hoping to tempt Naoise out of the hall, which will leave Deirdre unguarded?

20. *spy*: In 'The Fate of the Sons of Usnach' Conchubar sends first Levarcham, Deirdre's old nurse, and then Gelban of Lochlann to observe Deirdre and see if she is still as lovely as when he planned to wed her.

21. *entangled in a net*: This is Yeats's invention. In the saga Naoise and his brothers are captured by Druid magic and at their own request beheaded together with one stroke of Naoise's sword wielded by Maine Rough-Hand. A. N. Jeffares and A. S. Knowland suggest a parallel with the *Oresteia* of Aeschylus, where Agamemnon is murdered after being caught in a net by Aegisthus and Clytemnestra. This may be an echo in Yeats's creative imagination, but the tableau of Naoise's humiliation is wholly in keeping with Conchubar's sadism in wanting to shame his rival before Deirdre.

22. *There was one . . . her*: In the saga, Deirdre in her lament for the dead Naoise recalls how only once he caused her to know jealousy when he secretly kissed the daughter of the Lord of Duntreon in Scotland; she endeavoured to sail back to Ireland but Ainnle and Ardan swam after her and persuaded her to return; Naoise pledged undying fidelity.

23. *Pause*: This is a momentous silence, the more telling theatrically the longer the actress playing Deirdre can sustain it. When she turns next to Conchubar, she has measured out the situation, assessed the strength and scope of her adversary's will-power, devised a strategy to combat him and totally transformed herself in order to achieve it. The moment is Yeats's first experiment with the concept of the mask: assuming a persona that is the exact antithesis of one's self so as to come to terms with and vindicate one's innermost truth. It is a brilliant *coup-de-théâtre*, which requires the full resources of an actress's technical skill and panache if it is to be convincing, since Deirdre is given no soliloquy or aside to explain her decision. Subtly the ensuing action will intimate her purpose.

24. *We lay the dead . . . Usna*: Joseph Holloway thought this episode the highspot of Miss Darragh's interpretation:

> Some of her moments were delicious – her description of how she would set out the body of her dead lover I thought particularly so. Here her gestures were exquisitely appropriate. The way she extended her two hands in front of her with entwined thumbs to express the laying out of her lover's feet was perfectly lovely in conception.

25. *He has refused . . . dead face*: Holloway wrote of Mrs Campbell's performance here:

> Her cajoling Conchubar into allowing her to attend to the dead body of her beloved Naoise was a supreme piece of dramatic art, full of subtlety and emotionalism. Her savage outburst on his refusing her first request was superb in its tigerish savagery; · the baffled woman let loose the floodgates of her wrath on the loveless old man who waded through crime to attain her, and annihilated him into submission.

26. *Now strike . . . cock-crow*: Yeats much admired Shakespeare's scene where Cleopatra jokes with the clown who brings the asps with which she is to kill herself; this final speech for Deirdre, alive with double-meanings, is the closest Yeats came to

imitating that tone of quiet jubilation in the face of death. It affords a superb tonal contrast with Conchubar's obscene gloating to Fergus before the truth of the situation is revealed to him. Yeats's control of emotional tone in the closing moments of the tragedy is masterly: over some thirty-two lines, the mood shifts effortlessly from Deirdre's carefully veiled triumph, through the elegiac simplicity of the Musicians' epitaph for the lovers and their soft, wordless keening, to end in the bitter sarcasm with which Conchubar faces defeat and the violence of Fergus's threats of civil war.

At the Hawk's Well

'The form is a discovery and the dancing and masks wonderful,' Yeats wrote excitedly to Lady Gregory after the first performances in London of At the Hawk's Well (1 and 4 April 1916). 'Discovery', a favourite word with Yeats at this time, carries a range of meanings: the audiences were confronted with a style of dance-drama that was wholly innovatory in its use of dance, song, masks, ritual and an austere stylization in terms of design and staging; but the form also required them imaginatively to undergo a process of discovery, to experience through the drama and then to think about the choices made in the depths of self that determine one's individuality. There had been nothing remotely like this in English-speaking theatre; Yeats had made a real breakthrough in terms of dramatic structure and in the demands that structure made on performers, not least in requiring them through the wearing of masks wholly to depersonalize themselves as actors.

From the moment Ezra Pound introduced Yeats to Noh theatre, Yeats was inspired by the creative possibilities the form held for him; he was immediately anxious to know more about how the plays were staged than either Pound could surmise or Ernest Fenollosa's manuscripts reveal. Where Pound was fascinated by Fenollosa's collection of play-transcriptions as literature, Yeats recognized their astonishing theatrical potential. He was never to see a Noh play properly performed (Michio Ito gave him some idea of the posture, gliding movement and dance steps of the principal actor, or *shite*; and two of Ito's friends – Nijuichi Kayano, a dramatist, and Taminosuke Kume, a painter – attempted to demonstrate for him the operatic delivery adopted in reciting the text), but Yeats's intuitive grasp of the fundamental nature of Noh in performance was remarkably exact, as his essay, 'Certain Noble Plays of Japan' (1916), attests. Copying the Japanese prototype was never his intention: Noh was to provide a springboard to facilitate his leap into a new level of personal experiment and invention. *Yugen*, or perfect beauty, was described by Zeami, the fourteenth-century commentator on Noh, as chiefly residing in dramas about an old man, a woman or a warrior; he did not recommend that they should appear with equal dramatic stature within one play, as they do in At the Hawk's Well. Yeats saw the power of all the devices in Noh that make for an absolute concentration of focus and that turn the stage and the action taking place on it into a unified metaphor of considerable emotional and intellectual intensity; but he wanted freedom to use those devices to his own ends. The drafts for At the Hawk's Well show a confident grasp of form and of the placing and nature of ritual, song and dance within that form from the first: there was no protracted struggle to evolve a new style; it grasped Yeats's imagination fully structured and complete in its detail.

It is difficult to give a precise source for the play. Stories of wells with magical life-enhancing properties abound in Irish lore; several narrative romances by William Morris that Yeats was known to admire use 'well' and 'tree' as symbols of restored energy and fertility; and there was a Noh play amongst Fenollosa's papers, *Yoro, or The Sustenance of Age* by Zeami, which tells of a miraculous waterfall inhabited by a god of peace and bounty who endowed the waters with invigorating powers. None affords a precise parallel for Yeats's play: *Yoro* is in the form of Kami Noh, or 'god-play', and celebrates the god's munificence in showering blessings first on a local countryman and his son and then on the Emperor and his kingdom; the mood is wholly serene, quite without the anxieties, deceptions and underlying air of menace in *At the Hawk's Well*. Only one story in Lady Gregory's *Cuchulain of Muirthemne* approaches the theme of the play: in 'The Boy Deeds of Cuchulain' the hero in his youth overhears Cathbad the Druid saying that if any young man took arms that day, his name would be greater than any in Ireland but his span of life short; he demands that Conchubar allow him to take arms immediately and is granted his request; when Cathbad sees the ceremony he is filled with distress, remembering the last words of his prophecy; but Cuchulain is fearless: 'It is little I would care . . . if my name and the story of what I had done would live after me.' In the play Cuchulain's ambition in coming to the well is a quest for immortality; his wish is granted, but not in the way he expects; he is presented with a choice and instinctively accepts a future as a warrior hero with its promise of an enduring name in legend. The waters that 'plash' momentarily in the Hawk's Well are emblematic of a futile hope; they do not, like the waterfall in *Yoro*, sustain the Old Man but endlessly frustrate and enervate him. Wells in Irish lore tend to offer not immortality, but gifts of insight and prophetic vision; the Hawk's Well is not drunk from by Cuchulain, but in coming there he acquires self-knowledge and intimations of his destiny.

Yeats's major problem was finding the right collaborators to help him stage the play. Ito, fresh from his Dalcroze training in Paris and now performing regularly at the Coliseum, was available and willing to devise the choreography and play the Hawk-Woman; and in time he found Henry Ainley (formerly Naoise to Mrs Patrick Campbell's Deirdre and more recently the Leontes in Harley Granville-Barker's celebrated production of *The Winter's Tale*) and Allan Wade (the future bibliographer and editor of Yeats's work, but at this stage of his career a character-actor of some talent, who also had experience of working with Barker) to play Cuchulain and the Old Man respectively. An unsolved puzzle is why Yeats did not turn to Charles Ricketts for assistance with the design aspects of the production, particularly since Ricketts was an experienced and sensitive designer who had created a much admired array of costumes for Abbey revivals of *On Baile's Strand* and *The King's Threshold* the previous year (1915), and had a wide knowledge of Japanese art and principles of stylization. Ricketts had recently designed *King Lear* for a Tokyo-based company (with such success that they subsequently were to commission designs for a production of Wilde's *Salome*), and he had created costumes for Ito's solo performances. Did Yeats perhaps consider that Ricketts's designs showed too marked a Japanese influence, when he did not wish the Japanese origins of *At the Hawk's Well* to be stressed at the expense of his own invention? He turned instead to Edmund Dulac (then chiefly renowned for his book-illustrating) to design costumes, masks and make-up, to compose the music and to lead the chorus of actor–musicians.

The collaboration was not a total success. Yeats had little sympathy for his actors; the wearing of a mask for performers unaccustomed to doing so can be a disturbing experience which has to be prepared for with patience and sensitivity, and Yeats was not skilled to offer the right kind of assistance; he grew angry when Ainley in particular fell back on his traditional techniques to boost his flagging morale. But Ainley possessed a commanding, heroic stage-presence and a brooding intensity that were ideal for his role. Dulac's designs were felicitous: their bold, clear shapes enhance the body-lines of the performers, which is essential when masks are being used. His settings of the songs delighted Yeats; but, compared with Florence Farr's earlier settings of some poems and dramatic lyrics, Dulac's efforts do not sound so perfectly matched to the rhythm, accentuation, emotional pacing and colour of the words; they are adequate but not inspired. Overall the music is somewhat repetitive in its idiom and lacking in dramatic urgency. Nevertheless, Yeats retained the designs and music throughout the revivals that occurred during his lifetime: at a New York art gallery mounting an exhibition of Dulac's work in November 1916; at his home in Merrion Square in association with the Dublin Drama League (23 March 1924), when Lennox Robinson led the Musicians, Frank Fay appeared as the Old Man, Eileen Magee as the Hawk and M. J. Dolan as Cuchulain; at the Peacock Theatre on 18 November 1930 with a cast of students from the Abbey School of Acting; and at the Abbey (25 July 1933) when Ninette de Valois, wearing Ito's old costume, danced the role of the Hawk-Guardian and M. J. Dolan and W. O'Gorman played the Old Man and Cuchulain. Michio Ito long retained an association with the play: he staged it with Dulac's designs but with music by the Japanese composer Kosaku Yamada at the Greenwich Village Theatre in 1918 and in Japan in 1939. *At the Hawk's Well* has twice been translated into Japanese. It is the most frequently revived of the *Four Plays for Dancers*: T. S. Eliot at Pound's invitation saw the first performance in Lady Cunard's drawing room and felt himself inspired to attempt a 'drama of modern life' in which details would be 'accentuated by drumbeats' – an aspiration that arguably bore fruit in *Sweeney Agonistes*; and Samuel Beckett counted it his favourite amongst Yeats's plays, preferring 'a sup at the Hawk's Well' to a diet of Shaw.

Persons in the Play: In performance Cuchulain and the Old Man wore full-face masks, while the Hawk costume was made with a hood that lightly covered the edges of the face but left eyes, nose and mouth free; only the Musicians wore make-up. Alvin Langdon Coburn's photographs of the three principals show that the designs were realized with absolute accuracy.

Setting: The stage directions throughout this version of the text, printed first in *Four Plays for Dancers*, are exceptionally full. Read imaginatively, they graphically evoke what the first production must have appeared like to the specially invited audience at Lady Cunard's home.

1. *any bare space before a wall*: In a preface to the text printed in *Harper's Bazaar*, Yeats wrote: 'It has been a great gain to get rid of scenery, to substitute for a crude landscape painted upon canvas three performers who ... describe landscape or event ... we have many quarrels with even good scene-painting.' Yeats was never satisfied that the problem of staging outdoor scenes had been resolved at the Abbey, despite various attempts at stylized flats and backcloths.

2. *drum . . . gong . . . zither*: Noh plays are accompanied by a single flute and three types of drum.

3. *no mechanical means . . . from us*: In 'Certain Noble Plays of Japan' Yeats describes seeing Ito dance

> in a studio and in a drawing-room and on a very small stage lit by an excellent stage-light. In the studio and in the drawing room alone, where the lighting was the light we are most accustomed to, did I see him as the tragic image that has stirred my imagination. There, where no studied lighting, no stage-picture made an artificial world, he was able . . . to recede from us into some more powerful life. Because that separation was achieved by human means alone, he receded, but to inhabit as it were the deeps of the mind.

4. *First Musician*: The text printed in *Harper's Bazaar* (1917) and in *Four Plays for Dancers* (1921) was accompanied by Dulac's designs. This shows the appearance of all three Musicians:

16. Dulac's design for a costume for a
Musician in *At the Hawk's Well*.

It seems that in the event neither a zither nor a harp was used in 1916: one of the Musicians, according to a letter from Yeats to John Quinn, his American friend and patron, 'insists on a guitar . . . His instrument is to appear to-day disguised by Dulac in cardboard.'

5. *a folded black cloth*: There is no equivalent for this opening ritual in traditional Noh drama; it is entirely Yeats's own invention. Efficiently performed at a measured pace, it instils a wonderful concentration in an audience by imposing a hieratic mood over the theatre.

6. *gold pattern . . . hawk*: In *Four Plays for Dancers* the following design by Dulac for the Musicians' curtain-ritual was inserted into the stage direction by way of illustration:

17. Dulac's design for the Musicians' cloth in *At the Hawk's Well*.

7. *How little worth . . . birth!*: An ironic comment on the Old Man. Yeats returned to the idea in the fifth stanza of 'Among School Children' (1927), where he muses:

> What youthful mother, a shape upon her lap . . .
> Would think her son, did she but see that shape
> With sixty or more winters on its head,
> A compensation for the pang of his birth,
> Or the uncertainty of his setting forth?

8. *a square . . . well*: This extreme simplicity is wholly in keeping with the casual, almost childlike stylization of props on the Noh stage, 'where a ship', as Yeats observes in 'Certain Noble Plays of Japan', 'is represented by a mere skeleton of willows or osiers painted green, or a fruit tree by a bush in a pot . . . It is a child's game become the most noble poetry.' If the Guardian is wholly covered by the black cloak as Yeats prescribes, then her shapeless, unmoving form beside the representation of the well seems like an embodiment of the rocky, barren landscape that the Musicians are summoning before 'the eye of the mind'.

9. *hazel*: Hazelnuts are often associated in Irish lore with wisdom; but these boughs are significantly 'long stripped by the wind'.

10. *Old Man*: Dulac's design exactly captures the Musician's image of an ancient figure reduced to a near elemental state. Guardian and Old Man together create the forlorn landscape that is the play's actual and psychological setting.

18. Dulac's design for a costume and
mask for the Old Man in *At the
Hawk's Well*.

11. *His movements . . . marionette*: Yeats's inspiration here may have been Edward
Gordon Craig, who wrote of his desire to replace actors with *Übermarionettes*, by
which he seems to have intended not conventional string-puppets so much as beautifully
crafted, animated dolls rather like the Bunraku puppets of Japan. Or perhaps Yeats
was seeking to emphasize his concern that all movement on stage should be synchronized
with the music in order to avoid the risk of actors moving naturalistically and disturbing
the discipline of stylization that governs the conception of the play. The direction may
reflect Yeats's oft-expressed exasperation with Ainley and the subsidiary Musicians (a
Mrs Mann and a Mr Foulds) during rehearsals.

12. *the Sidhe*: The immortal ones in Irish lore, 'the holy shades/That dance upon the
desolate mountain', as the Old Man calls them elsewhere (p. 117).

13. *Young Man*: Dulac's design for Cuchulain subtly hints (with the wing-like decoration
at the shoulders and the helmet with its single horn and bull-like silhouette) at his
famed prowess at taming hawks and the reputation he will one day win for his part
in the war over the great Bull of Cuailgne:

19. Dulac's design for a costume and
mask for the Young Man in *At the
Hawk's Well.*

It is a hero's costume that defines Cuchulain's destiny. Yeats wrote to Quinn: 'Ainley
... wears a mask like an archaic Greek statue.' The Old Man quickly 'reads' the
costume with some accuracy: there will be times in Cuchulain's career when he will
be 'crazy for the shedding of men's blood' and 'for the love of women' (p. 116); it
could be said the sagas depict Cuchulain in just such terms. Yeats, however, is more
preoccupied with the mind of the hero and the relationship between fearlessness and
magnanimity, a quality in Cuchulain of which the Old Man is deeply suspicious.

14. *miraculous water*: At an early stage the play was called *The Well of Immortality*,
a phrase that appeared as a subtitle in the programmes of the first London performances.

15. *dancers*: It works considerably to Yeats's advantage that this was a popular term
for the supernatural beings of Irish legend and lore, since in the play the Guardian,
when possessed by the Sidhe, is compelled to express her strange 'otherness' through
the language of the dance.

16. *cry of the hawk*: All Yeats's and Ito's efforts to study the cries and movements of
hawks at London Zoo were in vain, since the birds were sleepy and would not respond
even to prods from an umbrella. Dulac, according to Ito, asked what the word for
hawk was in Japanese; he answered, '*Taka*!' This was decided on as theatrically more
thrilling than any of Ito's attempts at genuine bird cries. It is possible too for the
flautist amongst the three Musicians to produce a suitably eerie sound.

17. *It sounded . . . hood it*: It is a characteristic feature of myth and legend that heroes

approaching a situation that is to be a kind of rite of passage are challenged, often violently, by a figure who is actually a manifestation of the power that is shaping their destiny (Oedipus' encounter with the Sphinx, for example; or the episode in Wagner's opera in which Siegfried, climbing the mountain where he will find Brünnhilde, must first fight with the Wanderer, not knowing he is Wotan, to prove his heroic worth).

18. *Woman of the Sidhe*: She is given no name in this play, but in *The Only Jealousy of Emer* Cuchulain identifies the shape-changer, Fand of the Sidhe, who haunts him there, as the same supernatural woman whom 'long ago' he met 'on a cloudy hill' near 'old thorn-trees and a well':

> A woman danced and a hawk flew,
> I held out arms and hands; but you,
> That now seem friendly, fled away,
> Half woman and half bird of prey.

19. *The Guardian . . . hawk*: The sudden emergence of the Hawk-Woman like a bird startled into flight from the monumental masses of the black cloak is a spectacular *coup-de-théâtre*, akin to some of the miraculous transformations of costume (by the removal of cunningly placed tacking threads which allows the dress to turn virtually inside-out) that can be effected on stage in the Noh theatre when the character represented by the *shite* undergoes some experience of transcendence. Ito claims that Dulac's design for his hawk-costume was largely Egyptian in inspiration rather than Celtic. There is no denying its theatrical power, however, with the dancer's arms extended by short rods within the stiffened sleeves to give the effect of a vast wing-span.

Ito wore red tights (though Ninette de Valois recalls dancing in bare feet when she took the role); the front panel of the costume was cream with black markings: the back was brown with stylized feather designs in gold.

20. *dance moving like a hawk*: In the preface to *Four Plays for Dancers* Yeats honestly confesses regarding the whole group of plays: 'The dancing will give me most trouble, for I know but vaguely what I want. I do not want any existing form of stage dancing, but something with a smaller gamut of expression, something more reserved, more self-controlled, as befits performers within arm's reach of their audience.' Some commentators have criticized Yeats for this uncertainty but it is typical of his openness to the demands of collaboration within the theatre. This play is unusual amongst the group of dance-plays in not offering within the text some kind of scenario for the danced sequence, though in the manuscript-drafts the following account occurs: 'Chorus continues description of dance. How they go from rock to rock on the mountain side. Is it hate or is it love? Sometimes she leads him near the fountain, and then away. The fountain bubbles. At that moment the woman . . . breaks from him and runs out. He goes half way to the fountain, then hears the cry of the hawk and runs out after the woman.' Yeats trusted to Ito's choreographic skills, just as later he respected de Valois' improvisational gifts. He had initially envisaged some eight minutes of dancing within a play that runs, on Yeats's own assessment, for between thirty and forty minutes; but Dulac's score, which perhaps more accurately reflects what happened in the first performances, notes that the music for the dance 'ought to last about three-and-a-half minutes'. Ito's dance was admired by Yeats for his 'minute intensity of movement', which suggests a style close to that deployed in Noh. Ninette de Valois has described her choreography as more contemporary, and in the style known in the 1930s as

20. Dulac's design for a costume and
mask for the Hawk in *At the Hawk's
Well*.

'abstract expressionism'; she interpreted the text as requiring her to move through three distinct phases: 'from an evocation of brooding power, through suggestive seduction to the violent ecstasy of a wild bird'.

21. *Aoife*: Queen and leader of a warrior tribe in Scotland. She hovers as a powerful unseen presence behind the action of *On Baile's Strand* (where we learn she became Cuchulain's lover after he overcame her in battle and bore him the son, Connla, whom she trained to fight his father to the death), and she appears as an aged woman in *The Death of Cuchulain*.

22. *He comes . . . comes!*: It is interesting to compare this line with one on p. 116: 'I am named Cuchulain, I am Sualtim's son', which meets with the Old Man's deflating rejoinder, 'I have never heard that name.' Now we hear the exultant assertion of a man who has chosen his identity, but it is couched in the third person: Cuchulain has totally depersonalized himself in accepting his destiny as hero.

23. *Come to me . . . withered tree*: The closing lyric has a disturbing ambivalence: the Musicians have watched the action with us and seemed emotionally engaged with it

all; now they turn away from the vision they have conjured forth for us out of air in a bare space, seemingly disparaging both Cuchulain's choice and the Old Man's monomania as forms of absurd folly. It is a brilliant strategy, bringing us as audience sharply out of a state of concentrated reverie into awareness of a pressing need to articulate our own understanding and judgement of what we have just experienced. It is an alienation effect of a peculiarly exacting intensity, leaving us poised in indecision between the sensuous attractions of indolence and the bitter life that accompanies the pursuit of wisdom. Throughout their singing the Musicians quietly complete their ritual with the curtain; on one level the play ends, but in a fashion whereby Yeats ensures it lives on to 'dominate memory'.

The Dreaming of the Bones

Three weeks after the first performances of *At the Hawk's Well* on 24 April 1916, the Easter Rising, in which the Sinn Fein movement sought to establish an Irish republic and end 700 years of English domination, rocked Dublin; it brought savage reprisals from the British government. The event dominated Yeats's creative imagination and conscience for some years to come, as his work turned increasingly political, embracing both Irish and international perspectives. The historical past came to have a telling, challenging and often frightening immediacy for him to a degree that suddenly allowed him to exploit his new-found interest in the Noh drama in ways that had not perhaps at first occurred to him. A wealth of classical Noh plays focus on ghosts seeking release from passionate sins or errors of judgement committed when living; the past has a terrible hold on their consciousness, keeping them relentlessly poised in an ecstasy of spiritual pain from which there seems no escape. These are plays about states of unappeasable remorse, which only the Buddha's sublime compassion can ease. Though the central characters in these plays are often historical or legendary figures, the experience explored within the drama remains firmly subjective. By a masterstroke of invention, Yeats gave this form of ghost-play a forceful political impact which invested the personal dimension with a profound social relevance.

After the success of *At the Hawk's Well* Yeats at once began planning a further dance-drama about Cuchulain on the subject of the saga-tale, 'The Only Jealousy of Emer'; but, running into structural difficulties with it, he shelved that play temporarily as another drama about the origins and consequences of the British invasion of Ireland possessed his imagination in the months following the Rising. His new subject was one that Lady Gregory had explored in her tragedy, *Dervorgilla* (first staged at the Abbey in 1907 with Sara Allgood in the title role) and her preface to the text as printed in *Samhain* (November 1908) is a succinct account of the story:

> Dervorgilla, daughter of the King of Meath, wife of O'Rourke, King of Breffny, was taken away, willingly or unwillingly, by Diarmuid MacMurrough, King of Leinster, in the year 1152. O'Rourke and his friends invaded Leinster in revenge, and in the wars which followed, Diarmuid, driven from Ireland, appealed for help to Henry II of England, and was given an army under Strongbow, to whom Diarmuid promised Leinster as reward. It is so the English were first brought into Ireland. Dervorgilla, having outlived O'Rourke and Diarmuid, and Henry and Strongbow, is said to have died at the Abbey of Mellifont, near Drogheda, in the year 1193, aged 85.

Lady Gregory's play is set at Mellifont, where years of extreme piety and generosity cannot defend the dying Dervorgilla from the hatred of others engendered by her past, and most especially from 'the swift, unflinching, terrible judgment of the young'. This might be the outline of Yeats's scenario too, but for one major difference: Lady Gregory's play observes throughout the conventions of historical realism, and it is the anger of the next generation that her heroine faces. Yeats uses the tradition of the ghost-Noh to confront Dervorgilla and her lover with the anger of the Irish people as it has accumulated down the centuries, to be embodied now in a young Fenian soldier, pledged to the nationalist cause, who is seeking to escape capture by the British forces in the aftermath of the Rising. The English yoke is still in place; fear, disappointment and despair make this young man's anger implacable.

Interestingly this is the only one of his dance-dramas that Yeats referred to specifically as 'my Noh play'; and it is the one that most closely follows a Japanese model, Nishikigi by Zeami. Yeats wrote appreciatively of this particular Noh play in 'Swedenborg, Mediums, and the Desolate Places' (1914), recounting its plot-line in detail, which he had read in Pound's transcriptions from Ernest Fenollosa's papers. In the essay he begins to draw parallels between the play and stories of ill-fated lovers from Irish folklore. Yeats's imagination was alive to the creative possibilities of the story long before the Rising gave him the spur to develop from within it an original political theme. It is worth considering Nishikigi briefly to perceive both the resemblances and the contrasts with Yeats's The Dreaming of the Bones.

In Nishikigi a monk encounters a young couple he supposes are married; the man is selling love-tokens (nishikigi) and the woman narrow bands of woven cloth. The monk learns it is a custom of the district for men to court women with the nightly presentation of one of these love-tokens and that, were a man to continue the ceremony for a thousand nights, the woman was expected finally to relent and agree to marriage. The seller tells the monk a tragic tale of a man who followed the ceremony through but was still rejected; always his beloved, ignoring him, went on weaving bands of cloth; the lover died of grief and the woman he courted died shortly after out of remorse. The monk asks to see the graves and is escorted there by the couple (as Yeats observes, 'the chorus describes the journey to the cave'). Night falls; cold and alone now, the monk decides to pray that the lovers find union at last through divine grace; he sees the couple who were his guides suddenly transfigured in a vision and realizes he has been in the company of ghosts. He sees the lovers united in marriage in the world of spirits, but with the dawn the vision vanishes and the monk is left in 'a wild place, unlit and unfilled' where only the 'wind moves in the pines' (Pound's translation).

It is a delicate, atmospheric play, moving from remorse, through a hushed expectancy during the account of the journey, to a quiet exultation with the coming of the vision, while the final choruses evoke the strange emptiness that often follows states of heightened awareness. Nishikigi is somewhat unusual in that the leading actor, or shite, who plays the male lover is required to appear without a mask in the opening sequence when he takes on the semblance of a street-seller and only dons a mask for the vision which occupies most of the second half of the play. Acting without a mask is considered the supreme challenge of a Noh actor; Nishikigi is therefore especially revered in the Noh repertoire.

Yeats takes a number of details from his Japanese model, but puts them all to very different ends. The Young Man in The Dreaming of the Bones encounters a couple on the mountainside in the darkness, so cannot see, as the audience can, their other-worldly appearance denoted by their masks, heroic bearing and stylized movement. Attention at first is given to characterizing him and investing him with a complex political reality, which is markedly different from the Noh play, where the monk, played by a *waki*-actor, is not characterized at all initially, though as the action develops his voice becomes one of total, sensitive empathy. Where the journey in the Noh play is effortful but sustained by a rising hope, that in Yeats's play keeps the characters' nerves at a pitch of attention and sustains a sense of deep foreboding. In *Nishikigi* the landscape that comes into view is wild, barren grassland; in *The Dreaming of the Bones* it is a landscape laid bare by the ravages of continual warfare and reprisals. The monk is wholly sympathetic towards the lovers and is rewarded with a vision in which he sees how his compassion has brought them release from their centuries-long predicament; but the young soldier is full of horror and disgust as he realizes the identity of his companions and in a shaft of moonlight sees them trapped in their hellish condition, from which he can offer them no respite. Where the *shite*'s dance in *Nishikigi* is fast and intense, expressive of gratitude and exultation at the moment of his spiritual union with his beloved, that for Diarmuid and Dervorgilla involves an obsessive circling about each other as they are magnetized by desire but held back from passionately embracing by horror at the consequences of their longing – the dance is a terrifying image of a ravaging sexual frustration.

Importantly, where the dance in *Nishikigi* is a gift from the spirit world to a compassionate mortal, representing a momentary union of the two dimensions of reality, that in Yeats's play symbolizes the total breakdown of contact between the two worlds. It was through the close study of the Noh drama that Yeats evolved a philosophical proposition about ghosts which underlies this play; *Per Amica Silentia Lunae* (1918) where this idea is recorded, was written almost contemporaneously with *The Dreaming of the Bones*: the play is at one level an exploration of the concept. Considering why certain people are 'gifted' with the capacity to see ghosts, Yeats postulated: 'The dead, as the passionate necessity wears out, come into a measure of freedom and may turn the impulse of events, started while living, in some new direction, but they cannot originate except through the living.' The lovers' ghosts have a desperate need of human agency to 'turn the impulse of events'; they make a bold appeal for the young man's subjective emotion of pity and almost succeed, until knowledge of their identity rouses an objective patriotic fervour in him that suppresses all humane sympathy and he consigns them back to a hell of misery. The soldier renews his commitment to what he sees as political necessity and, to safeguard his integrity, he condemns the lovers for preferring passionate to political commitment. Brilliantly, Yeats resolves his play in a way that challenges the audience to make a personal decision, conscious always that (whether it is swayed by feeling or by ideology) such a decision requires the sacrifice of some part of one's humanity.

This strategy involving audience-response is admirably supported by another which relates to the use of masks within the play. How is one to interpret the fact that the soldier does not wear a mask or mask-like make-up, although his appearance as an Aran fisherman is soon revealed to be a disguise designed to aid his escape from the mainland? The issue is complicated by our perception of the ghosts' masks as 'heroic' (Yeats opined that the mask created by Dulac for Cuchulain in *At the Hawk's Well* would be ideal for Dervorgilla, and he had described that mask as 'like an archaic

Greek statue'). Throughout the play the nature of the action requires that the soldier be continually in close physical proximity to the ghostly lovers, and so the distinction regarding their facial features is kept to the forefront of our awareness. Is the implication of the play that the Young Man lacks heroic stature because he cannot achieve the necessary independence of mind which would allow him to rise free of political circumstance and make a gesture of magnanimity releasing the lovers? Or is their beauty like their elegance of movement and caressing voices part of an insidious charm calculated to seduce the soldier into a momentary forgetfulness, when they might take possession of his mind and bend it to their will? The stylized way in which Yeats requires the central journey to be played supports this view: three times the lovers conduct the Young Man in a circle about the stage, which has a powerfully mesmeric effect in performance, despite the Musicians' cries of alarm and their longing for cockcrow and the dawn that dispels ghosts. The impact is like the sealing of a magic spell. (Though Yeats does not specify this, in productions the direction of the circular movement is almost invariably anti-clockwise about the stage, the direction traditionally known as 'widdershins' in black magic, which is reserved for the darkest of enchantments.) As Yeats chooses to present them, these ghosts are morally as ambiguous as the ghost in *Hamlet* and potentially as dangerous. Unlike *Nishikigi*, which controls and directs an audience's sympathies to a clearly defined end, Yeats's play engages an audience imaginatively only to set their emotional and intellectual responses to the action in conflict.

What impresses is the richness of meaning that can be read into the play by virtue of Yeats's carefully calculated dramatic devices and strategies. That cyclic movement of the three characters about the stage may be interpreted simply as a journey, as the laying of a cunning enchantment, or as the shaping by Diarmuid and Dervorgilla of the historical process that tragically determines the Young Man's destiny. By stylizing the stage-action to such an austere degree, Yeats gives director, cast and audience considerable freedom over interpretation, allowing the play to be enjoyed on a narrative, symbolic or psychological level. For the first time in his career as dramatist, Yeats has discovered how a process of stylization can transform the entire stage-action into powerfully allusive metaphor. The process requires an audience to enter imaginatively into the world of the play and themselves shape the meanings and interpretation that they draw from the experience. Given the play's concern with the relation between history and politics, how one chooses to respond profoundly reflects one's own ideological sympathies. Yeats feared *The Dreaming of the Bones* was 'too powerful politically' to be staged while Ireland and England were still sensing the repercussions of the Rising, though he offered the play for publication in *Everyman*, a weekly review, affirming its topicality and suggesting the editor write a prefatory note 'either repudiating its apparent point of view or stressing the point of view'. Yeats was something of a publicist on occasions, but it seems clear from this letter that he saw the vitality of the play as residing in its provocative and contentious ambiguities. With *The Dreaming of the Bones* Yeats anticipated by some years Brecht's exploration of forms of Asian theatre in quest of a new style of alienated political drama that would none the less be aesthetically satisfying: the play is a landmark in the development of European theatre.

The Dreaming of the Bones was not staged at the Abbey until 6 December 1931, in a production by Udolphus Wright with W. O'Gorman as the Young Man and

J. Stephenson and Nesta Brooking as the lovers. Though Walter Morse Rummel wrote music for the songs and the journey-sequence in 1917, which was published in *Four Plays for Dancers*, the Abbey commissioned a new score for the production from J. F. Larchet.

1. *dizzy*: A felicitous epithet, given the circular patterns of movement that are soon to be established by the actors in the journey and in the final dance of the ghosts, when the lovers turn about each other with a growing rapidity that suggests they are trapped in a vortex.

2. *So passionate . . . agate cup*: This image may have been culled from Yeats's reading of *Nishikigi*. To quote his own account of the play: at the climax of the monk's vision of the lovers, 'he is shown the bridal room and the lovers drinking from the bridal cup. The dawn is coming. It is reflected in the bridal cup . . .'

3. *The little village . . . jade*: The play is set in the northern reaches of what is now Co. Clare.

4. *bawneen*: A home-spun flannel jacket.

5. *heroic*: See above for a discussion of the effect of these masks in performance.

6. *You have . . . Dublin?*: Eerily, the Stranger penetrates the Young Man's disguise at once, but the soldier supposes his voice whispering in the darkness comes from someone sympathetic to the republican cause and immediately relaxes his guard.

7. *Post Office*: The General Post Office was seized as a prime objective in the Rising and Patrick Pearse, the leader of the Fenian army, declared an independent Irish republic from there on 24 April 1916; it became the centre of much of the street-fighting that ensued before British forces quelled the rebellion over the coming week.

8. *Aran . . . Muckanish . . . Finvara*: Yeats firmly roots his drama in a specific locale: the Aran islands lie off the west coast of Ireland, as does Muckanish near Connemara; Finvara is a village in Co. Clare.

9. *Police . . . against us*: Animosity against the police (Irish volunteers working for the English authorities) is a recurring theme in Irish drama at this time and earlier; so too, surprisingly, is the feeling of respect for English opponents, 'who but did their duty' under orders. In *Reveries over Childhood and Youth* Yeats gives a moving instance of this attitude in writing about Ellen O'Leary (sister of his one-time mentor John O'Leary, whose sentence of twenty years' penal servitude was later commuted to fifteen years' exile from Ireland for his Fenian activities): 'No fanaticism could thrive amid such gentleness. She never found it hard to believe that an opponent had as high a motive as her own, and needed upon her difficult road no spur of hate.' Noticeably, when the Young Man begins to speak aggressively about people who betray their own countrymen, the Stranger rapidly interrupts with an offer to protect and guide him; this is a second tense and unexpected response, which begins to build dramatic suspense.

10. *born . . . midnight*: Gaelic lore is much preoccupied with liminal states of being caught at a precise point of temporal change, such as dawn, dusk or midnight, when the gift of supernatural vision was thought possible.

11. *My Grandam . . . lives again*: The Young Man is cynical about his grandmother's interpretation of the concept of purgatory and the Stranger appears to match his sarcastic tone until the haunting repetition like a refrain of the soldier's idea that 'some

but live through their old lives again' adds a sudden poignant note of pain. The Young Man is inclined to scoff but is soon to learn what exactly that process of living back entails when he experiences the labyrinths of remorse in which the two strangers are trapped.

12. *drinking blood*: Through death in battles fought against English invaders. Again the Stranger promptly changes the subject by drawing the soldier's attention to the speed of their progress.

13. *Aughanish ... Aughtmana*: Specific village-communities in the vicinity of Corcomroe.

14. *They go ... once*: Rummel gives this note about how the 'walk around the stage' should be timed in relation to his music: 'Two steps may be taken to each musical measure, making a very slow figurative step. This will mean about 24 steps to one walk around the stage (Round). The last two steps may be twice as long (*in time*), accompanied by certain movements of expectancy. In calculating that each step amounts to half a metre, the length of the stage would have to be of five metres.'

15. *Red bird of March*: In Yeats's thinking the coming of spring with the full moon in March was always a time of dynamic change. The young cock's aggressive crowing is yearned for to dispel the perplexities of the night, but the Musician's cry also suggests a longing for courageous, youthful insight to withstand and perhaps discard old troubles.

16. *Donough O'Brien*: Leader of a group of rebels against the authority of the King of Thomond in the early fourteenth century. Despite the support of Scottish troops, O'Brien was defeated at the Battle of Athenry; he escaped capture but died shortly afterwards (*c.* 1317) near Corcomroe.

17. *Young Girl*: It is a startling moment when the Girl suddenly begins to speak as the conversation turns steadily towards the lovers' own plight. From now on the appeal will be relentlessly directed at the Young Man's emotions and the intervention for the first time of a woman's voice in the play (Rummel's music for the First Musician, written after close consultation with Yeats, is cast in the baritone range) introduces a new tone of passionate urgency. It is a beautifully calculated dramatic effect, but Yeats considered it imperative to have a good dancer in the role of the Young Girl and advised that if the dancer did not wish to speak on stage then her lines might be taken by the actor playing the Stranger. He added, perhaps in the vain hope that Ito might return to England and play the role, that it was not essential that 'that masked dancer be a woman'.

18. *Although ... drives them apart*: This long speech, which is difficult to read, is very potent in performance. A series of modifying subordinate clauses delays the main subject, which exactly renders the Girl's psychological state: her consciousness has dwelt for so long on the pain of remorse that she hardly dares to contemplate the possibility that she might for a moment be 'blessed', were the soldier disposed to be kind. As his imagination is captured by the story she tells, her syntax becomes more direct.

19. *Helen*: Ironically, it is Helen as legendary beauty and adulterous lover of Paris (who abducted her from Sparta where she was queen to Menelaus) that the Girl recalls,

not the consequences of their love, which brought the Greek hosts to besiege and eventually sack the city of Troy.

20. *Diarmuid and Dervorgilla*: See above for the historical facts concerning these figures. Yeats often writes 'Dermot' for 'Diarmuid', which indicates how the name should be pronounced; Dervorgilla is pronounced with a hard g and with the strongest accentuation on the third syllable.

21. *You have told . . . well*: The Young Man still does not appreciate that he is keeping company with the very ghosts he vigorously denounces; the audience, however, reading the significance of masks, costumes 'of a past time' and 'ceremonial movement', are now completely enlightened, so the effect of his denunciation can be measured and judged.

22. *better push on now*: The Stranger's power is waning fast; the soldier initiates and leads this new circuit of the stage.

23. *I can see . . . most beautiful*: This speech, taken with the doleful repetition of the Girl's 'seven hundred years' shows Yeats carefully balancing the audience's sympathies here. The Young Man is not insensitive, uncouth or ignorant, and his rejection of the ghosts' appeal is seen to be rooted in a deep and passionate love of his country. Tragically, that love has to covet ruins as emblems of lost cultural possibilities, not take pride in cultural achievement. That this outburst on viewing the landscape far below him is intensely emotional is what finally defeats the ghosts: they learn to their cost that there is already a prior claim on his sympathies and sensibility.

24. *Why do you dance? . . . never reach it*: Some commentators have criticized Yeats for not offering lengthy prescriptions of the kind of dance he wanted. What he preferred, always respecting the creative skills of his performers, was to give as here a scenario in the form of a spoken commentary from an intermediary on stage, who watches the dance with the audience and tries to express the impact it has on him. (To some degree there is a precedent for this in Noh plays, where the chorus sometimes comment allusively on the dance being performed by the *shite* even as they accompany it.) The scenario is to be viewed as a sketch which the dancers are free to amplify through improvisation.

25. *I had almost yielded*: The play is the more disturbing and therefore the more challenging for an audience, the more the actor playing the Young Man can project the significance of this line through his whole performance.

26. *At the grey round . . . and crow!*: In 'Swedenborg, Mediums, and the Desolate Places' immediately before his discussion of ghosts in Noh plays and especially in *Nishikigi*, Yeats discusses Henry More's theory that the dead, or 'airy people', dance, play music and 'send forth musical sounds without the help of any terrestrial instrument'. It is this seductive, ghostly music, heard mysteriously in the night-time, that is evoked in the first of the songs; but increasingly the strangeness of the experience is disturbed by words intimating danger. The second song evokes a growing sense of nightmare that is dispelled by cockcrows announcing the dawn. Deftly the lyrics re-create the sequence of emotions through which the play has carried us, leaving us questioning whether this promised dawn will genuinely bring us release *politically* and freedom from the burden of the past.

The Cat and the Moon

Noh plays are performed in groups (often as many as five) in a traditional programme and, to give the audience some respite from the sustained intensity of the main dramas, short comic works, or *kyogen*, are played in the intervals between them. Yeats knew of this from Ernest Fenollosa and Ito, and turned to devising an Irish *kyogen* around the time of the completion of *The Dreaming of the Bones* in the summer of 1917. Yeats did not choose to include *The Cat and the Moon* along with his other Noh-inspired dramas in *Four Plays for Dancers* (1921) because 'it was in a different mood', but when he finally published the play in 1924, he observed in a note that he intended it 'to come as a relaxation of attention between, let us say *The Hawk's Well* and *The Dreaming of the Bones*'. Commentators have often questioned why he did not suggest the playing of the comedy between the two dance-plays relating to Cuchulain, but, composed when it was, it does clearly partake of the same creative impulse as *The Dreaming of the Bones* and *The Hawk's Well*, whereas it has little in common with *The Only Jealousy of Emer*, which has closer thematic and structural links with the composition of *Calvary*. Performed between the works Yeats recommends, *The Cat and the Moon* would afford a sharp, comic perspective on the theme which is treated in them in the tragic mode (the journey that, becoming a quest for some kind of inner transcendence or transformation, is either frustrated or achieved in a disturbingly ambiguous form); as such it would provide a lightening of tone but in a fashion that would heighten an audience's powers of discrimination. It makes a most rewarding programme in the theatre, as Raymond Yeates proved in a recent production at the Abbey.

Though Yeats acknowledged a Japanese influence on its conception, *The Cat and the Moon* is as different from the traditional *kyogen* as his dance-dramas are from traditional Noh. *Kyogen* generally involve broad, rumbustious farcical action and stylized knockabout or bawdy sequences, but they do not contain the sustained episodes of dance and comic character-dancing which Yeats's play requires; that is entirely his invention. With *The Cat and the Moon* Yeats was testing how versatile his new-found form of dance-play was and he proved the possibilities were limitless: it could even embrace that most popular of Abbey subjects – the folk comedy. What impresses is the way Yeats never loses touch with psychological realism (the tensions, animosities, grudging amity and relaxing moments of shared laughter that depict the long-standing friendship of Blind Man with Lame Man have a convincing accuracy of observation) while steadily transposing the tone of the play from the farcical to the miraculous.

Two beggars, one lame, one blind, visit a holy well in hope of a cure, which the Saint who presides over the well grants them. Effortlessly, Yeats adapts the conventions of his new dramatic form to convey the miracle: the Musicians, who are as usual established as commentators standing outside the action, speak for the disembodied voice of the Saint; and dance (at first tentative, then with ever greater vigour and daring) conveys the Lame Man's experience of what it means to be 'blessed' and have a saint for friend. It is the simplicity and obviousness of the theatrical devices used to evoke the miracle which make it wholly credible in the theatre. Yeats strengthens the impact on us of the image of a man once hobbling lame but now dancing by a powerful contrast: the Blind Man too undergoes a miracle and that miracle is also expressed through a dance; but his movements, though timed to a musical rhythm, still preserve the knockabout quality of farce, as he belabours the Lame Man for stealing his sheepskin. Though the Blind Man can now see, he is not changed in his nature. The Lame Man, choosing to be 'blessed' rather than cured, is given the gift of *grace*; and the spiritual and psychological change this brings is gradually made manifest in a new elegance of carriage and vivacity of movement. Before our very eyes, the Lame Man becomes the consummate dancer: he has found a proper human dignity, as his whole being (spiritually, mentally, physically) is suffused with joy and wonder.

Yeats described the text published in *The Cat and the Moon and Certain Poems* by the Cuala Press in 1924 as 'probably unfinished', because he felt unsure 'how the Lame Man is to move': was he to remain utterly still, crouching on one knee after descending from the Blind Man's back or was he to 'walk stiffly, or limp as if a leg were paralysed'? Only the rehearsal process leading to performance would show him what was required. (This text significantly omits all mention of a final dance like that just outlined; instead the main action finishes when the Saint climbs on the Lame Man's shoulder as he utters, 'Let us be going then, Holy Man.' The directions for the Blind Beggar's dance while beating the Lame Man are, however, given in full.) The play was first staged by the Dublin Drama League at the Abbey in May 1926 in a double bill with *The Only Jealousy of Emer*: Lennox Robinson directed a cast including M. J. Dolan and P. J. Carolan as Blind and Lame Beggar respectively, while Robinson himself led the Musicians. The text as printed here was first published in *Wheels and Butterflies* in 1934; the additions to the dialogue for Lame Man and Saint at the close of the action and the inclusion of a final dance, the progress of which is described in some detail, presumably reflect changes made for the 1926 production (the programme describes the director as working 'under the supervision of W. B. Yeats') when the poet finally got the chance to experiment with movement to find how best to evoke the miracle which provides the climax to the play.

Scene: Yeats, in the note to the 1924 edition, described Saint Colman's Well as 'within a couple of miles of my Galway house, Thoor Ballylee', the Norman castle he had acquired near to Lady Gregory's home, Coole Park. St Colman was patron saint of the ruined Kilmacduagh cathedral near by. Like *The Dreaming of the Bones* the play abounds in specific geographical references to give audiences a sense of actuality. One of the features that Yeats admired about Noh theatre was the powerful feeling for a distinct place that the plays generate through the texture of their poetry and the dialogue; this reflected his own desire through poetry and drama 'to bring back to certain places their avowed sanctity or their romance'.

1. *zither, drum, and flute*: Cymbals too are called for in the final dance (p. 144).

2. *The cat went ... animal blood*: The Musicians' songs had been published in advance of the main text of the play as a single lyric poem in *The Wild Swans at Coole* (1919). Taken together, the songs tell how the self-possession of the cat is disturbed by the elemental laws of change to which it is none the less subject. By contrast in the play that unfolds a chance miracle is seen as capable either of producing a total change in a human personality that is willing to relinquish selfhood or of simply confirming a wholly self-centred (albeit, shrewd and worldly-wise) identity.

3. *Kiltartan*: A local epithet derived from Coole. (Kiltartanese was the name devised

to describe the Irish-English dialect Lady Gregory created for many of her plays and translations.)

4. *They go round . . . drum-taps*: This stylized evocation of a journey provides a direct creative link with *The Dreaming of the Bones*. The halting, grotesque progress of the Beggars about the stage, which demonstrates their utter dependence on each other, is stressed for the audience by the ironic contrast it affords to the exquisitely disciplined movement of a cat as evoked by the accompanying song.

5. *flighty*: As Katharine Worth argues, this is a richly allusive epithet to apply to the Lame Man: it can mean short-sighted in the sense of 'telling lies that are bound to be found out', but it can also mean 'imaginative' and 'visionary', possessing an ability to see beyond the material world. In time the word gains particular resonance for us as audience, since the play continually requires us also to be 'flighty', imagining that we *see* the setting of the well and ash-tree, that the First Musician is an unseen saint, and that ultimately the illusion created by good acting is a genuine miracle!

6. *There is many . . . whole man*: As Martin and Mary Doul, the two blind beggars, discover when they are cured by a wandering Holy Man in Synge's *The Well of the Saints*; when their sight fades again, they choose to remain blind, to live a rich life in the imagination and to beg.

7. *holy man . . . Laban . . . lecher . . . Mayo*: This was private satire on Yeats's part at the expense of Edward Martyn and George Moore, one-time collaborators in the early years of the Irish Literary Theatre. Martyn, a devout and celibate Catholic, lived at Tillyra Castle, a few miles from Coole Park; Laban was the nearby townland where he went to chapel. Moore, whose family home was just across the border from Galway in Mayo, cultivated the reputation of ladykiller but was generally believed to exaggerate his conquests. Susan Mitchell, the Dublin wit, used to say: 'Some men kiss but do not tell; George Moore tells but does not kiss.' When the play was first written and performed Martyn and Moore were still alive and Yeats's note in the Cuala edition does not elucidate the reference here; by 1934 both writers were dead and in *Wheels and Butterflies* Yeats explains all, adding that he thought that Abbey audiences 'understood the reference'.

8. *the things . . . buttons*: Yeats's description of Saint Colman's Well notes that 'there are many offerings at the well-side left by sufferers; I seem to remember bits of cloth torn perhaps from a dress, hairpins, and little pious pictures'.

9. *rouse . . . against me*: If the play is performed in the programme Yeats devised, so that *The Cat and the Moon* follows *At the Hawk's Well*, an audience perceives a delightfully comic parallel here for the Hawk-Woman, who, after escaping from Cuchulain, similarly threatens to rouse the warring Aoife and her warrior-women against the hero.

10. *Let us be going, Holy Man*: The 1924 text gives the Lame Man's exit here: '*They go out to drum and flute as before*'; and the Musicians sing their final lyric. The final dance, which Yeats devised only when the play came into rehearsal in 1926, is what really makes *The Cat and the Moon* a miracle play. It is a superb instance of purposeful theatricality of a kind that can usually only be achieved successfully when the whole staging conditions of a play are realized during rehearsals and can provide the necessary spur to spontaneous creativity. Here we can detect Yeats, the man of the theatre, at work perfecting a play not as literary text but as text for performance.

The Only Jealousy of Emer

The completion of *The Only Jealousy of Emer* was disrupted by Yeats's impulse to write *The Dreaming of the Bones* in response to the contemporary Irish political situation. The break was seemingly welcome, since he was having problems in structuring his new subject. He had taken the saga-story that Lady Gregory entitled 'The Only Jealousy of Emer' in *Cuchulain of Muirthemne*, which tells how the hero, after attempting to capture two magic birds, was put into a mysterious sleep, in which he was transported to the kingdom of the Sidhe to help the goddess Fand win a victory over her enemies; Fand kept him for forty days before returning him to Emer, who was so overwhelmed with jealousy that she brought a band of armed women to try and kill her rival; Druids and Manannan, king of the sea and Fand's husband, had to weave spells so that Cuchulain would forget his other-worldly lover and Emer her jealousy. The original, a rambling story about magic and possession, is not promising material for a play, as was proved when the Abbey in 1907 staged Wilfrid Scawen Blunt's *Fand*, written at the invitation of Yeats and Lady Gregory. Blunt closely followed the narrative-line of the saga and found in it little scope for dramatic conflict or psychological depth: in Act One Emer trusts Fand with Cuchulain's spirit for forty days, then with scant motivation conceives a consuming jealousy in Act Three as their contract is about to end; Eithne, Cuchulain's mistress, is powerless for all her Druidic skill to bring Cuchulain out of his magical sleep, yet she contrives to spirit herself, disguised as a bard, in the central act into the land of the Sidhe, where her songs bitterly satirize Fand; but it is all to no recognizable thematic purpose. Yeats's play is a miracle of compression and theatrical flair by comparison, though in the process he treats his source material with a cavalier freedom.

From the time that he first read Lady Gregory's version of the Cuchulain stories, Yeats was profoundly impressed with the character of Emer. 'What a pure flame burns in her always,' he wrote in his preface to the published text of Lady Gregory's work; it is she, he opines, 'who will linger longest in the memory'. He had adapted her role in *The Green Helmet* to invest her with a heroic stature comparable with Cuchulain's by inventing the detail of her attempted suicide when her husband proffers his head to the Red Man. 'The Only Jealousy' is the one story in the sagas where Emer has a sustained prominent role, so Yeats's attraction to it is understandable. Some critics have suggested biographical parallels with current events in Yeats's emotional life at this time as his motive for exploring the subject: his long infatuation with Maud Gonne (Fand) and his more recent preoccupation with her daughter Iseult (Eithne) were ending, as his relationship with Georgie Hyde-Lees (Emer) progressed towards marriage. The initial problems must have centred on how to restructure the material to place the focus on Emer rather than on Cuchulain or Fand and how to motivate her jealousy. As happened with the two earlier dance-plays, Fenollosa's papers offered Yeats a useful model from Noh theatre.

Aoino-ue tells of the jealousy of the Princess Rokujo for the Lady Aoino-ue, a rival for her husband's affections, who has been virtually paralysed by an inexplicable illness (she is represented in performance by the simple device of a folded kimono laid on the stage floor). A priestess, praying for insight into the cause of the sickness, is shown a vision of the vengeful Rokujo, cursing and beating her rival with a fan; the spirit is an embodiment of the princess's malevolence, which is draining away her rival's strength. The priestess fails to pacify the spirit and a Buddhist saint is summoned; his prayers conjure forth the demon within Rokujo (there is a spectacular change of costume and mask by the principal performer at this point); there is a battle for control of Aoino-ue's consciousness in which the demon is defeated. Several features of Yeats's play can be found here: the inert body that is the largely silent focus of the action; a theatrically exciting metamorphosis on stage effected by an exchange of masks; the sense, as the action moves through clearly defined episodes, that we are moving into deeper and deeper reaches of the psyche; and a climactic conflict between malign and magnanimous forces, each motivated by a kind of love.

In *The Only Jealousy of Emer* the conflict is between an earthly and a supernatural lover for possession of Cuchulain. Emer wins because, unlike the self-obsessed Fand, she has the courage and magnanimity to see that possession is a diminishing of Cuchulain's freedom and individuality and that it is the better expression of her love to renounce any bond or claim on his affections out of respect for his human dignity. She restores Cuchulain's vitality and heroic stature and sustains her own self-respect, but at a terrible cost emotionally: awaking, Cuchulain turns joyfully to his mistress Eithne, unmindful of Emer's sacrifice or devotion.

This is the most overtly theatrical of Yeats's plays for dancers, yet the theatricality always advances the psychological theme. By a change of mask the figure of Bricriu seems to rise out of the form of Cuchulain as he lies comatose upon the bed: a withered, callous, bitter-tongued individual replaces one whom Yeats has several times characterized in plays as fierce but big-hearted. In the course of the action the one actor is to play both the contorted Bricriu and the heroic Cuchulain; the distinction is achieved simply by different masks and postures so that as audience we seem to see two images of one man. It is as if our faculty of perception has subtly been manipulated, just as in the play Bricriu touches Emer's eyes and gives her special insight into the spirit world. Her 'vision' is presented like a play-within-the-play: the verse form for this episode changes to plangently rhyming and echoing octosyllabic couplets from the blank verse that has prevailed till now and the performers move throughout to the rhythm of a seductive dance.

The play that Emer watches reveals Cuchulain not in his customary heroic and carefree stance but prostrate on his knees, his body sometimes caught up in adoration of Fand (who circles provocatively around him) and at times riven with pain at the memory of Emer, whose trust he has often betrayed, even as he is about to do now. Emer is shown how Fand's desire for Cuchulain is wholly self-centred; hers is a possessiveness that demoralizes the object of her love. The play-within-the-play acts as a mirror-image which shows Emer the nature of jealousy as a dangerous longing to control the affections of another, to use the beloved for one's own ends; and the visionary Cuchulain's calling out her name implicates her in the action and compels her imaginatively to engage with the meaning of what she is watching and to apply it to her own conscience. Emer confronts a world where the heroic has everywhere been displaced by the demonic: Bricriu and the figures in the play signify the ways that perception can be wholly distorted when a consciousness is in the grip of jealousy. Emer alone can restore proper proportions to this world; she has journeyed into the depths of herself and learned why she must renounce her hold over Cuchulain to save them both. The moment she gives voice to her decision, the stage clears of its delusory phantoms, Cuchulain is himself, and 'a pure flame' burns in Emer once more.

Recovering her integrity is a tragic process for Emer; it invests her with a beauty akin to Zeami's concept of *yugen* in the Noh theatre (which Yeats had encountered in Fenollosa's papers): a beauty heightened because permeated with a profound sorrow. Yeats was fond of quoting an observation culled from Castiglione that 'the physical beauty of woman is the spoil or monument of the victory of the soul'. That is the beauty we experience as we contemplate Emer's mask in the final moments of the play and read on its features all the complex emotions that we have been brought to sense imaginatively as registered there. It is the beauty celebrated in the final song of the Musicians, the closest Yeats came to writing a Noh-style lyric that is intricately allusive yet, to the alert spectator, deeply significant.

The Only Jealousy of Emer received its first performances in Amsterdam in 1922 when the director, Albert van Dalsum, commissioned masks from the sculptor, Hildo van Krop. Its first staging in Ireland was by the Dublin Drama League at the Abbey in May 1926: under Yeats's supervision Lennox Robinson directed a cast that included F. J. McCormick as the Ghost of Cuchulain, Arthur Shields as Bricriu, Eileen Crowe as Emer and Norah McGuinness, who also designed the costumes and masks, as Fand. Later Yeats wished to revive the play for Ninette de Valois, but as she always refused to speak on stage, he redesigned its structure so that Fand became wholly a danced role and he recast all but the Musicians' lyrics into prose. The result, *Fighting the Waves*, included more scenes for dancing: an opening prologue showed Cuchulain battling with the waves on Baile's Strand and a final sequence where Fand was seen mourning the loss of Cuchulain supplemented the central play-within-the-play that was now wholly conveyed by mime and dance. This version, using van Krop's full-head masks and music by George Antheil, opened at the Abbey on 13 August 1929; Robinson again directed, with M. J. Dolan as Bricriu, Meriel Moore as Emer, Hedley Briggs as the Ghost and de Valois as Fand, whom Yeats described as 'a strange, noble, unforgettable figure' in her mask. Antheil's music, scored for wind, strings, bells, piano, gong, wailing trombones and an unseen chorus but transcribed as a piano score, was published in *Wheels and Butterflies* with the text of the play in 1934; Yeats considered it 'the only dramatic music I ever heard – a very strong beat, something heroic and barbaric and strange' (though the reactionary Joseph Holloway dismissed it as 'noisy noise . . . like the falling of a tin tray on the flags').

Persons in the Play: The following woodcut appeared on the title-page of *Wheels and Butterflies* (1934) in which the text of *Fighting the Waves* was first published; it shows impressions of three of the masks, which Hildo van Krop originally made for the 1922 Dutch production of *The Only Jealousy of Emer*. Copies were given to the Abbey later for use in the 1929 production of *Fighting the Waves*, after Yeats had been shown photographs of replicas of the masks that the sculptor had cast in bronze. The illustration is of the masks for Cuchulain (left), Fand (centre) and Emer (right).

Yeats wrote: 'The masks get much of their power from enclosing the whole head; this makes the head out of proportion to the body, and I found some difference of opinion as to whether this was a disadvantage or not in an art so distant from reality.'

1. *faces made up to resemble masks*: Van Krop designed masks for all the characters of the play. Given the fluctuating emotional states that Emer experiences as the action

21. Design showing three masks for
The Only Jealousy of Emer and
Fighting the Waves from the title-page
of *Wheels and Butterflies* (1934).

progresses, it is a great help to the actress if she is given a mask which allows her to stylize these emotional responses into a series of bodily movements and postures; too much facial expressiveness by an unmasked actress could rob the play of that distance which Yeats aimed for.

2. *A woman's beauty . . . loveliness*: The opening lyric muses on the origins of true beauty, whether it is achieved by an intense and studied act of will on the part of the possessor or whether, as Castiglione proposed (see above), it is somehow perfected through the possessor's ability to transcend painful or tragic experience, its seeming frailty, like that of a shell or seabird, strengthened by its power to withstand the destructive force of chance and the elements. The song teases the audience's mind with images and shards of ideas that prefigure the conclusion of the play without robbing the action of suspense.

3. *all the rest . . . gone*: In the saga-story and Wilfrid Scawen Blunt's *Fand* Cuchulain's sleep has lasted a time and his bedside has been watched over by Laegaire, Conall Caernach, Lugaidh Redstripe and Eithne Inguba. In desperation they summon first King Conchubar and finally Emer to try to rouse the hero. Emer bids everyone depart; and immediately Fand appears to make her bargain with Cuchulain's wife.

4. *Towards noon . . . at this door*: Yeats ignores all the saga material about how Cuchulain came to be in his state of trance and, taking his cue from the fact that Fand is a sea-goddess, links the tale of Emer with the story on which he based his earlier tragedy *On Baile's Strand*, which ends with Cuchulain, mad with grief at the realization that he has killed his son, Connla, racing into the sea to fight with the waves which gradually overwhelm him. This is an altogether more plausible reason for Cuchulain's strange condition and for Fand's pursuit of him. (In *Cuchulain of Muirthemne* 'The Only Son of Aoife' is placed late in the cycle of stories after 'The Only Jealousy of

Emer'.) This summary of the action of *On Baile's Strand* allows *The Only Jealousy of Emer* to be played as a self-consistent work independent of the earlier play; but it also creates a good sense of continuity if the plays are acted either together or within the group of five plays about Cuchulain.

5. *sea-borne log*: In the chapter 'Kidnappers' in *The Celtic Twilight* Yeats recounts the tale of Mrs Ormsby, whose husband twice sickened but was saved from death by a 'faery-doctor'; the third time proved fatal, 'and ever after when she spoke of him Mrs. Ormsby shook her head saying she knew well where he was, and it wasn't in Heaven or Hell or Purgatory either. She probably believed that a log of wood was left behind in his place, but so bewitched that it seemed the dead body of her husband.'

6. *Manannan*: God of the sea, who according to some legends educated Cuchulain and Diarmuid of the Fianna in the use of the sword. He possessed a magic cloak that allowed him to transform his appearance, hence the frequent references to him as 'Shape-Changer' and 'old juggler'; the cloak when shaken before a mortal's face had the power to bring forgetfulness, especially of painful or compromising experience.

7. *I have that hope*: This is the secret of Emer's careful composure in the presence of a rival, but what is offered here as an explanation of her seeming strength is redefined later as a point of hubris in her which ultimately renders her vulnerable.

8. *Sidhe*: the immortal ones, supernatural beings.

9. *Bricriu – not the man . . . Sidhe*: Bricriu of the Bitter Tongue was a mortal whose palace rivalled Conchubar's Emain in splendour; Bricriu of the Sidhe is a figure in Irish lore akin to Loge in the Niebelung sagas, a god of mischief, malice and trickery. One reason why the composition of *The Only Jealousy of Emer* was protracted over nearly two years (where the other plays for dancers were completed within a matter of weeks) related to Yeats's difficulty in deciding 'who should be the changeling put in Cuchulain's place when he is taken to the other world. Who should it be – Cuchulain's grandfather, or some god, or devil or woman?' The choice of Bricriu was felicitous: it is deeply disturbing when his withered arm pulls aside the curtains to reveal him in Cuchulain's bed. The psychic shock occasioned by his grotesque appearance immediately transforms the elegiac mood that has prevailed till now, as his irony begins to challenge Emer's composure and expose it as rooted in a suspect sentimentality. The focus of the action has been brilliantly readjusted on to the psychology of motive.

10. *with his left hand*: The sinister side which opens up dark and troubling visions. Originally the text made this point more emphatically (as indeed the dialogue in *Fighting the Waves* does) with the reading, 'I have but to touch your eyes and give them sight; /But stand at my left side.' The cut was made for the *Collected Plays* of 1934.

11. *the metallic suggestion*: The effect is to make Fand seem utterly remote, 'other', even inhuman. This is augmented, once she speaks, by the sonorous, long vowel sounds that permeate the diction of her share of the dialogue.

12. *the moon . . . night*: The imagery of the waxing and waning moon that permeates this episode of the play in relation to Fand, seen as shimmering with radiance in her metallic costume and mask, draws on Yeats's steadily evolving philosophy (to be expounded at length in *A Vision* and in poems like 'The Phases of the Moon') that human personality in its quest for completion or unity of being undergoes similar

patterns of change. Yeats considered that, on reaching the equivalent of the fifteenth phase, or full moon, an individual was consummately subjective, wholly self-oriented, self-sufficient and self-possessed. This is the stage that Fand has almost reached in her evolution but considers that she requires the absolute devotion of a mortal to achieve a satisfying sense of perfection. The antithetical phase, equivalent to when the moon is wholly darkened, requires total abnegation of the self, a depersonalizing of one's identity. When Emer renounces all claim on Cuchulain's affections she undergoes such a process of abnegation, triumphs over Fand and achieves a tragic purity of being.

13. *A woman . . . knees*: Early printings of the text included reference to the dead Connla here as well as to Emer:

> A dying boy, with handsome face
> Upturned upon a beaten place;
> A sacred yew-tree on a strand;
> A woman that held in steady hand
> In all the happiness of her youth
> A burning wisp to light the door
> And many a round or crescent more;

These lines were cut and compressed in *Collected Plays* (1934) to focus attention wholly on Emer as the source of Cuchulain's anguish and guilt.

14. *I know you . . . bird of prey*: Cuchulain has an intimation that the supernatural Hawk-Woman encountered in Scotland (see *At the Hawk's Well*) was another manifestation of Fand, which she confirms. Yeats hoped that groups of his plays on the heroic world of the sagas might be played together (though he never consciously planned the five Cuchulain plays as a distinct cycle the like of Wagner's *Ring* or Shakespeare's two tetralogies based on English history). *The Only Jealousy of Emer* is the first to make specific links with other plays in the group.

15. *oblivion*: Cuchulain is promised the loss of all vestiges of a human identity if he will succumb to Fand's embrace, allowing her to perfect her selfhood.

16. *O Emer . . . married us*: This is as revised for *Collected Plays*. Earlier editions had a significantly different speech:

> Still in that dream I see you stand,
> A burning wisp in your right hand,
> To wait my coming to the house –

It is emotionally more powerful if the remembered ceremony on the threshold was a shared experience symbolic of marital union rather than one of a submissive Emer dutifully awaiting Cuchulain's return.

17. *No, never . . . cry*: Early editions of the play contain a very different sequence of events here: hearing Cuchulain speak of his memory of their wedded bliss, Emer makes her renunciation ('If he may live I am content'); the Ghost observes, 'What a wide silence has fallen in this dark!' and finds the strength to reject Fand ('That face, though fine enough, is a fool's face /And there's a folly in the deathless Sidhe /Beyond man's reach'); as the Ghost leaves her, Fand turns in fury on Bricriu, who scorns her threats as he falls back amidst the bedclothes. The revision makes for a more lucid climax that gives a heightened focus and due stage-time to Emer's momentous decision: the play-within-the-play remains intact; Fand leaves, drawing Cuchulain's ghost after her,

which intensifies the suspense and the pressure on Emer. This version, though simpler than the earlier one, is less fussy and consolidates our sense that the action is to be interpreted as portraying the movements of Emer's consciousness.

18. *the stage is bare*: Yeats does not indicate precisely how the ritual with the cloth is to be timed in relation to the Musicians' song, but it is important that the audience have time to register the full irony of the final tableau, as Eithne passionately embraces Cuchulain to the rear of the stage while to the fore Emer confronts her lonely destiny. Some commentators have tried to apply the final lyric exclusively to Fand or to all three of the women involved with Cuchulain. But it would seem more appropriate (given the stage-picture) to relate it to Emer, standing masked and solitary in her grief like a statue, from whom the reckless Cuchulain indeed turns his 'too human breast'; and we, as audience, are 'astonished' by the phenomenal courage of her choice, made confidently despite her certain knowledge that its 'bitter reward' will be the death of the heart.

Calvary

The Only Jealousy of Emer shows us a woman who sacrifices herself for the love of a man whom she knows will never recognize his obligation to her – a far more painful experience than his outright rejection. Yeats had become fascinated by the contrasts between what he termed objective and subjective individuals, and his next idea for a dance-play was clearly designed to exploit that contrast: in the same letter (14 January 1918) informing Lady Gregory that he had completed *The Only Jealousy of Emer*, he continued hesitantly with a scheme for a dramatic confrontation between a Sinn Fein soldier (who has unsuccessfully been attempting to persuade a sculptor to 'shoulder a rifle' in the Rising) and the ghost of Judas wandering through Dublin, 'looking for somebody to whom he may betray Christ in order that Christ may proclaim himself King of the Jews'. This idea, while it exploited a distinction between political commitment as objective behaviour (the soldier) and fanaticism as a subjective obsession (Judas), would seem closely allied to *The Dreaming of the Bones*; indeed it seems almost a commentary on that earlier play. As the play that was to become *Calvary* developed, however, the focus shifted away from Judas as active betrayer to Christ as passive sufferer; and the more closely the theme examined the nature of martyrdom as the making of a conscious choice to suffer for the sake of others, the more the play began to complement *The Only Jealousy of Emer*.

In *The Dreaming of the Bones* Yeats first explored the idea, found in a great deal of Noh drama, that the ghosts of individuals who died in states of passionate anguish linger about the places where they suffered in life, live endlessly through the experiences that brought them such intense grief in the hope of finding some release from spiritual torment, and thereby invest the places they so haunt with a distinct atmosphere. The difficulty was to convey the sense of relentless cycles of misery accompanying the process of dreaming back again and again over the past; Yeats solved this expertly by reiterating the phrase 'seven hundred years' throughout the play as a precise reminder of the distance in historical time between Diarmuid and Dervorgilla's betrayal of Ireland and the Easter Rising and by prescribing that all the patterns of movement should be in circular formations (first about the entire stage-space as symbolizing a journey and then, for the lovers' final dance, a continual weaving around each other).

The story of Christ's Passion presents less of a problem: it is enacted continually in the ritual of the Mass and there is a long European tradition of religious drama centring on the event. The process of dreaming back over the experience that took place on a particular hill called Calvary is an established and pervasive icon in Western culture, since Christ himself at the Last Supper imposed an obligation on Christians regularly to undertake that process in celebration of his sacrifice: for believers so to celebrate would confirm the worth of his endeavour. Yeats's play invites us imaginatively to start on the familiar re-enactment yet again. The First Musician sets the customary scene, with Christ appearing on cue carrying his cross, but then shocks us into contemplating whether another meaning can be read into the process of dreaming back, whether the fact of its endless repetition is not a proof of Christ's failure. Familiarity, as the proverb has it, breeds contempt, and mockery is the dominant tone throughout the action from the moment the jeering crowd is introduced into the setting of the scene.

While god-plays abound in the Noh tradition, there is none that provides a source for *Calvary*, with its pronouncedly sceptical stance: the gods appearing in Noh are always celebrated to endorse the Shinto and Buddhist values in which that theatre is deeply rooted. Yeats's inspiration here was a prose poem by Oscar Wilde, 'The Doer of Good', which tells how Christ came to a city and encountered several men and women whom he had healed physically or psychologically: but the one-time leper is now a drunken sot; the former blind man is an insatiable lecher, the woman taken in adultery thinks that, as her sins are forgiven her, she can continue in a life of relentless fornication; and Lazarus, raised from the dead, can only sit and weep.

Yeats carries the ironies of Wilde's poem to a far profounder level by making the challenges not to Christ's skill as healer but to his ambition to redeem all men through the sacrifice of his life; the need endlessly to 'dream His passion through' is terrible proof of the limits of his godhead. his sacrifice, conceived 'when the foundations of the world were laid', required a total abnegation of self; but, worse than the jeering crowd of onlookers enjoying his physical suffering, are Lazarus and Judas, who actively resist the obligations that they see Christ's consummate act of love as imposing on them. Both are obsessed with self (note how the word 'I' echoes through their speeches): Lazarus out of a loathing for life that makes him covet the anonymity of death; Judas out of ecstasy at his own intellectual prowess. They insist on being 'other', outsiders from Christ's universal schemes: having free will, that is how they choose to exercise it. They have no feeling whatever for Christ's pains, physical or spiritual, and no remorse either.

Finally, Yeats's Christ is left with the Roman soldiers who, coming from an alien culture, do not recognize the cross as any kind of significant emblem: crucifixions are all in a day's cheerful work to them. While Christ in dying tries to assert that all experience fulfils a divine plan, the soldiers set about playing dice for Christ's cloak and dancing with a wild abandon. Their whole existence is lived in praise of chance and recklessness; they cannot imagine that life might be determined by scrupulous choices and inhabit the moment without thought for any future. In dancing, they 'join hand to hand and *wheel* about the cross' (my italics) – an image of mindless energy and exuberant delight in the body. Their robust physical action is opposed to the passive Christ's strife with shadows within the life of the mind: the stage-picture is a terrifying emblem of futility, as Christ cries out, 'My Father, why hast Thou forsaken Me?'

It is a disturbing cry as recorded in the gospels, implying a recognition of failure and despair; but, as with the whole story of the crucifixion, there is a palpable risk that we will lose sight of the pain of it all because it is so familiar, even in its detail, through constant repetition as a cultural touchstone. Yeats's remarkable achievement with *Calvary* is to make an audience experience again the *passion* in the Passion, by confronting us not as we might expect with the physical horror of the event but, far more audaciously, with the mind of Christ in his intellectual suffering, as his magnanimity meets with rage, derision and complete indifference – attitudes that are portrayed with credible and sensitive insight. Like Wilde's poem, the play deliberately hovers on the edge of blasphemy for a purpose: to challenge an audience's potential apathy by stripping the Passion of every possible vestige of sentimentality. Yeats recognized that his audacity ensured that he would never see the play performed in his lifetime (and such was the case); yet that very audacity is what gives the play in performance today a vital immediacy quite lacking in more conventionally pious treatments of the subject.

Setting: No patterned screen or curtain, however stylized the design, is called for: it is essential to Yeats's dramatic strategy that each member of the audience should bring before the mind's eye his or her own imagined setting in response to the First Musician's terse words, 'The road to Calvary . . . Good Friday's come' – the particular setting shaped and informed by that individual's cultural background.

1. *round three sides . . . seated*: This is the first time Yeats suggests a preferred relation of stage with audience (though it is the configuration deployed in the initial performances of *At the Hawk's Well*). He envisages a deep thrust playing space so that the performers are acting almost in the round; if, as the directions to *At the Hawk's Well* indicate, conventional domestic lighting is used rather than some form of stage-lighting, then the audience are going to be very aware of each other. Yeats seems deliberately to be building devices that will keep his audience at a pitch of self-consciousness with this play (in 1918 this process of alienation would have been far more disturbing to audiences than today).

2. *the white heron . . . dream*: Yeats in his note to the 1921 edition of the play remarked of the Musicians' songs: 'I use birds as symbols of subjective life . . . Certain birds, especially as I see things, such lonely birds as the heron, hawk, eagle and swan, are the natural symbols of subjectivity.' As the lyric develops, the symbolic intent is clarified. The critic T. R. Henn mused whether a possible pictorial inspiration for this idea came from Yeats's interest in the paintings of Mantegna and in particular his *Agony in the Garden of Gethsemane* in the National Gallery, London, where a heron contemplating its reflection in the waters of a stream is to be seen near the figure of the agonized Christ.

3. *deathly face . . . field*: The contrast of macabre features and youthful, vigorous movement creates immediate suspense for Lazarus's entry prior to his announcing his identity. The story of his raising from the dead is found in John 11.

4. *chuckle*: The text of *Calvary* deploys a great deal of subtle repetition. 'Chuckle' is

a word both Lazarus and Judas resort to when describing their reaction to situations in which they feel totally alone, as if it is somehow a primal and essential expression of their different but equally subjective selves. It suggests a rather smug satisfaction at first; but through repetition by Judas the word comes to have rather eerie connotations intimating behaviour that verges on the manic.

5. *Martha, and those three Marys*: For a brief moment we are offered one of the more conventional pictures included in the Stations of the Cross, but any potential sentiment that builds here dissipates with the ensuing song with its distressing idea that the women have absolutely no individuality of their own whatever, no purpose in life without Christ as an object for their love and pity. They do not speak, or appear, except to the mind's eye; they exist only as attendant, grieving figures in the icon of the crucifixion.

6. *Judas*: The one disciple willing to betray Jesus to Caiaphas, High Priest of the Temple in Jerusalem. He showed the Temple guards where they could find Christ, since he knew Jesus intended praying amidst his followers in the Garden of Gethsemane on the Mount of Olives. To indicate which was Jesus among the group of disciples, he kissed him. Judas's reward was thirty pieces of silver; some accounts add that shortly afterwards, overcome by remorse, he hanged himself.

7. *He has been chosen . . . cross*: Judas supporting the crucified Christ is a powerfully ironic stage-picture, intimating that neither can be as totally free of the other as he would wish. They are a necessary pairing: the martyr has need of the betrayer to shape his destiny and the betrayer needs the holy man as a means to express his denial and rejection of faith. Each perfects the other's identity. This idea was clearly central to Yeats's composition of the play, since it reaches right back to the germ of inspiration Yeats confessed in a letter to Lady Gregory (when he thought of writing a play where Judas met with a Sinn Fein soldier): 'Judas is looking for somebody to whom he may betray Christ *in order that* Christ may proclaim himself King of the Jews' (my italics). It is particularly daring (and a sign of Yeats's mature dramatic skill) to offer so startling an icon to replace the traditional way of representing Christ's dying moments on the cross and to leave it as a purely visual statement to make its impact on an audience without further comment.

8. *Ephesus*: A brief mention of one of the great religious centres of the pagan world with its worship of Artemis/Diana in her aspect as earth-mother, goddess of fertility. The soldiers seem as uninterested in the significance of Ephesus as they are in the fact that Christ might himself be a god or have 'made the world'; all that matters to them is the game of dice.

9. *They dance*: The final whirling about the cross is a dramatic metaphor for the giddy world Christ came to save but which seems on the point of overwhelming him completely, even as Cuchulain, at the end of *On Baile's Strand*, is described by the Fool as 'mastered' by the waves. This is not an icon of the cross triumphant but an image of a tide of agony and doubt surging forth to challenge Christ's resolution and commitment to his ideal. What we watch here is the tragedy of Jesus the man being trapped in the inexorable demands of Christ as Messiah, God and Saviour.

Sophocles' King Oedipus

Staging *King Oedipus* had been one of Yeats's deep-seated ambitions from before the founding of the Abbey in 1904; several scholars were approached as likely translators; none produced work that satisfied Yeats. In 1905 Gilbert Murray refused to provide a literal translation for Yeats to make stageworthy, because he thought the play overrated and unrelievedly cruel. Yeats shelved the project temporarily until the actor, Murray Carson, expressed a wish to play the title role; for two years Yeats negotiated a production and again began seeking out an actable translation, even settling on one by R. C. Jebb which had been staged in Cambridge, but in 1911 Carson withdrew. Nugent Monck came at this time to work at the Abbey at Yeats's invitation to extend the actors' range; he mounted productions of medieval dramas, experimented (the most successfully of Abbey directors to do so) with Craig's system of screens, and took workshop sessions on *Oedipus* using Jebb's text. His efforts so delighted Yeats that he began thinking of dates when Sophocles' tragedy might enter the repertory. It was only at this point that Yeats began seriously to work on the text himself, giving as his reason his anxiety that 'existing translations won't *speak*'.

This was a valid criticism: period translations pursued a grand style, verbose, syntactically contorted, full of superfluities and archaic references, which were designed to give readers (rather than audiences) as literal an experience of the Greek text as possible; little of the theatrical and dramatic spirit of the original survived. At first Yeats merely put style on Jebb's work, which Monck had cut quite heavily in rehearsal in the interests of actability; but what began as a dilettante chore soon took possession of his imagination. A total overhaul of the dialogue, amounting to a rewriting of Jebb, was completed by the spring of 1912, when Yeats unaccountably lost interest in the venture before attempting versions of the choruses. (Max Reinhardt staged a spectacular production with Martin Harvey and Lillah McCarthy at Covent Garden in January that year, which would have taken the novelty off a version at the Abbey and might have drawn unfavourable comparisons from critics. Also the Abbey at that date was without an actor with the physical scope, tonal range, versatility of technique and sheer rugged stamina necessary to accomplish the demanding central role.) Yeats's manuscripts were stored away.

One can appreciate why Yeats should have been so keen to stage a Greek tragedy in these years: Craig had excited his interest in masks, and his own most successful plays (*On Baile's Strand* and *Deirdre*) had found a place for ritual and song, and had deployed choric figures to frame the action. It is conceivable that Yeats would soon have returned to his Greek project had Pound not introduced him to Noh theatre, sparking off a burst of creativity of a highly innovative kind (though using the masks, dance, song, stylization and ceremonial which would have been essential to a proper staging of Greek tragedy). But only one of those new works had been staged – and that privately and in London – an ironic fact that must have nagged Yeats when in 1923, receiving the Nobel Prize for Literature, he chose as the principal subject of his address his work in establishing the Abbey as a 'people's theatre'. In 1924 the Abbey in fact became a national theatre receiving state subsidy, but Yeats's involvement continued as Director not as practising dramatist. Two years later that situation changed when an acclaimed and unexpectedly popular dramatic success initiated a whole new phase of playwriting. The key to it all was Mrs Yeats's discovery of the *Oedipus* manuscripts and her prompting her husband into a renewed interest in the play.

The choruses were quickly finished and the entire play underwent substantial revision while Yeats was preparing the text for duplication as actors' copies ready for Lennox Robinson's production, which, 'set in an arrangement of Craig Screens', opened on 7 December 1926, with F. J. McCormick, a superbly accomplished tragedian, as Oedipus, Eileen Crowe as Jocasta, Barry Fitzgerald as Creon and M. J. Dolan as Tiresias. Immediate acclaim set Yeats to work on *Oedipus at Colonus*, where (as he informed his friend, Olivia Shakespear) his version became 'bolder'; beside it *King Oedipus* left him 'shocked at my moderation'; he continued, 'I want to be less literal and more idiomatic and modern.' Once *Colonus* was finished, Yeats immediately set about revising them both, consulting now, with Lady Gregory's help, a French translation of the plays by Paul Masqueray. Always the impulse was to achieve a text that would, when spoken, be immediately comprehensible; he wanted a speech that was 'bare, hard and natural like a saga'. Yeats admired the sheer implacability, the inexorable drive of Sophoclean tragedy, and he wanted nothing to stand in the way of that powerful theatrical impact. Becoming ever bolder, he shortened the choruses and finally – his most astonishing adaptation – reduced to a few lines Oedipus' long justification to the Chorus of why he blinded himself. Yeats had noted that McCormick was visibly strained by the closing episode at the dress rehearsal ('so much that he could hardly act in the last great moments'). Olivia Shakespear, to whom he confided this, replied that she thought unactable the final speeches in which Oedipus moves slowly from anguished self-pity to a quiet acceptance of his fate. Yeats agreed: 'It is so on our stage but I cut all of it out but a few lines.' This revised version of his original text of *King Oedipus* was played together with *Oedipus at Colonus* in September 1927 and published the following year.

'A version for the modern stage' is Yeats's careful description of his work: it is not a translation in the academic sense of the word. He wrote rather 'for an audience where nobody comes for self-improvement or for anything but emotion ... I put readers and scholars out of my mind and wrote to be sung and spoken. The one thing that I kept in mind was that a word unfitted for living speech, out of its natural order, or unnecessary to our modern technique, would check emotion and tire attention.' What gives Yeats's work its power is the remarkable compression: everything was to be trimmed away that did not advance the action, and so he developed a technique for encompassing the spirit of the original Greek text by the most economical of means. The result is a muscular prose which is taut, spare, rhythmic, which readily follows the inflexions of the speaking voice and works effortlessly for stresses that excite psychological and emotional insights: a prose that is dramatic and characterful. The gain for Yeats's subsequent dramatic work was far-reaching: adapting Sophocles taught him a great deal about ways of compressing syntax for intensity of effect, which owed no kind of debt to Shakespeare's more familiar patterns of grammatical compression.

But the gain was not confined to the evolution of new forms of diction and dramatic syntax. Completing the *Oedipus* project was as momentous a landmark in Yeats's development as playwright as his discovery of the Noh. Sophocles' tragedy explores a theme that had begun to preoccupy Yeats with the later dance-plays: the interweaving of chance and choice in shaping the individual life-experience. Oedipus and Jocasta at various times in the action assert their free will and voice a belief that their lives are subject to chance or luck, and yet the intricate structure of the play shows that the god Apollo has total control of events and is shaping the destinies of all the characters to his own ends. A seemingly random series of consequences is found to be part of a most exacting design: Apollo is nowhere seen in the play, but the plotting of the action even to its finest detail is a sustained and relentless manifestation of his power. The plotting, the story-line, is, therefore, profoundly symbolic to the extent that Yeats felt, watching the play, 'a sense as of the actual presence in a terrible sacrament of the god'. Many characters in Yeats's earlier plays (the Wise Man, Deirdre, Diarmuid and Dervorgilla, Emer and Christ) had been preoccupied with the need to shape their stories to an appropriate ending and one preferably of their own choosing. This issue in the final phase of his playwriting becomes an acutely pressing concern, where Yeats sets about exploring the nature of destiny as individuals come to experience it in their lives, either resisting or accepting it as a force powerfully affecting their sense of a personal integrity.

In 1904 Yeats had intended the staging of *Oedipus* to be a means to creating the taste amongst Dubliners by which his own plays might be enjoyed; completing *Sophocles' King Oedipus* in 1927 as 'a version for the modern stage' created the context in which his own late plays might best be understood. A favourite theme in the poetry of his last years is of the need in the artistic life continually to 'remake' the self; completing the long-standing *Oedipus* project effected just such a process of inspirational renewal.

1. *Cadmus*: The legendary founder of Thebes who, on killing a dragon, by Athene's advice sowed the creature's teeth, from which sprang forth an army of armed men; these he set to fight each other till only five survived, who became the fathers of the Theban nation.

2. *Zeus*: Father and ruler of the gods, believed to reside on Mount Olympus.

3. *riddling Sphinx*: A mythological creature, half lion, half female, who was sent to Thebes by Hera, queen of the gods, to ask the citizens a perplexing riddle ('What goes on four legs at dawn, two at noon and three in the evening?'), the answer to which was 'Man'. Anyone failing to answer the test was killed by the monster, but Oedipus solved the puzzle and killed the sphinx. The priest reminds Oedipus of that show of superior intelligence and questions whether it was just luck then with the sphinx or whether he still has gifts of insight rare in humankind.

4. *Pythian House of Phoebus*: Delphi was the centre of worship of Phoebus Apollo, god of the sun and light, music, healing and prophecy. His priestess, the Pythia, was possessed by the god and uttered oracular pronouncements from a special shrine. As the critic and translator Robert Fagles writes, 'The oracle maintained contacts with peoples and rulers all over the Greek and barbarian worlds; it promoted revolutions, upheld dynasties, guided the foundation of colonies – its wealth and political influence were immense.'

5. *Speak before all*: Not in the event a politic decision, but a decent one. Oedipus' continuing refusal to hide anything from his fellow-citizens builds and sustains audience sympathy for him.

6. *dark things plain*: Yeats, as the action progresses, exploits the words 'light' and

'dark', both in their literal and complex figurative senses, building up intricate levels of irony since Apollo was god both of the sun and of enlightenment.

7. *The Chorus*: At the Abbey these Theban elders were six in number including their leader, who was an actor from the company, the rest being members of a liturgical choir. The music (all the choruses were sung) by Dr J. F. Larchet was scored for a tenor-voiced leader, one at baritone and the remainder at bass pitch.

8. *Golden House*: The treasury of the temple at Delphi.

9. *Delian God*: Apollo, whose birthplace was traditionally believed to be the island of Delos in the Cyclades.

10. *God-trodden western shore*: The Atlantic (believed in ancient times to be the edge of the world); this too is the 'formless deep' of the next stanza.

11. *Master of the thunder-cloud*: Zeus, who is generally depicted wielding lightning and thunderbolts as symbols of cosmic power and authority.

12. *Artemis*: Apollo's sister, patroness of hunting and childbirth.

13. *Maenads*: Wild followers of the god Dionysus, whose mother, according to a different cluster of myths surrounding Thebes, was Semele, a daughter of Cadmus. She was seduced by Zeus, who, appearing in his divine glory at her request, caused her to be burned to ashes. The story of the coming of Dionysus to Thebes is the subject of a tragedy by Euripides, *The Bacchae*, where he is shown punishing Cadmus, his other daughter, Agave, and her son, Pentheus, for their failure to believe in his godhead.

14. *Lysian king . . . face'*: Yeats for once in conflating the Greek original gives rise to some confusion here. The Lysian king refers to Apollo, and his emblem, appropriately, is a golden bow; Sophocles crowns Bacchus (another name for Dionysus, god of wine and theatre) with the golden head-dress. The whole chorus is considerably compressed compared with the original, where each of the gods whose aid is entreated, the horrors of death by plague, and the vast wastes of the Atlantic are all described at greater length.

15. *Tiresias*: According to myth, Tiresias, on striking a pair of coupling snakes with his staff, had been transformed for part of his life into a woman. He was turned blind by Hera when, questioned by the gods as to whether men or women got more pleasure from love, he answered that (on his experience) women did. Zeus made him a learned seer to compensate for Hera's cruelty.

16. *wise and suffer for it?*: This whole scene with Tiresias underwent extensive revision by Yeats till he had got the precise tone he sought for: one poised between mounting anger at Oedipus' stubbornness, fearfulness of the gods and their decrees, and pity for the king's fate. Tiresias, as Yeats presents him, is a man trapped by the demands of his calling, at once keen to preserve his integrity as seer yet pained by the sight of suffering humanity. He is confident of his knowledge yet realizes all too well how his insight is dangerous to everyone, and particularly to himself.

17. *No, I came . . . any birds*: There is an echo here of Judas in *Calvary*, vaunting himself with constant repetitions of the word 'I'.

18. *Loxias*: One of the many descriptive titles given to Apollo; the meaning of the Greek ('to one side' or 'at a tangent') may refer to the cryptic, riddling nature of most of the oracle's pronouncements. This is an apt name for Apollo at this moment, since

Tiresias as Apollo's spokesman immediately launches into a very shrewdly disguised version of the truth about Oedipus' situation. Repeatedly throughout Yeats's version of the play characters (especially Jocasta) refer to Apollo as Loxias when they are commenting on a statement from the oracle which they believe they understand or which they feel they can disprove.

19. *an alien*: Everyone, including Oedipus himself, believes the king is Corinthian by birth.

20. *The Delphian rock*: Yeats again compresses the chorus to less than half its length in the Greek, concentrating on the idea of Fate and the oracle calling for the tracking down of the murderer, which is the substance of the first two stanzas in the original. Sophocles adds further stanzas pondering the nature of the prophetic art and Tiresias' particular skills; praise of Zeus and Apollo as the all-seeing ones; and a touching assurance from the Chorus of their trust in their king that prevents them thinking the worst of him. Yeats presumably cut these to intensify the sense of Apollo's relentless pursuit of his victim.

21. *Parnassus*: A mountain overlooking Delphi, which Sophocles actually describes as 'snow-capped', not 'cloudy'.

22. *Fates*: The Furies, avenging spirits, protective of the rights of victims of murder.

23. *crossing-place . . . navel . . . world*: It was believed that Apollo's shrine was placed at the very centre of the world; the sacred white stone that marked the site, the *omphalos*, was termed 'the navel'.

24. *justly said*: Yeats preserves a vein of quiet reasonableness in Creon's speeches at first that makes Oedipus' accusations seem the more offensive and rash. Ironically, though he himself does not appreciate the fact, Creon's words in the ensuing scene touch the truth of Oedipus' nature and situation with a relentless accuracy, simply because of his sensitivity of judgement. There is no malice in his nature, only a desire, such as Tiresias expressed, to safeguard his own integrity.

25. *Helios*: The sun-god, worshipped in his own right but sometimes identified with Apollo in his aspect as god of light.

26. *Our land . . . is over*: I have cut here a stage direction reading '*Exit leader of Chorus.*' This is not required by Sophocles' text, but is a reflection of the way the play was staged by Lennox Robinson at the Abbey. The Chorus of five men was situated within what was customarily the orchestra-pit, below the level of the stage; only the leader appeared on stage with the named characters and at this point he was required to withdraw to allow a more intimate scene for wife and husband. Surviving typescripts of the play as performed in 1926 and 1927 (which must have been used as prompt copies during rehearsal) carry pencilled annotations in Robinson's hand showing how the characters were disposed about the stage in the various episodes in relation to each other and the Chorus.

27. *bound its feet together*: Sophocles is more explicit, describing the father as fastening the child's ankles together with a pin or spancel.

28. *What the God would show*: Jocasta is always careful to distinguish between the all-knowing, infallible god and his fallible (because human) agents who tend the oracle or claim the gift of prophecy.

29. *What restlessness of soul . . . mind!*: Jocasta's kindly intentioned effort to dispel Oedipus' alarm unwittingly serves only to kindle fresh agony from a new source. It is part of the acute painfulness of this tragedy that from the time of Oedipus' birth individuals with the best of intentions have endeavoured to avoid Apollo's decree, only to find now that in so doing they have but augmented the ensuing catastrophe.

30. *He was tall . . . to you*: In the original there are two speeches preceding Jocasta's description of her first husband, which Yeats decided to cut. First Jocasta responds to Oedipus' cry of dread at what the future may hold with a pointedly maternal concern, which Oedipus then brushes aside as he asks her to tell him what Laius looked like and what his age was. The transition appears rather abrupt on the page but in performance the effect created is that the couple are in such a rare state of compatibility that the wife can read her husband's mind unerringly.

31. *I fear . . . question him*: Early drafts of the play reiterate words relating to the idea of reason and its opposite, madness and folly, but most of these were cut after the first performances, suggesting that Yeats made a particular artistic decision in the light of his experience of the play in production. One can but guess at the motive but it is possible that Yeats considered such loaded, judgemental words were too emphatic a statement of the theme of the play and so too overt a directive to the audience. This particular line was one that was amended at this time. Formerly it read: 'I fear, Lady, that I have spoken folly; and therefore I would speak with him.' In its revised form, it has become much more self-centred: Oedipus is too preoccupied to indulge in polite forms of address even to Jocasta; he appreciates he has been behaving intemperately, but even if he thinks he has behaved foolishly, Oedipus is not the man to lose face by admitting as much and so he searches for a more guarded phrase; and finally 'question' establishes Oedipus firmly in a position of power, where 'speak with' implies a more relaxed exchange. The revision is psychologically more complex because the expression is tauter: Oedipus is revealed as a man who, seeing himself at bay, needs the comfort of asserting his authority. Simple changes have opened up whole new dimensions of meaning behind an apparently simple sentence of explanation about why Oedipus suddenly needs to see Jocasta's former slave. This is creative translation at its finest, where the characters invented by one dramatist are completely inhabited by the adapter's imagination.

32. *Nobody is more . . . evil luck*: Brilliantly within one sentence Yeats captures the strangely shifting tones of adoration and deference that characterize Oedipus' attitude to Jocasta; even before he knows the truth, he responds to her as wife and mother.

33. *Sibyl*: The Pythia, or medium-like prophetess, through whom Apollo's oracular decrees were communicated.

34. *For this one thing . . . dance?*: Yeats again shortens the chorus, trimming it of poetic embellishment to clarify and sharpen the line of argument, as the Theban elders express their dread of coming chaos should the power of the Delphian oracle be called into question.

35. *He has come . . . dead*: Yeats originally wrote 'no longer lives' – a typical circumlo-cution in giving news of an adverse kind, which allows the recipient a brief time to adjust to shock and likely grief. The revision to a stark statement that Polybus is dead is more apt, since Jocasta is more concerned to allay Oedipus' fear of oracles than to

observe niceties of decorum. All her consciousness is directed with maternal solicitude
at securing Oedipus' peace of mind. Even when later she guesses at the awful truth
about their precise relationship, she tries her hardest to save Oedipus from the anguish
of discovering it too. Interestingly, Robinson's extant sketches in the prompt books
of the first and second productions show that he kept Jocasta in the dominant central
position on stage throughout the following scene, once Oedipus had entered; though
she says less and less as the action develops, her intelligence far outstrips Oedipus' in
realizing the import of what the Messenger is saying. Robinson's blocking of the scene
would allow the actress to make clear the motivation that compels Jocasta to make
her sudden terrified exit into the palace.

36. *Hades*: The underworld, kingdom of the dead, which was ruled by the god Pluto.

37. *bold words*: In the Greek original these 'bold words' refer to a far longer speech
from Jocasta which Yeats has surprisingly cut. In it she consoles Oedipus with the
thought that many a man has dreamed of sharing his mother's bed with no disastrous
consequences. (It was the passage on which Freud based his famous interpretation of
the play and his concept of the Oedipus complex.)

38. *Cithaeron*: A mountain separating the state of Thebes from Eleusis. Its lower
reaches are marked by long glens; it was here that Dionysus brought his Maenads
when they descended on Greece from Asia.

39. *name you bear*: Oedipus means 'swollen foot', but to Greek ears the name also
embraces the word *oida*, meaning 'I know.'

40. *Oedipus' nurse . . . adored*: Yeats again reduces the chorus in Sophocles to a fraction
of its length, giving just the outline of its development: Cithaeron is celebrated for
nursing the child Oedipus who, grown to manhood, is now so famous that the elders
believe he must have been fathered by a god – Pan, Apollo or Dionysus ('the mountain
Lord').

41. *woman-breasted Fate*: The Sphinx.

42. *What can . . . heartbroken Oedipus*: Though intensely compressed, this is a superb
evocation of Sophocles' great elegiac chorus about the vanity of human life and
ambition. Yeats's epigrammatic terseness and the sonorous triple rhymes to each short
stanza give the despair underlying the threnody a profound, stoic grandeur.

43. *Ister . . . Phasis*: The great rivers creating the borders of the northern lands of
Thrace and Colchis beyond Greece.

44. *The curtain is parting*: Sophocles' messenger observes that the palace doors are
opening; Yeats's version reflects more accurately the setting used at the Abbey. The
programme notes that the setting was created from the Abbey's set of Craig screens,
but they were notoriously difficult to move once in position. Presumably they were
arranged in a perspective formation to create a central doorway of some height within
which curtains were hung to make a more practicable entrance. Yeats wrote elsewhere
of playing *Oedipus* 'before a purple curtain'.

45. *Enter Oedipus*: From here to the end Yeats made his most drastic cuts to Sophocles'
text, reducing some 335 lines of Greek verse to little more than a hundred lines of
prose. The original is a long aria of suffering for Oedipus which the chorus partly
share in pitiful sympathy and partly distance themselves from through shock, a sense
of sacrilege, and sheer uncertainty of how properly they should behave, till Creon

appears and coolly takes control of the situation, assuming a kingly authority. At the time of the first Abbey production of the play the episode was more substantial; but the performance troubled Yeats, who was not alone in doubting whether a modern actor could sustain interest through so long an exposition of pure grief and horror. Joseph Holloway, generally a fervent admirer of McCormick, had some reservations about the ending, even though he thought both production and impersonation overall worthy of the term 'great': 'McCormick was very dignified in bearing and impressive of speech in the opening episodes; his sudden change when blind at the end might be considered too pronounced, and his voice too whiningly pitched, though his episode with the children was moving in the extreme.' In revising the play for publication and the second production at the Abbey, Yeats cut the final scene to its present length, notably leaving only the sequence with the daughters at a length commensurate with the Greek text. Sophocles has Oedipus tell over again the terrible story of his life at a pitch of shame and self-loathing. Yeats leaves much to the imagination as his Oedipus speaks sparingly of his self-mutilation, the patricide and his incest; and, to shift the focus of the speech at the points where he makes his major deletions, he invents short speeches for the Chorus (p. 190), seemingly to help redirect Oedipus' thoughts, as if the Theban elders cannot bear to witness such a prolonged act of public humiliation. The brief, tense phrases or short sentences that make up Oedipus' speeches graphically evoke a man struggling for breath against bursts of unimaginable pain. Yeats next cuts Creon's expressions of disgust at the obscenity of seeing Oedipus in public and his account of seeking the gods' permission to assume the throne of Thebes, so that nothing distracts attention from Oedipus' anxiety that due rites of burial be given to Jocasta and that his innocent children should be properly cared for. From the entry of Antigone and Ismene, Yeats follows Sophocles closely till the final choric song, which pares the Greek down to a stark, pithy but magnificent epigram. As an acting text for the modern theatre, despite the liberties taken in the rendering of the final scene, Sophocles' King Oedipus has few rivals.

The Resurrection

During the summer of 1926, when Yeats was completing his translation of the choruses for King Oedipus, he wrote to Olivia Shakespear: 'I have lots of subjects in my head including a play about Christ meeting the worshippers of Dionysus on the mountain side.' Scenarios survive from this time outlining schemes for a large-scale dance-play: figures are seen rolling back the stone from the entrance to the sepulchre; Christ comes forth and has his grave-clothes unwound by the three Marys. He then dreams back over his life and death in conversation with the figures who reveal themselves to be Buddha, Dionysus and a third divinity; they tell him about the numerous gods who died to save their followers, and Christ cries out against the endless misery and pain of humankind for whom gods die in vain; all but Buddha and the three Marys steal away; the women kneel at his feet, as Christ spreads his arms wide while speaking the closing line: 'I am the way and the life.' The idea of this confrontation of divinities has considerable dramatic potential, but the implicit theme of the piece offers little advance on the subject of Calvary. By late May, Yeats was composing the songs that were to become the Musicians' lyrics framing the action; and, seemingly while working on *Oedipus at Colonus*, he excitedly dashed off what he was later to dismiss as 'a chaotic dialogue', which he published in the *Adelphi* magazine in June 1927.

This text, entitled *The Resurrection* (a play of ideas and not a dance-drama), bore little relation to the scenarios: three young men talk in an antechamber of the Upper Room, where the apostles sit in despair after the crucifixion; they argue about Christ's status as human or divine, propounding conflicting philosophies to support their individual conceptions of godhead; outside a crowd of wild, Bacchic worshippers are heard celebrating the savage death, dismemberment and miraculous rebirth of Dionysus; Jesus appears in the chamber and is believed at first to be a phantom till one of the men has the courage to touch him, when he finds to his horror that 'the heart of the phantom is beating'. Yeats and subsequent commentators have tended to disparage this work; it lacks dramatic tension, certainly, and Yeats insists didactically on his theme instead of giving it theatrical life; but all the constituent features of *The Resurrection* in its revised form (as completed in December 1930, published a year later and staged in 1934) are already present in this early version; what is wanting is a tight structure within which those elements might achieve a maximum impact. Revision transformed what in the 1927 version is a theological disquisition cast in the form of a dialogue into an astonishing performance-text: *The Resurrection* has to be experienced rather than simply read.

When the Messenger in *King Oedipus* arrives to tell of Jocasta's death and Oedipus' blinding, he prefaces his story with an expression of hope that his memory can adequately encompass the full details of it all so that the chorus may learn the extent of the king's and queen's sufferings. Yeats's translation of this moment is not strictly accurate but graphically succinct: 'so far as words can serve, you shall *see* it' (my italics). Narrative is to appeal directly to the imagination, which will transform the material into a play to be watched by the mind's eye. This principle is set to work in *The Resurrection* to a highly sophisticated degree. The dance-dramas had regularly invited audiences to enter the world of the play by envisaging for themselves within the bare playing space an imaginary setting; it was a cunning strategy to fine-tune their responsiveness to the spoken word. *The Resurrection* pushes this strategy to an extreme.

We are in a bare room with two young men in a state of exceptional tension, because they fear at any moment that room may be invaded by Temple guards, Roman soldiers or an angry mob; they are alert to every sound. Soon that given stage-space expands in our imaginations. Yeats's plays often exploit the idea of what lies, literally and symbolically, beyond the confines of the stage; here what constitutes the *beyond* is excedingly complex. First we are led to imagine off to our left the Upper Room, and we people it with a tableau of the eleven apostles in postures of despair; then, as if glancing out of a small window, the men look over our heads towards a distant horizon where they say one can see Calvary with its three crosses. These are familiar icon-like images which we can quickly bring to mind; but what happens next is wholly outside traditional expectations concerning this situation. We seem to be surrounded by strange wild drumming and the chilling sound of rattles as the young men's attention is called to the foreground of the view from the window, where the followers of Dionysus come to enact their ritual. Again and again they seem to approach only to retreat, but each approach comes nearer, threatening to erupt on stage. What we are encouraged to imagine is in fact nothing less than a dance-play: men, bizarrely dressed and made up as women, are dancing themselves into an orgiastic frenzy, as others sing and mime an intricate ceremony, a primitive mystery about death and renewal that requires of its celebrants a total self-abandon.

Our sensitivity to this dimension of reality is suddenly disturbed by a loud knocking, and a third young man is admitted to the room whose breathless narrative evokes yet another scene: the garden on the hillside, the deserted sepulchre and Jesus' appearance to the three Marys. Like the images of Calvary and the apostles in the Upper Room evoked earlier, this last scene is more comfortable to imagine than the Bacchic rite because made more familiar by a long iconographic tradition of pictorial representation; yet, paradoxically, none of these three images has the immediacy or dynamism of the imagined dance-play, which we envision as much in response to a tumult of exotic sound as to descriptive language. Startling, because wholly unexpected, it sets our pulses racing and generates in a performance a tense expectancy. More unnerving still is the dancers' sudden silence *without*, at the moment when they seemed to have come closest to us; almost simultaneously a new figure enters the stage, masked and moving at a slow, stylized pace. Our imaginations have been worked on to such a degree that we are unsure what dimension of reality we are now inhabiting, as we confront this spectacle of the risen Christ; the figure seems to partake more of the world of the dance-play than of the play of ideas that has ostensibly been the focus of the stage-action.

It is a finely conceived strategy to oppose two different styles of theatre in the context of a discussion about the nature of religious belief, so that an audience is left to ponder whether faith is subject to reason (as the young men believe, at least initially) or whether, being mystical and therefore irrational, it requires a leap of the imagination. Yeats shows how in its origins Christianity was closely related to numerous long-standing cults devoted to rituals celebrating death and magical rebirths, and sacrificial feasts in which the worshippers partook of the body of the slain god. It is not the images of Calvary and the resurrection institutionalized by centuries of Christian art that stir us most profoundly in experiencing the play but the highly theatrical, if disturbing, evocation of the Bacchic dancers who suddenly come to a pitch of attentiveness as they sense the risen Christ passing through their midst to enter the Upper Room: He is the reborn God whose mysterious presence they have long sought for through the irrational pursuit of trance, frenzy and ritual. Yeats is not asserting the superiority of the pagan religions over Christianity but revealing their strong kinship, of which later ages of more systematized piety can easily lose sight. He insists on the irrationality of Christian faith as its most potent force precisely because it requires of the believer an exercise of the imagination to encompass its subtle ambivalences. In the introduction to the reprinting of *The Resurrection* in *Wheels and Butterflies*, Yeats observed, 'It has seemed to me of late that the sense of spiritual reality comes whether to the individual or to crowds from some violent shock.' The play in performance exploits the arts of the theatre with audacious skill to effect (if it is scrupulously directed) just such a psychic shock on its audiences, compelling them to contemplate Christ's resurrection with a cleansed and pristine vision.

1. *ordinary stage scene . . . at left*: This is a return to the simply functional Abbey setting Thomas Sturge Moore and Robert Gregory first suggested and designed for Yeats's *The Hour-Glass* in 1903.

2. *studio . . . dance plays*: If presented in a small room in this fashion under natural or domestic lighting conditions and with the actors who play the Hebrew, Greek and

Syrian passing to and fro through the audience as Yeats's directions specify, then *The Resurrection* becomes truly an example of total theatre.

3. *Peacock Theatre*: In 1926 the Abbey acquired the whole of the Mechanics' Institute building which they had only partly occupied since 1904. The Board agreed that the architect Michael Scott should convert the former library on the first floor into a studio theatre seating 102 patrons, with a small stage raised by two steps above the front level of the raked auditorium floor. Yeats called it his stage for poetry. At ground level a café was situated at first, but in time it became the home of the Abbey School of Acting, while the Abbey School of Ballet took over the top floor.

4. *I saw . . . called*: According to J. G. Frazer's *The Golden Bough*, which much influenced Yeats in the composition of this play, Dionysus, Zeus' son, was lured away to a wood by the Titans during their war with the gods, where he was brutally dismembered; Pallas Athene, the 'staring virgin', seized the child-god's heart, which she carried to Zeus. Zeus consumed the heart, then gave Dionysus a second birth by begetting him on Semele, a virgin mortal. Yeats saw parallels between this story and that of the annunciation, crucifixion and resurrection of Christ, and so the Muses sing to herald the start of a new era, 'Magnus Annus', at the time of the nativity, when a familiar cycle begins over again like the ritual re-enactment of some cosmic drama. Virgil wrote of this cyclic pattern in history in his fourth *Eclogue* (which has traditionally been interpreted as foretelling the birth of Christ), suggesting that ancient history would repeat itself in some new guise with new wars being fought as at Troy and new quests undertaken like Jason's in his ship, the *Argo*, in search of the mythical Golden Fleece. Christ's nativity will undermine the ordering stabilities of the Roman world, when once again a mortal virgin conceives the child of a god which will be celebrated astrologically with the appearance of a new star. 'Fabulous' is richly allusive in the context of the whole play, where faith is seen to demand belief in miraculous events which might otherwise appear matter for fiction or fable.

5. *the dead . . . cemeteries*: Matthew records that at the time of the crucifixion and resurrection graves opened and yielded up their dead.

6. *the Eleven*: The remaining disciples since Judas's betrayal of Christ, desertion and suicide.

7. *divided . . . them*: The institution of the Last Supper, on which the Mass and Eucharist are patterned.

8. *Is it true . . . denied it?*: All four gospels give the story of how, after Christ's betrayal and capture, Peter three times denied being a follower of Jesus, who had earlier predicted his disciple would do this.

9. *What makes you laugh?*: Eerie laughter reverberates throughout this play, unsettling characters and audience alike. Laughter, which to the Greek is an expression of Neoplatonic sarcasm that the image or shadow of a god could be taken for a palpable fleshly reality, is to the Hebrew crude blasphemy and sacrilege. The Greek sees his laughter as the expression of a consummate reasoning power; the Hebrew interprets it as madness, irrationality.

10. *The utmost possible . . . no statues*: Now the Greek dismisses the Hebrew's view of the Passion as irrational because rooted in a morbid obsession with death and disgust for the human body.

11. *three days ago*: The gospels of Matthew and Luke specify that Christ claimed he would rise on the third day after his death and burial.

12. *A sound of rattles . . . continuous*: Significantly, the Bacchic worshippers arrive at the precise moment the Hebrew speaks of his dread of the idea of an absolute renunciation of the self to allow his god a complete possession of his being. (The pain of such a sacrifice is the subject of *Calvary*.)

13. *a full moon in March*: In ancient times deemed the start of the new year and therefore a time of potential cataclysmic change.

14. *Astrea*: A daughter of Zeus, much lauded by Virgil as embodying ideals of justice and compassion in the Golden Age; she was transformed into the constellation Virgo.

15. *When the goddess . . . hair*: Yeats was fond of this image from Homer's *Iliad*, when Athene came to Achilles' aid.

16. *Lucretius*: A Roman philosopher of the first century BC, who in his *De Rerum Naturâ* set out rationally to question why humankind should continually live in fear of the gods, since they inhabited only the world of dreams and had no influence on the natural world.

17. *Man too remains . . . privacy*: This is the argument Lazarus and Judas raise against Christ in *Calvary*: they yearn for a metaphysical 'privacy' they feel he has denied them.

18. *Something incredible has happened*: For the Syrian's account of the resurrection which follows, Yeats took details from all four of the gospels.

19. *They stooped . . . feet*: This was the image with which the projected dance-play about the risen Christ was to end.

20. *Why are you laughing?*: Again the phrase is repeated. The Syrian's laughter, soon to be merged into the laughter of the Dionysiac dancers, expresses a state between hysteria and joy as his mind tries to come to terms with a miracle that, overthrowing all that his trained mind has learnt, suggests the onset of utter chaos; the Bacchic laughter, however, that we have heard throughout portions of the play is a token of ecstatic acceptance and abandonment to rapture.

21. *The heart . . . beating!*: In the introduction to the play included in *Wheels and Butterflies* Yeats wrote, 'Years ago I read Sir William Crookes' *Studies in Psychical Research*. After excluding every possibility of fraud, he touched a materialised form and found the heart beating. I felt, though my intellect rejected what I read, the terror of the supernatural described by Job.'

22. *Thomas . . . the heart is*: John's gospel tells of the apostle Thomas, who was not present with the others when Christ first appeared to them and who doubted his resurrection; when Jesus next appeared, Thomas was summoned and bidden to place his finger in the wounds in Christ's hands and side.

23. *Athens, Alexandria, Rome*: The great centres of learning in classical times.

24. *Heraclitus*: A philosopher of Ephesus (*c.* 500 BC) who expounded the belief that the universe was governed by a law of antinomies, or patterns of interrelated opposites; since fire was the primal element in creation, everything existed in a state of continual flux. Man and god are deemed by him to be one such pair of opposites.

25. *In pity . . . has fed*: The final lyric evokes the consequences of Christ's resurrection as initiating a new cycle in world history that would in time challenge and overthrow the

achievements of all the classical disciplines of learning: science, astrology, philosophy, mathematics and architecture. The second stanza looks compassionately in human terms at the significance of Heraclitus' theory of transience and flux.

The Words upon the Window-Pane

The ambiguities, uncertainties and deliberately veiled mysteries surrounding aspects of Swift's life, especially in respect of his long, seemingly platonic relationships with Stella and Vanessa, have fascinated Irish writers since his tragic death. Satire, gossip, conjecture (based on fancy or on the dark hints that Swift himself dropped about his difficult temperament and nature) and the awful circumstances of his last years (ill, lonely, his brain gone with the onset of senile decay) have led to both bizarre and compassionately sensitive theories about why he never married either of the women who were clearly devoted to him. The fierce, uncompromising realist, who was one-time Dean of St Patrick's Cathedral in Dublin, has become the object, since his demise in 1745, of a wealth of myth-making and the subject, this century, of a deal of playwriting. Yeats's *The Words upon the Window-Pane* was one of the first; and it remains one of the finest.

Structurally, the play, which Yeats completed with remarkable rapidity, has much in common with *The Resurrection*, though it is undeniably bolder in its control of audience-response. It must have been intensely galling for Yeats that his highly innovative dance-plays had not become an established part of the Abbey's repertory (though *Fighting the Waves*, his adaptation of *The Only Jealousy of Emer*, had been an unqualified success on the main stage in 1929); plays in the realist tradition seemed to hold the monopoly with the National Theatre Society. *The Words upon the Window-Pane* cunningly remedies that situation by a series of brilliantly designed, subversive strategies.

Yeats had never liked Shaw's comedies (least of all Shaw's gift to the Abbey, *John Bull's Other Island*, which made cruel sport of contemporary Irish movements to initiate an intellectual and cultural renaissance to which Yeats himself was deeply committed). In *The Resurrection* we have a Shavian-style play of ideas ostensibly taking place before us; yet always there hovers on the edges of our perception the dance-play involving the Dionysiac worshippers which approaches and recedes, getting ever closer with each advance, finally threatening to invade the stage, but the irrational in the form of a ghost enters instead to silence those three earnest talkers, Hebrew, Greek and Syrian.

The Words upon the Window-Pane involves a spiritualist seance, which Yeats treats with dispassionate realism. Again at first we seem to be engaged in a play of ideas, as metaphysical propositions concerning good and 'hostile' spirits are elaborated and discussed; and there is a sufficient leavening of satirical comedy at the expense of most of the characters attending the seance which makes it difficult to gauge at first how serious Yeats's intentions are. We seem to be watching a well-made play about Dublin life in what in the 1930s was the currently conventional Abbey mould. But the one character invested with a measure of authority, Dr Trench, while talking about the nature of the afterlife, introduces the concept of passionate ghosts 'dreaming back' or reliving 'some passionate or tragic moment of life', which Yeats had incorporated from Noh drama into *The Dreaming of the Bones* and *Calvary*. When the seance begins, the medium, Mrs Henderson, is possessed by one such passionate ghost, who through her body and voice undergoes just such a purgatorial process of dreaming back, to the utter consternation of the actual characters in the drama. They are helpless before the insistent power of the ghost's anguish. Like the messengers of Greek tragedy, the medium becomes the means of communicating what is conventionally unstageable; but here it is in a dramatic, not a narrative form, for Mrs Henderson plays in her person all the characters in the dream-play, effectively silencing everyone else. The stage is invaded by angry, bitter ghosts, who manipulate Mrs Henderson's body like a marionette; the Abbey style of comic realism is totally displaced by a dance-drama, but by one which we are in large measure required to imagine.

Yeats has taken possession of the Abbey in a wonderfully apt and idiosyncratic manner, shaping it wholly to his creative will. In the process he devised one of the most technically demanding roles for a mature actress conceived this century. The part requires the accomplished projection of four quite distinct voices, covering a range from high soprano (for the child, Lulu, the medium's 'control' in the spirit world) to harsh baritone (for Swift), and two distinct styles of movement: naturalistic (for the medium in her everyday self) and stylized (to evoke the medium's state of trance and her subsequent possession by Swift at various stages of his fraught life in middle and old age). May Craig, who was coached in the role by Yeats himself, played Mrs Henderson to immense acclaim in the first production of November 1930 and continued to play the part in revivals at the Abbey until the 1960s. The cast of Lennox Robinson's original staging included P. J. Carolan as Trench, Arthur Shields as Corbet, F. J. McCormick as Abraham Johnson and Shelah Richards as Miss Mackenna.

The relationship between *The Words upon the Window-Pane* and *Four Plays for Dancers* is not confined to *The Dreaming of the Bones* and *Calvary*, for the whole structure of the new play bears close links too with *The Only Jealousy of Emer* in its deployment of the device of the play-within-the-play. In the dance-play the device carried us into the deepest reaches of Emer's psyche; here, a group of people dabbling in spiritualism for largely trivial and selfish ends are suddenly confronted through the device with insights into the spirit world which compel them to view their concepts of an afterlife with an awesome seriousness. The play-within-the-play, like any drama in performance, excites a wealth of varied responses from its on-stage audience: some are humbled, some thrilled, some shocked into compassion, some convinced that it is all fascinating trickery and illusion. Requiring us to watch an audience who are themselves experiencing a play in performance challenges us to investigate our own responses and explore both what exactly motivates us to go to a theatre and how we expect to be affected by what we see there. Do we simply admire an actress's technically accomplished impersonation? Do we relish the theatrical illusionism of it all? Or do we invest the experience with imaginative credence and ask ourselves why the world we envisage in the mind's eye through the play-within-the-play seems more *real* than the world we see physically represented on stage? Noticeably several of Yeats's letters over this period refer to Pirandello's investigations in terms of theatre of the nature of illusion and appearance; three of Pirandello's plays at least had been staged by the Drama League over the preceding six years – *Henry IV*, *The Pleasure of Honesty* and *The Rules of the Game* – at times when Yeats was resident in Dublin; Yeats, always versed in the best of contemporary modern theatre, would seem here to be offering a very personal exercise in Pirandellian metatheatricality.

All this fund of provocative experience resides in a play which is principally about Swift (*The Words upon the Window-Pane* is a feat of compression and allusive structuring) and yet is made to seem a wholly appropriate frame for that subject. Yeats presents Swift as a man possessed by a vision of classical Rome, the world of Brutus and Cato, as admirably ordered because founded on stoic fortitude wherein joy resided exclusively in the life of the mind. He has sought to impose the sharing of such a vision on Stella and Vanessa as proof of their love for him ('When I rebuilt Rome in your mind it was as though I walked its streets'). Stella, submitting to the implied emotional self-discipline of Swift's vision, has found a degree of personal freedom, as the poem etched by her into the window-pane and the beneficent atmosphere generated simply by her sudden presence in the room proves. But Vanessa rebels against the required physical restraints ('Why should we not marry like other men and women?'); and Swift is racked by a crisis of conscience over his insistence that they both conform to his wishes. It is a portrait of emotional tyranny and insidious male chauvinism; but our potential horror is offset by a growing sensitivity to the complex motivation that underlies Swift's need for his vision. That vision of a world given over wholly to reason and a high seriousness of decorum in personal behaviour is shown to be the product of irrational fears of insanity, the body, disease, loneliness and death; as a mere vision it is too a product of Swift's imagination, which selects, excludes, idealizes in ways that give Vanessa strong grounds for opposition and criticism ('I am a woman, the women Brutus and Cato loved were not different') and allow her to attempt to tyrannize over him in turn by psychological blackmail ('You are growing old. An old man without children is very solitary'). The imagination in Swift is seen to be so entirely shaped by negative emotions that, far from enriching his life, its workings render him vulnerable to conscience and remorse.

At every level the play brings us back to considering how the imagination operates, to distinguishing its kinds of truth, to discovering the frightening ways in which its creativity can be abused. Always there is that imagined play-within-the-play going on in our minds during the performance, which quite overpowers in interest the theatrical spectacle at which we are ostensibly looking. It is against that disrupting of our customary modes of perception that we must measure any scepticism we may feel about ghosts, seances or spiritualism, and any romantic tendency we may have to value the imagination as sacrosanct or as the quintessential expression of some ideal or 'higher' self. In *The Words upon the Window-Pane* Yeats, like Pirandello, explodes all our conventional expectations of theatre to find a convincing means of showing us the intricately subtle ways in which the mind will succumb to delusion. In performance the play is at once challenging, chastening and exhilarating to experience: it is the work of a dramatist now flamboyantly in control of the art that is theatre and of ways of establishing a creative engagement between stage and audience.

Dedication: Lady Gregory died at Coole Park on 22 May 1932: her friendship with Yeats had lasted for some thirty-six years. The play was completed by October 1930.

1. *Myers' . . . Doyle*: Frederick William Henry Myers (1843–91) wrote *Human Personality and Its Survival after Death*, which was published posthumously in 1903; Sir Arthur Conan Doyle, the creator of Sherlock Holmes, wrote two relevant works,

A New Revelation (1918) and a *History of Spiritualism* (1926). The first is probably the volume referred to by John Corbet.

2. *Lord Dunraven . . . Home*: A. N. Jeffares notes that the Earls of Dunraven also carried the title Viscount Adare, and suggests that Yeats is probably referring here to the third Earl, 'Edward Wyndham-Quin . . . who was a scholar, interested in archaeology and literature'. He presumes also that Yeats made an error over the name of the famous spiritualist and probably intended to refer to Daniel D. Home (1833–86), the Scottish medium.

3. *Mrs. Piper*: Lewis Spence's *Encyclopedia of Occultism* describes Mrs Piper as starting her career as a professional clairvoyant in the early 1880s, but she was best known for her trance utterances and writings. From 1889 she regularly visited England. At first her customary control was a Dr Phinuit, but F. W. H. Myers also became a spirit guide for her after his death in 1891. Her trance impersonations were the subject of tests by psychical researchers, her most remarkable and frequent being a spirit manifestation of the American author George Pelham. Spence observes that the wide range of certifiable fact and reference in her trance utterances and scripts was generally unintelligible to Mrs Piper herself, who was not an educated woman. Mrs Henderson would appear to have been modelled to a considerable degree on Mrs Piper.

4. *A state . . . dead persons*: Yeats, as an initiate of the Order of the Golden Dawn and a disciple for many years of Madame Blavatsky, was perhaps more committed to Theosophy than to spiritualism, though his wife practised automatic writing and he visited seances occasionally throughout his life, preserving always a degree of enlightened scepticism as recorded in his essay 'Magic' (1901). In the introduction Yeats wrote in 1931 to the published text of the play, he observed pithily: 'mediumship is dramatisation' and admitted 'even honest mediums cheat at times either deliberately or because some part of the body has freed itself from the control of the waking will, and almost always truth and lies are mixed together'. He did, however, sometimes take the advice of mediums he trusted.

5. *The poet Blake*: Yeats had worked with Edwin Ellis, one of his father's circle of artist friends, on an edition for Bernard Quaritch of William Blake's prophetic books between 1889 and 1893; Yeats's contributions included an interpretation of the romantic poet's philosophical symbolism, to which he subsequently made frequent reference in his own writing.

6. *Swedenborg*: The Swedish scientist Emanuel Swedenborg (1688–1772) was a philosopher who, like Blake, devised a complex theosophical, symbolic and mystical system which fascinated Yeats, especially during the years when he was preparing and drafting his own similar system, *A Vision*.

7. *Harold's Cross*: A suburb south of Dublin with a noted racecourse.

8. *Miss Mackenna . . . hall*: Usually in a Yeatsian drama what lies beyond the immediate playing space is poignantly shrouded in mystery, but here Yeats takes care to establish a naturalistic sense of the tenement house, the geographical location of its various rooms and its history. The use of the hallway, with people arriving and passing to other rooms, contributes considerably to a believable verisimilitude. This is an ordinary, inhabited space, very like countless other Dublin houses with eighteenth-century origins; the mystery in the play is to well up from within the space itself, not encroach on the setting by some strange power from without.

9. *Grattan:* Henry Grattan (1746–1820) was a statesman committed to achieving Ireland's independence and an orator of superb eloquence. He was bitterly opposed to William Pitt's plans to unite the Irish and English parliaments, and was a champion of Catholic Emancipation.

10. *Curran:* John Philpot Curran (1750–1817) was called to the Irish Bar in 1775 and defended many of the leading United Irishmen in the 1790s, especially those arrested after the rebellion of 1798. As an MP he attacked the Union as 'the annihilation of Ireland'. He was a friend of Byron, Godwin and Sheridan.

11. *Jonathan Swift:* Swift (1667–1745) was Dean of St Patrick's from 1713; he thought he was left deliberately in exile in Ireland after the fall of the Tory ministry at the time of the death of Queen Anne. His writings include the *Drapier's Letters* (1724), *Gulliver's Travels* (1726) and 'A Modest Proposal' (1729). He believed fervently that 'government without the consent of the governed' is slavery.

12. *Stella:* This was the private name Swift called his close friend Esther Johnson (1687–1728), whom he met while he was acting as secretary to Sir William Temple at Moor Park. She followed Swift to Ireland, where she became (in his words) 'the truest, most virtuous and valuable friend that I . . . was ever blessed with'. They are buried beside each other in St Patrick's Cathedral. Many supposed they were secretly married, but there is no record of such a ceremony. Swift would only see her privately in the company of another woman, usually her companion Rebecca Dingley. Denis Johnston, the Irish barrister and dramatist, deduced from this and other evidence that Swift, like Stella herself, was an illegitimate child of Sir William Temple and that he lived in mortal fear of accusations of incest as well as gossip about his bastardy, which even as rumours would undermine his authority and probity within the Church; Johnston made this view of Swift the subject of a play, *The Dreaming Dust* (1940, revised 1954), but it remains a hypothetical supposition.

13. *Journal to Stella:* Dating from 1710, this comprises a series of delightfully conversational letters written to Stella and Rebecca Dingley by Swift about his and their everyday lives.

14. *Vanessa:* Another pseudonym devised by Swift, this time for the young woman Hester Vanhomrigh (1690–1723), whom he met in London in 1708. Falling passionately in love with the Dean, she pursued him to Ireland, where she settled after 1714 at Marlay Abbey, Celbridge, on the River Liffey. Swift's long poem *Cadenus and Vanessa* (an account of their frequently strained relationship) endeavours wittily to give platonic friendship a mythological status and decorum.

15. *a poem . . . birthday:* This poem of fifty-eight lines in rhyming couplets, extracts from which are quoted at various times in the play, was entitled 'Stella to Dr. Swift on his birth-day November 30, 1721'.

16. *Donne:* John Donne (1572–1631), a Dean of St Paul's Cathedral, London, was a leading Metaphysical poet, though most of his works were only published posthumously.

17. *Crashaw:* Richard Crashaw (1612–49), another of the Metaphysical school of poets, whose works, generally expressive of his devout Roman Catholic faith, were much influenced by Spanish mystical poetry.

18. *I hope to prove . . . than England:* This theme about the golden age of the Protestant

Ascendancy in Ireland is taken up at length in the introduction to the published text of the play, where Yeats observes that it is 'the overstatement of an enthusiastic Cambridge student, and yet with its measure of truth'. But it was a view that his late writings show that he shared fundamentally.

19. *Bolingbroke, Harley, Ormonde*: Henry St John Bolingbroke (1678–1751), a notable orator and politician, was largely responsible for effecting the Peace of Utrecht in 1710 but went into exile in France after his dismissal on the accession of George I. Robert Harley (1661–1724) was Earl of Oxford; though a confirmed Tory, he contrived to serve in a Whig ministry for some years. He aided Bolingbroke and the Tories in achieving the Peace of Utrecht, but was summarily dismissed from office in 1714. James Butler, Duke of Ormond (1665–1746), was three times Lord-Lieutenant of Ireland like his father before him but, after being impeached, he too went into exile in France. The first two men were amongst Swift's circle of friends; the third he much admired. Yeats claimed descent from the Dukes of Ormond, and Butler was commonly used as a Christian name within his family.

20. *Brutus and Cato*: Marcus Junius Brutus (85–42 BC) joined the conspiracy to assassinate Julius Caesar out of honourable concern for the future health of the republic, once Caesar (after triumphing over his rival, Pompey) began to assume tyrannical powers. (This is the subject of Shakespeare's tragedy *Julius Caesar*, which concludes with Brutus taking his own life after defeat at the Battle of Philippi, where he fought against Caesar's supporters Mark Antony and Octavius.) Marcus Porcius Cato Uticensis (95–46 BC), a renowned stoic, supported Pompey against Caesar to the extent of accompanying Pompey and his confederates into exile in Africa; after the complete demise of their political fortunes, he committed suicide. Both men were politicians who shaped their lives (and deaths) to accord with their ideals.

21. *the ruin . . . Revolution*: In his introduction to the published text of the play, Yeats writes as a gloss to Corbet's comment: 'Did not Rousseau within five years of the death of Swift publish his *Discourse upon Arts and Sciences* and discover instinctive harmony not in heroic effort, not in Cato and Brutus . . . but among savages, and thereby beget the sans-culottes of Marat?' Jean-Jacques Rousseau (1712–78) wrote a number of provocative philosophical studies, but it was *The Social Contract* of 1762 that helped create the climate in which the French Revolution became possible.

22. *Gulliver*: *Gulliver's Travels*, published in 1726, had occupied Swift from 1720 onwards. The four books of travels (to lands peopled by midgets, giants, mad inventors, philosophical scientists, horses and the like) initially allow the author to satirize specific current political practices and abuses, but subsequently the perspective widens to engage with the follies and obsessions of humankind.

23. *saeva indignatio*: As the text next implies, these are words from Swift's epitaph in St Patrick's: 'Ubi saeva Indignatio Ulterius Cor lacerare nequit.' While drafting this play Yeats also completed a verse translation of the epitaph:

> Swift has sailed into his rest;
> Savage indignation there
> Cannot lacerate his breast.
> Imitate him if you dare,
> World-besotted traveller; he

Served human liberty.

24. *Moody and Sankey*: These two celebrated American Evangelists had died in 1899 and 1908 respectively. In their preaching they encouraged choral and solo singing to create moods of religious fervour, and Sankey compiled a collection of suitable works for this purpose entitled *Sacred Songs*.

25. *Sometimes . . . reason for it*: See *The Dreaming of the Bones* and Yeats's essay 'Swedenborg, Mediums, and the Desolate Places' (1914), published in *Explorations*. In *A Vision* (1937) Yeats writes:

> In the *Dreaming Back*, the *Spirit* is compelled to live over and over again the events that had most moved it; there can be nothing new, but the old events stand forth in a light which is dim or bright according to the intensity of the passion that accompanied them. They occur in the order of the intensity or luminosity, the more intense first and the painful are commonly the more intense, and repeat themselves again and again. In the *Return*, upon the other hand, the *Spirit* must live through past events in the order of their occurrence, because it is compelled by the Celestial body to trace every passionate event to its cause until all are related and understood, turned into knowledge, made a part of itself.

26. *incident . . . Odyssey*: A passage in 'Pages from a Diary in 1930', published in *Explorations*, explains this reference: Yeats is discussing kinds of spirits and gives as an example, 'the shade of Heracles in the *Odyssey* drawing its bow as though still in the passion of battle, while the true spirit of Heracles is on Olympus with his wife Hebe'. In *A Vision* (1937) Yeats again refers to 'the Homeric contrast between Heracles passing through the night, bow in hand, and Heracles, the freed spirit, a happy god among the gods'.

27. *requiescat in pace*: May he or she rest in peace.

28. *Job . . . quotation*: Job 4: 13–15.

29. *Hymn 564*: The words are by John Keble. The singing heightens the mood considerably and establishes a sense of ritual.

30. *in a child's voice*: The graphic detail of the snoring followed by Lulu's high-pitched voice is finely calculated by Yeats to provide an outlet for any impulse for nervous or cynical laughter that some spectators may experience. Generally in performance the more an audience laughs at the earlier passages of satirical comedy with characters like Patterson or Johnson and at the eerie transitions from the sublime to the ridiculous here, the more startled and unnerved they will be shortly when a harsh baritone unexpectedly issues from Mrs Henderson's lips. Lulu's 'Nobody must laugh', which seems strangely to break out of the confines of the stage-world and embrace the audience, invariably commands a tense silence throughout the theatre.

31. *No, I do not recognise her*: The oddly dressed spirit is in fact Vanessa, who has been thrown to the floor by an irate Swift. Trench's line is one of the most ambiguous and disturbing in the play. Is he merely responding to Lulu's description? Or, possessing psychic powers, does he actually see the tormented spirit beside him? The actor has to decide on an interpretation, but it can prove a chilling moment in performance, again expertly preparing for Swift's eruption into the play. The rapid transitions of tone here keep an audience in a state of tense expectation.

32. *Lord Treasurer*: Harley, the Earl of Oxford.

33. *Plutarch*: A Greek biographer who wrote comparatively of the lives of celebrated Greek and Roman nobles, soldiers and politicians.

34. *surfeit of fruit*: So Swift believed: 'I got my giddiness by eating a hundred golden pippins at a time at Richmond . . . four and a quarter years [later] . . . I got my deafness.'

35. *I have something . . . London*: Yeats glosses this line in his introduction to the play; after outlining 'several theories to account for Swift's celibacy', he continues, 'Lecky suggested dread of madness – the theory of my play – of madness already present in constant eccentricity.' But he concludes with a careful reservation: 'There is no satisfactory solution. Swift, though he lived in great publicity . . . hid two things which constituted perhaps all that he had of private life: his loves and his religious beliefs.' Modern doctors suppose from the frequent references in his letters from his youth onwards to attacks of giddiness, deafness, fluxes and tinnitus that he suffered from Ménière's disease, which is caused by a disorder of the inner ear or labyrinth. The symptoms were not recognized as a precise disease until the 1860s.

36. *Dr. Arbuthnot*: John Arbuthnot (1667–1735) was Queen Anne's personal physician. Pope as well as Swift claimed him as a friend.

37. *line of Dryden's*: From *Absalom and Achitophel*.

38. *If some poor . . . down in sin*: Another verse of Keble's hymn that was begun earlier in the play.

39. *Chrysostom*: A fourth-century Father of the Greek Church, author of commentaries on several books of the New Testament.

40. *How from my heart . . . fading eyes*: Stella's need to wear spectacles is the subject of some banter in the *Journal*; but Swift seems to have been fascinated by Stella's eyes. In several of the poems written by him to celebrate her birthday there occur lines expressing ideas very akin to this in her poem for him, such as his verses for 1721:

> And every virtue now supplies
> The fainting rays of Stella's eyes.

In a poem praising her nursing of him when sick, Swift notes Stella's particular gifts in ministration: 'My sinking spirits now supplies /With cordials in her hands and eyes'.

41. *you will live long after me*: Swift, who was twenty years her senior, was to live on for seventeen years after Stella's death in 1728.

42. *His brain had gone*: Swift appears to have succumbed to senile decay rather than madness in the last three years of his life.

43. *Perish . . . born!*: Job 3:3: 'Let the day perish wherein I was born.' It is not Swift but Lulu who has been dispelled; Swift has become Mrs Henderson's 'control', compelling her into states of trance so that his anguish can manifest itself and find renewed expression. The ghost now has absolute mastery of a woman's mind, but will lay waste its composure, not build an imaginary Rome there; this is a diabolical corollary for what Swift set out to achieve through Stella and Vanessa and a realization of all that he is shown in the play as most dreading. Wanting too desperately to play the good angel has betrayed him into becoming its evil counterpart.

The King of the Great Clock Tower

This, the last and undeniably the finest achievement of the long collaboration between Yeats and Ninette de Valois, has a complicated history. A first version in prose with an elaborate colour-scheme for the masks, costumes and setting was staged at the Abbey on 30 July 1934, when (under Lennox Robinson's direction) de Valois played the Queen, F. J. McCormick the King and Denis O'Dea the Stroller. Yeats was immensely pleased with the performances, which were given in a double bill with *The Resurrection*, and began immediately to cast the play into verse. Both versions were published; the second, wholly poetic one that is printed here was never to be staged in Yeats's lifetime. Some weeks later in the summer of 1934 Yeats met Margot Ruddock, an actress–dancer who yearned to establish a poets' theatre; their friendship matured rapidly and Yeats by October was redesigning the play, giving the Queen a speaking role and in time eliminating the character of the King. This third version of the material was substantially so different from the original that Yeats retitled the play, *A Full Moon in March*. Various directors were approached with a view to a staging, including Ashley Dukes, Rupert Doone and Nancy Price; but none of these schemes matured; and, though Margot Ruddock was to act in a production of *The Player Queen* and be a reciter for Yeats in several of his BBC broadcasts about poetry, she was never to appear in the play devised for her. She also had qualms, seemingly, about the dancing requirement of the role of the Queen (presumably fearing comparison with de Valois); but Yeats suggested that, as the actress would be masked, an identically dressed dancer could substitute for her in the latter, danced half of the play; the published text of *A Full Moon in March* recommends this way of handling what might otherwise be a very demanding (but not insuperable) role.

Yeats always expressed a preference for *A Full Moon in March* and often spoke or wrote in derogatory terms of *The King of the Great Clock Tower*; critics have tended to follow his lead. Ironically, he chose to view the two plays as virtually identical in terms of subject matter, when in fact the elimination of the character of the King from the later play ensures that there are major differences between them. Certain narrative features are common to both works (the wooing of a Queen by a commoner, a beheading for his presumption, her dance with the severed head that culminates in the head magically singing), and both plays inhabit the strange world, at once naïve yet emotionally intricate, of fairy-tale or folklore. At a deeper thematic level, the difference is marked. The rivalry of King and Stroller and the changing responses of the Queen to each of the men ensure that *The King of the Great Clock Tower* remains a study of the psychology of courtship and sexual fulfilment, whereas *A Full Moon in March* stays closer to the subject of one of Yeats's sources, Wilde's *Salome*, and examines 'virgin cruelty' and the idea of a feared but necessary 'desecration' in 'the lover's night'. After the beheading in this version the Queen reappears with a stylized pattern of 'red blotches upon her dress' and wearing 'red gloves', as if covered in blood. At the climax of her dance, when the head begins to sing and she kisses its lips, 'her body shivers' and she fulfils the Swineherd's prophecy uttered before his death:

> There is a story in my country of a woman
> That stood all bathed in blood – a drop of blood
> Entered her womb and there begat a child.

Perhaps Yeats's most penetrating comment on the plays was his observation to Edmund Dulac, 'I don't like the *Clock Tower* which is theatrically coherent, spiritually incoherent.' With all due respect to Yeats, theatrical coherence should be a prime consideration in composing a play. Of the two works, *The King of the Great Clock Tower* is the finer performance-text; and it is by no means spiritually or symbolically incoherent, though it is less complex than *A Full Moon in March*. The later play has excited a wealth of critical interpretations because of that complexity: T. R. Henn, for example, has written of it as a sacred rite revolving around the 'mother-goddess and the slain god' and Frank Kermode has viewed it as an aesthetic allegory about the *poète maudit* (the Swineherd), his inspirational image (the Queen) 'out of time and deathless', and the creative process that gives birth to a poem. (Both interpretations are fully justified by Yeats's own comments on the play.) It is possible to pursue such intellectual constructs in a reading of the text, but difficult for a director to give them a viable theatrical immediacy in the imaginations of an audience, when in performance the play, through its language, sign-systems and ritualized action, is insistently physical, sustaining a focus of attention on blood, dung, virginity and a concern with the body's 'desecration' through sexuality and the urge to procreate. There is a wide gap between the readily accessible significance of the staged action and possible thematic and symbolic levels of meaning; the obsessional intensity of the play is such that, as Peter Ure opines, a performance risks being 'silly, shocking or monstrous'. (Significantly, Yeats himself wrote, 'I do not understand why this blood symbolism laid hold upon me, but I must work it out.') *The King of the Great Clock Tower* poses none of these problems relating to audience-reception; Yeats, ever sensitive to such matters, might well have revised his opinion about the relative merits of the two plays, had he once seen *A Full Moon in March* staged.

Of the two versions of *The King of the Great Clock Tower* the one in verse is in all respects preferable to that in prose, particularly for its use of distinctive rhythms to characterize the two men: the King's verse is full of heavy stresses and is sharply emphatic, with the syntax continually framed into rhetorical questions; that for the Stroller is light, mellifluous and flowing, rising at times to a quiet ecstasy. The verse meticulously defines two styles of masculinity: the one chauvinist, violent, obsessed with knowing, with displays of authority and power; the other acutely sensuous, confident but reverential, profoundly intimate yet respectful of the Queen's dignity and independence. The Stroller speaks of love but without wishing to violate the Queen's innermost reaches of selfhood; the King speaks only of his rights, insists on understanding the Queen utterly and suspects her continuing silence as the product of a guilty and secretive conscience. It is the Stroller, wholly accepting the sanctity of her silence, who elicits a response from the Queen and that through the medium of the dance, which communicates through the language of the body beyond the need for words. They communicate with a scrupulous delicacy through metaphor – his spoken or sung, hers expressed in movement with the whole being – and the King is rendered powerless either to comprehend or to intrude.

The opening chorus (inviting us to imagine the joys of love-making through the traditional metaphor of the dance), the bold colour-scheme together with the refined stylization of the staging, and the contest between the men for the attention of the Queen (where the exact nature of their differing sexual identities lies implicit within their respective modes of speaking) together create a dramatic technique which from the first requires an audience to interpret the perceived stage-action as metaphorical. We must work to create the thematic dimensions of the play for ourselves; and this deftly prepares us for the latter half of the play, where speech ceases to be the prime medium of communication as dance, song, mime and tableaux continue and complete the action. We must open ourselves completely to the experience of the play in performance, and become alert to the power of the human body to convey meaning; we must learn to read a new language, which is wholly the language of theatre. We ultimately shape whatever meaning we read into the play. This argues a wonderful respect and trust on Yeats's part in the interpretive skills of his performers and his audience. Compared with *The King of the Great Clock Tower*, *A Full Moon in March* as a performance-text lacks such a keen sense of scruple and decorum.

Given the preoccupation of *The King of the Great Clock Tower* with the most intimate of relations between the sexes, Yeats's deployment of dramatized metaphor shows a careful tact. The King desires the Queen simply to confirm his sense of self and, though she remains outwardly impassive, the Queen feels only revulsion. The Stroller willingly dies rather than deny his love, and his sacrifice of selfhood earns the Queen's gratitude; without shame she dances her adoration and through the dance comes steadily into possession of an inner strength which compels the King to recognize his vulnerability; aggression is of no avail and he finally lies prostrate before her. The final tableau and the ensuing image of the Queen standing at the gap in the curtains as if on the threshold of whole new realms of experience, which is sustained while the Musicians sing their closing lyric, are richly enigmatic symbols. Has the woman triumphed at the cost of both men? Has she discovered warmth and compassion through having the courage to find her own unique mode of self-expression? Has the King undergone a journey of self-discovery by the end or has he been totally destroyed, emotionally and psychologically? Is his last posture an emblem of reverence or exhausted defeat? Is the outcome tragic or creative? The play uses masks to create a sense of the magical and miraculous when the 'head' begins to sing. Which of the characters achieves a state of transcendence through emotional fulfilment? There are no simple answers to these questions, because the dramatic action wholly respects the ever-changing mystery of sexual relations. Different performances will suggest different meanings, all of them possible within such an open-ended dramatic conceit. That is the play's great strength as a text for theatre.

Dedication: Ninette de Valois was born Edris Stannus in 1898. This Irish dancer had begun her professional career dancing with Diaghilev's Russian Ballet; by 1926 she had a dance school in London, and later that year took to designing the movement work for her cousin Terence Gray's productions at the Festival Theatre in Cambridge. It was there that she met Yeats when he came to see Gray's production of *The Player Queen*. Yeats invited her to go to Dublin to found an Irish School of Ballet and help him revive his plays for dancers. This she did on a regular basis until 1934, when she gave up most of her other projects to concentrate on creating a full-scale English ballet company as part of Lilian Baylis's grand enterprise involving the Old Vic and Sadler's

Wells theatres. That company became in the fullness of time the present Royal Ballet.

Setting: These directions suggest that Yeats envisaged the play being performed at the Peacock Theatre, though the initial prose version had been staged at the Abbey. Note that, though instructions are given for the masks for Queen and Stroller, no mask is specified for the King; in performance this helps to create an immediate rapport between the first two characters and to isolate the third, who seems by contrast more vulnerable, for all his aggressive speech. The performance is to be accompanied by percussive instruments only: there is no flute to create a melodic line as in the earlier dance-plays; a rhythmic drumming and the resonating of a gong suffice here. The text of the prose version which was first printed in *Life and Letters* (November 1934) gives details of the colour-scheme which was devised by Dorothy Travers Smith for the Abbey staging: the King is described as 'dressed in red', the Queen as 'dressed in orange with details in black or red', the Stroller as 'dressed in black with details in red'; the 'inner curtain' patterned with dancers was 'pale purple in colour'; the attendants 'dressed in black' were both male, the first had a bass voice, the second a tenor.

1. *Tir-nan-oge*: Literally 'The Country of the Young'; paradise in Celtic lore, eternity. The following lyric celebrates a timeless world of transcendent experience and draws for some of its imagery on Yeats's early narrative poem *The Wanderings of Oisin*.

2. *beating of a bell*: A symbol of Time, which always threatens to intrude on transcendent states of being. This theme was expressed in a form that related it more closely to the play which follows in a first version of the Musicians' song (which Yeats sent in a letter to Olivia Shakespear):

> I call to mind the iron of the bell
> And get from that my harsher imagery,
> All love is shackled to mortality,
> Love's image is a man-at-arms in steel;
> Love's image is a woman made of stone;
> It dreams of the unborn; all else is nought;
>
> To-morrow and to-morrow fills its thought;
> All tenderness reserves for that alone.

3. *When the curtains . . . screens*: Again the printed text of the prose version gives details of the original Abbey production, specifying that 'the background and the cubes are a rich blue', while the semicircle of curtains or of Craig's screens were to be 'so painted that the blue is darker below than above'.

4. *Boyne Water*: The prose version adds by way of explanation, 'where the old Gods live'.

5. *Aengus*: The god of youth, beauty, poetry and love in Celtic mythology.

6. *'On stroke . . . dies*: This was at midnight on the night of the full moon in March.

7. *The Queen begins to dance*: What appears in the reading a short conclusion to the play ideally in performance occupies as long a playing-time as the spoken dialogue which precedes and provides a framework for it. If the psychological progression is properly to be understood, then audiences need time to watch and interpret the stages of the dance, the song, the mime and final tableau. Yeats gives an outline scenario here and leaves the detail to be evolved entirely through the improvisational skills of his performers.

8. *Mortal men . . . are*: A Neoplatonic idea: from a transcendent standpoint, mortals seem but shadows. This is the perspective that the ensuing song adopts throughout.

9. *Sacred Virgil*: The reference is to the fourth *Eclogue*, traditionally considered a prophetic book, but nothing there compares with the marvels of eternity in the eyes of the singer. However, he silences himself ('there's a stone upon my tongue'), before he can reveal anything that is part of his new visionary state of awareness.

10. *Castle Dargan's ruin all lit*: Castle Dargan near Sligo was frequently visited by Yeats in his childhood. In section XXI of *Reveries over Childhood and Youth* the poet records many experiences by night where he has suddenly seen strange phantom lights, torches, fires. In the introduction to *The Words upon the Window-Pane* Yeats writes, 'The Irish countrywoman did see the ruined castle lit up'; the very same image was to inspire a later play, *Purgatory*.

The final lyric complements that which opened the play; where the first celebrated immortality, this tells of moments of ecstasy or supernatural awareness when humankind can seemingly get a brief glimpse of eternity. Our austere last image of the Queen, 'framed in the half-closed curtains', is richly allusive, ensuring that the sense of her presence lingers on in the memory, a potent challenge both inviting and resisting definition.

The Herne's Egg

'A wild, fantastic, humorous, half-earnest play' was how Yeats described *The Herne's Egg* to a friend during its composition; to another he confided that it was 'very Rabelaisian'. Conceived at first as a full-length play, it was pared away in the writing to six short scenes which have the exultant ferocity and drive of good farce. 'Farce' might seem an odd categorization for the one play amongst Yeats's last works for the theatre which owes the clearest debt to his long-standing preoccupation with Sophocles' *Oedipus the King*. *The Herne's Egg* examines the ways the power of a god is made manifest in the lives of mortals; the presence of the Great Herne, the heron god, is – like Apollo in the Greek tragedy – everywhere felt behind the developing action but never seen directly (though the legs of a giant bird rising out of mountain mist are depicted in a crude cartoon style on the backcloth in the opening two scenes and its huge shadow passes to and fro over the stage in the third).

But the Sophoclean influence has been merged in Yeats's inspiration with another that reaches even further back into his creative past: in 1896, in the company of Arthur Symons, Yeats saw in Paris the first performance of Jarry's *Ubu Roi*, itself in part a parodic rewriting, as the title suggests, of *Oedipus*. This was an encounter with one of the most provocative and revolutionary expressions of Modernism. Symons defined Jarry's play as 'a symbolic farce'. Yeats, who at that date saw himself as one of the last romantics, was both mesmerized and appalled. The impression the performance made on him could still be graphically recalled over twenty years later when he was writing *The Trembling of the Veil* (published 1922); he viewed the moment as a turning-point in cultural history, when 'comedy, objectivity . . . displayed its growing power once more'; he carefully listed all the subtleties so prized by established artists in the 1890s that he saw threatened by this brash new spirit of the age, and ended by ruefully submitting to the change implicit in Jarry's innovatory energies as inevitable: 'After us the Savage God.' The Great Herne, like Père Ubu, is a manifestation of that savage god.

The melding of Sophocles with Jarry in Yeats's inspiration sharpened the cruelty inherent in the Greek tragedy. In consequence, what Yeats invented in *The Herne's Egg* was one of the first instances in European theatre of an absurdist black farce: the human characters each struggle to shape an independent identity but find their efforts continually frustrated by an unseen force whose hold over their existence is ruthless and absolute. They must either submit or suffer miserable defeat. It is as grim a vision as one finds in the plays of Boris Vian or Eugène Ionesco, but it is put across with enormous comic zest. The dialogue is trenchantly direct on account of Yeats deploying a strong driving rhythm to the verse, which gathers terrific energy as it propels expression through very short verse lines. The terse syntactical compressions this technique requires make for some hilarious effects, particularly in the patterned dialogue of the opening scene and in the use throughout of the character of Mike, the sergeant-figure in Congal's army. Energy is also generated in the first four scenes by the constant changes of tone and style that advance the action at breath-taking speed, repeatedly surprising an audience by the audacity of the juxtapositions. We hover precariously on the edge of blasphemy and sacrilege, but our laughter at the bizarre vitality of it all is meticulously provoked and controlled to keep shock or disgust at bay. *The Herne's Egg* is a play in which seemingly anything might happen, yet every moment of the action is implacably bringing Congal closer to his death.

Nothing that happens in *Oedipus the King* means quite what the characters suppose it might mean. Until the terrible catastrophe brings them all to enlightenment, only the blind seer, Tiresias, has paradoxically the necessary inner vision to understand the significance of events. Sophocles shows us the difference between seeing and perception. Yeats as dramatist had similarly begun to make drama out of the nature of this difference from the time that he decided to explore Deirdre's tragedy in terms of role-play and acting. Theatre is about giving credence to what is known to be illusion; and from his dance-plays onwards Yeats pushed the possibilities involved in audience-engagement with theatrical illusion to ever more challenging extremes. With the dance-plays we are required to imagine the settings and to read complex psychological states into the apparently impassive features depicted on masks. In *The Resurrection* and *The Words upon the Window-Pane* we are invited to imagine a play taking place simultaneously alongside the play that we are actually watching in the theatre; and, as this complex situation develops, Yeats dares to make what we imagine become increasingly more powerful and more *real* than what we see. With *The King of the Great Clock Tower* Yeats exploits all the arts of the theatre (poetry, dance, mime, song, the patterning of body movement within space, masks, ritual, colour-symbolism) to bring us to a pitch of awareness where we can interpret all that we see as an intricately evolving metaphor for what would be otherwise completely unstageable: the psychology of the sexes during the experience of courtship and coition. *The Herne's Egg* presents us with a series of bizarre situations which the characters involved in them perceive in decidedly different terms. Perception might be said to be what defines a particular identity as unique, but that is to argue that it is highly subjective and therefore of only relative value. There has to be a shared system of belief within a community to help determine a common mode of perception, if anarchy and conflict are not to prevail. But to submit to such a system of belief could be seen as curtailing one's individual freedom of expression. That is the dilemma that the play explores.

The comradely world of the rival kings, Congal and Aedh, and their armies involves a set of shared assumptions about the value of fighting, so experience falls neatly into predictable patterns. When the swaggering Congal invades the domain of Attracta, the nun-like priestess who guards the shrine of the Great Herne, a conflict of values sets in, to his confusion. What he claims is a soldier's right to grab the heron-eggs to grace his feast, she insists is sacrilege; her sacrificial curse he interprets as a futile threat; where she views herself as the Great Herne's promised bride, he views her as a frigid girl fantasizing about gods out of sexual frustration. He cheerfully proffers seduction by himself or one of his men as 'cure'. Attracta's claims about a sacred marriage with a bird seem ludicrous (particularly when the details of the experience are discussed by her and her three friends) until a strange wild flute music sends her into a trance in which she begins to whirl about the stage as if her being were suddenly possessed. The three girls continue to chatter animatedly about the finer points of consummation with a bird, while Attracta undergoes a transformation in front of our eyes: at first the effect, making her appear like a puppet on a wire, is comic and grotesque; but as the pace of the whirling increases to a frenetic dance that culminates in long sweeping leaps, the mood becomes positively awesome.

Continually Yeats changes our perspective to challenge how we perceive what we watch. First we observe Congal (a figure known to Irish audiences from history and the heroic sagas) reduced to 'a weather-stained, war-battered/Old campaigner', a 'robber of sheepfolds and cattle trucks', stealing eggs, getting blind drunk . . . and doing battle when the need arises with a broken-off table-leg. At the start of the second scene we see a life-size toy donkey, yet its owner talks to it as real, remarking about its 'rapscallion eye', and keeps a careful distance from its hoofs to avoid being kicked on the shins; in the stage-world it has the kind of reality we invest in a pantomime creature, and yet at the end of the play we will *hear* its stentorian braying as it spies a mate, breaks its tether and abandons itself to a joyful copulation. At one point we watch a drunken Congal and his men confront the still entranced Attracta; grimly, they prepare to rape her in turn, while she, from the depths of her trance, sings ecstatically of her mystic union with the Great Herne. In the following scene the men, sated, boast of their sexual conquest; she claims she lay with the god and answers their derision by calling on the Herne to vindicate her; three thunder claps reverberate in her support. We, as audience, laugh at first at the sound effect coming pat on cue; but our response quickly changes as the men fall prostrate with terror, and Attracta, growing in authority, ominously summons Congal to return to the holy mountain at the full moon. Powerful acting can give both the strangest of experiences and obvious theatrical trickery a compelling verisimilitude.

That full moon in the final scene is painted with a comic grinning face; it lights a place where Congal finds a ragged fool arming himself to do battle with a cauldron lid for shield, cooking pot for helmet and spit for spear. Attracta's curse foretold that Congal would die at the hands of a fool, but this fool is quickly vanquished; and Congal decides to elude destiny by taking his own life. The only implement to hand is the kitchen spit, on which he decides to impale himself; but he is fraught with anguish lest he is himself the promised fool of the curse. Congal began the play insisting that humankind shape their own lives to their own objectives, but his confidence in this position has been undermined by circumstance till he is terrified at the prospect that all along he has been a pawn manoeuvred by the Great Herne in an elaborate game of the god's devising.

By richly exploiting theatrical illusion Yeats has brought the audience to share Congal's distrust of perception and judgement. Is his suicide heroic or grotesque (in performance we cannot ignore that vast grinning moon on the backcloth)? Should we experience empathy and tragic pathos or the detachment of laughter? By what scale of values can we any longer determine the exact quality of any experience we witness so as to gauge the appropriate response? Yeats has pitched us into an absurdist nightmare that grows stranger and more disconcerting by the minute (particularly in the closing episode, where the god is imagined as pursuing his vengeance over Congal even into the afterlife). Rarely has the proximity of farce to tragedy been more pointedly and creatively explored. Perhaps the most surprising shift of tone and perspective comes in the final scene, where, as Congal and Attracta begin to recognize and speak of the pain they are experiencing through the god's cruelty, they are invested with a measure of human dignity. Absurd though the predicament is that entraps them, he is not at the last without courage, nor she without compassion. It is as if suffering makes them see each other as individuals for the first time: briefly the dialogue between them touches a note of dispassionate tenderness, before we are left staring at that cynical moon to the sound of the donkey's triumphant braying.

Not surprisingly, the Abbey fought shy of staging the play during Yeats's lifetime. This was somewhat to his relief, since he feared it might well provoke a riot amongst Dublin audiences, given the cultural and religious climate in 1936. (The text of the play as printed contains a number of minor textual problems, which would have been corrected had *The Herne's Egg* been directed by Hugh Hunt, as Yeats wished.) It was first performed by Austin Clarke's Lyric Theatre Company in 1950, with a cast that included George Green as Congal, Eithne Dunne as Attracta, and the young Jack MacGowran as Mike; settings and costumes were by the poet's daughter, Anne Yeats. In recent years Jarry's *Ubu* plays have attracted the attention of many notable directors; *The Herne's Egg* equally merits revival. It demands a virtuoso's skill from each of the actors and the director, and a great flexibility and openness from the audience. When the ideal conditions are met, the result is an exuberant exercising of the imagination.

Persons in the Play: The historical Congal was a king in Ulster (not Connaught as in the play) supporting the cause of Druidism, who was slain at the Battle of Moyra in 637 in which the triumph of Christianity was assured. He was the subject of one of the sagas, which in modern times was published in a verse adaptation by Sir Samuel Ferguson (reviewed by Yeats in 1886). In this version Congal rebels against his High-King because of what he considers an insult when he is given a hen's instead of a goose's egg at a feast; his fiancée, Lafinda, enters a convent; after his defeat on the battlefield Congal is killed by an idiot called Cuanna, but is comforted in his dying by Lafinda. Yeats treats this source with considerable freedom.

Aedh (pronounced *Ay* as in 'day'; the word means 'fire') was another historical figure (566–93) but not a king in Tara, which was the seat of the High-Kings of Ireland. In Ferguson's poem Congal fights with Aedh's son.

There is a series of textual cruces surrounding the '*Connacht soldiers*'. The text in *Collected Plays* list 'Mike, Pat, Malachi, Mathias, Peter, John' as Congal's army at this point. Though Peter is listed in some of the entrances for the group of men, he only speaks once, in Scene V. Malachi has several speeches assigned to him but his name is often omitted from the stage directions listing the soldiers, most crucially in Scene V, when the soldiers involved in the rape all in turn assert the fact. James is not listed amongst the 'Persons in the Play' but has a developed cameo role of considerable importance in Scene IV. The situation is further complicated by the fact that Congal often refers to himself and his troop of 'seven men', suggesting that he and his army together number eight. In Scene IV, where the men prepare for the rape, Congal includes himself amongst the 'seven men' who will do the deed, and the stage directions refer to seven men who throw their caps at Attracta. Had Yeats supervised a production of the play, he would doubtless have ironed out this problem, which is presumably one of oversight. In the event it is perhaps best to substitute James or Malachi for Peter as occasion demands and give Malachi Peter's line in Scene V; I have emended the text in this way. (An enterprising cast and director might make a wealth of comic by-play out of Congal's uncertainty as to how many men he has fighting for him, especially when they are all befuddled with drink in Scene IV and some deliberate counting of bodies has to take place.)

SCENE I

1. *herne*: A heron.

2. *All should be suggested . . . realistically*: Yeats generally disliked painted backcloths, particularly for outdoor scenes. Here he is deliberately emphasizing the theatricality of the whole proceedings – but even then the painting must be done with style.

3. *The battle*: There is enormous comic potential in this sequence, if Yeats's prescriptions are followed exactly.

SCENE II

4. *your present shape*: Cunningly, Yeats introduces the idea of reincarnation and metempsychosis (and in respect of a donkey having led a wicked life as a thief and a roué in a previous existence) before the subject becomes a dramatic issue in Scene V.

5. *Go pack . . . eggs*: Congal does not wait for permission but casually assumes he will get it.

6. *Ovid . . . upon the grass*: Ovid, a Roman poet, lived in the age of Augustus (43 BC–AD 18). His *Metamorphoses* is a series of stories largely telling of gods pursuing mortals out of love or lust, in which either the god transformed himself in order to gain access to the lady or the woman was transformed for rejecting the god's advances. Two such stories are then referred to. Danaë was shut by her father in a tower of bronze; Zeus came to her there in a shower of gold; and the child of their union was the hero Perseus. Zeus appeared as a swan to Leda and raped her; their offspring were Clytemnestra and Helen of Troy, Castor and Pollux; Leda's story was the subject of a poem by Yeats included in *The Tower* (1928). Congal, the male chauvinist, argues that these women secretly desired their rape, where Ovid distinctly describes them as victims. It is ironic that Congal should criticize Ovid for misunderstanding the psychological nature of metamorphosis, given the transformation he will undergo himself at the end of the play.

7. *Seven men*: Here the seven decidedly does not include Congal. (See the note on the *Connacht soldiers* above.)

8. *A doll upon a wire*: The dance here picks up an image Yeats frequently uses in his dance-plays: inspired no doubt by Edward Gordon Craig and his theories about the desirability of replacing actors with what he called *Übermarionettes*, Yeats wrote that he wished the actors in his *Four Plays for Dancers* consistently to move to drum-taps like marionettes. It is important in performance that due playing-time is accorded to the development of the dance and that the dialogue be carefully orchestrated into the stages of that development.

9. *She has still my little egg*: There is again a slight textual crux here as a result of revision: it was in fact Kate who earlier presented the basket of eggs.

10. *The moon was full*: Always in Yeats's thinking a time of significant change, of supernatural or metaphysical experience of profound value.

SCENE III

11. *All go through . . . suggest them*: Yeats again exploits a device of theatrical illusion: well-choreographed mime here for Congal and his men should help an audience 'see' both the vast bird that twice sweeps over the stage and the shower of stones they hurl at it. If accompanied by music like the opening battle, the sequence has the potential to be funny and eerie at once.

SCENE IV

12. *concertina*: This is an inspired suggestion: the concertina can be made to exude wonderful wheezing sounds that, appropriately for a play full of patterns and mirror-images, are not unlike the braying of a donkey.

13. *A servant . . . egg there*: As is the case in Ferguson's *Congal*.

14. *Aedh takes . . . fighting*: The fight here must suggest a drunken brawl, however stylized, a very different affair from the orderly combat of the opening scene.

15. *Enter Congal . . . Mathias etc.*: The direction here includes Peter, though he is not named later by Congal (p. 243) when he lists the seven who will take part in the ritual rape. The text has been emended to include James, who is listed later.

16. *Maybe . . . done it*: Congal's mind, befuddled with drink and disturbed by grief at the loss of his old enemy, for the first time admits the possibility that the Great Herne might exist and wield the power Attracta ascribes to him.

17. *He begins to count . . . the drum*: As Andrew Parkin observes, this is 'a vivid stage representation of phallic cruelty. The harshness also involves a maudlin rhetoric about the cause of the sentence, the death of Aedh. His murderers are hypocritically blaming Attracta for his death.'

18. *She may . . . woman should*: The male chauvinist view: that a woman only 'lives' when submissive to a man's phallic desire. Congal cannot conceive that Attracta might find fulfilment by some other means.

19. *I name the seven*: The 'seven' include Congal himself and exclude Peter, though he is specifically listed as entering with the other soldiers in early editions.

20. *Men carry . . . dignity*: There is a profound irony here, if one envisages the stage-picture at this point. A drunken rabble intent on rape hardly possess dignity; the only dignified presence on stage is the still, silent figure of Attracta, whom they have consistently reviled.

SCENE V

21. *Congal . . . enter*: Early editions specify 'Congal, Malachi, Mike etc.' as entering here; but Malachi is not given any words in the ensuing scene. Peter, however, is given one short speech asserting he took part in the rape, though Peter is not included amongst the seven men that Congal names when instituting the ritual of the rape in Scene IV, whereas Malachi is so named. I have substituted Malachi's name for Peter's throughout the scene.

22. *The bride . . . a liar*: Generally I have followed the text of the 1952 edition of the *Collected Plays*, which incorporates some changes, additions and revisions made in holograph by Yeats in a copy of the first edition of the play (published in 1938); these were never printed in his lifetime. Mrs Yeats supervised the 1952 edition and that gives the text printed there considerable authority, which I have largely respected. This speech is a vexing case, however, and what I have given here is the text of Corney's speech as it appears in the 1938 text. Yeats's manuscript revisions include the addition of three further lines, included in *Collected Plays*, which read:

> A king, a king, but a Mayo man.
> A Mayo man's lying tongue can beat
> A Clare highwayman's rapscallion eye,
> Seven times a liar. .

This is tortuously expressed: presumably Yeats wished to begin preparing for the final episode of the play by connecting Congal with Corney's donkey, which we have heard is wicked because it possesses the transmigrated soul of a Clare highwayman (the lines here deliberately pick up the phrasing of Corney's description of the donkey in Scene II). But the connection is made so tersely and in so confusing a way that it does not really carry that desired effect in performance. The text of 1938 is crisper and dramatically more effective and so is the one given here.

23. *I lay . . . said is true*: Yeats's poem 'Leda and the Swan' describes the rape and imagines the tragic consequences that are to ensue with the birth of Helen and Clytemnestra, who will bring both Troy and Argos to destruction. The sonnet ends by posing a question about Leda's consciousness while being overmastered by the metamorphosed Zeus:

> Did she put on his knowledge with his power
> Before the indifferent beak could let her drop?

Here Attracta is seen to be completely transformed by her sacred 'marriage'; she has acquired an awesome dignity and the skills of seer and sibyl; knowledge and power are hers now and she can withstand Congal's chauvinist raillery with a grave composure and assurance, which she decidedly lacked when she first tried to resist his cocky, subversive attitude in Scene II. The actress must show this growth in Attracta's character, which is as much a matter of inner strength as of vocal grandeur. The stage-space is now wholly hers to command.

24. *Slieve Fuadh*: In the Fews mountains in Co. Armagh, associated in *Cuchulain of Muirthemne* with Conall Caernach, the Ulster chieftain.

25. *One man . . . gods*: This revision of a line, which in the 1938 text reads 'I would have one man among those gods', greatly enhances Attracta's new-found authority: she asserts her will with implacable conviction.

SCENE VI

26. *the moon has just risen . . . face*: The 1938 text differs significantly: there the moon 'is about to rise' at the start of the scene so the light is dim; the 'round smiling face' is not actually seen till Attracta enters for the second time to confront the dying Congal. This fulfils her prophecy in the previous scene that they would meet again 'just as the moon comes round the hill'. Thus Yeats's cynical, smiling moon is withheld till late in the action, when it appears in direct response to Congal's challenge to the Herne:

> Are you up there?
> Your chosen kitchen spit has killed me,
> But killed me at my own will, not yours.

A director must experiment in rehearsal and decide how best to time this effect. It undoubtedly produces laughter when first viewed, and Yeats may have felt on reflection that that would be an inappropriate audience-response immediately after Congal's grue-some suicide with its stylized impaling. The whole sequence of events in this final scene is a manifestation of the Herne's cruelty and power, so Yeats may have considered it right for the smiling moon to preside over the action throughout. It would provoke laughter before any dialogue was spoken and then, remaining a constant presence in an audience's view of the stage, would become increasingly disturbing as the action develops.

27. *When beak . . . lying there?*: The simple change of tense for the verbs in these words (now spoken, but first heard as the closing lyric of Attracta's song in Scene IV) effects a further transformation in the priestess. The oracular assurance of the previous scene has gone, leaving Attracta a vulnerable woman meditating on an experience only hesitantly apprehended, not properly understood. This prepares expertly for the compassion she is suddenly to begin to feel for the dying Congal.

28. *He won . . . second*: The first bout in Congal's imagining was the confusion over the eggs that led to Aedh's death; the second was the rape of Attracta.

29. *They arrange stones . . . spit in*: In Scene III Congal and his men tried to kill the Herne with stones and swords, now an arrangement of stones and the sword-like spit are prepared for Congal's death. Andrew Parkin observes that a heron's beak is long and sharply pointed exactly like a cooking spit.

30. *But I have beaten . . . seven men*: Congal is unrepentant and dies asserting his victory over the Herne, which from the perspective of the grinning moon is the final proof that the self-determining hero is really a fool. As Corney's final reaction demonstrates, the last laugh is at Congal's expense, since he dies in the belief that another human being, Attracta, can assuage his fear and protect him from a god's vengeance. But in his appeal to her Congal finally acknowledges Attracta's skill and power, and ceases to see her simply as a sexual object, and that serves in part to redeem him on a human, if not a metaphysical, level.

31. *Come lie . . . cool*: Ironically, it is as woman and not as sacred bride and priestess that Attracta seeks to frustrate the Herne's design for Congal; for her presumption she is taught the meaning of failure and grief, proving the truth of her earliest pronouncements (in Scene II): 'There is no reality but the Great Herne' and 'There is no happiness but the Great Herne.' Measuring her will against the god's brings swift defeat and punishment; and she rapidly loses the supernatural powers she acquired as the god's 'darling'.

32. *All that trouble . . . donkey*: The stage-picture presents us with a divided focus: to one side lie the dead Congal and the exhausted, mourning Attracta, while above and beside them are a smiling moon and a man helpless with laughter at the thought of the joke that he splutters out as the play ends. It is a challenging moment for the audience, as if Yeats is defying us in the context of that stage-picture to find Corney's joke funny. Being confronted relentlessly by such an absurdist vision, we have by now lost all sense of decorum that would help us to decide the appropriate response. We are learning what it is like to be under the sway of a savage god.

Purgatory

Many aspects of Yeats's earlier dramatic practice came together and found a new form of expressiveness in *The Herne's Egg*, as he pursued his investigations into the nature of perception and its relation to identity. Yeats poured an abundance of materials into the play, but he miraculously found an ordering narrative structure to contain them all and give them meaning. On every level of creativity, it was a prodigiously extravagant achievement; and one he hugely enthused over in the writing. *Purgatory*, his next venture, was the exact antithesis: it was to be a spare, unrelievedly dark, tightly structured, one-act tragedy of neoclassical intensity, where the action is precisely commensurate with the playing-time (even though the experience being explored embraces fifty years or more of the central character's lifetime). One of the disturbing features of that character, the Old Man, is his ability to live seemingly outside the pressures of chronological time: time past has an almost palpable immediacy in his present awareness. Memory, fantasy and current circumstance are equally *real* to him. Once again Yeats is conducting us on a journey into the deepest reaches of a particular consciousness to explore how a distinctive mode of perception comes into being. What impresses is how he contrives to give to such a state of intense subjectivity a viable dramatic form.

Many Noh dramas involve the summoning up of a ghost (played by the leading actor, or *shite*) by a figure (played by the subsidiary actor, or *waki*) who is deeply moved by the atmosphere of a place to which that ghost, when a living being, was profoundly attached. The ghost relives the circumstances from its past which explain why it must haunt that particular territory; and the human spectator of its anguish (the *waki*-figure) feels compelled by sympathy to pray to Buddha for the ghost's release from its torment; usually Buddha's compassion is stirred and the ghost finds rest. In *Purgatory* Yeats returns to this form of Noh, which he had previously adapted to his own ends in *The Dreaming of the Bones, Calvary* and *The Words upon the Window-Pane*. The Old Man, like a *waki*-figure, returns to a place (the ruined shell of a house) that has special significance for him; his coming there activates the appearance of two ghosts associated in his mind with the house. But here the resemblance to the Noh prototype ends: these ghosts appear but are not played by the leading actors, and they do not speak for themselves. In Yeats's ghost-play, the *waki*-figure usurps the role of the *shite*: the Old Man interprets the motive for the ghosts' appearances, tells the story of their past, expresses what he senses must be their anguish and voices their desperation and hope of release. We see the ghosts, but must decide whether to take on trust the Old Man's account of their purgatorial suffering. Excitingly, Yeats plunges us, as in

The Herne's Egg, into a dilemma about perception by setting what we see markedly in conflict with what we hear and, hearing, are required to imagine.

The ghosts appear separately: first we observe a seemingly joyous, young girl waiting in anxious anticipation and then a debonair young man, drinking alone in a mood of quiet satisfaction. There is nothing about these two images, as they appear framed in the burnt-out window of the ruin, which suggests psychological torment. Yet the Old Man tells us a terrible tale: of a socially ill-matched marriage; of the wife's death in child-birth; of the father's bankrupting her estates through wild, extravagant living; of the son's murder of his father, whose corpse he then hid in the burning home which the father had set recklessly on fire; of the son's belief that his mother's soul must be suffering endless torment for the consequences of her passion for a coarse, illiterate groom who sired the child destined to be his murderer; and of that son's consummate desire to find the way to end her agonies and free her soul into rest. The story, we finally learn, is the Old Man's autobiography: the ghosts are his parents, the ruined house his former home and his the burning ambition to end the chain of consequences for the mother's sake. Compared with the restless movement of the ghosts in *The Dreaming of the Bones* and *The Words upon the Window-Pane*, these two are noticeably still, as we see them framed within the window and in postures suggestive of those conventionally adopted in family portraits. It is difficult to read into their representation the dark history that the Old Man insists is the truth of their past.

All stories capture the imagination if well told and this one engrosses the mind, because it unfolds at such a measured rate, with such precision of detail and a steadily developing logic, despite its horror. But the telling of the tale neither follows the theatrical convention of the messenger-type narrative monologue addressed directly to the audience nor does it stay confined within the intimate ruminating of the soliloquy, but shifts uneasily between those two forms and tones of address. The Old Man has a companion, his sixteen-year-old son, to whom he seems as anxious to confide the tale as to end his mother's purgatorial suffering, though aspects of the story in its telling often seem to take possession of the teller, requiring him to dwell and meditate over them. The Boy is a genial rascal and not at all a willing listener: he initially opines his father is 'a silly old man' whose 'wits are out again', but becomes randomly interested in those parts of the story that concern his grandfather, of whom he heartily approves ('My grand-dad got the girl and the money'). Like the ghosts when they appear, the Boy continually offers a challenging perspective on the Old Man's preferred view of events, and this has the effect of making the audience concentrate as much on the manner of telling the story as on the narrative itself.

The Old Man talks of purgatorial anguish, remorse and necessary expiation as if they were a ritual cycle; though his mind appears wholly focused on the past, he is noticeably watchful of the Boy's responses and is quick to seize him when he tries to steal his father's money and run away. The Boy is the first to notice the seeming coincidence that he is himself the age at which his father committed murder and, when the Old Man gets the better of him in the struggle for the money, threatens that history might repeat itself. But the Old Man is fearless; it seems as if he is testing the Boy to prove a point and with a particular end in view. It is at this moment that the male ghost appears and the Boy sees this apparition of his grandfather, with whom he has continually identified. As if that is somehow his expected cue, the Old Man performs a second murder ('My father and my son on the same jack-knife!'), believing that this will have 'finished all that consequence' so his mother's guilt will be appeased. Like Abraham, the Old Man has brought his son to a secret place to sacrifice him to the object of his worship; for a moment the stage fills with a strange light as he experiences the ecstasy of accomplishment; but then a new implacable attack of remorse sets in. The hoof-beats of a phantom horse, which always announce in the Old Man's consciousness that the ghosts are to recommence their haunting, reverberate in his imagination once again.

Only now do we understand the significance of why so terrible a story should have been told in such rational and measured tones and with such attention to a logic of process defining a sequential patterning of cause and event. The whole experience that we have witnessed in the play has been a ritual devised by the Old Man, a rite of purgation, centring on what he believes will be a cathartic act of cleansing. The shock of the murder compels us to reappraise everything that we have seen and heard and find our own patterns of meaning free of the subjective perceptual bias of the Old Man's narration. There is a decidedly different interpretation of it all, which shows the guilt to be wholly and inescapably his, and his the purgatorial torment and anguish. The Old Man's final words are a prayer for divine help in the form of grace, but one is left wondering whether the precise appearance of the ghosts – so different from how he imagines them – is not already a metaphysical aid to encourage him to interpret the past afresh and not project his guilt so cruelly on to his mother under the guise of redeeming her wrongs. His mind is permeated with sexual disgust and misogyny, the full extent of which we appreciate only at the close of the play; but that diseased psyche wholly controls the Old Man's mode of perception and powers of reasoning, impelling him to the belief that the detachment to be achieved by ritualizing one's actions, however heinous, frees one from culpability and blame. Till the closing moments of the play, we have inhabited a consciousness which is lethal, sharing its ways of seeing itself, its present world and its past.

Purgatory was completed very rapidly in what seems to have been three compositional bursts. Yeats began devising the scenario during late March 1938; by the beginning of April he wrote of being 'in the middle of my one act play'; and on 3 May of needing 'three or four more days to finish my play'. From its first performance at the Abbey in August 1938 *Purgatory* was considered a masterpiece. M. J. Dolan played the Old Man and Liam Redmond the Boy (though Yeats considered him too old for the part) in a production by Hugh Hunt with designs by Anne Yeats. T. S. Eliot admired the play, considering that future poet–dramatists were forever in Yeats's debt for devising a style of free verse that could move swiftly from a near naturalistic idiomatic flow to formal intensity, as the need arose. Given the particular nature of Eliot's own developing concern with the drama at this time, he must also have been impressed at the brilliance with which Yeats created a believably modern drama that clearly and effortlessly sustained its roots in classical Greek tragedy. Whereas in Sophocles' *Oedipus the King* the inexorable logic of the action is proof of a god's absolute power, in *Purgatory* the implacable logic is the manifestation of a mind that, longing to play at being a god, is wholly evil. In both plays a would-be saviour of others from a terrible pollution is found to be the corrupting source of that pollution himself. Yeats's work on Sophocles continued to prove richly inspirational for his own dramatic writing. Comparison with the Greek tragedian is not to Yeats's detriment.

Setting: This is the nearest Yeats ever came to evoking the principal features of the Noh stage in his theatre. Noh is performed on a bare wooden scaffold-like stage, on the rear wall of which is traditionally painted a stylized representation of a pine-tree. Here, however, the bare structure is a windswept ruin and the tree, stripped leafless, is decaying.

1. *Half-door . . . talk*: It was in the very latest stages of composition and redrafting that Yeats hit on this highly effective, naturalistic opening with the Boy's voice, disgruntled, weary and resentful, which affords an immediate and stark contrast with the Old Man's quietly authoritative tone.

2. *Upon others . . . bring help*: This is the Old Man's private justification for everything that ensues in the play, which he sees as essential for his mother's salvation. The play ends with him steadily realizing that his own desperate need is for 'the mercy of God'.

3. *Curragh*: A district of Co. Kildare where there are numerous stud farms and stables for the breeding and training of racehorses; there are regular race meetings there.

4. *Great people . . . this house*: Yeats seemed to have memories of Coole Park firmly in mind when writing of the past glories of this establishment; certainly the ensuing lines which qualify this one recall many images and phrases from Yeats's several poems and random comments in his letters and prose writings describing Lady Gregory's home. The accounts of library, breakfast room and parkland in Lady Gregory's own book, *Coole* (not published until 1971), also have a bearing on this passage. Perhaps even the tree, now stripped of its leaves that were once 'thick as butter', is a reference to Lady Gregory's own favourite catalpa, under which she frequently rested in her garden. The Coole estate had been sold after Lady Gregory's death and the house razed to its foundations, an act of cultural vandalism that Yeats had foreseen as possible in his poem 'Upon a House shaken by the Land Agitation' (first published in 1910).

5. *Aughrim and the Boyne*: The Protestant William of Orange defeated the Catholic James II at the Battle of the Boyne in July 1690; virtually a year later a Williamite force led by General Ginkle suppressed an Irish army under French command at Aughrim.

6. *Or came . . . in the park*: Lady Gregory's *Journal* for 3 June 1922 contains the entry: 'Everything is beautiful, one must stand to look at blossoming tree after tree; the thorns in the Park that William used to come over from London to see at this time of the year best of all.' The 'William' referred to was her late husband, one-time Governor of Ceylon.

7. *There were old books . . . by the ton*: See Yeats's 'Coole Park and Ballylee, 1931' with its account of the library there:

> Beloved books that famous hands have bound,
> Old marble heads, old pictures everywhere.

8. *Puck Fair*: Held annually at Killorglin in Co. Kerry, 9–11 August. Some commentators, computing from the date of the play's first performance (10 August 1938), have decided that the Boy was born on 10 August 1922, the year of the founding of the Irish Free State; they have then deduced that there is a complex historical symbolism underlying the play, which relates to Yeats's fears that Ireland had entered a period

of degeneration from that time in her history when civil war erupted. Yeats often wrote such symbolic agendas into his dramatic works, but they do not often impinge on an audience's awareness during a performance and certainly do not do so here, where one's attention is wholly caught up in the immediate action. As he wrote of another work at this time, 'My "private philosophy" is there but there must be no sign of it.'

9. *I stuck . . . knife*: This brutally powerful line took some time to evolve. At first Yeats thought of strangling as the method of effecting the murder and, when he revised this to stabbing with a knife, next wrote a more detailed description of driving the weapon in 'between the third and second rib'. The final version exactly captures the grim impulse that motivated the murder and the complete hatred of son for father; 'stuck' suggests the butchery of a pig.

10. *Listen to the hoof-beats!*: In the introduction to *The Words upon the Window-Pane* Yeats refers to a supernatural phenomenon that was told to him: 'The gamekeeper did hear those footsteps the other night that sounded like the footsteps of a staga where stag has not passed these hundred years.'

11. *A window . . . girl*: This use of a lighted window on an otherwise darkened stage recalls, as Katharine Worth has observed, a similar technical effect deployed by Maeterlinck in his play *Interior* (significantly the one play by the Flemish dramatist to be staged at the Abbey in March 1907). A group of villagers, seen as dim presences standing in the darkness of a garden, watch through the lighted window of a house a family happily engaged in their various evening pastimes; they wait with mounting pathos, knowing that the family is soon to receive news that the eldest daughter of the house has drowned herself. It is a poignant, atmospheric play that requires an audience to listen to characters who are hardly visible and closely observe others who are never heard. In *Purgatory* Yeats exploits his audience's faculties of hearing and seeing to far more intricate effect than tragic irony and pathos.

Some directors of late have experimented with leaving the two ghosts to the imagination of the audience, like the sound of the hoof-beats, but this considerably reduces the complexity of Yeats's theme about perception. It becomes all too easy (if we do not see the ghosts too) to dismiss the Old Man as mad from this point on, which robs the final murder of its power to shock.

12. *Tertullian*: A Christian writer, living at the end of the second century, who composed a treatise, *De Anima*, which argues that pleasure and remorse exist alike in the soul at and after death.

13. *They struggle . . . at each other* and *The window . . . into a glass*: The text included in *Collected Plays* runs these two stage directions together and places them all after 'I will break your fingers.' The manuscripts, extant typescripts, the first Cuala edition of *Purgatory* in *Last Poems and Two Plays* (1939) and the text, proof-read by Yeats, that was printed in the Longford edition of *On the Boiler* all hold back the stage direction concerning the appearance of the male ghost in the lighted window until after the Boy has threatened to murder his father, just as the Old Man when young murdered the Boy's grandfather. Dramatically this is the apt place for the ghost's entry, the implications of the timing of the supernatural manifestation being powerfully ironic. The pacing of the effect in theatrical terms is better too: if the apparition occurs during the fight between father and son, the impact is lessened by there being so much

other activity on stage. I have, therefore, followed the ordering of dialogue and stage-action as printed in the first edition.

14. '*Then the bride-sleep . . . Adam*': Line 165 of Dante Gabriel Rossetti's 'Eden Bower' reads: 'Yea, where the bride-sleep fell upon Adam (*Alas the hour!*)'.

15. '*Hush-a-bye . . . bright*': The nursery rhyme crooned over the dying son is bitterly ironic in the context of the relationships and the social standing of the characters so far revealed. This eerie effect was incorporated in the text from the time of the first verse draft of the play, though it does not appear in the scenario.

16. *I am . . . harmless*: There is a marked echo here, which Yeats may well have intended deliberately, of King Lear's humbling himself before Cordelia: 'I am a very foolish, fond old man' (IV.vii.60). But where Lear's words express a genuine humility, the Old Man's are suffused with self-pity and total self-delusion. Again this third quotation or near-quotation was part of Yeats's structuring of this climactic episode from the first verse draft.

17. *Release . . . dream!*: The Old Man is unregenerate; the haunting has started again with the onset of the hoof-beats but he still cannot face the reality of himself, or understand why he keeps himself perpetually a victim to the process of dreaming back over the past. This is the bleakest journey Yeats essayed into the territory of the mind to explore a consciousness that is beyond the reach of anyone's pity or capacity to help. It was, significantly, a favourite play of Beckett's whose later works, like *Not I*, return to the same darkly sinister terrain with a similarly clear, dispassionate vision.

The Death of Cuchulain

The night after the first performance of *Purgatory* the Abbey revived *On Baile's Strand* as part of a Theatre Festival, which was also a celebration of Yeats's achievements with the drama. Yeats's letters of the next few days express his excitement at the success of his most recent play, but also carefully record his pleasure in seeing again one of his earlier works: 'I have not seen it for years and it seemed to me exactly right'; the Cuchulain was 'magnificent'; and to his immense satisfaction his daughter's designs 'were greatly admired'. To Dorothy Wellesley he confided a further insight: ' "Cuchulain" seemed to me a heroic figure because he was creative joy separated from fear.' That observation appears to have become rooted in Yeats's mind, germinating there into a last play which was to complete the series devoted to saga-themes and provide a summation of a lifetime's thinking about the practice of theatre. He had thought of writing 'a long Noh play on the death of Cuchulain' in the autumn of 1937, but there is no further reference to this plan until exactly a year later, when he informed Edith Shackleton Heald that he 'was in the middle of a play about Cuchulain's death', feeling that it was 'necessary to wind up my plays on that theme'. Wrestling with difficulties over structuring the action fatigued him, but he had completed a prose draft by early November and was in a position to read Dorothy Wellesley a poetic version when she visited him at his hotel in Cap Martin where he was spending the winter. The play was finished around Christmas-time, but Yeats continued to add revisions to a clean typescript almost until the day of his death on 28 January 1939. He never supervised proofs or printed text, and the play was not performed till December 1949 (and then

not by the Abbey but by Austin Clarke's Lyric Theatre Company in a production by
Evelyn MacNeice with designs by Anne Yeats and music by Arthur Duff).

Yeats took as his source the last two chapters of Lady Gregory's *Cuchulain of
Muirthemne*, which tell how his enemies throughout Ireland (human and supernatural,
many the sons and daughters of one-time heroes whom Cuchulain had slain) joined
forces under the command of Queen Maeve and marched to attack him in the plain
of Muirthemne; how Emer and Cathbad the Druid endeavoured to keep the hero from
joining battle till Conall Cearnach could bring his forces in Cuchulain's support by
sending his current mistress to seduce him into love-making; how his enemies sent a
magic phantom in the mistress's form with the contrary message that Cuchulain should
go out and fight; how he ignored ill omens and eluded the trickery of Morrigu, the
war-goddess, designed to keep him at home but went into battle; and how, receiving
numerous fatal wounds, he tied himself upright to a pillar-stone to meet his end, was
beheaded and mutilated by his enemies but avenged by Conall, who brought to Emer
the heads of all the men who participated in her husband's death. Yeats treated his
sources with considerable freedom, taking only random episodes to suit his purpose
and inventing others that would allow him to draw material from the span of the
hero's lifetime into the process of Cuchulain's dying so that he could explore the way
the mind prepares itself for death through a cycle of expiations. Cuchulain's death
becomes a ritual severing of his passionate attachments of life, to find peace within
himself.

After the tightly knit form of *Purgatory*, the new play is startling for its fractured
structure, which is deliberately brought to our attention by a repeated series of dramatic
devices. *The Death of Cuchulain* is in three scenes, with a prologue and epilogue making
five episodes in all; the time shifts precariously between the audience's immediately
historical and cultural present and the heroic world of Celtic mythology; each episode
has its own particular style (drily bitter satire; poetic realism; a mesmerically controlled
ritual; an extremely stylized dance-drama; and a raucous, popular street-ballad sung
to the accompaniment of pipe and drum). There is little here that is reminiscent of the
Noh drama beyond the requirement of 'a bare stage'; song, ritual, dance, choric
commentary feature in the work but not in the ordered and integrated fashion of the
Four Plays for Dancers. The fragmented impact is positively stressed by the prescription
in the stage directions that, as each episode ends, pipe and drum music should begin
as the stage is plunged into darkness. This is to continue for a set period of time till
the lights come up sharply again. Silence should immediately prevail and be sustained
for a considerable duration ('half a minute' is recommended on the first occasion that
this direction occurs) before actors appear to commence the new scene. Each episode
independently etches itself in an audience's memory. It is as if Yeats is asking an
audience to engage imaginatively with the experiences that make up the play and find
for themselves the artistic unity within which all the material coheres.

Sometime early in 1935 Ethel Mannin had introduced Yeats to the German
expressionist playwright Ernst Toller, who was then living in exile, being in fear of
Nazi persecution. By early April, Yeats was writing to Mannin that (in terms of his
private reading) the 'great sensation of recent weeks has been Toller's *Seven Plays*',
that he considered Toller 'a greater technical innovator than Pirandello' and was
impressed by the German's 'intellectual power'. Toller had advocated the structuring
of plays around climactic moments of action which he called 'stations' after the manner

of the Stations of the Cross. These scenes were to be independently shaped to achieve their own internal coherence; and much of the power of the plays in terms of audience-impact was to come from the aesthetic and intellectual surprise caused by juxtaposing a range of such scenes conceived in different theatrical styles. This was the technique Toller himself pursued in such plays as *Masses and Man*, *Transfiguration* and *Hoppla!* In *The Death of Cuchulain* Yeats would appear to be following Toller's example, but to be pushing the technique to an extreme that Toller himself never attempted, deliberately and flamboyantly asserting the illusory nature of theatre while relishing the rich diversity of dramatic styles and conventions that the art of illusion can deploy.

The play starts with a scoffing, teasing prologue (somewhat in the manner of one of Ben Jonson's inductions) telling us roughly what we can and cannot expect to see, as a figure looking suspiciously like a travesty of the elderly Yeats sets about combatively twitting the audience regarding his own and their theatrical likes and dislikes. We are to have poetry, fine dramatic acting, mythology, music, severed heads and dance (proper, inspired dancing, that is, not the artificialities of classical ballet); and that is precisely what we get.

The first scene is the one most closely modelled on saga material: it is a miracle of compression from what is a highly complicated plot in *Cuchulain of Muirthemne*. Eithne, Cuchulain's mistress, comes to the hero with a message, ostensibly from Emer, ordering him to go out and fight, but she carries in her hand a letter from Cuchulain's wife commanding him for his safety to stay at home in Eithne's company till Conall joins him. The conflicting messages are a challenge to Cuchulain's perspicacity, particularly when Eithne claims she has suddenly been gifted with vision, can see the Morrigu, the war-goddess, beside them, and knows instinctively that they are caught up in the goddess's scheming. What is he to believe? He suggests the trickery is perhaps of Eithne's own devising to rid herself of an old love before taking 'a younger man, a friendlier man'; but he offers that interpretation without any show of jealousy or anger, accepting the idea of the waning of Eithne's affections as inevitable in a transient world. His impulse is gently compassionate (proof in fact of his deep regard for her) but Eithne is horrified that he shows none of his customary violence at having his passions thwarted. The change in him to a wholehearted generosity she sees as certain evidence that he is marked for death and dreads that he will die thinking her a traitor to him. When a trusted servant enters, Cuchulain explains to him the lovers' dilemma as essentially a matter of perception. The man asks if Eithne's confession is true and Cuchulain, insisting that only the kindliest interpretation be put on her words, replies: 'I make the truth!' The hero elects to go to battle; but, mindful of Eithne's anguish, arranges with utter composure for her to be drugged to sleep, then, in the event of his death, to be given to Conall, 'because the women /Have called him a good lover'.

Confronted by an intricate web of deceptive appearances, Cuchulain, deciding on his best course of action, calmly asserts, 'I make the truth'; and the scene builds inexorably towards that psychological climax. Congal in *The Herne's Egg* asserted the truth as he chose to perceive it, as did the Old Man in *Purgatory*: and the consequences for both men were disastrous. But Cuchulain noticeably makes a different order of truth when confronted by Eithne; he chooses to act not in a manner that vindicates himself but in one that puts the best interpretation on her conduct, so relieving her of any future possibility of guilt. Cuchulain vindicates his perception of Eithne's integrity and that is the measure of the distance between him and either Congal or the Old Man. In a joking fashion in his prologue Yeats informed us about the narrative content of the play, so that our attention would more profitably focus on the thematic life of the drama. That simple but profound statement, 'I make the truth', becomes the ground-base for each of the following scenes, which are all Yeats's own invention.

Aoife comes to the dying Cuchulain, intent on vengeance for the killing of their son; far from being aggressive in his own defence, Cuchulain accepts that she has an absolute right to kill him. She binds his hands with her veils; then, instead of sadistically lingering over his demise as one might expect, asks for a true account of her son's death. They begin to talk of their past, of the circumstances of their son's conception, of how he became the victim of the hatred that replaced their love. The talk is simple, dispassionate, without any pressure to ascribe blame and provoke guilt. Once in their youth when warrior-enemies, they had met and love had flourished where hatred might have been expected to seek expression. As the process of shared recall continues, that same emotional ease together recurs, stilling any urge in them to be vindictive. The quiet, even tone that settles over the scene is the token that they have implicitly accepted joint responsibility for the tragic experience they have brought each other to endure.

The Blind Man offers a sharp contrast to Aoife; he is utterly callous, intent on murder for material gain and delighted to find that someone else has trussed Cuchulain firmly to the pillar-stone, since that makes his task all the easier. He is a terrible companion for a hero's death: reductive, malicious, so wholly self-centred as to be quite without respect for his victim's basic human dignity, as his hands search over Cuchulain's body for the most vulnerable place to insert his knife. This is the darkest challenge yet to Cuchulain's status as hero. Like Shakespeare's Cleopatra, who jokes with the Clown who brings her the asps with which she will take her life (a scene Yeats much admired), Cuchulain too rises to a genial humour while under the pressure of death, agreeing without any hint of sarcasm that twelve pennies is indeed a good fee for a murder and asking whether the Blind Man's knife is kept sharp enough to do the job. The magnanimity that Cuchulain found in the presence of Eithne does not desert him in facing either Aoife or the Blind Man; steadily Yeats defines magnanimity for us as a willing depersonalizing of the self (a process neither Congal nor the Old Man could undergo), a cleansing from perception of all tendencies to subjectivity. Unexpectedly, Cuchulain is rewarded in the moment of death with a visionary intimation of his 'soul's first shape, a soft feathery shape' and his last cry is not despairing but ecstatic: 'I say it is about to sing.'

The Morrigu next appears to give a truculent account of the facts of Cuchulain's death and Conall's pursuit of vengeance as recorded in the sagas (she is surrounded by symbolic representations of severed heads); she tersely concludes with the observation, 'I arranged the dance.' If she embodies destiny in the universe of the play (and her intrusions into the action give her that weight of significance) then she may be said to have controlled the narrative patterning of the action. But the prologue to the play, as we have seen, suggests that Yeats wished to concentrate our attention less on the plot than on the issue of 'making' the truth. The Morrigu may have arranged the circumstances of Cuchulain's death but she has no power to control the actual manner of his dying: to the last Yeats has Cuchulain experience that 'creative joy separated from fear' which the dramatist considered the essence of true heroism, and his death is wholly liberating in consequence.

The Morrigu's image of the dance leads us straight into Emer's scene of mourning. At first her movements suggest blind rage against the heads of Cuchulain's enemies, a predictable response; but the nature of the dance changes, as Emer directs her consciousness towards her husband. Her body no longer expresses intense grief (a largely subjective emotion) but moves as if in adoration, which suggests that her inspiration now comes from a growing imaginative identification with Cuchulain. As through empathy and intuition she begins to share within some deep reach of the mind in the process of his dying, Emer's form is suddenly lifted spontaneously into a posture suggesting acutely attentive listening. In the stillness and silence she hears 'a few faint bird notes'. The dance in its various stages enacts in a different dramatic medium a process of depersonalizing the self which exactly complements Cuchulain's own inner progress and Emer is similarly rewarded by a moment of visionary enlightenment.

The final scene returns us to the present day as folk band and singer erupt on to the stage, joyously celebrating others in recent times whose lives have been gifted with a visionary sense of Cuchulain's presence, as they have themselves risen to the demands of heroism. It is neither the violent nor the passionate Cuchulain that the present age has chosen to immortalize in a statue, but (more significantly for Yeats's purpose) the dying hero, as sculpted by Oliver Sheppard to commemorate the Easter Rising of 1916. The whole argument of the play is that it was in his dying that Cuchulain proved himself the absolute hero. Availing himself of Toller's technique of a deliberately fragmented structure allowed Yeats to explore and test that premise through a whole range of theatrical styles and means of dramatic expression. Daring and innovatory, *The Death of Cuchulain* was a triumphant demonstration of Yeats's control over all the arts that go to the making of theatre.

1. *A very old man . . . mythology*: This figure is often described as Yeats parodying himself and there is some truth in that view. But, as Liam Miller argues, the ideas expressed by the Old Man are strikingly like those expressed in print by one of Yeats's old friends, Edward Gordon Craig, son of the actress Ellen Terry and a one-time actor himself who could therefore with some degree of credibility describe himself as a 'son of Talma'. The resemblance to Craig is especially strong in the final stages of the opening speech, when the subject turns to the merits of different styles of dancing, about which, as a former lover of Isadora Duncan (one of the creators of the modern movement in dance), he felt fully equipped to pronounce with regularity. Craig, like Yeats by this date, was craggy-looking and white-haired. That the character embraces some aspects of Craig is strengthened by the fact that in the drafts of the play the Old Man had initially a more expanded role and was often referred to as the 'producer', operating the lights, giving the cues for the music and donning a hooded cloak to appear in minor parts such as the Servant in the scene between Eithne and Cuchulain, which could be seen as Yeats's gentle satire on Craig's desire (as outlined in his first book, *The Art of the Theatre*) that one individual should be in total charge of all aspects of the production process. Yeats himself, of course, also took an autocratic line when directing rehearsals; George Moore's autobiography, *Hail and Farewell*, and Joseph Holloway's *Diaries* offer numerous wickedly satirical instances of Yeats's pretensions as producer. It seems best to view the Old Man as an amalgam of individuals of Yeats's acquaintance who had an involvement in theatre direction (including a sly look at himself).

2. *Talma*: François Joseph Talma (1763–1826), a renowned French actor who strongly supported the French Revolution, himself effected a considerable revolution in Parisian theatre practice, since he instituted reforms of speech (preferring the sense of the verse rather than the poetic metre to determine dramatic pauses and their duration), of stage costume (Jacques Louis David, the painter, made designs for him from classical models) and of acting style (he suppressed the elaborately declamatory use of gesture).

3. *an audience . . . or a hundred*: Fifty had been Yeats's expressed preference in relation to audiences for his *Four Plays for Dancers*, but the Peacock Theatre, his stage for poetry, seated 102 persons.

4. *Milton's Comus*: This masque was staged at Ludlow Castle on 29 September 1634, before the Earl of Bridgewater, who was then President of the Council of Wales and Lord-Lieutenant. The Earl's children took the central roles of the Lady and her two brothers, and their tutor, Henry Lawes (who also composed the music), played the Attendant Spirit.

5. *sciolists*: In 'J. M. Synge and the Ireland of his Time' Yeats wrote of Synge's attraction to the Aran Islands: 'Here above all was silence from all our great orator took delight in, from formidable men, from moral indignation, from the "sciolist" who "is never sad", from all in modern life that would destroy the arts; and here . . . he could love time as only women and great artists do and need never sell it.'

6. *Drum and pipe . . . silence*: It is clear from the early drafts of the play that Yeats originally thought of bringing the musicians actually on stage at this point, when the ragged ballad-singer would perform what in the published text is the first stanza of the song now positioned in the final scene.

7. *the music . . . Homer's music*: In Yeats's 'The Tower' he refers to the wandering and blind Irish poet Anthony Raftery (1784–1834) who wrote a poem celebrating the beauty of Mary Hynes; and he muses on this:

> Strange, but the man who made the song was blind;
> Yet, now I have considered it, I find
> That nothing strange; the tragedy began
> With Homer that was a blind man,
> And Helen has all living hearts betrayed.

8. *I had thought . . . carved*: Like those designed and sculpted by Hildo van Krop for *The Only Jealousy of Emer* and *Fighting the Waves*.

9. *I could have got . . . she has gone*: The manuscripts make it clear that the reference is to Ninette de Valois, who, after working with Yeats in Dublin (helping to direct his dance-plays and supervising the Abbey School of Dance) for part of each year for over six years, had left in 1934 to fulfil her long-standing ambition to establish a classical ballet company at the Sadler's Wells Theatre in London.

10. *upon the same neck . . . and death*: This seems a beautiful invocation of the dance required for the central role of the Queen in *The King of the Great Clock Tower*, which de Valois improvised in the first performances, to Yeats's total admiration. He subsequently dedicated that play to her in gratitude.

11. *Degas*: Hilaire Germain Edgar Degas (1834–1917) was one of the most respected and feared of the artists of the Nouvelle Athènes in Paris. His life was devoted to his art and he would not tolerate fools, sycophants or amateurs, for whom he reserved

his most biting wit. Degas evolved his brilliance of technique and execution through years of painstaking study, often painting and repainting the same theme or subject till he expressed it to perfection. He was particularly attracted to capturing the most ephemeral of experiences, hence in part his delight in painting scenes of evanescent movement at the ballet. The Old Man's observation is accurate: Degas the realist often paints coarse-grained faces on the otherwise sylph-like forms of his dancers.

12. *Rameses the Great*: Pharaoh of Egypt (1311–1245 BC).

13. *I spit!*: Katharine Worth suggests that here Yeats may be subliminally recalling a climactic moment at the end of Maeterlinck's *The Death of Tintagiles*, of which he was fond. The princess, Ygrainne, frustrated in all her efforts to save her brother from the cruelty of their grandmother, the Old Queen, has no means left to express her refusal to submit other than by spitting at the bolted iron door which blocks her chance of following the Queen's guards, who are taking the child away to an unknown fate.

14. *Eithne Inguba*: In the saga sources Cuchulain has many lovers, and it was one called Niamh who was magically impersonated by the sorceress Badb, so that she might persuade Cuchulain to fight. When Niamh herself came to him with a message from Emer, urging him to go with her to the Valley of the Dumb where they would be safe from Maeve's enchantments, Cuchulain refused to stop preparing for battle. Yeats changes the identity of the mistress involved in the confusion of messages, presumably to allow continuity with the other plays in the Cuchulain series (and especially with *The Only Jealousy of Emer*, which directly precedes this, where Eithne has a significant role) if the five plays are staged as a cycle.

15. *Maeve*: Queen of Connaught, implacable enemy of the champions of Ulster.

16. *Emain Macha*: The capital of Ulster, which was sited somewhat to the south-west of present-day Armagh.

17. *Muirthemne*: Cuchulain's territory was situated in part of what is modern-day Co. Louth in the lands bordering the sea between the Boyne and Dundalk.

18. *Conall Caernach*: Champion of Ulster, second only to Cuchulain; he avenged Cuchulain's death by killing and beheading every enemy chieftain who participated in the battle waged against the hero. After he had laid these before Emer and recited their names to her, he dug Cuchulain's grave and raised a pillar-stone over it. (He appears in *The Green Helmet*.)

19. *The Morrigu*: Goddess of war and fate, who had the power to transform herself into a crow. In most of the sagas she is described as Cuchulain's enemy on account of his murdering her magician-father, Calatin. She and her sisters, Badb and Macha, had but one eye each in the middle of their foreheads. Maeve adopted these monsters and taught them magic to further her plans to destroy Cuchulain.

20. *When I went mad ... you turned*: These brief lines summarize the subject matter of the two preceding plays in the Cuchulain series, *On Baile's Strand* and *The Only Jealousy of Emer*.

21. *Women have spoken ... death*: The tone and phrasing are beautifully poised to express Cuchulain's doubt and reservation without directly accusing Eithne. Cuchulain throughout the scene is made scrupulously careful not to judge his former mistress. Eithne feels this shows a lack of the passion she deems 'necessary to life' and so fears that Cuchulain must be 'about to die'.

22. *Aoife*: See the texts and notes for *At the Hawk's Well* and *On Baile's Strand* for details about this leader of a tribe of warrior women whom Cuchulain encountered in his youth in Scotland. After he defeated her in battle, they became lovers; unknown to Cuchulain, who had returned to Ireland, she bore him a son, whom she trained to be an expert fighter before sending him to Dundealgan to challenge Cuchulain to mortal combat. The consequences of that tragic fight are explored for the last time here.

23. *six mortal wounds . . . pool*: In *Cuchulain of Muirthemne* Cuchulain is described as driving in his war-chariot several times through the whole host of his enemies, each time decimating their numbers; but first his charioteer, Laeg, is killed; then one of his two favourite horses, the Grey of Macha, is wounded and 'with half his harness hanging from his neck' plunges into 'Class-linn, the grey pool in Slieve Fuad'; and finally Cuchulain himself receives the full force of Lugaid's spear through his bowels; his other horse, the Black Sainglain, rides away. Cuchulain begs leave of his enemies to go and drink from the lake, which they allow on condition that he comes back to them for a last encounter. After drinking and washing, 'he called to his enemies to come and meet him. There was a pillar-stone west of the lake, and his eye lit on it, and he went to the pillar-stone and he tied himself to it with his breast-belt, the way he would not meet his death lying down.' His enemies are in dread of approaching him, after the Grey of Macha rides mysteriously out of the lake, circling the pillar-stone before three times attacking them and killing 'fifty men with his teeth and thirty with each of his hoofs'.

24. *She has wound . . . him*: This is a powerful image, suggesting on the level of realism that Cuchulain is now totally weakened since he can be held by such flimsy materials. Visually the effect at first suggests that Cuchulain is wholly at Aoife's mercy (the stage-picture evokes memories of Judith and Holofernes or Samson and Delilah); but, as the scene develops, a strangely meditative tone of shared reverie between the elderly woman and the dying man, the action of binding the man in the woman's veils, begins to carry other, less sadistic overtones. The image seems in time to undergo a transformation and to carry resonances of the ending of one of Yeats's earliest plays, *The Shadowy Waters*, where Dectora envelops Forgael, the once violent pirate, in her hair as an emblem not of possession but of complete union. A favourite image in Yeats's later poetry for the union of the male and female energies was occasioned by the gift to him of a Japanese sword, the scabbard of which was bound in a length of fraying brocade from a woman's kimono.

25. *I will keep . . . kill you*: Many commentators have considered this a dramatically weak motive for Aoife's leaving the stage; but this is not necessarily the case if the actors involved are properly attentive to the mood of the scene they share. There is nothing aggressive or vindictive about Cuchulain and Aoife's dialogue together; they neither accuse nor seek to apportion blame for the tragedy they have created in the death of their son. Recalling their shared past instils instead a mood of cathartic peace, which the sound of approaching footsteps painfully disrupts. Aoife wishes to sustain that mood rather than take a quick revenge, because it is balm to her soul tortured with remorse for the past. Given this motivation, her decision to hide is wholly credible.

26. *Twelve pennies! . . . Twelve pennies!*: The Blind Man's short interjection creates a superb tension for the audience between Cuchulain's two exclamations. Is his cry,

as one might expect in the context, one of sarcasm, disgust, despair? The repetition and the ensuing observation ('What better reason for killing a man?') turn what in a lesser man might have been a spiritual defeat into an expression of heroic objectivity.

27. *I say . . . sing*: Birds are often in Yeats's poems both emblems of the soul and, more importantly, symbols of self-fulfilling ecstasy where being (existence) is wholly transmitted into art (song); and this would seem a fitting end for the hero whom Yeats described as representing 'creative joy separated from fear'. In one of his last poems, 'Cuchulain Comforted', which is based on a dream Yeats experienced while composing the play, the hero is greeted in the afterlife by numerous shades or ghosts, 'convicted cowards all', who bid him sew his shroud while they entertain him with their singing. They proffer linen and thread his needle. The final line reads: 'They had changed their throats and had the throats of birds.'

28. *She is the Morrigu*: Yeats had some difficulty with this sequence while drafting the play. The manuscripts show that he first thought of bringing back the Old Man here as 'attendant' or 'producer' to arrange the severed heads while cheerfully singing the nursery rhyme, 'Sing a Song of Sixpence', with its refrain about the 'four and twenty blackbirds' coming directly and with shrill irony after Cuchulain's dying line. It was only with the third draft that Yeats decided to reintroduce the Morrigu here as a figure of destiny, claiming to have organized Cuchulain's last battle even as she now supervises the mourning rites. A change of tone was dramatically necessary; the cold, oracular detachment of the Morrigu is more shocking to an audience's susceptibilities here than the Old Man's now familiar truculence would have been. The Morrigu has no emotional or imaginative engagement with the facts of which she speaks, which affords a marked contrast with Emer, who through the medium of the dance grows into a state of complete spiritual identification with her husband in his moment of dying.

29. *Maeve's latest lover*: A manuscript draft gives the Old Man a line that explains the situation: 'Our army says that her lovers were beyond counting but soldiers are liars when they talk about women.' In the sagas Maeve's amorousness is continually stressed.

30. *She is about to prostrate . . . faint bird notes*: In the first sketch for the scenario of the dance, the ordering of the climax was slightly different: 'she is about to prostrate herself before it [the head] when the sound of a bird's song is heard above her head. She prostrates herself before the head of Cuchulain, she then hears the bird and moves between that and the head; she finally stands transfixed, listening.' Here the audience hear the sound before Emer and the sense of some transcendent communication between husband and wife is lost. The revision presents us with a subtler psychological line: Emer loses all sense of self as she prostrates herself before the head in adoration; her whole body seems suddenly to be borne upright by some strange impulse till she is caught up into a posture of attentive listening – one that exactly mirrors Cuchulain's figure at the moment of his death; only then does she hear the bird notes.

31. *loud music*: Austin Clarke's production (1949) apparently brought on the band of the Transport Workers' Union playing a stridently rollicking jig!

32. *the stage brightens*: There is something to be said for making the lighting for each of the scenes set in heroic times progressively dimmer till Emer is last seen in a single shaft of light. After the required pause in total darkness, a dazzling burst of light

coming simultaneously with a great burst of music plunges us firmly back into the twentieth century with a tumultuous shock. The ballad-style lyric that the Street-Singer performs refers to modern-day individuals who have had a sense of Cuchulain's presence being made manifest dimly in their company at a time of trial and conquest over themselves or when in the throes of artistic inspiration. The suggested lighting plot would bring the audience to a state of mind where the heroic past would seem to have been intuitively apprehended as a force working in the depths of consciousness to enrich their modern-day awareness. This would help them relate the concluding song to their experience of the play on a fittingly sensory level, since (as happens with the final stages of *The King of the Great Clock Tower*) the spoken word has ceased for some time now to be the prime means of communication.

33. *Usna's boys*: Naoise, the lover of Deirdre, and his brothers Ainnle and Ardan were the three Sons of Usna.

34. *I meet . . . great horses*. 'Under Ben Bulben' in *Last Poems* uses these same images for which Yeats drew on a local belief amongst Sligo communities that the sounds of galloping supernatural horses could be heard in 'the wintry dawn' on the mountainside and that these phantom-riders were a 'pale, long-visaged company' of immortals from Ireland's heroic past.

35. *I both . . . loathe*: Yeats several times quotes what he terms 'Blake's old thought', namely that 'sexual love is founded on spiritual hate'.

36. *Post Office*: The General Post Office in Dublin had been the scene of the Easter Rising of 1916, of the proclamation of an independent Irish state, and of the rebels' surrender. Part of the theme of this song is summed up by two lines from Yeats's poem 'The Statues':

> When Pearse summoned Cuchulain to his side,
> What stalked through the Post Office?

37. *Pearse and Connolly*: Patrick Henry Pearse (1879–1916), schoolteacher, poet and editor of the weekly newspaper of the Gaelic League, *An Claidheamh Soluis* (*The Sword of Light*), was one of the leaders of the Easter Rising who, on reading the proclamation of independence, was named President of the provisional government. Shot subsequently by the British, he was often seen by Yeats as willing himself into the role of martyr in seeking a kind of mythical heroic status. Yeats's observation to Edith Shackleton Heald that Pearse and some of his followers made 'a cult' of Cuchulain was certainly true. James Connolly (1870–1916), an Irish trade-union leader and one of the chief organizers of the Irish Citizen Army, was similarly shot for his involvement in the Easter Rising.

38. *Oliver Sheppard*: The sculptor (1864–1941) had been a fellow student with Yeats and George Russell ('AE') at the Metropolitan School of Art in Dublin. Invited to create a suitable memorial to the martyrs of the Easter Rising that would be cast in bronze, he produced several designs relating to aspects of the life of Cuchulain. His depiction of the hero's death tied to the pillar-stone with a raven hovering at his shoulder (exactly as described in Lady Gregory's *Cuchulain of Muirthemne*) was the subject eventually chosen by the government; on completion the statue was situated in the central hall of the rebuilt Post Office in what is now O'Connell Street. Yeats is claiming that artists (like Sheppard with his sculptures and, by implication, Lady

Gregory with her adaptations of the old sagas and himself with the writing of plays like his Cuchulain series) have played as crucial a role as political revolutionaries in shaping history to create a new Ireland. This final ballad is a fitting epitaph to Yeats's achievements as playwright and theatre practitioner.